Thinking with Assent

Thinking with Assent

Renewing a Traditional Account of Knowledge and Belief

MARIA ROSA ANTOGNAZZA

OXFORD
UNIVERSITY PRESS

OXFORD
UNIVERSITY PRESS

Great Clarendon Street, Oxford, OX2 6DP,
United Kingdom

Oxford University Press is a department of the University of Oxford.
It furthers the University's objective of excellence in research, scholarship, and education by publishing worldwide. Oxford is a registered trade mark of Oxford University Press in the UK and in certain other countries

Published in the United States of America by Oxford University Press
198 Madison Avenue, New York, NY 10016, United States of America

British Library Cataloguing in Publication Data
Data available

Library of Congress Control Number: 2023952447

ISBN 978–0–19–883151–8

DOI: 10.1093/oso/9780198831518.001.0001

Printed and bound in the UK by
Clays Ltd, Elcograf S.p.A.

To Sophia

Contents

Acknowledgements

I have been thinking about the views advanced in this book for over three decades, starting from my undergraduate studies in Milan. Over such a long period of time, my debts to a great many people have grown incrementally. First of all, I would like to acknowledge my impersonal and indirect but nevertheless very important debt to the philosophical thought of Sofia Vanni Rovighi (1908–1990), whose writings have shaped my formative years, and whose way of doing philosophy through the history of philosophy has reached me via her students, notably Mario Sina (my *Doktorvater*) and Maria Grazia Zaccone. At a time in which women had to prove themselves much harder than men, Vanni Rovighi was elected, in Milan, first to the chair of Medieval Philosophy (1951), then to the chair of History of Philosophy (1959), and finally to the chair of Theoretical Philosophy (1973), making her one of the first women in Italy to hold such senior academic positions in philosophy. The fact that her work is little known today may not be independent of the tendency, in her lifetime, to underrate the original contribution of women.

In more recent times I worked closely with Michael Ayers, especially on the relationship between knowledge and belief from Plato to Locke; Chapters 1 and 2 build on a paper we have co-authored and which appeared in Ayers's *Knowing and Seeing* (Oxford University Press, 2019). Over and above this collaborative work, however, my whole project owes a great deal to many inspirational conversations with Michael. Those conversations, for which I am hugely grateful, have stimulated and shaped key aspects of my work. It is a pleasure and a privilege to record my thanks. The encouragement of Robert M. Adams, with whom I discussed this project especially in its early stages, has also been a key factor in the journey which has led to this book.

Peter Adamson, Maria Alvarez, Bill Brewer, Massimo Mugnai, and Andrea Robiglio have read a complete draft or have regularly discussed the whole project with me, contributing many insightful comments. I owe them an enormous debt of gratitude for their help and generosity, as well as for their friendship over the years. Many more friends and colleagues have read and commented on parts of my draft, and have discussed, challenged, and helped me revise various aspects of my proposal. They include Francesco Ademollo, Fabrizio Amerini, John Callanan, Lucy Campbell, Simon-Pierre Chevarie-Cossette, Nilanjan Das, Julien Dutant, David Galloway, Adrian Haddock, John Haldane, John Hawthorne, Chris Hughes, John Hyman, Andrea Kern, Michael Kremer, Jessica Leech, Clayton Littlejohn, Paul Lodge, Guy Longworth, Rory Madden, M. M. McCabe, Carlo

Nicolai, David Papineau, Gaston Robert, Gonzalo Rodriguez-Pereyra, Thomas Pink, Sebastian Rödl, Matthew Soteriou, James Stazicker, Hamid Taieb, Mark Textor, Cecilia Trifogli, Giovanni Ventimiglia, Daniel Whiting, and, especially, Raphael Woolf and Shaul Tor. 'Give belief its due!' was the expression used by Peter Momtchiloff at OUP to summarize our first discussion of this project. I am most grateful to Peter for his insightfulness and support all the way through.

Seminars and workshops have been crucial for the development of some features of my view. In addition to the constant source of intellectual stimulation provided by the weekly staff seminar at King's College London (KCL), a workshop on 'Knowledge and the First Person', organized by Ursula Renz and Johannes Roessler at Warwick University in September 2019, and a workshop on Michael Ayers's *Knowing and Seeing*, organized by Naomi Osorio-Kupferblum at the University of Vienna in February 2020, have been at the origin of various versions of Chapter 6. I had precious opportunities to present aspects of my work-in-progress at a number of visiting-speaker seminars, including during my tenure as Leibniz-Professor at the University of Leipzig in 2016; during a visiting professorship at Oxford University and Oriel College in 2019–2020 (including at an All Souls College seminar organized by Dmitri Levitin and Noel Malcolm and at the Oxford Epistemology Group organized by Nick Hughes); during a visit to the University of Milan as Senior Research Fellow (May and September 2021); and during my tenure at the St Andrews University as Scottish Philosophical Association Centenary Fellow (April 2022). I am very grateful to participants for their insightful feedback. The KCL students who attended my BA and MA classes on Epistemology in 2020–2021 and my work-in-progress MPhil/MPhilSt research seminar in March 2022 have challenged and helped me with their perceptive questions and comments (among others, those of Philip-Thomas Edwards and Barry Quek). Of course, none of the people mentioned here bear any responsibility for any shortcomings or misunderstandings in the way in which I have developed and executed my project.

From a more institutional point of view, it is a pleasure to record my thanks to the Mind Association for supporting work toward this book with a Mind Senior Research Fellowship in 2019–2020, to the Leverhulme Trust for granting a one-year Research Fellowship (declined to take up the Mind Fellowship), and to King's College London for two periods of institutional research leave (September–December 2020 and July–December 2022). It should also be noted that Part I of the book develops and extends views anticipated in 'The Distinction in Kind between Knowledge and Belief', *Proceedings of the Aristotelian Society* 120/3 (2020): 277–308; Chapter 6 reworks material from 'Subject, Object, and Knowledge as First-Person', *Grazer Philosophische Studien* 98/4 (2021): 516–29; and Chapter 14 is based on material from 'Belief, Religious Belief, and Faith' in a special issue on 'Kinds of Belief' in *Rivista di Filosofia* 110/2 (2019): 283–306, and 'Knowledge and Religious Belief', *Think* 20/58 (Summer 2021): 39–52. I am very grateful to the anonymous referees who evaluated the original proposal, and to the anonymous advisers who read and commented on the complete manuscript, all of them secured by Oxford University Press, for their invaluable comments and challenging questions. This book has been improved by my attempt to answer their points and to incorporate their suggestions.

I finally turn to thank those who are and have been most important to me, starting from my mother and father, Giuseppina Cremona and Gian Luigi Antognazza, for the constant inspiration they have provided with their practical wisdom. As always, my greatest debt is to Howard Hotson, who, over many years, has encouraged and supported me at every step of this project. His attentive and insightful reading of various drafts has been invaluable in helping me to clarify the structure and sharpen the argumentative line of the book. His comments have led to substantial changes of some aspects of my proposal. In brief, his help has been immense. John Antognazza Hotson and Francesca Antognazza Hotson have added a fresh perspective to our dinner table conversations while enduring with good grace their parents' seemingly endless appetite for these matters. This book is dedicated to Sophia Antognazza Hotson (Aberdeen, 31 May 1999–Oxford, 7 March 2018). Through her extra-ordinary life, Sophia made me realize (among many other things) that cognition is broader, richer, and more diverse than I thought, and that its best mode is powered by love.

Maria Rosa Antognazza

Oxford
23 March 2023

Editor's Preface

A brief note is called for regarding the circumstances in which this book was prepared for publication.

On 21 February 2023, the author was unexpectedly diagnosed with a rare and untreatable condition and given only three to six months to live. Six months earlier, she had submitted a mature draft of this book for review by the Oxford University Press, and her primary professional objective during her final months was to polish it for publication. By mid-March she had obtained and responded in detail to the readers' reports commissioned by the Press and adjusted the text in a number of significant respects. She then intended to read the penultimate draft through one more time with fresh insights in mind from her most recent reading; but during the following week a dramatic acceleration in the progress of her illness halted this final review at an early stage. She died at home on 28 March, just five weeks after her initial diagnosis.

When it became clear that she would be unable to continue, she entrusted to me the task of polishing for publication the manuscript which I had already read in two previous drafts. Her precipitous decline prevented careful planning: she simply asked that I 'delete all the queries' and read the volume through 'for coherence'. Fortunately, the manuscript was found to be in a very mature state. Although the number of clearly marked queries was large, most of these pinpointed minor details in the footnotes and Bibliography. In other cases, her notes indicated precisely what needed to be checked or completed. The only category of queries which could not be dealt was her plan to insert references to, and perhaps discussions of, about a dozen pieces of philosophical literature which the Bibliography indicated that she was still planning to read.

In consultation with her friend, colleague, and head of department, Maria Alvarez, a plan was devised to send the three sections of the book to appropriate experts currently or formerly at King's College London. We are grateful to Peter Adamson for reviewing Part I, Clayton Littlejohn and Mark Textor for reviewing Part II, and Zita Tóth for reviewing Part III. John Callanan has scrutinized the sections on Kant; and Michael Ayers, Susan James, Mogens Laerke, David Owens, Lucy Sheaf, Sarah Tropper, and Cecilia Trifogli helped with more specific questions.

In addition to dealing with the specific queries flagged by the author, the members of this informal editorial panel were invited to make only the most minimal of changes when they found obscurities of expression, errors of fact, or the kind of nuances of misinterpretation visible only to specialists. In only one respect was it found necessary to make more extensive insertions into the text. The Abstracts (for the online version) of the last ten chapters could be readily digested from the Introductions to Parts II and III, but equally clear signposting was lacking both from the Introduction to Part I and from the introductions and conclusions to some of the first five chapters. Continuing work on previous drafts (where I had advised on presentational issues of this kind), I have inserted what was lacking, keeping as close as possible to the author's own formulations, and vetting the new material with Peter Adamson, whose collaboration and advice were invaluable. The meticulous reader (who wishes to avoid ascribing to the author any statements not actually written by her) may wish to be aware that the longest of these insertions are the conclusion of the Introduction to Part I (numbered I.5), the opening paragraphs of Chapters 1–5, and the conclusions of Chapters 1–3 (that is, sections 1.3, 2.4, and 3.3).

Although this book was deprived of a final polishing by the author herself, she repeatedly expressed satisfaction during her last few days of work on it, and I believe that this published text is very nearly what she would have accomplished if she had been given sufficient time to complete the task unassisted. It has been a great consolation to her husband and a few of her friends to prepare this culmination of her philosophical legacy for publication in the months immediately after her premature death.

Howard Hotson

Oxford
28 June 2023

General Introduction

Epistemology is currently in ferment. What was recently regarded as the 'standard account' of knowledge is no longer consensual, yet no new paradigm has emerged to replace it. The aim of *Thinking with Assent* is to propose an original account of cognition by reframing the contemporary debate in the light of insights deriving from the history of epistemology. In so doing, the focus of this project is on identifying and outlining the most important cognitive modes which characterize our cognitive life.

For several generations, anglophone epistemological debates have centred on a conception of knowledge as a kind of belief which meets certain criteria. The *Stanford Encyclopedia of Philosophy* still informs us that 'much of epistemology revolves around questions about when and how our beliefs are justified or qualify as knowledge'.[1] Ever since Plato, according to the familiar textbook story, knowledge was conceived as justified true belief (JTB); but in 1963 a short paper by Edmund Gettier blew a huge hole in this supposedly 'traditional' account by showing that having a justified true belief is not sufficient for having knowledge. The key task which Gettier left to subsequent epistemologists was to repair this hole; and this they have attempted to do mostly via a series of increasingly sophisticated analyses which (typically) address the issue of how the third condition for knowledge (to be added to true belief) should be reconceived.[2] Yet an

[1] Entry 'Belief' (Schwitzgebel 2019).

[2] See Shope 1983 and 2002 for a sophisticated discussion of almost countless attempts; Lycan 2006 for an overview of attempted solutions to the Gettier problem; and Zagzebski 1994 for a discussion of the inescapability of Gettier problems. According to Zagzebski, the problem is located in the gap between justification (of both an internalist and an externalist kind—call it X) and truth. No matter how small the gap, as long as justification does not guarantee truth, it is always possible to have cases in which the normal link between X and true belief is broken by 'bad luck', but due to some accidental reason which has nothing to do with X, the belief in question may turn out to be true ('good luck'). Zagzebski considers two opposite ways of avoiding Gettier problems (Zagzebski 1994: 72): 1. Give up the independence between the justification condition and the truth condition (consequence: only true beliefs are justified); 2. Make the justification condition and the truth condition almost completely independent (consequence: true belief is enough for knowledge). Rather, in her view, the way forward is to acknowledge that fallibility is present in knowing. According to Greco 2003, knowledge is intellectually creditable true belief; Gettier subjects do not have it, hence they don't know. According to Sosa 2007, knowledge is apt belief, but Gettier subjects do not believe aptly, so they do not know. More recently, Turri 2011: 7 claims to have solved the Gettier problem by proposing the following account of knowledge: 'knowledge is adept belief, but Gettier subjects don't believe adeptly, so they don't know'. Sayre 1997 advances a ground-breaking view according to which while believing takes propositions as objects, knowing takes states of affairs. Knowledge cannot therefore be belief with the addition of other factors such as justification.

Thinking with Assent: Renewing a Traditional Account of Knowledge and Belief. Maria Rosa Antognazza, Oxford University Press. © Maria Rosa Antognazza 2024. DOI: 10.1093/oso/9780198831518.003.0001

adequate repair has proved elusive: the ongoing attempt to find the necessary and sufficient conditions which turn belief into knowledge continue to face counter-examples and charges of circularity.

In light of this recurrent failure, an increasing number of philosophers have called for the exploration of alternative accounts of knowledge. Notably, Timothy Williamson, in his ground-breaking *Knowledge and Its Limits* (2000), argues for a new 'knowledge-first epistemology'. Williamson's key manoeuvre is to invert the previously 'standard' relationship: rejecting the twentieth-century orthodoxy that regards belief as conceptually prior to knowledge, Williamson advocates the conceptual priority of knowledge to belief. Knowledge, he argues, can be characterized without reference to belief, while belief can be characterized by reference to knowledge.[3] Knowing, Williamson maintains, is a state of mind: the most general truth-entailing or 'factive' mental state.[4] On the other hand, 'believing p is, roughly, treating p as if one knew p'. 'Knowledge', he continues, 'sets the standard of appropriateness for belief.... [T]he further one is from knowing p, the less appropriate it is to believe p. Knowing is in that sense the best kind of believing. Mere believing is a kind of botched knowing.'[5] In short, for Williamson, knowing entails believing, but this entailment does not imply that the concept of knowledge is reductively analysable in terms of the concept of belief plus some other supposedly more basic notions.[6]

Another present-day proposal that decisively breaks with the twentieth-century (J)TB+ orthodoxy is John Hyman's original account of knowledge as the ability to be guided by the facts.[7] Hyman opposes the view that knowledge is a species of belief and argues that belief should be defined in terms of knowledge: 'we can define the belief that p', he writes, 'as the disposition to act (think, feel) as one normally or generally would if one knew that p'.[8] Contra Williamson, however, Hyman rejects the view that the concept of knowledge has a primary or basic role or position in our system of mental and logical concepts.

I propose to push this revolt against post-Gettier epistemology further, in a more radical manner, and in a way which differs in key respects from both

[3] Williamson 2000: 4–5. Cf. Guttenplan 1994, arguing that knowledge, as opposed to belief, is the central propositional attitude: according to Guttenplan, instead of the usual explanation of knowledge as belief plus something we should think of belief as knowledge minus something (that is, minus the 'factivity' of knowledge).

[4] A conception of knowing as a mental state is also defended by McDowell 1995.

[5] Williamson 2000: 47.

[6] The type of analysis at issue is a *reductive* conceptual analysis (cf. Williamson 2000: v, 33). The distinction between reductive and non-reductive forms of conceptual analysis is stressed by Strawson 1992. Cf. also Cassam 2009: 24–5.

[7] Hyman 1999, 2014, 2015 (esp. pp. 159–90), and 2017. For a brief discussion, see especially Chap. 9, sect. 9.2.3. Other proposals include Quine 1969; Craig 1990; Kornblith 2002.

[8] Hyman 2017: 285.

Williamson and Hyman's accounts.[9] Although there are significant differences between the many versions of (J)TB+ analyses of knowledge,[10] the shared features of these theories on which I will focus are the lack of a distinction in kind between knowledge and belief, and the reductive analysis of knowledge in terms of belief plus additional conditions.

My first step, in Part I of this book, will be to challenge the crude history of philosophy underling the entire Gettier paradigm. A careful survey of ancient, medieval, early modern, and modern epistemology will reveal that the allegedly 'standard' or 'traditional' analysis of knowledge as justified true belief is in fact neither standard nor traditional. On the contrary: it is difficult to find major philosophers, going back over thousands of years, who framed the problem of knowledge and belief in these terms; and what the main historical movements and authors did say about human cognition is typically strikingly at odds with this so-called 'standard' analysis.[11] In fact, leading representatives of the Western philosophical tradition do not merely reverse the relationship between knowledge and belief, in the manner proposed by Williamson's knowledge-first epistemology: they conceive knowledge, belief, and the relationship between them in a very different way. According to these genuinely traditional views, knowing and believing are distinct in kind in the strong sense that they are mutually exclusive mental states: the same cognitive subject cannot, simultaneously and in the same respect, be in a state of both knowing and believing the same thing. Knowing is not 'the best kind of believing';[12] nor is believing to be understood derivatively from knowing as 'knowledge minus something'.[13] In brief, in modern parlance, these traditional views propose a disjunctivist account of knowing and believing:[14] either one is in a mental state of knowing or one is in a mental state of believing. Knowing does not entail believing because knowing and believing are mental states which are different in nature.

Having reclaimed this historically well-attested account of cognition, my project involves reframing contemporary debates in the light of this account. My emphasis will not be on providing detailed criticisms of present-day rival

[9] Although some differences are already indicated below, the diversity of my proposal will become fully apparent in the course of this book.

[10] Notably, they divide between internalist and externalist approaches to justification, and include (among the latter approaches) reliabilist theories according to which knowledge is true belief formed in a reliable or truth-conducive way. Even the latter broad umbrella covers, however, significantly different proposals. For instance, in her pioneering work on virtue epistemology, Zagzebski (1996: 271) defines knowledge as a state of true belief arising out of acts of intellectual virtue.

[11] Cf. Antognazza 2015: 165–72; Dutant 2015; Ayers and Antognazza 2019.

[12] Williamson 2000: 47. [13] Guttenplan 1994: 297.

[14] As noted in the insightful discussion offered by Soteriou 2016, the distinctive claim of disjunctivism is its denial that cases of perception, illusion, and hallucination all have the same nature. According to disjunctivism, the kind of experience one has when perceiving the world does not have the same nature as the experience one has when hallucinating. On disjunctivism about perception cf. Hinton 1967, 1973; Snowdon 1980; McDowell 1982.

proposals but on developing what is (I suggest) a better alternative.[15] This alternative will be pursued in particular in Part II by revisiting and renewing historical insights which deserve, in my view, to be recovered. The core of this project will propose an account of developed human cognition according to which knowing and believing are irreducibly distinct ways of 'thinking with assent'. According to this proposal, knowledge is ontologically prior to belief and, crucially, is not a kind of belief—not even 'the best kind'. In turn, 'mere believing' (that is, on Williamson's account, believing without knowing) is not 'a kind of botched knowing'[16] but a mental state fundamentally different from knowing, with its own crucial and distinctive role in our cognitive life. Contrary to the claim that belief aims at knowledge,[17] I will argue that the *specific* contribution of belief to our cognition is that of aiming at truth where and when knowledge is out of our cognitive reach (either for objective or for subjective reasons). In this framework, therefore, the paradigmatic aim of belief is truth, not knowledge, although in some cases belief may well aim also at knowledge.

The final chapters (in Part III) are devoted to deploying this newly rehabilitated paradigm to address a range of controversial questions, including the taxonomy of belief, the role of the will in belief, testimony and collective knowledge, and religious epistemology. In religious epistemology, it will be argued that the conception of knowledge and belief as two irreducibly different cognitive modes is especially important in safeguarding the distinctive epistemological status of religious belief. In particular, *Thinking with Assent* will offer an account of religious belief alternative to that advanced by the influential movement known as Reformed Epistemology.

Before embarking on this venture, some clarifications are in order about what this project is, and, conversely, what it is not. First of all, 'knowledge' can be taken in different ways. This book takes it as the act of knowing by an individual. *Thinking with Assent* is about *individual* knowing, that is, it is concerned with what an individual knows as opposed to justifiably believes.[18] As convincingly argued by Alexander Bird, there is another type of knowing—social knowing—which is *analogous* but distinct from individual knowing.[19] As such, social (or collective) knowing has its own distinctive features—features which are not proper of, and do not simply transfer to, individual knowing. The epistemic humility suggested by the approach which will be proposed in this book is a

[15] I agree with Cassam and Williamson that 'the most effective way to demonstrate the limitations of the post-Gettier tradition'—and (I would add) of rival proposals more generally—'is by developing a better alternative' (Williamson 2009: 291; cf. Cassam 2009).

[16] Williamson 2000: 47.

[17] Williamson 2000: 47–8. See also Williamson 2000: 1: 'the point of belief is knowledge'. Cf. Greenough and Pritchard 2009: 1.

[18] In what follows, knowledge or knowing refers tacitly to individual knowing unless otherwise specified.

[19] Bird 2022. Cf. also Hyman 1999: 433; 2015: 159.

Socratic humility directed at claims of knowledge by individuals. If anything, it magnifies rather than diminishes the importance of collective knowing.[20]

Second, the account which will be presented is a *philosophical* account of human cognition. It is a proposal on how to think of cognition, knowledge and belief, with philosophical rigour, not an attempt to preserve common-sense views of what is meant by knowledge, or loose ways of speaking of knowledge and belief. We all have some pre-theoretical and pre-philosophical conception of what, broadly speaking, counts as knowledge and how this is distinct from belief. Such pre-theoretical and pre-philosophical conceptions are the point of departure of a philosophical investigation of human cognition but not its point of arrival. The over-preoccupation with offering an account of cognition which preserves what 'we' mean by knowledge in everyday discourse risks conflating what 'I' and my cultural and linguistic milieu mean by knowledge with some idealized 'we' who is supposed to hold widely, if not universally, shared views. At its best, the claim to capture what we all mean by knowledge is a piece of purely descriptive cultural history. At its worse, it is a piece of cultural imperialism which assumes that the culturally, socially, linguistically, and historically conditioned assumptions of my pre-theoretical world view are somehow the common views of humanity at large. By the same token, I am not especially keen to build on so-called 'intuitions'—the risk is, once again, to mistake for truth, or at least for the views of humanity at large, what are in fact culturally conditioned currently held opinions. As I see it, a key task of philosophy in general, and of the history of philosophy in particular, is to keep us alert to the fact that what people commonly endorse at a certain point in history may not be at all what we should embrace.[21] The project pursued in this book is therefore in line with what seems to me the task of any philosophical account more generally, namely, the task of giving rigorous answers to some fundamental questions which occur to most people—answers which, ultimately, may or may not closely align with pre-theoretical assumptions. The point is not to legislate (absurdly) on how people should use words but to show that, whatever people might ordinarily say or agree to, if they reflect in a sustained way on their initial views, they will come to the conclusion that some aspects need revision, others are best illuminated when observed from a different perspective, while still others might need to be abandoned altogether. In short, my ambition is to provide a philosophical account which makes sense, *upon reflection*, of our experience.

Third, the aim of this project is not to adjudicate what we call (or should call) what, but to identify what are the most fundamental modes of our cognition, whatever they are called or have been called in present discourse or in the history of human thought.[22] The claim is that—across time, languages, and different

[20] See Chap. 5, sect. 5.3.2, and Chap. 12 for further discussion.
[21] I have argued for this view in Antognazza 2015.
[22] *Pace* Dutant 2015: 112 and Pasnau 2017: 219.

philosophical systems—a prominent strand of thought can be traced which identifies in a broadly similar way some key distinctions in human cognition. In my view, the very fact that, despite different cultures, different languages, and vastly different philosophical commitments, certain patterns keep reappearing provides a good indication that these patterns are tracking something which is phenomenologically manifest prior to further metaphysical and epistemological claims such as realism or idealism, empiricism or rationalism, and so on. In other (currently fashionable) words, there is a good chance that these distinctions are carving nature at its joints, whatever the labels used in different languages and historical periods. As it will become apparent especially in the first part of this book, there is no clean translation from one language to the other, or from one historical period to the other, of what is called what. The same term may be used by different authors or in different periods to indicate quite different things. Different languages, or families of languages, may employ more fine-grained terminological distinctions which are not available in other languages. And yet, a careful study of the history of philosophy shows that there are some remarkably recurrent ways of identifying the fundamental modes of our cognition which resurface across otherwise sharply distinct philosophical views and terminology.

To indicate these cognitive modes, I have employed commonly used terms but in a precise, philosophical way—that is, as (to some extent) technical terms of the account I am proposing. In doing so, I am mindful of Locke's warning that, in our philosophical inquiries, we should not expect to be able to reform the languages of the world. Furthermore, I agree with Leibniz in taking the view that new terms of art should be avoided as much as possible. As he notes:

> when we write about something commonly discussed, and we do not labour under a lack of terms, it is either the mark of the foolishness of one who does not wish to be understood, or the malice of one intending to deceive, or the arrogance of one hoping, without reason, to drive others to his fabrications, to think up terms which are ours alone, or peculiar uses of them.[23]

It seems to me that, typically, good philosophical technical notions neither create fully new terms nor hijack a commonly used word to apply it to something altogether different. Rather, they use a common word in a technical manner to limit, sharpen, and shape an amorphous area still broadly recognizable in relevant ways as picked out by that term.[24] In particular, in this project, I will use

[23] Leibniz, *Elementa juris naturalis* (A VI, 1, 461). Trans. Lucy Sheaf, in Leibniz, *Elementa juris naturalis* (forthcoming).

[24] Indeed, it seems to me that Leibniz was an absolute master of the art of using common terms in a richer and deeper philosophical way. This does not mean, of course, that the introduction of new terms of art is always inappropriate (Leibniz himself introduced quite a few): it only means that they should be kept to a minimum.

'cognition' as a general category under which fall more specific categories such as 'knowledge' and 'belief'. Moreover, I will often use the term 'knowledge' as shorthand for a family of cognate cognitive modes picked out by terms such as *epistēmē, noesis, nous, katalēpsis, 'ilm, scire, scientia, intellectus, intelligere, intuere, intuitus* (with their derivatives in Romance languages), *wissen, Wissen, begreifen, knowing, knowledge, understanding,* and *intellection.*[25] Likewise, I will often use 'belief' as shorthand for a family of cognate cognitive modes picked out by terms such as *doxa, pistis, zann, opinio, opinari, fides, credere* (with their derivatives in Romance languages), *Glaube, glauben, Meinung, meinen, belief, believing, opinion, opining,* and *credence.*[26] In turn, as a shorthand, the notion of 'assent' will map onto terms such as *sunkatathesis, hupolēpsis, taṣdīq, assensio, assentio (ads-), assentire* (with their derivatives in Romance languages), *Fürwahrhalten, Anerkennung, Bejahung, Zustimmung, Setzung, assent, agreement, affirmation, assertion, assenting,* and *positing.* Moreover, I will speak of 'epistemology' from ancient philosophy onwards. Although the term 'epistemology', used in the modern sense of theory of knowledge, was introduced in the mid-nineteenth century, it does not follow that before the mid-nineteenth century there was no proper theory of knowledge—it only follows that it was not called 'epistemology'. Likewise, from the fact that pre-twentieth-century conceptions of knowledge were different from the main mid-twentieth-century orthodoxy, it does not follow that there was no proper 'epistemology' before the introduction of 'our' modern conception of knowledge.[27]

Finally, as an historian of philosophy by training and by passion, I take the view that philosophy has a great deal to gain from a deep engagement with its history.[28] Methodologically, *Thinking with Assent* is an illustration of this view. A distinctive feature of this project is its ambition to contribute to contemporary debates by rediscovering and renewing some key historical insights. The modes of thought we use today are the result, modification, rejection, and so on, of past modes of thought, although we may have lost track of why and how we have come to think in these ways as opposed to other possible (and sometimes more productive)

[25] I take it that this use of 'knowledge' as shorthand for a family of cognate cognitive modes is consistent with Williamson's proposal that knowing is the most general factive mental state, and that other factive mental states are more specific ways of knowing (cf. Williamson 2000: esp. 33–41, 48).

[26] A discussion of the important differences between cognate cognitive modes in these broader families, as well as between objects and acts of cognition, is offered throughout the book. There are of course significant variations on how specific authors use these terms: e.g., in Parmenides, *pistis* (intended as 'trust', 'reliance') typifies the relationship between the knower and the known as opposed to 'the opinions (*doxas*) of mortals, in which there is no real trust' (B1.30). (Thanks are due to Shaul Tor for drawing my attention to this example.)

[27] Cf. Pasnau 2017 and Carriero 2013, raising the question of whether there is any epistemology, in our sense of the term, in Spinoza or Leibniz. Note that, in Italian, until very recently 'epistemologia' mostly referred to the philosophy of science and not to the theory of knowledge, which was instead called 'gnoseologia'; in German, the theory of knowledge is still called *Erkenntnistheorie*, a term which (as Carriero reminds us) has a longer history than the term 'epistemology'.

[28] See Antognazza 2015.

ways. *Si parva licet*, in this recovery of historical insights I follow Leibniz's lead in focusing on what philosophers agree on, rather than on what they disagree about.[29] I do realize that this approach runs against what is customary in analytical philosophy but I take this very fact as an attempt to recover different and complementary ways of thinking. By my lights, the identification of patterns of agreement across different philosophical systems, historical contexts, and intellectual agendas, is heuristically fruitful for those more interested in finding out what is right than in pursuing what is original. To conclude, as Michael Ayers has recently reminded us, one of the key reasons for studying the past is simply 'to increase our "sample size" in modes of thought, for we need all the help we can get'.[30] We are dwarfs standing on the shoulders of giants:[31] the humility of the history of philosophy is also its strength.

[29] See Antognazza 2015. [30] Ayers 2019: 200, citing Stephen Jay Gould 1992.
[31] This metaphor has been traced back at least to Bernard of Chartres (eleventh-twelfth century).

PART I
KNOWLEDGE AND BELIEF
A Distinction In Kind

Introduction to Part I

I.1 The Contrast between Seeing and Not-Seeing

The view that knowledge and belief are distinct in kind in the strong sense that knowing and believing are mutually exclusive mental states is routinely dismissed in contemporary literature as so obviously implausible as to deserve little or no discussion.[1] Dissenting voices challenging the claim that knowing entails believing are few and far between.[2] My proposal breaks decisively with this trend by showing that a strong distinction in kind between knowledge and belief is well-attested in the history of epistemology and provides the basis for an account of cognition that avoids many of the pitfalls encountered in recent literature. Furthermore, my investigation will uncover that an important, and even dominant, historical strand not only has construed knowing and believing as mutually exclusive; it has also distinguished two elements of cognition which are, nowadays, typically conflated: namely, assenting and believing. Part I of this book explores salient aspects of these distinctions throughout the long history of Western philosophical thought, identifying some shared views.

It will be argued that, according to a persistent and genuinely traditional strand of thought which should be recovered, there are two fundamentally distinct modes of cognition which can be roughly characterized by the contrast between *seeing* and *not-seeing*. A remarkably clear formulation of this contrast is found in Aquinas:[3]

> the reason why the same thing cannot simultaneously and in the same respect be known and believed, is that what is known is seen whereas what is believed is not seen [ea ratione non potest simul idem et secundum idem esse scitum et creditum, quia scitum est visum et creditum est non visum]. (ST IIa IIae, q. 1, art. 5 ad 4)[4]

[1] E.g., Williamson 2000: 42; Alston 1991: 70–1; Pasnau 2017: 219.

[2] Myers-Schulz and Schwitzgebel 2013 challenge the standard view that knowledge entails belief, arguing that there are cases in which a subject knows some proposition *P* without (determinately) believing that *P* (I am grateful to Michael Kremer for drawing my attention to this paper). Black 1971 questions the received wisdom according to which knowledge entails, includes, involves, or necessitates belief.

[3] Hawthorne 2013: 127–31 acknowledges the seen/unseen contrast in Aquinas, noting that this contrast 'gets at some primitive distinction between a fact being present to the mind and its not being present to the mind', but finds it unhelpful 'to identify that kind of presence with knowledge'. I disagree: as I will argue in the course of this book, we will do well to recover this earlier conception of knowledge. For a recent defence of knowing as seeing, see Ayers 2019.

[4] Unless otherwise stated, translations are my own. On the contrast between seen/unseen as regards different modes of cognition see also Aquinas, *Scriptum super Sententiis*, lib. 3 d. 23 q. 2 a. 2.

In this tradition, the mental state of 'seeing' (or 'grasping') is regarded as the most fundamental, primitive cognitive mode. At first pass, this mode of cognition is usually indicated by terms such as *noesis, nous, katalēpsis, epistēmē, intellectus, intelligere, intuere, intuitus, scire, scientia* (with their derivatives in Romance languages), *begreifen, wissen, Wissen, understanding, intellection, knowing,* or *knowledge.*[5] In this tradition, knowledge derives directly from its object, which is present in a primitive and irreducible way to the mind of the knower. That is, knowledge, at its most basic, is a primitive perception or irreducible mental 'seeing' or 'grasping' the object of cognition with no gap between knower and known. Knowing is, most fundamentally, a *sui generis* cognitive contact between a subject and an object.[6]

This mental state is contrasted within this tradition with another mode of cognition in which the object of cognition is *not* directly seen or grasped. This cognitive mode is usually indicated by terms such as *doxa, pistis, zann, opinio, opinari, fides, credere* (with their derivatives in Romance languages); *Glaube, glauben, Meinung, meinen, belief, believing, opinion, opining,* or *credence.*[7] For this tradition, belief is a mental state or a cognitive mode in which precisely the perception or presence of the object which characterizes knowledge is lacking.[8] Therefore, knowledge cannot be a species of belief for the simple reason that 'seeing' cannot be a species of 'not-seeing'. Aquinas is again remarkably clear on the mutual exclusivity of these two mental states: either one is in a state of knowing or one is in a state of believing. The same person cannot be in both states at the same time and in the same respect:

> all knowledge [scientia] is acquired through some self-evident, and therefore 'seen', principles [principia per se nota, et per consequens visa]. And for that reason it is necessary that whatsoever is known is, in some way, seen [quaecumque sunt scita aliquo modo esse visa]. Now, as stated above, it is not possible that the same thing should be believed and seen by the same person. Hence it is indeed impossible that the same thing be known and believed [scitum et creditum] by the same person. Nevertheless it may happen that what is seen or known [visum vel scitum] by one, is believed by another. (ST IIa Iiae, q. 1, a. 5)

5 These terms involve further important distinctions, notably the distinction between act and object of cognition (discussed in Part II) and the distinction between non-discursive and discursive cognition (discussed esp. in Chaps 1, 2, and 5).

6 I take this traditional position to be in line with Williamson's claims that 'factive mental states' (of which knowing is the most general) are 'states whose essence includes a matching between mind and world' (Williamson 2000: 40), and that 'the most salient feature of knowing... is that it is a world-involving state' (Williamson 2014: 3).

7 Important differences in this doxastic family of cognitive modes are discussed esp. in Part III.

8 Cf. Antognazza 2015: 165–72 and Ayers and Antognazza 2019.

It is crucial to note that 'believing' here does not imply speculation determined by something other than convincing reasoning. The grounds for believing may be very strong, and belief can be true and strongly justified—and still, on this traditional account, such belief would not be knowledge but a different mental state or cognitive mode. Much traditional epistemology would certainly have agreed that justified true belief (JTB) is not sufficient for knowledge—not because something else should be added to true justified beliefs, but because the mental state of knowing is fundamentally different from the mental state of believing.

I.2 Belief as a Catch-All Category

Contrary to this long tradition of distinguishing in kind between knowing and believing, late-twentieth-century anglophone epistemology has instead been characterized by 'an inflated use of "believe"' in which 'the term "belief" has been allowed to spread over any positive propositional attitude'.[9] Or to adapt Hegel's metaphor, the notion of belief as used in much anglophone epistemology during the past six decades 'is like a night in which all cows are black'.[10] It has obscured the richness of cognition owing to its covering in an ambiguous way very different elements of our mental life. As the first part of this book will show, this blanket use of 'belief' was, however, far from standard in the philosophical tradition stretching back to antiquity. Nor was it is approved by the very architect of anglophone epistemology, John Locke, who took such great care in ensuring that the term 'belief' was not a general term which also covered knowledge.

How then did 'belief' become a catch-all category for all sorts of mental states? This book will argue that the catch-all conception of belief is the consequence of a sceptical attack against the older philosophy of cognition according to which there is a primitive contact between mind and world. More specifically, I will contend that the inflated use of 'belief' in twentieth-century philosophy has its roots in Humean scepticism. Once Humean-type scepticism declared that all putative knowledge is really, at bottom, belief—that is, a state traditionally conceived as lacking a direct presence to the mind of the object of cognition—the scene was set for a conception of belief as the umbrella under which to group all cognitive modes. The subsequent attempt to rescue knowledge from this sceptical attack via the specification of the necessary and sufficient conditions belief must meet to qualify as knowledge led precisely to the post-Gettier conception of knowledge as (J)TB+ criticized by this book and increasingly regarded as a philosophical cul-de-sac.

[9] Alston 1996: 20. By late-twentieth-century anglophone epistemology, I mean the epistemological literature which has been produced especially in the USA and in Britain primarily since Gettier 1963.

[10] Hegel used this metaphor in the 'Preface' of the *Phenomenology of Spirit* (§ 16) to criticize Schelling's Absolute.

I.3 The Conflation of Assent and Belief

Moreover, it will be argued that some of the key problems which have afflicted late-twentieth-century epistemology, and continue to afflict current debates, are rooted not only in this rebranding of knowing as a type of believing but also in the conflation of two other elements of cognition that a long tradition has kept distinct: namely, assent and belief. The first, assent, is an implicit, simple, and indivisible, mental 'yes' which applies generally to all affirmative, positive, or assertive cognitive mental acts/mental states—irrespective of whether such a cognitive mental state is compelled or not compelled by 'clear sight'. The second, belief, is a specific cognitive mental state which has degrees, and on the basis of which something *not* directly seen or grasped may nevertheless be affirmed for epistemic and non-epistemic reasons of varying degrees of strength. The former element is marked in the history of philosophy by terms such as *sunkatathesis*, *hupolēpsis*,[11] *taṣdīq*,[12] *assensio*, *assentio* (*ads-*), *assentire* (with their derivatives in Romance languages), *Fürwahrhalten*, *Anerkennung*, *Bejahung*, *Zustimmung*, *Setzung*, *assent*, *agreement*, *affirmation*, *assertion*, *assenting*, or *positing*. The latter element is marked in the history of philosophy by the family of terms already listed above: *doxa*, *pistis*, *zann*, *opinio*, *opinari*, *fides*, *credere*, *Glaube*, *glauben*, *Meinung*, *meinen*, *belief*, *believing*, *opinion*, *opining*, or *credence*.

The conflation, instead, of assent and belief manifests itself, among other things, in the sliding between treating belief as an on/off state and acknowledging that belief has degrees. How uncomfortable this sliding is, is shown, for instance, in the work of acute epistemologists such as William Alston and Robert Audi. In a seminal paper, Alston writes: 'I must confess to some uneasiness about the whole notion of degrees of belief. I am inclined to think that unqualified, flat-out belief that *p* requires that it seem unquestionable to S that *p*.' Despite this uneasiness, Alston opts to 'go along with the common view that beliefs come in all degrees of strength, from complete certainty at the top all the way down to a mere inclination to suppose that *p*'.[13] Similarly, Audi is inclined to think that 'an attitude properly

[11] Moss and Schwab 2019 show the centrality in Aristotle's epistemology of the notion of *hupolēpsis* as taking-to-be-true, noting that 'Many Ancient interpreters connect *hupolēpsis* with the Stoic notion of assenting' (p. 13; cf. also pp. 28–9 for the closeness between *hupolēpsis* and Stoics's assent or *sunkatathesis*). However, since Moss and Schwab identify 'belief as nowadays understood' with taking-to-be-true, their proposal is to translate *hupolēpsis* with belief. My proposal is that, in technical philosophical contexts, taking-to-be-true (or thinking with assent) should be kept distinct from 'belief'. This is due to the widespread ambiguous use of 'belief' as both: (1) a generic taking-to-be-true which applies to all affirmative cognitive mental states, including knowledge, and (2) a specific mental state incompatible with knowledge. Notably, also Moss and Schwab 2019: 8 acknowledge that '"belief" in English does double-duty'.

[12] *Taṣdīq* ('assent' or, literally, 'deeming something true') is the technical term used in Arabic philosophy from al-Fārābī (*c.*870–950) onwards to indicate affirming a proposition. On *taṣdīq* ('assent') and its contrast with *taṣawwur* ('conceptualization') see Black 1998. I am grateful to Peter Adamson for drawing my attention to the notion of assent in the Islamic tradition.

[13] Alston 1996: 6.

considered belief' is a 'flat-out' state which is difficult to reconcile with the notion of degrees of belief: 'For most of what we believe, it may well be true that we believe it unqualifiedly.... Granted, it is also true of belief that it does not preclude *some* degree of doubt, but typically, if one believes *p*, one does not doubt it.'[14] Another manifestation of the categorical versus graded conception of belief is the divide between the Bayesian approach to belief which dominates decision theory and formal epistemology, and according to which belief is primarily a quantitative and not a qualitative notion, and those who insist instead on the primacy of its qualitative nature.[15]

This tension between on/off belief and degrees of belief has recently been tackled in anglophone epistemology through the distinction between 'belief' and 'credence', used, respectively, for 'binary' (that is, on/off, categorical, full) belief and 'scalar' (or graded) belief.[16] This new terminological policy has been remarkably swift in supplanting talk of 'belief' as a state which has degrees—talk to be found (in a quite natural and common-sense way) in a vast amount of still fairly recent epistemological literature.[17] It is worth stressing here, however, that this new epistemological distinction has no basis in 'ordinary language' or etymology: 'belief' (from the Germanic side of the English lexicon and cognate with modern German *Glaube*) and 'credence' (from the French side, descended from the Latin *credere*) are essentially synonymous, sharing similar etymological origins in terms meaning 'to hold dear', 'to give credit', 'to confide', 'to trust'.[18] There is no analogy to this pair of synonyms in Romance languages, which are directly descended from Latin without an admixture of German, because there was no need to generate two terms meaning the same thing.

To be sure, the creation of technical vocabulary is a perfectly standard and acceptable practice in academic philosophy. What matters is not which terms we use but the mental states to which these terms are supposed to refer. However, whatever we may choose to call them, the current terminological fashion has correctly identified a problem—that is, the fact that elements of cognition which have incompatible features have been subsumed under the same notion (belief)—but has proposed a botched solution. One could of course continue to use 'belief' ambiguously to indicate both a binary state and a state which has degrees, or one could continue to mask this ambiguity by using two different (but broadly

[14] Audi 2011: 69, 72. Cf. also Maher 1986: 363. [15] Cf. Engel 1998: esp. 144.

[16] On current debates regarding the relationship between belief and credence see for instance Jackson 2020, 2019a; Buchak 2014: 59–71.

[17] Recent epistemological literature argues, for instance, for 'belief without credence' (Carter, Jarvis, and Rubin 2016), and forges related ad hoc terms such as C-evidence—'evidence that is credence-generating'—and B-evidence—'evidence that is belief-generating' (Jackson 2019b).

[18] Cf. Bénveniste 1969: 171–9; *OED*; Kurath, Kuhn, Lewis, and McSparran (2000–). Note that, unlike 'belief' and 'credence', 'assent' does not share these etymologies—this is another important indication that belief/credence and assent should not be conflated, as it will be argued in the course of this book.

synonymous) terms. But I see no advantage in this equivocal use in a *philosophical* context when there is an historically well-attested way to mark the key distinctions outlined above, as well as, most importantly, historical and theoretical reasons which explain why the equivocal and inflated use of 'belief' is not philosophically neutral.

In brief, what I would like to highlight is that the whole issue of 'binary' versus 'scalar' belief results from having conflated two elements of cognition which important strands of epistemology (including Stoicism, Aristotelian–Thomist Scholasticism, Kantian philosophy, and Newman's original brand of British empiricism) have kept distinct.[19] As *technical* philosophical vocabulary goes, the traditional distinction between assent and belief remains, in my view, a much better way, not merely of *solving* the problem, but of *eliminating* the problem in the first place.

I.4 Knowing, Believing, and Thinking with Assent

This brings us to the title chosen for this book. The key inspiration for that title is provided by Aquinas's explanation of two fundamentally distinct ways in which, in developed human cognition, the mind thinks with assent—two distinct ways that track, in turn, the distinction in kind between knowledge and belief crucial to the present proposal. Knowing is a mental state in which assent is moved 'by the object itself', that is, by the presence or presentation of the object of cognition itself to the mind (the object is 'seen'). Believing is a fundamentally different cognitive mode in which the object of cognition is not present (it is not 'seen'). Therefore, assent to a certain state of affairs being such-and-such is not sufficiently moved by the presence of the object itself and needs to be determined by reasons extrinsic to the object (reasons which may be of an epistemic or a non-epistemic kind):

> Now the intellect assents [assentit] to something in two ways. One way, because it is moved to assent by the object itself [ab ipso objecto], which is known either through itself [per seipsum cognitum] (as in the case of first principles, of which there is understanding [intellectus]), or through something else already known [per aliud cognitum] (as in the case of conclusions, of which there is knowledge [scientia]). In another way, the intellect assents to something, not because it is sufficiently moved to this assent by its proper object, but through a certain voluntary choice turning toward one side rather than the other. And if this is done with doubt or fear of the opposite side, there will be opinion [opinio]; if, on

[19] The difference between these two elements of cognition is discussed, in particular, in Chap. 2, sect. 2.1.2; Chap. 4, sect. 4.2.5; Chap. 11; and the General Conclusions of this book.

> the other hand, this is done with certainty [cum certitudine] and without such fear, there will be faith [fides]. Now those things are said to be seen [videri dicuntur] which, by themselves, move our intellect or the senses to knowledge of them [ad sui cognitionem]. Wherefore it is evident [manifestum est] that neither faith nor opinion can be of things seen [nec fides nec opinio potest esse de visis] either by the senses or by the intellect. (ST IIa IIae, q. 1, a. 4)

I.5 Milestones in a Traditional, Non-Sceptical Philosophy of Cognition

What follows in the next five chapters is a highly selective attempt to track some prominent cases of the strand of thought which endorses a distinction in kind between knowing and believing across very different epistemic traditions, historical periods, linguistic communities, and cultural domains. This shows (I claim) that a conception of knowledge as, most fundamentally, an immediate mental apprehension of reality—a 'seeing' or 'grasping' of 'what is'—cuts across a vast cultural, linguistic, historical, and (crucially) philosophical space, including the epistemological divide between rationalism and empiricism and the metaphysical divide between idealism and realism. Such a conception is therefore logically prior to *further* claims regarding the *nature* of what is seen or grasped, and is therefore compatible with different ontologies (for example, with idealism or realism about the nature of the reality which has been grasped). Likewise, the enormous expanse of this conception suggests that it is grounded in a feature of human experience deeper than language, culture, or mere philosophical tradition. Moreover, the gradual refinement and development of this basic position over time produces a rich variety of material which can be redeployed to introduce this traditional conception into contemporary epistemological debates (in Part II).

Chapter 1 begins this historical survey by revealing a deep epistemological consensus among ancient Greek philosophers. After finding the first traces of it in three leading pre-Socratics, it focuses particular attention on Plato. Rejecting the interpretation that *Meno* and *Theaetetus* propose a JTB analysis of knowledge, it argues that, for Plato and the polymorph philosophical tradition descending from him, knowledge is, most fundamentally, an apprehension of 'what is' distinct in kind from belief. Although Aristotle broke with his teacher on other key epistemological doctrines, the two were perfectly aligned in thinking that knowledge latches on to 'what is' or to reality, whatever their further views on the nature of this reality. A similar view of knowledge and belief underlies Epicureanism and Stoicism. Most interesting for present purposes, moreover, is the Stoics' clear early example of conceiving 'thinking with assent' as a broader, general category of which other cognitive modes—grasping, knowing, and believing—are either cases or epistemic components.

Chapter 2 shows how this same deep epistemological consensus resurfaces in medieval scholasticism, survives the transition to early modern philosophy, and bridges the divide separating rationalists and empiricists. Thomas Aquinas articulates with great clarity the ancient epistemological consensus that 'what is known is seen, and what is believed is not seen'. He then develops it further into a fine-grained analysis of different types of cognition. For him, cognition rises from the sense-perception of particulars via the sort of discursive cognition which he calls *aestimativa* in non-rational beings and *cogitativa* in rational beings to the fully-fledged cognitive modes of understanding (*intelligere*), knowing (*scire*), and knowledge (*scientia*) which, together with belief, qualify as different modes of 'thinking with assent'. Standard historical narratives might lead us to expect that Descartes might break with this pre-modern approach to epistemology. But, in fact, Descartes shares with the scholastics the fundamental conception of knowledge as an immediate mental apprehension, a primitive grasping or seeing, and the irreducible presence of the object of cognition to the cognizer. Locke too distinguishes between knowledge and belief as the difference between directly perceiving and not directly perceiving (in his case, the connection between ideas). In Leibniz, we find a broadly similar approach to this fundamental point, albeit with a closer analysis of the difference between degrees of knowledge. As knowers, he argues, we normally have only a partial grasp of fully determinate objects of cognition. Because we are unable (even in principle) distinctly to enumerate all the predicates which can be attributed with truth to the object of cognition, we do not know everything about the object. Nevertheless, whatever we do know is perfectly known.

In Chapter 3, ancient and modern Scepticism is portrayed as a response to the tradition outlined in the previous two chapters. Ancient Sceptics typically accept the Platonic distinction between reality and appearance but, unlike Plato, hold that we have access only to appearances. Hume also sharply distinguishes belief (however probable) from knowledge in the traditional manner; but he follows the ancient Sceptics in concluding that, in practice, the fallibility of our reason means that knowledge is beyond our grasp. This leaves only beliefs of greater or lesser probability. The disputed issue in ancient and early modern epistemology is therefore *not* whether some beliefs count as knowledge. Neither Sceptics nor their opponents adopt the supposedly 'standard' or 'traditional' view that knowledge is justified true belief. Rather, the point at issue is whether knowledge, understood as a *sui generis* primitive cognitive contact between knower and known, is possible for humans. Sceptics deny or at least doubt this possibility, either in principle or in practice. However, once cognition has been reduced, de facto, to belief and probability, it may seem to a much later generation that the only way to avoid scepticism is to redefine knowledge as a special kind of belief. This is precisely what (J)TB+ theories of knowledge have tried and (now according to many) failed to do. This recurrent failure is unsurprising, since such theories are ultimately the offspring of scepticism.

Chapter 4 sketches aspects of the distinction in kind between knowledge and belief after Hume. Kant retains the Platonic conception of knowledge and belief as two kinds of cognition that often have different objects and cannot one be a species of the other; but he inverts what we can know and what we can only believe: knowledge has phenomena as its objects; belief alone can extend to the noumenal world. Moving on to the early twentieth century, the historical survey then finds that the distinction in kind between knowledge and belief was reaffirmed in uncompromising terms by such diverse philosophical movements as Oxford Realism and neo-Scholasticism. These striking similarities between diverse philosophical movements are less surprising if one considers their common source in Aristotle and other aspects of ancient philosophy. This does not mean, of course, that contributors to these movements were in total agreement on epistemological questions. The disagreement of a prominent Oxford Realist with a prominent Catholic philosopher working within aspects of the scholastic tradition helps to clarify the crucial issue of whether assent admits of degrees.

On the basis of the traditions briefly retraced in Chapters 1 to 4, Chapter 5 draws some important conclusions about the significance for a non-sceptical philosophy of cognition of the distinction in kind between knowledge and belief. Here it will be argued at greater length that the main line of battle in the history of epistemology runs between those who affirm a natural mental state in which there is a *sui generis* contact between mind and reality, and those who reject such a natural mental state. For the former, we do enjoy a mental state which is different in kind from belief; for the latter, all our cognition is belief, and the question is how and when belief is permissible. The battle against scepticism (I conclude) is therefore won at the outset by observing that human beings share with other animals capable of sense perception a natural, primitive, effective contact between cognizer and cognized which apprehends those features of the environment which are in principle open to exploration by that particular kind of perceiving being. Once this initial contact is granted, higher forms of cognition can then be evaluated within a framework which does not start by assuming a gap between cognizer and cognized. Admittedly, this proposal sets the bar for knowledge high; but the charge that it sets the bar *too* high can be dealt with in two ways. The first response is to stress the crucial social dimension to knowledge: what a community knows is whatever some group or individual within the community has contacted cognitively in the manner required for knowledge. The second, complementary response is to acknowledge the crucial contribution made to our cognition by belief: the key point here is to recognize belief as a cognitive mode, irreducibly different from knowledge, but complementary of it and essential to our cognitive life, which offers a different but generally successful way to engage with reality and/or the world when rigorously governed by its own standards.

1
The Apprehension of 'What Is'

1.1 Knowledge, Belief, and the Apprehension of 'What Is'

If we wish to uncover the 'standard' or 'traditional' account of the relationship between knowledge and belief, the obvious place to begin is at the beginning of the Western philosophical tradition: in ancient Greece.[1] Doing so reveals that there *was* a standard account of this relationship among otherwise competing Greek philosophical schools, but that this account was completely at odds with the recently fashionable view that knowledge is a kind of belief (or, for that matter, that belief is a botched form of knowledge). The alternative view, reconsidered in this book, that belief and knowledge are fundamentally distinct and mutually exclusive modes of cognition, goes back at least as far as leading pre-Socratic philosophers such as Xenophanes, Parmenides, and Empedocles,[2] and underlies subsequent Greek philosophical traditions as diverse as Platonism, Aristotelianism, Epicureanism, Stoicism, and (as discussed in Chapter 3) Scepticism.

1.1.1 The Pre-Socratics

A sharp distinction between knowledge and belief as different in kind and involving different objects and faculties goes back to the earliest philosophers who wrote in ancient Greek. In his only preserved work, for instance, Xenophanes regards knowledge and belief as different in kind, associates the former but not the latter with sight, and suggests that they are set over different objects.[3] But the most prominent early example is surely Parmenides. Parmenides's only preserved work (a hexameter poem) proposes a similarly sharp distinction between 'the way of

[1] Cf. Ayers and Antognazza 2019: 5–14 and Vanni Rovighi 1963–1979: 11–39.

[2] Arguably, some intimations of this distinction are traceable even earlier, e.g., in the invocation of the Muses in *Iliad* 2.485–486: 'for you are goddesses and you are present and know all things, but we hear only report [*kleos*] and know nothing'. Thanks are due to Shaul Tor for this reference.

[3] The key text is DK21 B34: 'And that which is clear and certain no man has seen [*iden*]; nor will there be anyone | Who knows [*eidôs*] about gods and what I say about all things; | For even if, in the best case, someone succeeded in speaking what has been fulfilled, | Still he himself does not know [*oide*]; but belief [*dokos*] is fashioned for all'. Note that the Greek words for 'seen' (*iden*) and 'knows' (*eidôs*) in this text are cognate. Strictly speaking, the Greek *oida* (= 'I know') is the perfect tense of *eidon*: i.e., it literally means 'I have seen'. I am very grateful to Shaul Tor for the latter remarks and for drawing my attention to this text. On Xenophanes see Lesher 1992; Tor 2017: 128–33; Tor 2020: 20–3.

Thinking with Assent: Renewing a Traditional Account of Knowledge and Belief. Maria Rosa Antognazza, Oxford University Press. © Maria Rosa Antognazza 2024. DOI: 10.1093/oso/9780198831518.003.0002

truth' (*alētheia*) and 'the way of belief' (*doxa*).[4] Furthermore, in his famous and controversial Fragment 3, a close connection is established between 'intellecting' (*noein*) and being (*einai*).[5] Whether or not this fragment supports a metaphysics which identifies thought and being in a way which leads to idealism,[6] it seems to me beyond doubt that, for Parmenides, true cognition (or what we may call 'knowledge') makes contact with 'what is' (*to on*), or 'truth'/'reality' (*alētheiē*), whatever his conception of the ontological status of this reality. Indeed, Parmenides not only describes a mode of cognition that involves successful contact between mind and reality but also overtly distinguishes it from a qualitatively different cognitive mode labelled 'the beliefs of mortals' (*brotōn doxas*, B1.30). The latter takes as its objects other kinds of items, namely the multiple and heterogeneous items of everyday experience (for example, B10, B16). The bottom line is that these are distinct ways of thinking or distinct modes of cognition, and only the former allows us to grasp 'what is' (*to on*).[7]

In Empedocles we also find the idea that cognition is constituted by some sort of contact between the subject and object of cognition, conceived in terms of a physical or material assimilation of the object by the subject, grounded in a likeness between them.[8] This cognitive model is underpinned by a metaphysics which is therefore very different, and even opposed, to that of Parmenides. Yet both philosophers maintain that there is a mode of cognition in which we latch on to reality—a reality constituted, for Empedocles, by bodies which affect a perceiver through 'effluences'. Most importantly, Empedocles's insight that there must be likeness between cognizer and cognized has momentous consequences for a theory of what can, or cannot, be known[9]—a key insight which will be shared by very diverse thinkers, including Plato himself.[10]

[4] It should be noted that these are labels introduced by scholars as a way to summarize Parmenides's text rather than Parmenides's own labels. Moss and Schwab 2019 argue that *doxa* is not best understood as belief but as something closer to mere opinion. The reason why they challenge the common association of *doxa* with belief is that, in turn, they associate 'our' generic notion of belief with 'taking-to-be-true'. I fully agree with them that *doxa* is not generic taking-to-be-true, but a mental state 'incompatible with knowledge' (Moss and Schwab 2019: 4, 7–8, 10). I propose, however, to keep the notion of taking-to-be-true (or what I call 'thinking with assent') distinct from that of belief, precisely to avoid the pitfalls which derive from an ambiguous use of 'belief' as both 'taking-to-be-true' (or as an implicit mental affirmation) and as opinion.

[5] DK 28 B 3: '*τὸ γὰρ αὐτὸ νοεῖν ἐστίν τε καὶ εἶναι*'.

[6] For further discussion, see for instance Wedin 2014: chap. 22 ('Was Parmenides an Identity Theorist? On *νοεῖν* and *εἶναι* in Fr. 3').

[7] See Tor 2015 and Tor 2017.

[8] See DK 31 B 109/LM D 207: 'For it is by earth that we see earth, by water water, By aether divine aether, and by fire destructive fire, And fondness by fondness, and strife by baleful strife.'

[9] For the consequences I draw from this insight, see Chap. 15, sect. 15.3.2. As documented in a splendid note in Tor 2017: 175 (n. 22), the like-by-like principle almost certainly predates Empedocles, although Empedocles offers its clearer articulation in archaic Greece: expressions intimating this principle are found in the *Iliad* and *Odyssey*, as well as in some Hippocratic medical texts, while Theophrastus ascribes it (with good reason) to Parmenides.

[10] Cf. *Republic* VI 490b and *Phaedo* 78b–79e. The idea that there must be some sort of similarity between cognizer and the objects of cognition is found also in Aristotle (cf. for instance, Aristotle, *Nicomachean Ethics* 1139a10). I owe these references to Gaston Robert. For further discussion see Chap. 7, sect. 7.2.

1.1.2 Plato: 'What Is', 'What Is Not', and What Both 'Is and Is Not'

With Plato, we encounter the first ancient Greek philosopher whose works have been preserved in sufficient quantity and quality to found an enduring and hugely influential philosophical tradition which shapes Western thought. As this tradition evolves, it assumes many different forms, due not least to its mingling with other influential philosophical strands. Despite this diversity, certain distinctive features justify the labelling of aspects of otherwise importantly different philosophical systems as 'Platonist'. Among the most important and influential of these is the manner in which Plato not merely distinguishes sharply between knowledge and belief, but anchors this epistemological distinction in his idealistic metaphysics.

The most extended and explicit development of this view is found in *Republic* V–VII,[11] where it is underpinned by Plato's metaphysics.[12] According to Plato, knowledge is of 'what is' (ὄν) (476e7–477a1) and is therefore directed toward ('set over'; ἐπί) 'what is' (477a9). On the opposite extreme, ignorance is of 'what is not' (μὴ ὄν) (477a2–4) and is therefore set over 'what is not' (477a9–10). Between 'what is' and 'what is not', there is, however, something which both 'is and is not', such as beautiful things which are also in some respect not beautiful, or just things which are also in some respect not just (479a5–d2). Belief is the faculty or power directed toward (set over) what both 'is and is not'. Considered as powers or faculties (*dunameis*), knowledge (*epistēmē*; *gnōsis*) and belief (*doxa*) are therefore sharply different due to their having different cognitive functions (they do different things) and their being directed to two different kinds of objects (478a3–b2).[13]

Here three points require emphasis. First, anyone who knows achieves a cognitive contact with 'what is' or with reality: that is, knowledge latches on to entities which have real being (whatever those entities might be, 478a). Second, belief accomplishes something different: 'more obscure than knowledge but clearer than ignorance' (478c/Griffith 183). It is not mere ignorance, since ignorance has no object, but another type of cognition which is still 'set over' some kind of object (478b–c). The objects toward which belief is directed are images (*eidōla*),

[11] According to the standard division of Plato's works, *Republic* belongs to Plato's middle-period and is situated between the earlier *Meno* and the later *Theaetetus*. For Plato's original texts, including *Republic*, see *Oxford Classical Texts* (*OCT*).

[12] This traditional reading of *Republic* V–VII has been challenged by Fine 1979 and Fine 1990. In these controversial pieces, Fine argues that Plato aligns with contemporary epistemology in correlating knowledge not with objects but with propositions, thus leaving open which objects these propositions are about (that is, there could be knowledge of sensibles and mere belief about forms). In her view, Plato did not hold that knowledge involves 'any special sort of vision or acquaintance' (2000: 219) but was instead a coherentist. Fine's 'extremely unorthodox' reading has been convincingly rejected, to my mind, by Gonzalez 1996.

[13] Cf. Gonzalez 1996: 246–8 for a careful and detailed textual presentation of the argument. On the reading of 'is' as 'exists' see Ayers and Antognazza 2019: 6–7, where a summary of the argument is also offered.

copies (that is, entities which only indirectly and partially signal what really is), or *nomima* (that is, 'conventions', things which exist by convention or postulated states of affairs).[14] Although their status of 'being' and 'not being' what they signal is potentially misleading, *eidōla* or *nomima* still have a role to play in the cognitive journey towards grasping what fully is. Third, the mutual exclusivity of knowing and believing is grounded in their having distinct cognitive functions: they are different capacities which are directed at different objects.[15]

This account is echoed in the later *Timaeus* (51d3–52a7), where true belief (or true opinion, true judgement: *doxa*) and intellection (*nous*, considered as equivalent to *epistēmē* at *Tim.* 37c2 and 46d7) are distinguished as two kinds (*genē*) with distinct origin and nature (51d–e/Lee/Johansen 43; trans. slightly modified):

> If intellection [*nous*] and true belief [*doxa*] are different in kind, then these 'things-in-themselves' certainly exist, forms imperceptible to our senses, but apprehended only by intelligence; but if, as some think, there is no difference between true belief and intellection, what we perceive through our body must be taken as the most certain reality. Now there is no doubt that the two are different, because they differ in origin and nature.[16]

The famous discussions of the Idea of the Good (504b–509c), the Divided Line (509c–511e), and the Cave (514a–521d) expand and illustrate these views in such an iconic way that they became emblematic of what is traditionally regarded as 'Platonism', namely, the view that knowledge and belief 'are two entirely separate states of mind or faculties, each dealing with its own distinct set of objects'.[17] In Plato's ontology, these two sets of objects are, respectively, the unchanging Forms of the intelligible world and the sensible world (that is, what 'becomes' without ever being).

One of the reasons behind the attempt to fit Plato's texts into a twentieth-century epistemological framework seems to have come from a reaction against an extreme reading of this two-world ontology. According to Gail Fine, if we embrace the traditional interpretation of Plato's distinction in kind between knowledge and belief, and its underpinning in a two-world ontology, we arrive at the patently absurd consequence that 'no one can know even such mundane facts as that

[14] 479d3–5. This reading of *nomima* is defended in Ayers and Antognazza 2019: 7–8.

[15] Cf. 478a–b/Griffith 182/LCL 237: 557–9: '"Will the object of knowledge and the object of belief be the same thing? Or is that impossible?" "Yes, it is impossible, from what we have agreed—that is, if it is the nature of different capacities to be directed at different objects, and if knowledge and belief are both capacities, and if each is different from the other, as we claim".' On knowledge as having a different nature or essence than belief cf. Gerson 2009: 9–10. Moss 2021 argues that, for Plato, *epistēmē* is cognition of 'what is' (namely, it is a deep grasp of ultimate reality) while *doxa* is cognition of what seems, and that this distinction between cognition of what is and cognition of what seems is the most salient feature of Plato's epistemology. Cf. also Moss and Schwab 2019.

[16] Attention to these passages in *Timaeus* is drawn by Sedley 2004: 179. See also Sedley 2019.

[17] Sedley 2004: 179.

they're now seeing a tomato, or sitting at a table'.[18] As Francisco Gonzales notes, however, this consequence is absurd only if one assumes a twentieth-century conception of knowledge according to which knowledge amounts to justified belief in true propositions. By contrast, for Plato, knowledge (*epistēmē*, *noēsis*) is, primarily, a *non-propositional* form of *acquaintance*, that is, a 'direct acquaintance with what truly exists as truly F'.[19] This primitive seeing is explicitly explained by Plato through extensive analogies with sight in sense-perception.[20] 'Nothing Socrates says', Gonzales concludes, 'rules out the possibility of our having justified true belief that we are seeing a tomato': the crucial point is that such a justified true belief is *not* what Plato means by knowledge.[21] As emphasized by Lloyd Gerson, Plato's account could hardly be more different from the framework of the so-called 'standard analysis':

> for Plato if knowledge is the inerrant or infallible mental seeing of Forms or essences, it is not a representational state. It is not of propositions. When representations occur, belief, including false belief, is possible. A non-representational cognitive state like knowledge is one in which (1) what is known is present to the knower and (2) the knower is aware of that presence.... The content can be represented or expressed to oneself and to others, but the knowing itself is not the representation or expression.[22]

Regarding cognition more generally, the image of the Line provides the most detailed account of its richness and complexity as envisaged by Plato. The Line is divided into two main sections: 'one representing the visible kind, the other the intelligible' (509e/Allen 223). The first main section (corresponding to *doxa*)[23] is in turn divided into two modes of cognition: *eikasia* (imagination, conjecture), which has shadows, images, reflections as its objects, and *pistis* (belief),[24] which has sensible things (such as animals, plants, and artefacts) as its objects. The second main section is likewise divided into two types of cognition: *dianoia* and *noēsis* (intellection, understanding) (509c–511e; see also 533c–534a). The translation of *eikasia*, *pistis*, *dianoia*, and *noēsis* in these passages is notoriously difficult and controversial.[25] As Plato himself states, however, it does not matter which terms we use (533e); what matters is that the Line identifies four different states of

[18] Fine 1990: 96. Cf. Trabattoni 2016 for an interpretation which downplays the distinction, in Plato, between *doxa* and *epistēmē*.

[19] See Gonzalez 1996: 257–8, 262, 271. Cf. Bluck 1963: 259.

[20] Cf. especially the analogy between the Sun and the idea of Good (504b–509c).

[21] Gonzalez 1996: 271.

[22] Gerson 2009: 41. Cf. Gonzalez 1996: 274–5 and Gonzalez 1998.

[23] Cf. 533e–534a.

[24] *Pistis* is often translated with the Latin word *fides* (faith) and associated with religious faith. In the Platonic context at hand, however, *pistis* is simply used to indicate a kind of *doxa*.

[25] See especially 511e and 533e–534a. Griffith translates 'conjecture', 'belief', 'thinking', and 'understanding'; Grube/Reeve translates 'imagination', 'belief', 'thought', and 'understanding'; Allen translates 'Imagination', 'Belief', 'Understanding', and 'Thought'; Gerson 2009: 34 translates *noēsis* as

mind ('four conditions arising in the soul' 511d/Griffith 219). In *Symposium* (209e–212a) Plato appears to add a further stage of the cognitive ascent through a mystical intuition which goes above and beyond rational cognition and seems to be powered by an appetitive principle (love) rather than by a purely cognitive principle. Its purpose, Diotima explains, 'is to reach the final vision of the mysteries' (210a/Gill 47).[26]

To summarize the message of *Republic*: knowledge is a state of mind in which—contrary to what happens with *doxa*—what really is, is *seen*. Or, thinking of it as a power or faculty, knowledge is the power to see the Forms, as opposed to opinion as the power to judge of appearances. Like the freed prisoner of the cave, it is only by turning away from *doxa* and appearances towards the world of being that knowledge is achieved. This two-worlds ontology, even if granted, need not imply a total separation between worlds: the enlightened philosopher who returns to the cave after seeing the Forms is now able to discover imperfect images of the Forms in sensible things.[27] In other words, knowledge of what is truly F makes sensible things intelligible qua imperfect imitations or instantiations of F, as opposed to being merely appearances grasped through sense-perception.[28] But be that as it may, what is important here is that, for Plato, knowledge and belief are two mutually exclusive mental states or two different faculties with distinct cognitive functions: knowledge is a non-propositional acquaintance or cognitive apprehension of what really is; belief is a judgement about what appears to be.

1.1.3 Gettier and Plato

Unfortunately, a tentative remark in a footnote of Gettier's short paper of 1963 sparked an opposite interpretation which has been as dominant in analytical epistemology as the myth that justified true belief is the 'standard' or 'traditional' analysis of knowledge. Attempts 'to state necessary and sufficient conditions for someone's knowing a given proposition', Gettier writes, can be summarized as follows: '(a) S knows that P IFF (i) P is true, (ii) S believes that P, and (iii) S is

'intellection' and *dianoia* as 'understanding or thought'. Plato himself slides between calling the highest or fourth part of the line *noēsis* (511e) and *epistēmē* (533e–534a), in the latter case collecting both part four (*epistēmē*) and part three (*dianoia*) of the line under the category of *noēsis*, as opposed to parts two and one (*pistis* and *eikasia*), both categorized as types of *doxa*. Gerson 2009: 34 (note 10) notes that the word *dianoia* (and the prefix *dia-*) implies discursiveness while the word *noēsis* indicates a direct or immediate type of cognition.

[26] It is worth noting, in this connection, that the Form of the Good is said to be 'beyond being' at *Republic* VI 509b. I am grateful to Raphael Woolf for drawing my attention to this passage.

[27] 520b–c; Griffith 226: 'So you must go down, each of you in turn, to join the others in their dwelling-place. You must get used to seeing in the dark. When you do get used to it, you will see a thousand times better than the people there do. You will be able to identify all the images there, and know what they are images of, since you have seen the truth of what is beautiful and just and good.'

[28] Cf. Gonzalez 1996: 273–4.

justified in believing that P.' 'Plato', Gettier claims in his first footnote, 'seems to be considering some such definition at *Theaetetus* 201, and perhaps accepting one at *Meno* 98'.[29]

But is this what Plato is actually doing in these texts?[30] In *Theaetetus*, Plato does indeed consider an account of knowledge (*epistēmē*) in the neighbourhood of the (JTB) analysis formalized by Gettier, but only to reject it. This dialogue, from Plato's middle period, has three parts.[31] The first part presents and criticizes a definition of knowledge as sense-perception (*aisthēsis*) (151d–186d). The second part is concerned with a definition of knowledge as true belief or true opinion/true judgement (*alēthēs doxa*) as opposed to false belief/false opinion/false judgement (187a–201c).[32] The third part (201c–210a) considers the definition of knowledge as 'true belief plus an account [*logos*]'.[33] The dialogue, however, ends with the rejection of all three of these attempts to define knowledge. Already this fact shows that, far from endorsing an analysis of knowledge as JTB (in the form of true judgement/true belief plus an account), Plato considered such a conception and was not satisfied with it. If anything, rather than being the father of the JTB analysis discredited by Gettier, Plato anticipates (by a couple of millennia), at the very outset of the Western philosophical tradition, Gettier's criticism by noting that 'true belief plus an account' is not sufficient for knowledge.[34]

Furthermore, in his discussion of the third definition, Socrates seems to be objecting (among other things) to the very idea of an analysis of knowledge, thereby providing a much more radical criticism than mere dissatisfaction with this or that analysis. This is one of the key upshots of his critique of the so-called 'Dream Theory' (201b6–206c2) according to which knowledge is explained bottom-up as the combination of more basic elements: on this model, to know something would be to give an account of it by breaking it down into components which are not further reducible. Crucially, according to this theory, these ultimate

[29] Gettier 1963: 121. [30] Cf. Ayers and Antognazza 2019: 5–11.

[31] This division of Plato's corpus and tripartition of the *Theaetetus*, although not uncontroversial, constitutes the current convention among scholars. See Sedley 2004: 1–3 and Gerson 2009: 44.

[32] As noted by Sedley 2004: 118, the Greek word *doxa* and its cognate verb *doxazein* can be translated, respectively, as 'judgement'–'judge'; 'belief'–'believe'; 'opinion'–'opine'. Although Sedley favours 'judgement'–'judge' as a translation, he himself sometimes substitutes it with 'belief'–'believe' without warning. I note that a translation of the words *doxa–doxazein* (as used by Plato in *Theaetetus*) as 'judgement'–'judge' already puts some significant distance between Plato's second and third definitions of knowledge and Gettier's justified true belief. Nevertheless, I am happy to grant that (even in this translation) the definitions can still be regarded as in the neighbourhood of the JTB analysis.

[33] Also translated as 'true judgement plus an account'; 'true opinion accompanied by reason', or 'by a rational explanation', cf. 201c; 202c.

[34] Cf. *Theaetetus* 208b/LCL 123: 'Soc. There is, then, my friend, a combination of right opinion with rational explanation, which cannot as yet properly be called knowledge? Theaet. There is not much doubt about it. Soc. So it seems that the perfectly true definition of knowledge, which we thought we had, was but a golden dream.' Dutant 2015: 4 notes that *Theaetetus* 'ends with the suggestion that a true belief with an "account" is not sufficient for knowledge'. According to Gerson 2009: 44–55, in the *Theaetetus* Plato 'does not merely maintain the position he held in *Republic*, he also shows why knowledge cannot be as the Standard Analysis has it.'

components are themselves unknown and unknowable precisely because they cannot be further analysed (and knowledge, it is alleged, consists in giving an analysis). In his reply, Socrates rejects the view that knowledge can result from something which is itself unknown. His conclusion is that *knowledge* of the elements must be prior to knowledge of the complexes constituted by these elements, and that, therefore, the elements themselves must be primitively known in a direct and underivative way.[35]

As far as I can see, an implication of Plato's criticism is that knowledge cannot be explained by breaking it down into more primitive elements because those elements must themselves be *known*. Knowledge is already presupposed by any analysis and cannot, therefore, be explained by it. In modern parlance, one may say that Plato embraces a knowledge-first epistemology according to which successful cognition must be founded upon the direct, underived knowledge of at least some things: knowledge has ontological priority as well as cognitive primacy over other cognitive modes.[36]

In the same vein, Socrates ends his assault on a conception of knowledge as 'true belief plus an account' by showing that it is circular, since giving an account (or rational explanation) of the truth of a certain belief (or judgement) amounts to *knowing* why that belief is true. Once again, the notion of knowledge is already presupposed by this conception rather than being explained by it.[37]

The *Theaetetus* ends in 'the declared failure of the entire investigation',[38] but in so doing does not fail to achieve some important negative and positive results. Negatively, it already shows that: (1) justified true belief (or some conception in that neighbourhood) is not sufficient for knowledge; (2) that such a conception already presupposes the notion of knowledge and is, therefore, circular; and (3) that knowledge cannot be reductively analysed. Positively, it seems to suggest that knowledge is a primitive mental state which constitutes the foundation of any successful cognition. At any rate, it certainly does not endorse a JTB analysis of knowledge.

What about the earlier *Meno* 98,[39] tentatively charged by Gettier with having accepted the JTB analysis of knowledge (as opposed to having merely entertained

[35] Cf. Sedley 2004: 167.

[36] Gail Fine (1979) is right to point out that, for Plato, 'knowledge must be based on knowledge'. However, I follow Sedley (2004: 166–8) in disagreeing with her reading of this principle as proposing a circular, coherentist conception of knowledge as opposed to a hierarchical system.

[37] Cf. *Theaetetus* 201a–b/LCL 123: 'Soc. Then, it seems, if asked, "What is knowledge?" our leader will reply that it is right opinion with the addition of a knowledge of difference; for that would, according to him, be the addition of reason or explanation. Theaet. So it seems. Soc. And it is utterly silly, when we are looking for a definition of knowledge, to say that it is right opinion with knowledge, whether of difference or of anything else whatsoever. So neither perception, Theaetetus, nor true opinion, nor reason or explanation combined with true opinion could be knowledge.' Sedley 2004: 175–8 offers a detailed discussion of this circularity, identifying it also as Plato's fatal objection against the conception of knowledge proposed at *Meno* 98.

[38] Sedley 2004: 3.

[39] On the standard division of Plato's corpus see Sedley 2004: 2–3.

it)? At first blush it may appear that the following remark by Socrates proposes a JTB theory of knowledge according to which true beliefs are turned into knowledge by the addition of an explanatory account or reason (*aitias logismos*):

> [true beliefs] are not worth much until you tether them by working out the reason [*aitia*] ... Once they are tied down, they become knowledge and are stable. That is why knowledge [*epistēmē*] is more valuable than right opinion [*orthē doxa*]. What distinguishes one from the other is the tether.[40]

The problem is that Socrates goes on to say:

> And yet I myself am speaking not as one who knows, but as one who is guessing. What I *don't* think is pure guesswork is that correct judgement and knowledge are different. If there's anything else that I would claim to know—and there are precious few things of which I would claim that—this is one thing that I would add to the list of those that I know.[41]

Far from endorsing the notion that knowledge is justified true belief, at the very beginning of the Western philosophical tradition, the famously cautious Socrates clearly states that one of the very few things he knows is that knowledge is *not* a kind of belief because knowledge and correct judgement are two different things. More specifically, what Socrates claims to know is *that* knowledge and correct judgement (or true belief) are different, not *how* they are different. The explanatory account of how they are different just given at *Meno* 98a in terms of the addition of a reason (*aitias logismos*) to true belief, is straightaway demoted to guesswork at *Meno* 98b. Most importantly, there is something which Socrates *knows* (namely, that true belief and knowledge are different) without having an account of this difference. It follows that at least some knowledge is more primitive and already presupposed by the process of 'working out' the reason or logos of certain beliefs or judgements. In short, the *Meno* already bears the suspicion of circularity towards a JTB type of account which will be brought to the forefront in the third part of the *Theaetetus*.[42] The bottom line is that knowledge is not a complex and, therefore, derivative entity resulting from something else (that is, true belief, judgement, opinion) plus the addition of some other ingredient.

As David Sedley lucidly summarizes, 'the Platonist path that lies ahead is one on which knowledge—although nowhere formally defined—will be recognised as a state of mind that differs far too radically from true judgement to be defined as a

[40] Meno 98a; trans. Fine. [41] Meno 98b; trans. Sedley 2004: 176–7.

[42] This point is convincingly argued by Sedley 2004: 176–8. Cf. Ayers and Antognazza 2019: 9–10 and Gerson 2009: 28–30.

species of it'.[43] Gerson is even more trenchant in pointing out that Greek philosophers in general did not think of knowledge as a belief which meets certain criteria and that Plato in particular rejects the basis for a JTB analysis of knowledge 'on the grounds that knowledge is not a sort of belief; it is not belief—even *true* belief—'plus' something else'.[44]

Neo-Platonic thinkers such as Plotinus, in turn, latched into the Platonic insight that knowledge and belief belong to two distinct epistemic spheres and are irreducibly different. For Plotinus 'there is no knowledge of that which can be otherwise'.[45] Knowledge (intended as the highest mode of cognition or as thinking in its primary sense) is non-propositional and non-representational: it is a mental 'seeing' or a 'direct contact with—and, hence, identification with—that which is knowable. What are knowable are the paradigms of intelligibility, those entities which make it possible to understand that two things can be the same, though they are different. The sceptical challenge is addressed by denying that knowledge is belief that is justified by evidence.'[46] In short, the main thrust of a broadly Platonic and Neo-Platonic way of thinking is alien to the view that an account of knowledge can be given that starts from belief with the addition of appropriate conditions. On the contrary, as an underived cognitive contact with 'what is' or an intellectually 'seeing' the Forms, knowledge has ontological priority over other modes of cognition.

I conclude by noting that both the *Meno* and, more generally, the entire maieutic programme of Socrates, point at a further feature of knowledge: namely, its being fundamentally or essentially first-person.[47] The slave boy in the *Meno* does not have anything more than true belief until he grasps the geometrical proof by himself (85d3–4: 'he will know, having recovered the knowledge himself from himself [*autos ex hautou*]'). Being told that the proof is true is not the same as seeing it first-hand when one finally understands what follows from what. Only the latter state of mind counts, strictly, as knowledge. Moreover, what provides the tether which stabilizes true belief is 'working out' (that is, understanding, grasping) the reason, not merely being told.[48] Rather than belief being *turned into* knowledge, belief is *stabilized by* knowledge. Finally, Socrates's maieutic approach does not provide third-person answers: each one of us has to find out the answer for herself. This essentially first-person character of knowledge tallies with its

[43] Sedley 2004: 179. [44] Gerson 2009: 3.

[45] Gerson 2009: 141. Cf. Aristotle, *Posterior Analytics*, Book I, chap. 33, 88b. Gerson's discussion is based on the third treatise in *Ennead V*: 'On the Cognitive Hypostases and That Which is Beyond' (referred to as 5.3). Intellect and Soul are the cognitive hypostases; the One is the hypostasis 'which is beyond' Intellect and Soul.

[46] Gerson 2009: 134–51 (here p. 141). On Plotinus see also Gerson 1994 and 1996.

[47] For a discussion of individual knowledge as essentially first-person see Part II, Introduction, and Chap. 6. Cf. also Chap. 12 on the issue of testimony. This first-personal character should not be confused with solipsism or with a denial of the interpersonal nature of a Socratic maieutic approach.

[48] Cf. Ayers and Antognazza 2019: 9–10.

being, at its most fundamental, a non-propositional acquaintance: a *seeing* 'what is', or a presence of reality to the mind.

It may be tempting to brush aside the above discussion by dismissing it as an historian of philosophy's pedantry. Gettier was, obviously, not doing history of philosophy, and neither are modern analytic philosophers. No need therefore to get upset or to write long refutations. Instead, let it be taken for granted that an innocent historical mistake was made in attributing the JTB analysis to Plato, and that equally innocently, this mistake mushroomed into the orthodox view for generations of epistemology students. The next editions of epistemology textbooks can leave out any mention of Plato and all will be well. In what follows in Chapters 1 to 5, I will try to show that, if there are any truly innocent mistakes in history, this is not one of them.

1.2 *Nous, epistēmē*, and *katalēpsis*

Plato and Aristotle are commonly regarded as founders of two opposing philosophical schools, notably (for the matter at hand) as regards their approach to sense-perception. But although profoundly diverging on the latter as on many other issues, they seem to me perfectly aligned in thinking that knowledge latches on to 'what is' or to reality, whatever their further views on the nature of this reality.

1.2.1 Aristotle: Sense-Perception and Intellectual Perception

Nous and *epistēmē* are of course, for Aristotle, high-end cognitive achievements which require the intellectual ability to grasp universals. At its most basic, however, cognition is for him one of the natural states or natural activities of which certain kinds of living beings are capable. It is set apart from other natural states or activities of living beings by a peculiar feature, namely, the kind of *unity* which the cognitive act establishes between perceiver and perceived, or (in higher types of cognition) between knower and known—a kind of unity in which the ontological distinction between perceiver and perceived, knower and known, is at the same time maintained. This unity is observed by Aristotle, first of all, in sense-perception:

> The actuality of the object of perception and of the senses are one and the same, but their being is different. I mean, for example, actual sound and actual hearing. For it is possible for someone who has hearing not to be hearing; and what has sound is not always making a sound. But whenever what is able to hear is in actuality hearing and whatever is able to sound is sounding, then actual hearing

> and actual sounding come about simultaneously.... And since there is one actuality of the sensible object and what is capable of perceiving, though their being is different, it is necessary that what is spoken of in this way as hearing and sounding perish or be preserved at the same time. (*De Anima*, Book III, chap. 2, 425b, 426a; Shields, 52–3)[49]

I suggest that the core of Aristotle's position as outlined in the passage above is as follows: the act of perceiving consists in a pure presence or presentation of the object of perception to the perceiver with no gap between them. In *this* respect, intellectual 'perception' or intellectual knowledge is analogous, for Aristotle, to sense-perception:[50] 'Both reasoning and understanding seem to be a sort of perceiving, for in both of these cases, the soul discriminates [*krinei*] something and comes to know [*gnōrizei*] things that are [*ta onta*]' (*De Anima*, Book III, chap. 3, 427a; Shields, 55).[51] That is, despite the key differences between the capabilities of the senses and of the intellect, in intellectual cognition there is a unity between knower and known which is analogous to the unity between perceiver and perceived in sense-perception.[52] Thus, also theoretical knowledge is a pure presence of the object of cognition to the mind (in this case, 'objects which involve no matter',[53] that is, intelligible things such as, say, abstract mathematical objects). In this cognitive act there is a peculiar kind of identity between the knower and the known. Later on, the Scholastics translated Aristotle's view as the doctrine that *cognoscens in actu et cognitum in actu sunt unum* ('the knower in the act of knowing, and what is known in its being known, are one'), and called this identity 'intentional'.[54]

In brief, to be known is to be present to the mind, and to know is this presence of the object to the mind.[55] Aristotle even suggests that the 'mind' (*nous*, 'intellect') or 'that whereby the soul thinks and judges' is not a 'thing' but a capacity whose actual being *resolves into* this presence of the object of cognition in a cognitive act.[56]

[49] Smith, 687 translates (426a): 'Since the actualities of the sensible object and of the sensitive faculty are one actuality in spite of the difference between their modes of being, actual hearing and actual sounding appear and disappear from existence at one and the same moment.'

[50] In an insightful paper, Bengson (2015) argues for a 'quasi-perceptualist view of intuition' according to which intuitions are not hunches, inclinations, seemings, but 'presentations' to be understood, on a certain level of abstraction, as the same type of mental state as perceptual experiences.

[51] Aristotle goes on to rejects the *identification* between sense-perception and intellectual cognition ('thinking', *to noein*) to be found in ancient materialism (e.g., Empedocles). The problem, as Aristotle sees it, is that 'all of these suppose that reasoning is corporeal, just as perceiving is, and that both perceiving and understanding are of like by like' (*De Anima*, Book III, chap 3, 427a; Shields, 55). On the analogy between sense-perception and intellectual cognition see also the beginning of chapter 4 in Book III of *De Anima*.

[52] Cf. *De Anima*, 430a; Smith, 683: 'Actual knowledge is identical with its object.' Shields, 61 translates: 'Knowledge in actuality is the same as the thing.'

[53] *De Anima*, 430a; Smith, 683.

[54] For a detailed discussion of intentionality see Chap. 7.

[55] Attention to these passages and to this conception of knowledge is drawn by Vanni Rovighi 1962: 113–15 and Vanni Rovighi 1963–1979: 25.

[56] See *De Anima*, Book III, chap. 4, 429a; Smith, 682.

There are, however, key differences between sense-perception and intellectual cognition (or what Aristotle generally calls 'thinking', *to noein*). Sense-perception is always and only of particulars (corporeal objects, plants, animals),[57] that is, of the really existing things or 'things that are' with which the senses put us in contact in a variety of ways. On the one hand, sense-perception therefore relates the perceiver to 'something which is'; on the other hand, this contact with reality is limited to the 'here' and 'now', with no grasp of *why* the individual is the way it is.[58] Imagination (*phantasia*) extends this cognitive contact beyond what is immediately present to the senses, filling the gaps between perceptions.[59] Like sense-perception, however, imagination is also always and only of particulars. In turn, sensitive memory retains the images produced by imagination.

It is only with intellectual cognition that the cognizer is able to understand why things are as they are by grasping their intelligible form or essence. As Aristotle puts it succinctly in *De Anima*, the key difference between sense-perception and intellectual knowledge is that 'actual perception is of particulars, whereas knowledge [*epistēmē*] is of universals' (Book II, chap. 5, 417b; Shields, 34). In intellectual knowledge, the knower connects not only with 'things that are' but with their essences, that is, with the necessary, stable core which explains what they are beyond the accidental differences manifested in sense-perception.[60] Of course, these essences are discovered by the intellect in sensible things and are no longer the separate forms of Plato's ontology (they 'are, in a sense, within the soul', Aristotle writes).[61] Their apprehension in an act of intellection (*nous, noēsis*) seems analogous, however, to the act of intellectual *seeing* of a Platonic form.[62] Or, to use another striking metaphor found both in Plato and Aristotle, the simplest and most immediate act of thinking *touches* a corresponding, existing entity.[63]

1.2.2 Aristotle: *Nous, epistēmē*, and *hupolēpsis*

Book VI of the *Nicomachean Ethics* lists *nous* and *epistēmē* under the 'states of mind by which we have truth and are never deceived'.[64] These are distinguished as

[57] Cf. *De Anima*, Book II, chap. 5, 417b. [58] Cf. *Posterior Analytics*, Book I, chap. 31, 87b.

[59] On Aristotle's account of imagination see especially *De Anima* Book III, chap. 3, 428a–429a.

[60] Cf. Crivelli 2022: 608: 'in Aristotle's view a thinker thinks about an entity by immediately grasping its essence'. See *De Anima* 3.4, 429b16–18; 7, 431b2; 8, 431b28–432a3 (cited by Crivelli 2022: 608 n.).

[61] *De Anima*, Book II, chap. 5, 417b (McKeon, 566). [62] Cf. Ayers and Antognazza 2019: 11.

[63] See Aristotle, *Metaphysics*, Book 9, 10 (1051b24); cf. Plato, *Theaetetus* 190c6, d10, 208d8 and *Timeus* 37a6 (cited by Crivelli 2022: 611, where *Metaphysics*, Book 9, 10 is discussed in detail). As noted by Crivelli, 'to touch' is the only verb 'corresponding to the five canonical senses that cannot be construed with a 'that'-clause'.

[64] The other two 'states of mind by which we have truth and are never deceived' are *sophia* (philosophic or theoretical wisdom, conceived by Aristotle as the combination of *nous* and *epistēmē*) and *phronēsis* (practical wisdom). In book VI, chap. 3, Aristotle distinguishes five states 'by virtue of which the soul possesses truth by way of affirmation or denial': *technē, epistēmē, phronēsis, sophia,* and *nous* (1139b15; Ross).

the following two different kinds of truth-entailing states: (1) intuitive reason (*nous*) which 'grasps the first principles' from which all demonstrative knowledge follows, and (2) discursive or demonstrative knowledge (*epistēmē*), that is, 'judgment about things which are universal and necessary, and the conclusions of demonstration'.[65] Moreover, *Posterior Analytics* clarifies that intellection (*nous*) is more accurate (*akribesteron*) than demonstrative knowledge,[66] in line with the view that error does not originate in simple apprehension but in the process of combining or dividing simple objects of thought (hence the Scholastics' conception of judgement as *componere et dividere*, echoed by Locke's notion of agreement and disagreement between ideas).[67]

Judgement or taking-to-be-true (*hupolēpsis*) is, in turn, the generic cognitive mode under which, in *De Anima*, Aristotle groups more specific cognitive modes, including *epistēmē* and *doxa*.[68] Whereas knowledge (*epistēmē*) has as its object that which 'cannot be other than it is',[69] *doxa* is concerned 'with what can be otherwise'.[70] The difference in kind between *epistēmē* and *doxa* is grounded in this difference in kind between their objects, 'for when the objects are different in kind, the part of the soul naturally related to each is different in kind'.[71] Indeed, for Aristotle, 'it is not possible to *doxazein* [to have or form a *doxa* about] and to know the same thing at the same time'.[72] It is, at any rate, perfectly clear that Aristotle's *epistēmē* is not a matter of having justified true beliefs. If anything, as a grasp of demonstrations or as an explanatory capacity, *epistēmē* is closer to understanding than to justified true belief.[73] Finally, belief, for Aristotle, while

65 Aristotle, *Nichomachean Ethics*, Book VI, chap. 6; Ross.

66 *Posterior Analytics*, Book II, chap. 19, 100b. Cf. Gerson 2009: 72.

67 *De Anima*, Book III, chap. 6, 430b; Smith, 684–5: 'falsehood always involves a combining; for even if you assert that what is white is not white you have combined not-white... the thinking of the definition in the sense of what it is for something to be is never in error... but, just as while the seeing of the special object of sight can never be in error, seeing whether the white object is a man or not may be mistaken, so the belief that the white object seen is a man or not may be mistaken, so too in the case of objects which are without matter' (that is, in the case of intelligible objects). For Aristotle, there are two kinds of simple objects: essences (that is, natural kinds such as the kind horse) and incorporeal substances (God and perhaps some incorporeal intellects) (see Crivelli 2004: 6).

68 *De Anima*, Book III, chap. 3, 427b; Smith 680: 'within the field of judgement itself we find varieties—knowledge [*epistēmē*], opinion [*doxa*], understanding [*phronēsis*], and their opposites'. A few lines below, under the faculties or states of mind by which we discriminate and which are either right or wrong, Aristotle lists sense-perception (*aisthēsis*), belief (*doxa*), knowledge (*epistēmē*), and intellection (*nous*). Cf. Gerson 2009: 67–71 and Moss and Schwab 2019: 14–15.

69 *Posterior Analytics*, Book I, chap. 33, 88b. Trans. Gerson 2009: 67.

70 *Nicomachean Ethics* 1140b; Crisp 108. Cf. *Posterior Analytics*, Book I, chap. 33, 88b.

71 *Nicomachean Ethics* 1139a10; Crisp 104. I am grateful to Gaston Robert for drawing my attention to this passage.

72 *Posterior Analytics* 89a38–39. Quoted from Moss and Schwab 2019: 5, where it is convincingly argued that for both, Plato and Aristotle, *epistēmē* and *doxa* are 'mutually exclusive' (p. 4).

73 In his translation of the *Posterior Analytics*, Barnes translates *epistēmē* with 'understanding', in line with Burnyeat (1984)'s widely accepted proposal according to which Aristotle's *epistēmē* is closer to the meaning of the English word 'understanding' than to 'knowledge'. See also Moravcsik 1979 for *epistēmē* as understanding in Plato and Kosman 1973 for *epistēmē* as understanding in Aristotle. Significantly, Burnyeat's move is partly motivated by the need to differentiate Aristotle's conception of

being a cognitive mode different from knowledge (*epistēmē*) and understanding/intellection (*nous*), is still a species of rational judgement.[74] As such, it belongs only to beings endowed with reason, unlike sense-perception or imagination which is shared with non-rational animals.[75] To put it another way: although sense-perception and imagination, insofar as they are also powers to *discriminate*, are analogous to judgement, proper *judgement* requires the ability to discover universals. As a type of judgement, belief is proper therefore only to rational beings.

1.2.3 Epicureanism and Stoicism: *Energeia, katalēpsis, epistēmē*, and *doxa*

After Aristotle, Hellenistic philosophies such as Epicureanism and Stoicism develop complex and sophisticated epistemologies underpinned by naturalistic commitments.[76] As regards their metaphysical frameworks, these philosophical systems conceive 'what is', or what is ultimately real, in ways which are fundamentally different from the accounts provided by Plato or Aristotle. Epicurus reduces everything to atoms and void, reviving the ancient, pre-Socratic atomism of Democritus. The Stoics agree that the world with which we have our primary epistemic contact is a world of bodies, although they also argue that this world of bodies is totally governed by divine reason and providence. It is, therefore, all the more remarkable that, notwithstanding their alternative metaphysical models, they concur with Plato and Aristotle in drawing a sharp distinction between knowledge and belief, and in identifying the former with a mental state in which cognitive subjects are in contact with 'what is'. Irrespective of whether the ultimately real is conceived as intelligible objects or as material objects, for these very diverse philosophers there is a fundamental cognitive mode constituted by the presence of those objects to a cognitive subject. Belief, by contrast, is regarded as a different mental state in which there is no such direct apprehension of 'what is'.[77]

epistēmē as a capacity to give explanations from a 'modern' conception of knowledge as having a true justified belief. Cf. Lesher 2001: 45 and Gerson 2009: 89: 'Aristotle's account of thought in general drives his conclusion that knowledge is distinct from belief, and even from true belief.'

[74] Cf. *Posterior Analytics*, Book II, chap. 19, 100b.

[75] *De Anima*, Book III, chap. 3, 428a; Shields, 57: 'every case of belief implies conviction, while conviction implies being persuaded, and persuasion implies reason [*logos*]; yet among the beast some have imagination, but none has reason [*logos*]'.

[76] Gerson 2009: 90.

[77] Given their materialistic commitments, Epicureanism and Stoicism would of course not contrast knowledge and belief in terms of being directed toward different kinds of objects. Still, the contrast between knowing and believing as two different mental states in which one does, or does not, make contact with 'what is' is clear.

In his lost *Canon*, Epicurus distinguishes between the immediate grasp of what is true or 'evident', and what is 'non-evident'. The notions of *energeia* ('evidence') and *epibolē* (the 'act of attending') take central stage. On the basis of his materialist conception, Epicurus thinks of sense-perception in terms of fine configurations of atoms (that is, 'images', *eidōla*) which stream from the objects to the organ of sense (for example, to the eye) or to the mind, producing a 'presentation' (*phantasia*).[78] This process amounts to an encounter with an object which is real, and which is the source of the incoming arrangement of atoms impinging on the sensory organ that attends to it. The resulting 'presentations' or 'evidences' show what is true.[79] 'What is present already in perception', Epicurus stresses, must be carefully distinguished from 'what is waiting' to be verified,[80] that is, beliefs. Verification of beliefs is by 'witnessing':

> Witnessing is an apprehension by evidence (*katalēpsis di' enargeias*) that what is believed is such as it was formerly believed. For example, when Plato approaches from afar, I guess and believe, by reason of the distance, that it is Plato. When he has come near, it was witnessed in addition, when the distance was eliminated, that it is Plato, and this was witnessed by evidence (*di' enargeias*) itself.[81]

In brief, a primitive cognitive contact with reality (as conceived by Epicureanism) provides the foundation of all cognition as well as the 'measuring stick' or *kanōn* for measuring beliefs about what is non-evident (namely, things or states of affairs with which we are not in an immediate cognitive contact).

The Stoics agree with the Epicureans in grounding the possibility of knowledge in an immediate contact with reality given by 'cognitive impressions' (*phantasiai katalēptikai*).[82] Crucial to their epistemology is the notion of *katalēpsis* (literally, 'grasp'), introduced by the founder of Stoicism, Zeno of Citium (*c*.335–263 BCE), as a technical term to indicate the immediate *sense-perceptual* or *intellectual* grasp which provides the foundation of all cognition. Interestingly, one of the ways in which Cicero translates *katalēpsis* is *perceptio*: cognition is, at its most basic, a primitive perception (either sense-perceptual or intellectual) of 'what is'. Or, as Michael Frede puts it: 'in having a cognition the mind is in touch with things so as to grasp them'.[83] A 'cognitive impression' is, literally, a 'grasping revelation' (from *phantazein*, 'to reveal', and *katalambanein*, 'to seize or grasp'): it reveals the reality

[78] Asmis 1999: 260–6. [79] Asmis 1999: 269–72.

[80] Epicurus, *Kyriai doxai* 24 (quotation from Asmis 1999: 283).

[81] Sextus Empiricus, *Adversus Mathematicos* VII.212–13 (quotation from Asmis 1999: 283). Conversely, 'It is an impact by evidence that what is believed is not such as it was believed. For example, when someone is approaching from afar, we guess, by reason of the distance, that it is Plato, but when the distance has been eliminated, we have learned by evidence that it is not Plato' (*Adversus Mathematicos* VII.215; quotation from Asmis 1999: 284).

[82] Cf. Diogenes Laertius, *Vitae Philosophorum* (*Lives of Eminent Philosophers*) 7.54.

[83] See Frede 1999: 295–9 (here p. 298) and Ayers and Antognazza 2019: 12–13.

with which the mind comes to be in touch. In Cicero's words, cognitive impressions 'manifest, in a certain particular way, those objects which make the impressions'.[84] Despite the profound difference between the ontologies of Plato and of the Stoics, Chrysippus (*c.*280–206 BCE) is reported to have conceived this 'revelation' of reality to the cognizer in terms which are strikingly similar to Plato's account of the illumination of 'what is' in the intellectual vision which constitutes knowledge: 'The word '*phantasia*' is derived from '*phōs*' (light): just as light reveals itself and whatever else it includes in its range, so impression (*phantasia*) reveals itself and its cause.'[85]

Epistēmē, that is, knowledge or understanding which resists any argumentative attack and of which only the wise are capable, is built upon the foundation provided by *katalēpsis* (the sense-perceptual or intellectual grasp which is possible for any rational being). This is a distinction which seems to me analogous, in many respects, to the distinction between non-discursive intellection (*nous*) and discursive, demonstrative knowledge (*epistēmē*; *dianoia*) embraced by Plato and Aristotle. According to the striking metaphor proposed by Zeno, *epistēmē* is more secure than *katalēpsis* because the one who has *epistēmē* (namely, the wise person) not only 'grasps' the object with her fist but also grasps that fist with her other fist.[86] The image seems to indicate a state which involves further understanding (or a further, second-order grasp) of what is immediately apprehended (and is available to apprehension by anyone).[87] In turn, *doxa* (belief) is a different mental state which cannot be turned into knowledge. As Frede writes, for the Stoics, 'there is no way to get from mere belief to knowledge, however cogent one's arguments may be'.[88] In a key passage, Sextus summarizes as follows the relationship between *epistēmē*, *katalēpsis*, and *doxa* in Stoicism:

> For they [the Stoics] hold that three things are linked to each other: knowledge, belief and placed between these, grasping. Of these, knowledge is sure and stable grasping unalterable by reasoning; belief is weak and false assent [*asthenēs kai pseudēs sunkatathesis*]; and grasping is what is between these, assent to a graspable presentation. According to the Stoics, a graspable presentation is true and such that there could not be a false one just like it. They say that knowledge is present only in the wise, belief is present only in base men, but that grasping is common to both groups[.][89]

[84] Cicero, *Academica* I.41 (trans. Frede 1999: 297). Cf. Gerson 2009: 102 translates *katalēptikē phantasia* as 'graspable presentation'.

[85] Long and Sedley 1987: I.237 (sect. 39 B, Aetius). Cf. Ayers and Antognazza 2019: 13.

[86] Cicero, *Academica* 2.145.

[87] Cf. Gerson 2009: 110 and Frede 1999: 322.

[88] Frede 1999: 297.

[89] Sextus Empiricus, *Adversus Mathematicos* VII.151–2/SVF I.68–9. Trans. Gerson 2009: 104.

The common factor in *epistēmē* and *katalēpsis* is 'grasp'. What sets *doxa* (belief, opinion) apart from these two mental states or cognitive modes seems to be precisely the *lack* of such a grasp. What links all three is *assent* (*sunkatathesis*):[90] *epistēmē, katalēpsis,* and *doxa* all involve assent but the Stoics take a very dim view of belief since, on their account, this is a mental state in which assent is given without being in contact with 'what is'—something the wise person would never do. Needless to say, assent (*sunkatathesis*) and belief (*doxa*) are not the same thing and should not be confused with one another. Stoic epistemology, I suggest, is perhaps the clearest early example of conceiving 'thinking with assent' as a broader, general category of which other cognitive modes—grasping, knowing, and believing—are either cases or epistemic components.

To begin drawing positive, analytical conclusions, I do not mean to argue that 'knowing' and 'believing' are species of the genus 'assenting'. Rather, I regard knowing, believing, and assenting as mental acts which are essentially different. For instance, knowing and believing are on/off while believing is scalar; and knowing and believing are involuntary while assenting covers *both* involuntary and voluntary aspects of cognition. Therefore, knowing and believing are not species of a mental act which is on/off and may comprise both voluntary and involuntary elements. Rather, knowing and believing are the epistemic components of assenting.

1.3 Conclusions

This first chapter has briefly reviewed some highlights in the history of ancient Greek notions about knowledge, belief, and the relationship between them. What analytical implications can be drawn from this brief historical survey?

The most obvious one is that Gettier was careless, to say the least, in his interpretation of Plato. Far from *endorsing* the conception of knowledge as justified true belief, Plato carefully considered and then *decisively rejected* such a conception. So decisive was this rejection that one of the very few things Socrates claimed to know was the contrary position: that knowledge and correct judgement are two very different things. Moreover, Socrates and Plato not only rejected knowledge as (J)TB: they also rejected knowledge as (J)TB+, at least in the form of justified true belief plus an account (*logos*), and they did so (like many epistemologists in recent years) on the grounds of circularity.

The second and equally arresting conclusion is that Plato was not alone in sharply distinguishing belief and knowledge in this manner. On the contrary: a

[90] Gerson 2009: 104: 'Minimally, the "linkage" that exists between belief, grasping and knowledge is that they all require assent.' On the different kinds of assent in Stoicism see Frede 1984 and Barnes 1982.

similar distinction was already implicit in several leading pre-Socratics; it was maintained by Aristotle, despite his well-known disagreements with his teacher on other epistemological matters; and it was equally apparent in very different later philosophical schools such as Epicureanism and Stoicism. This raises the unsettling possibility that the six-decades-long attempt to 'rescue' the 'standard' account of knowledge after Gettier was misguided, since the (J)TB model was never standard. On the contrary: if there is a 'standard' account of knowledge in the founding phase of the Western philosophical tradition, it is not the position (considered and rejected by Plato) that knowledge is justified true belief: it is the doctrine, articulated in various ways by all of these philosophical schools, that belief and knowledge are two different cognitive states, relying on two different cognitive faculties, which may even be directed at two different kinds of objects.

Moreover, these ancient philosophical schools do not merely adopt or transmit this basic distinction: they progressively develop it. The pre-Socratics identify a basic contact between the mind and reality, characterize it by metaphors of sight, and first intimate the idea that it is grounded in a likeness between knower and known. Plato further identifies this kind of intellectual 'seeing' as a non-propositional, non-representational, primitive mental act which is essentially first-person. Aristotle further analyses the unity of knower and known, clarifies the distinction between sense-perception (of particulars) and intellectual cognition (involving universals), and further distinguishes the intuitive reason which grasps first principles from the discursive or demonstrative reasoning based on them. The Stoics extend the metaphors of sight to those of touching and grasping and develop the conception of 'thinking with assent' as a general category of which other cognitive modes—grasping, knowing, and believing—are cases or components.

The third conclusion of this first chapter, in other words, is that the history of this perennial distinction between knowledge and belief is not merely the endless recapitulation of the same basic idea: this history also documents the incremental refinement of that notion and its embedding in increasingly sophisticated philosophical contexts. The fact that this process of recapitulation and refinement continues despite the vast philosophical differences between these thinkers and schools suggests that the distinction between knowing and believing is grounded in some fundamental aspect of human experience (as will be further suggested in Part II).

2
Seeing and Not-Seeing

The deep epistemological consensus underlying so much ancient philosophy was not confined to the figures documented in the previous chapter: it survived the translation from Greek to Latin, from the pagan cultural milieu to the Christian world, and from the informal schools of antiquity to the formally constituted universities of the European Middle Ages. More remarkably still, it outlived the supposedly epoch-making epistemological shift between medieval and early modern philosophy, to remain foundational to the thought of such diverse philosophical giants as Descartes, Locke, and Leibniz. The process of gradual refinement of this traditional epistemology outlined in the first chapter therefore continues seamlessly in this second one.[1]

2.1 Thomas Aquinas: *Scire*, *credere*, and 'thinking with assent'

After the recovery of Aristotle between the twelfth and the thirteenth centuries, the distinction between knowing (*scire*) and believing (*credere*, *opinari*) was spelled out in remarkably clear terms by a philosopher and theologian who could hardly be suspected of wishing to undermine belief (and, in particular, religious belief): Thomas Aquinas. In the Middle Ages, Aquinas was by no means an undisputed authority. His philosophical positions were often at odds with other medieval views—not least those of medieval thinkers who drew their principal inspiration from Augustine and his Christianized neo-Platonism rather than Aristotle. On the other hand, there can be little doubt that Aquinas's thought had an enormous impact on the Latin West.[2] In particular, his conception of knowing and believing as different ways of 'thinking with assent' is, for present purposes, of great enduring interest.

[1] This brief introduction was lacking from the author's draft and has been added by the editor.

[2] As noted by Marenbon 2007: 245–6, Aquinas's thought achieved exceptional prominence following its institutionalization by the Catholic church after the Protestant Reformation. Since the mid-twenty century, the study of Aquinas has enjoyed an extraordinary renaissance in Anglo-American analytical philosophy, giving rise to so-called 'analytical Thomism'. Leading contributors include G. E. M. Anscombe, Peter Geach, Anthony Kenny, Brian Davies, John Haldane, Norman Kretzmann, Eleonore Stump, and Robert Pasnau. Literature on Aquinas in this analytical tradition is vast: for widely read overviews of Aquinas's thought see, for instance, Davies 1992 and Stump 2003. My own understanding of Aquinas is rooted, however, in an earlier Thomist renaissance which flourished especially in Germany, France, Belgium, and Italy from the mid-nineteenth century onward.

Thinking with Assent: Renewing a Traditional Account of Knowledge and Belief. Maria Rosa Antognazza,
Oxford University Press. © Maria Rosa Antognazza 2024. DOI: 10.1093/oso/9780198831518.003.0003

2.1.1 Thinking

In *Summa Theologiae* IIa IIae, q. 2, a. 1, devoted to the nature of believing ('*Quid sit credere*'), Aquinas starts from the ecclesiastical authority with whom any Christian theologian, at some point or another, must engage: Augustine. In *De Praedestinatione Sanctorum Liber Unus* 2.5, Augustine provides the framework for future discussions by noting that thinking is prior to believing since no one believes something without first thinking that it should be believed. To believe, Augustine concludes, is itself nothing other than thinking with assent ('ipsum credere, nihil aliud est, quam cum assensione cogitare'). Aquinas agrees but develops Augustine's point by inserting it into a broader account of cognition in which believing (*credere*) is compared with other cognitive modes—notably, knowing (*scire*).[3]

Thinking (*cogitare*), Aquinas notes, can be taken in three ways.[4] First, it can be taken in a broad, general way, as signifying any cognitive act. Second, it can be taken in a narrower sense as the discursive thinking which precedes the full understanding given by the certainty of seeing ('per certitudinem visionis'). In this narrower sense, thinking is the process of deliberation ('motus animi deliberantis') not yet perfected by fully seeing the truth ('per plenam visionem veritatis'). It is through this process of discursive thinking that human beings eventually arrive at knowledge ('id, quod scimus'). The culmination of this process is the formation of a mental word (*verbum*). That is, complete or fully 'formed' understanding requires conceptual thought (*verbum mentis*).[5] This *verbum mentis* finds its expression in natural languages (or in some other communicable system of signs) but is prior to any of them. Third, if thinking is about the apprehension of particulars, 'thinking' is taken as the act of the 'cogitative power' (*virtus cogitativa*).[6] By introducing the *cogitativa* into his account of cognition, Aquinas acknowledges that the senses are proper cognitive powers already *by themselves*, without the intervention of the intellect. There is cognition, therefore, before the introduction by the intellect of any concepts and (a fortiori) before any linguistic expression of concepts. As Aquinas boldly writes in ST I, q. 14, a. 1: 'Sense is cognitive [Sensus, autem, cognoscitivus est]'. Even more strikingly, the existence of an analogous cognitive power—called *aestimativa*—is also acknowledged in non-rational animals.[7]

[3] Cf. Aquinas, *Scriptum super Sententiis*, lib. 3 d. 23 q. 2 a. 2 ('Utrum credere sit cum assensu cogitare').

[4] ST II IIae, q. 2, a. 1.

[5] QDP Q. 9, a. 9 co.: 'Understanding [intelligere] itself is not complete unless something is conceived in the mind of the one who understands [aliquid in mente intelligente concipiatur], and this is called "word" [verbum]; for before some conception is established in our mind, we are not said to understand [intelligere], but to think in order to understand [cogitare ad intelligendum].' Cf. Shields and Pasnau 2016: 240–1, where attention to this passage is drawn.

[6] ST II IIae, q. 2, a. 1.

[7] Cf. ST I, q. 78, a. 4. On how this account tallies with Aquinas's naturalistic philosophy of mind or, more broadly, philosophical psychology, see Chap. 8, sect. 8.1.

Read against the Platonic and Aristotelian background, Aquinas is clarifying two important points, which stake out his own original position: (1) there is a meaning of 'thinking' (*cogitare*) which is broader than the Aristotelian (or the Platonic) *nous*, and that extends to all cognitive acts; most importantly, as we will see below, it also includes the kind of cognition that Plato and Aristotle called *doxa*; (2) even taken in a narrower sense of discursive thinking, *cogitare* is broader than Aristotelian and, especially, Platonic discursive thinking (*dianoia*) insofar as it includes not only intellectual reasoning but also pre-conceptual (and, a fortiori, pre-verbal) cognition grounded in sense-perception (what Aquinas calls *cogitativa* in human beings and *aestimativa* in non-rational animals).

Moreover, one of the key features which, according to Aquinas, distinguishes divine knowledge from human knowledge is the absence in the former of any discursive thinking:[8] the divine word (*verbum Dei*) is not the result of a process of thought but of complete understanding given by immediately and fully seeing the truth; divine knowledge (*scientia Dei*) is perfect intuitive knowledge or *scientia visionis* (knowledge of vision)[9] in which there is immediate clear sight (*manifesta visio*) of everything: God 'simul, et non successive omnia videt' (ST I, q. 14, 7). In human beings, a kind of cognition which gives us a glimpse of this 'knowledge of vision' is the intuitive, immediate grasp of self-evident truths.[10] Were our cognition closer to divine knowledge than it is, we would be able to grasp individual beings in all their individual determinacy, that is, we would be able to grasp not only that a certain living being is, say, a child, but also *all* the properties that can be attributed to that individual child[11]—something that, for the Aristotelian Aquinas, we are unable to do (perfectly adequate knowledge of individuals is, for Aquinas, beyond our ken).

2.1.2 Thinking with Assent

Aquinas's next move is to comment on 'thinking with assent'. His suggestion is that, taken in a broad sense, 'thinking with assent' is a category to which knowing, understanding, believing, suspecting, doubting, opining, and so on all belong. 'Thinking with assent' does not capture therefore what is distinctive of believing

[8] See ST I, q. 14, a. 7; ST I, q. 14, a. 14; ST II IIae, q. 2, a. 1.

[9] Cf. ST I, q. 14 a. 9: 'God knows all things [omnia]...Granted that certain things are not now actually existing, they have nevertheless existed or will exist; and all these God is said to know by knowledge of vision [scientia visionis]. For since God's understanding, which is his being, is measured by eternity, which exists without succession embracing all time, the present intuition of God [praesens intuitus Dei] takes in all time and all things which are in any time as present to himself.'

[10] According to Aquinas, there are first principles which are 'per se nota' and of which there is immediate grasp or understanding (ST II Iiae, q. 1, a. 5: 'principia per se nota, et per consequens visa'). Cf. also ST II Iiae, q. 1, a. 4.

[11] See ST I, q. 14, a. 11 ('*Deus cognoscit singularia*') and ST I, q. 14, a. 14.

(*credere*) as a cognitive mode, since also the person 'who considers the things that she knows [scit] or understands [intelligit], thinks with assent'.[12] In order to clarify what is distinctive of believing, one has to consider *how* assent is determined.

Now, some acts of thinking are characterized by 'clear sight' (*manifesta visio*) which compel assent. Such is the case of someone considering things she knows ('ea, quae scit') or understands ('vel intelligit'). As Aquinas puts it, understanding (*intellectus/simplex intelligentia*) and discursive demonstrative knowledge (*scientia*) are 'fully formed' cognitive acts.[13] This category is contrasted with another type of mental acts which are still 'unformed'—I take this to mean acts of thinking that are not characterized by clear vision and in which assent to a certain state of affairs is eventually reached as a sort of decision resulting from a discursive process of judgement. This second type of acts is divided in turn into subcategories depending on the degree of certainty with which assent is given. As Aquinas writes in the *Scriptum super Sententiis* (lib. 3 d. 23 q. 2 a. 2, qc. 3, co.), 'certainty is nothing else than the determination of the intellect to one [side] [certitudo nihil aliud est quam determinatio intellectus ad unum] and it is greater in proportion to the strength of what causes this determination [Tanto autem maior est certitudo, quanto est forties quod determinationem causat]'. Thus, 'to doubt' corresponds to a basic epistemic neutrality as regards giving assent to one or the other alternative; 'to suspect' is to be inclined to assent to one alternative on account of some slight motive; 'to opine' is to assent to one alternative but not without fear that the other may be true.[14] What is distinctive of the act of believing (and, in particular, of religious belief) is, on the one hand, its similarity to knowledge and understanding as regards the firmness of assent; on the other hand, its similarity to doubting, suspecting, and opining as regards the lack of clear sight. The following key passage in Aquinas's taxonomy of cognition deserves to be quoted in full:

> the act of believing cleaves firmly to one side, and in this respect a believer has something in common with one who knows and understands [in quo convenit credens cum sciente, et intelligente]; and yet his cognition [eius cognitio] does not have the perfection of clear sight [non est perfecta per manifestam visionem], and it has, in this respect, something in common with one who doubts, suspects, and opines. It is in this manner that it is proper of the believer to think with

[12] ST II Iiae, q. 2, a. 1: 'si ergo cogitare sumatur communiter secundum primum modum, sic hoc quod dicitur cum assensione cogitare, non dicit totam rationem ejus quod est credere: nam per hunc modum etiam qui considerat ea, quae scit, vel intelligit, cum assentione cogitat'.

[13] ST II Iiae, q. 2, a. 1: 'cum aliquis considerat ea, quae scit, vel intelligit, talis enim consideratio jam est formata'. Cf. Aquinas, *Scriptum super Sententiis*, lib. 3, d. 23, q. 2, a. 2, qc. 1 co.

[14] ST II Iiae, q. 2, a. 1: 'quidam vero actus intellectus habent quidem cognitionem informem absque firma assensione; *sive* in neutram partem declinent, sicut accidit dubitanti; *sive* in unam partem magis declinent, sed tenentur aliquo levi signo, sicut accidit suspicanti; *sive* uni parti adhaereant, tamen cum formidine alterius, quod accidit opinanti'.

> assent; and this is the way in which the act of believing is distinguished from all acts of the intellect that are about what is true or false. (ST IIa IIae, q. 2, a. 1)[15]

Furthermore, Aquinas clarifies that believing belongs to intellectual cognition and not to cognition limited to sense-perception ('cogitare non sumitur hic, prout est actus cogitativae virtutis, sed prout pertinent ad intellectum' ST II IIae, Q. 2, a. 1, ad secundum). The implication seems to be that non-rational animals are capable of sense-perceptual cognition, including a kind of discursive cognition based purely on the senses (the *aestimativa/cogitativa*), but not of belief, since belief is a type of discursive thinking which requires at least some grasp of universals (that is, some conceptual thought).

Finally, when assent is not simply compelled by clear sight (as in knowledge and understanding), the factor which determines the intellect to assent to one or the other alternative is the will:[16] 'the intellect of a believer [intellectus credentis] is determined to one side not by reason but by the will [non per rationem, sed per voluntatem], and therefore assent is taken here as an act of the intellect as determined by the will' (ST II IIae, q. 2, a. 1, ad tertium). I do not think Aquinas is recommending here doxastic voluntarism or is suggesting that one can believe things at will. For one thing, it is important to remember that when the object of cognition does by itself compel assent due to 'clear sight', as in the case of knowledge and understanding, the will has no role to play.[17] For another thing, when 'clear sight' of the object of cognition is lacking, the intellect is still *inclined* but not *determined* to assent to a certain state of affairs being one way or the other. The strength of this inclination depends, in turn, on the strengths of reasons in favour of one or the other side (and hence the distinction between doubting, suspecting, opining, and believing). In the absence of a full determination of assent *ex parte objecti*, however, some other factor is needed—namely, some conative or appetitive reasons (such as desire, trust, hope, love...) which in combination with cognitive or epistemic reasons ultimately determine the intellect to assent to the obtaining of one of the alternative states of affairs. In brief, what is needed is the will—that is, for Aquinas, the human rational version of the conative or appetitive power to be found in all sensitive beings. It is this appetitive power which drives sensitive beings towards what is good for them, or (at least) appears good to them.[18] Thus, believing remains an act of the intellect, whose specific aim is to reach truth; in some cases, however, assent to the obtaining of a certain state of

[15] Cf. ST Iia Iiae, q. 4, a. 1 and *Scriptum super Sententiis*, lib. 3, d. 23, q. 2, a. 2, co.

[16] The relationship between belief and will is specifically discussed in Chap. 11.

[17] Cf. ST Iia Iiae, q. 2, a. 9 ad secundum: 'now the assent of knowledge [assensus scientiae] is not subject to free will because the person who knows [sciens] is compelled to assent [cogitur ad assentiendum] by the force of demonstration'. Cf. *Scriptum super Sententiis*, lib. 3, d. 23, q. 2, a. 2, co.

[18] On the relationship between cognitive and conative/appetitive aspects of life, intellect, and will, see Chap. 6 and Chap. 9, sect. 9.2.4.

affairs may need to be finally determined by the conative/appetitive power which drives us towards what is (or appears) good.[19]

This model is crisply outlined in the key passage from the *Summa Theologiae* already quoted in the Introduction to Part I:

> Now the intellect assents [assentit] to something in two ways. One way, because it is moved to assent by the object itself [ab ipso objecto], which is known either through itself [per seipsum cognitum] (as in the case of first principles, of which there is understanding [intellectus]), or through something else already known [per aliud cognitum] (as in the case of conclusions, of which there is knowledge [scientia]). In another way, the intellect assents to something, not because it is sufficiently moved to this assent by its proper object, but through a certain voluntary choice turning toward one side rather than the other. And if this is done with doubt or fear of the opposite side, there will be opinion [opinio]; if, on the other hand, this is done with certainty [cum certitudine] and without such fear, there will be faith [fides]. Now those things are said to be seen [videri dicuntur] which, by themselves, move our intellect or the senses to knowledge of them [ad sui cognitionem]. Wherefore it is evident [manifestum est] that neither faith nor opinion can be of things seen [nec fides nec opinio potest esse de visis] either by the senses or by the intellect. (ST IIa IIae, q. 1, a. 4)

To summarize—for Aquinas, 'what is known is seen, and what is believed is not seen [scitum est visum, et creditum est non visum]' (ST IIa IIae, q. 1, a. 5, ad quartum). Sense-perception is a cognitive mode characterized by the presence of the object of cognition to the cognizer in which assent to a state of affairs being so-and-so is directly moved by this presence.[20] This type of cognition is only of particulars and is achieved without conceptual schemes provided by the human intellect. The senses afford, however, also a sort of discursive cognition restricted to particulars, named by Aquinas *aestimativa* in non-rational beings and *cogitativa* in rational beings: this is a power of discrimination analogous to judgement but it is not properly judgement due to the lack of universals/conceptual thought. In turn, understanding (*intelligere*) and knowing (*scire*)/intellection (*intellectus*) and knowledge (*scientia*) are the fully-fledged cognitive modes characterized by 'clear sight [manifesta visio]'. By contrast, belief—together with a family of

[19] Cf. also ST IIa IIae, q. 2, a. 2: 'since to believe [credere] pertains to the intellect, just as the drive toward assenting [motus ad assentiendum] comes from the will'; ST IIa IIae, q. 4, a. 1: 'Now the act of faith is to believe, as stated above (*q. 2. a. 2 and 3.*), which is an act of the intellect determined to one side [determinati ad unum] by the command of the will; hence an act of faith is related [habet ordinem] to both the object of the will, which is the good and the end, and the object of the intellect, which is the true.'

[20] I side with interpretations of Aquinas as a (qualified) direct realist, notably, Kretzmann 1993 (esp. pp. 138–42) and Perler 2000, 2004. For a different interpretation, see Pasnau 1997, 2008. This aspect is further discussed in Chap. 7, sect. 7.2.

cognate cognitive modes such as doubting, suspecting, opining—is a type of cognition in which 'clear sight' is lacking. Belief is, nevertheless, an intellectual type of cognition, that is, a type of discursive thinking which requires grasp of universals or conceptual thought (hence there is no belief in non-rational animals). Notably, this position neither disparages belief (as in Platonic *doxa*) nor conceives belief as botched knowledge. Finally, all these cognitive modes qualify as 'thinking with assent' either broadly taken as embracing any cognitive act, or narrowly taken as referring more specifically to discursive thinking.

2.2 Descartes: *Intuitus* and Evidence

Although it is common to emphasize the discontinuity between medieval and early modern Western thought, the transition between the Middle Ages and modern times is a long and complex process with no clean breaks.[21] To be sure, transformative processes commonly known as the Protestant Reformation and the scientific revolution reshaped the intellectual landscape of the sixteenth and seventeenth centuries, eventually feeding into the multinational and multilayered movements conveniently grouped under the label of Enlightenment. Yet the natural emphasis of actors and historians on innovation can result in an underestimation of the continuity between medieval and early modern philosophy. A striking example of such continuity is the continuing evolution of thinking regarding the distinction in kind between knowledge and belief.

Contrary to the textbook historiography which regards early modern epistemology as dominated by the 'traditional' conception of knowledge as justified true belief (JTB),[22] in central early modern texts one encounters the view that knowledge can start only by turning away from beliefs and opinions (Descartes). Instead of finding knowledge as a species of belief, one finds that knowledge is a state of mind irreducibly different from belief, since it is *seeing* (perceiving) what in the state of belief we *cannot see*, for example, it is sense-perception of external, bodily objects and/or mental *perception* of connections between two or more ideas (Locke). At the opposite end of the metaphysical spectrum, knowledge (in its adequate, full form) is conceived as a revised version of the traditional *visio Dei* (the vision of God) or beatific vision—that is, a vision of all things in God (Malebranche) or (in a more radical reconception) intuitive knowledge (*scientia intuitiva*) of God as the only one substance of which everything else is a mode

[21] Cf. for instance Marenbon 2013. I am very grateful to Michael Ayers for comments on an early version of the following two sections. On theories of knowledge and belief in the seventeenth century see Ayers 1998a.

[22] By 'textbook historiography' I mean the frequent claim in the late twentieth century that knowledge has been traditionally conceived as 'justified true belief'. For dissenting voices see Carriero 2013; Antognazza 2015; Dutant 2015; Ayers and Antognazza 2019.

(Spinoza).[23] Both the Epicurean/Stoic/Empiricist strand and the Platonic/neo-Platonic/Augustinian/Rationalist strand of seventeenth-century epistemology think of knowledge as a kind of seeing (by the senses or by the intellect). Neither of these strands thinks of knowledge as a kind of belief with the addition of certain conditions.

2.2.1 *Intuitus* as Immediate Mental Apprehension

Descartes is a particularly significant case in point. Already in the early *Regulae ad directionem ingenii*, Descartes declares that 'we ought to investigate what we can clearly and evidently intuit [intueri] or deduce with certainty, and not what other people have thought or what ourselves conjecture [suspicemur]. For knowledge [scientia] can be attained in no other way' (Rule Three: AT X, 366/CSM I, 13). Knowledge does not start from an attempt to justify our beliefs and opinions. Quite the opposite. As in the Platonic allegory of the cave, the first step towards knowledge is to free ourselves from beliefs and opinions, turning away from the 'fluctuating testimony of the senses [fluctuantem sensuum fidem] or the deceptive judgement of the imagination' (AT X 368/CSM I, 14), and to 'look'. As noted by the translators of the *Regulae*, 'intueri' means literally 'to look, gaze at' and is used by Descartes as a technical term for immediate mental apprehension. As noted in turn by J. Laporte in his classic *Le rationalisme de Descartes*, for Descartes 'savoir se réduit à voir' (Laporte 1945: 21)—knowing is reduced to seeing. To this immediate mental apprehension, to this *intuitus*, is also reduced the only other certain 'mode of knowing [cognoscendi modum]' (AT X, 369): *deductio*.[24] That is, the epistemic value of discursive reasoning is ultimately to be found in the *intuitus* by which we *see* that one link in the chain is necessarily connected to the next link (see Rule Three: AT X, 369–370/CSM I, 14–15): 'The self-evidence and certainty of intuition is required not only for apprehending single propositions, but also for any train of reasoning whatever.' Even if 'we held in our memory all the demonstrations of others [omnes aliorum demonstrationes memoriâ teneamus]' (AT X, 367), this would still not count as knowledge because we would not have seen for ourselves how one thing necessarily follows from another. Being founded in *intuitus*, *deductio* can never be wrong even though it is possible that we omit

[23] Cf. esp. Book III of Malebranche's *De la recherche de la verité* and Spinoza's *Ethica*, Part II, Propositions 40–7.

[24] The following are Descartes's definitions of *intuitus* and *deductio* in Rule Three: 'By "intuition" I do not mean the fluctuating testimony of the senses [fluctuantem sensuum fidem] or the deceptive judgement of the imagination as it botches things together, but the conception of a clear and attentive mind, which is so easy and distinct that there can be no room for doubt about what we are understanding [quod intelligimus]' (AT X, 368/CSM I, 14); 'deduction, by which we mean the inference of something as following necessarily from other propositions which are known with certainty' (AT X, 369/CSM I, 15).

something 'if we do not see it [si non videatur]' (AT X 365/CSM I, 12). In other words, failure in deductive reasoning comes from not seeing what is the case.

As usual, Descartes claimed that he was breaking completely new ground (see AT X, 369). In fact though, a conception of knowledge as ultimately an immediate mental apprehension, a primitive understanding, grasping, or seeing an intelligible truth,[25] was a central feature of the Scholastics's theory of knowledge. In *Summa Theologiae* I, q. 79, a. 8, Aquinas writes: 'For to understand is simply to apprehend intelligible truth: and to reason is to advance from one thing understood to another, so as to know an intelligible truth. [Intelligere enim est simpliciter veritatem intelligibilem apprehendere. Ratiocinari autem est procedere de uno intellecto ad aliud, ad veritatem intelligibilem cognoscendam.]' One could hardly miss the parallel between Descartes's *intuitus* and *deductio* and Aquinas's *intellectus* (the immediate intellectual perceiving or grasping of intelligible truth) and *ratiocinatio* (discursive, demonstrative reasoning). In Aquinas as in Descartes, the latter is a strength (due to its power to extend knowledge) but also a weakness, insofar as connections between one thing and the other are only mediately seen and ultimately rely on the *intuitus*, intellection, or primitive apprehension of each single connection in the chain. Angels, Aquinas continues, who have more perfect cognitive powers, do not need discursive reasoning, that is, they 'have no need to advance from one thing to another; but apprehend the truth simply and without mental discussion [sed simpliciter et absque discursu veritatem rerum apprehendunt] ... Reasoning, therefore, is compared to understanding [intelligere], as movement is to rest, or acquisition to possession; of which one belongs to the perfect, the other to the imperfect.'[26]

One might object that, for Descartes and other early modern authors, the objects immediately present to the mind are ideas, rather than things themselves. It should be noted, however, that this type of objection is fuelled from very early on by attacks on 'the way of ideas'. Not least for polemical reasons, these attacks do not acknowledge that 'ideas' can be construed as the things themselves as they are present to the cognizer.[27] That is to say, ideas are things themselves as perceived or thought by the mind (for example, my idea of the sun is the sun *itself* as I perceive, or as I conceive it). This construal of 'idea' is not so far from Aquinas's key statement that 'Cognition is brought about by the presence of the

[25] E.g., understanding why if a = b, and b = c, then a = c (even if one is unable to explain or give reasons why it is so). Cf. Ayers 2019: 195. In my view, it is utterly implausible to equate the immediate understanding of this truth to 'believing' it with conviction. To put it another way: anyone who has experienced such an understanding, and has not yet been indoctrinated with the theory that it must be some kind of belief, is very unlikely to think of it as 'strongly believing' that if a = b, and b = c, then a = c.

[26] Cf. Aquinas's conception of divine knowledge as perfect intuitive knowledge (*scientia visionis*) which does not require any discursive reasoning (briefly discussed above in sect. 1.1). See further Scribano 2006.

[27] Cf. in particular Antoine Arnauld's position in *Des vraies et des fausses idées*, discussed below in Chap. 7, sect. 7.3.2.

cognized thing in the cognizer. But the cognized thing is in the cognizer according to the mode of the cognizer.'[28] In fact, the scholastic distinction between formal and objective reality (that is, between the psychological and the intentional aspect of mental phenomena) plays a crucial role in Descartes's and Spinoza's conception of ideas.[29] But be this as it may, the point here is that, for both Descartes and the scholastic tradition, to know is, ultimately, a primitive and irreducible presence of the object of cognition (be it construed as ideas or things) to the cognizer.

2.2.2 Evidence

The invitation to turn away from opinions and the *fluctuantem sensuum fidem* is one of the leitmotifs of the *Discourse on the Method* and fills the first of Descartes's *Meditations*. In these key texts of Descartes's philosophical maturity, the conception of knowledge as evidence comes fully to the fore. Evidence is taken in its primary (and nowadays often overlooked) sense, derived from the Latin *ex* (from) + *videre* (to see).[30] 'Evident', in this classic, primary sense, is the quality of being 'distinctly visible', 'conspicuous', 'obvious to the sight' (OED). In turn, the original meaning of the term 'evidence', from the Latin *evidentia*, is 'manifestation', 'display', 'obviousness' (OED). That is, evidence is only secondarily a set of reasons for believing something; primarily it is a 'visibility' or 'seeableness' which allows an immediate apprehension by the mind. In its traditional definition, 'evident is what is seen [*evidens est quod videtur*]'.

Descartes's *Discourse*, echoing the early *Rules*, sets evidence taken in this primary sense as the cornerstone of the new method for discovering truth:

> The first [precept] was never to accept anything as true if I did not have evident knowledge of its truth [ne recevoir iamais aucune chose pour vraye, que ie ne la connusse evidemment estre telle]: that is, carefully to avoid precipitate conclusions and preconceptions, and to include nothing more in my judgements than what presented itself to my mind so clearly and so distinctly that I had no occasion to doubt it. (AT VI, 18/CSM I, 120)

Aquinas would have called this a cognition which is perfect 'due to clear sight' ('per manifestam visionem') (cf. *Summa Theologiae* IIa IIae, q II, art 1). This 'seeing very clearly' is what allows Descartes to affirm the *cogito* as the first truth:

[28] ST I, q. 12, a. 4: 'Cognitio enim contingit secundum quod cognitum est in cognoscente. Cognitum autem est in cognoscente secundum modum cognoscentis.'

[29] For further discussion see Chap. 3 on 'Intentionality'.

[30] For an illuminating discussion of the primary versus the secondary sense of evidence see Ayers 2019: 34, 66–7, 115–16, 118–19, 194.

> I considered in general what is required of a proposition in order for it to be true and certain; for since I had just found one that I knew to be such, I thought that I ought also to know what certainty consists in. I observed that there is nothing at all in the proposition 'I am thinking, therefore I exist' to assure me that I am speaking the truth, except that I see very clearly that in order to think it is necessary to exist. (AT VI, 33/CSM I, 127)

That is, certainty (as presented in this key passage) is not a subjective feeling but the objective certainty given by *seeing* (mentally grasping) the necessary connection between the subject and the predicate of a proposition (in the case of the *cogito*, to 'see very clearly' that thinking implies existing). In brief, the clear and distinct perception of what *presents itself* to the mind (AT VI, 18/CSM I, 120) is not a purely psychological, internal event which provides the subject with an internal justification for his belief (as it has been routinely interpreted by justified true belief theorists, only to castigate it as hopelessly subjectivist and internalist). Descartes is of course aware that sometimes we are mistaken in thinking that we are clearly seeing something when we are not.[31] Not even for him are we infallible in the sense that we never mistakenly take for clear and distinct what it is not so. But our error rests on mistakenly assuming to see what we are not seeing, not on assuming that what we *do* (intellectually) see in a clear and distinct way is true.

Translated into current philosophical language, this position seems consistent with the view of Williamson (2000: 23–6) that mental states (including knowing) are not transparent in the specific sense that one is not *always* in a position to know that one is in the relevant mental state. Likewise, it provides grounds for rejecting the sceptic's requirement that, to have knowledge, a subject should *always* be able to discriminate between the mental state of the good case and the mental state of the bad case. The key point is merely that—at least in some central, paradigmatic cases of knowing—one knows of knowing; and although this is not enough for infallibility, it is enough for certainty.

2.2.3 Knowing as Seeing

It is worth pausing at this point to extract from this traditional understanding of 'evidence' a proposal worthy of renewed philosophical attention: namely that, in cognition, everything ultimately rests on *seeing* what is the case.[32] At bottom, there is nothing else which can be done but *to see*—for example, to see that an argument

[31] Cf. AT VI, 33/CSM I, 127: 'So I decided that I could take it as a general rule that the things we conceive very clearly and very distinctly are all true; only there is some difficulty in recognizing [bien remarquer] which are the things that we distinctly conceive.'

[32] For a magisterial discussion of the relationship between knowing and seeing see Ayers 2019.

is cogent; to see that a premise is missing; to see what follows from what. Moreover, I contend that this is what anyone who advances any position whatever does, including those who reject appeals to seeing as naïve, or misguided, or unhelpful.[33] What is it that these attackers are doing but *showing* the flaws of the attacked position, so that also others can *see* (thanks to the attacker's sophisticated discussion) how naïve, misguided, and unhelpful the attacked position is? On what grounds does the attacker's rejection rest but on *seeing* (perhaps at the end of a long argument) that the rejected position is mistaken? Even those who deny the very existence of any foundational or grounding element in cognition, and propose instead a radically coherentist position, do so by trying to show the merits of coherentism so that those supporting foundationalism can eventually *see* how unsustainable their position is. Anyone who, thanks to a careful analysis, is finally convinced of a mistake is doing nothing else but finally *seeing* this mistake. Even the sceptic who affirms the radical uncertainty of everything, or the impossibility of knowing anything, is implicitly granting that she has shown (and that others should therefore *see*) the radical uncertainty of everything, the impossibility of knowing anything. The only real alternative to the appeal to seeing is silence. But then, as Aristotle famously said regarding attempts to deny the principle of non-contradiction, there would be no point in seeking 'to give an account of our view to one who cannot give an account of anything'.[34] In short, no one can deny, except verbally, the ultimate recourse to *seeing* what is (or is not) the case, and this appeal to seeing is nothing else than the appeal to what is evident.

The ubiquitous (and much maligned) visual metaphors are unavoidable not only for the generic reason that natural language is all imbued with metaphors but also for the specific reason that visual metaphors extend to other modes of cognition one of the most fundamental ways in which a sentient being relates to the world (another one being 'grasping', with its own attendant intellectual metaphors). According to the account of cognition which will be proposed in this book, there is continuity between basic animal cognition and more developed forms of cognition. It is therefore only natural that notions which describe the most primitive forms of contact between a sentient being and its environment—seeing and grasping—find an analogous application to more sophisticated cognitive modalities. If one accepts this continuity, it is to be expected that the experience of sense-perception (which is shared with other animals) helps to make intelligible to the human animal higher kinds of cognition.[35]

The real problem, I contend, is not the metaphorical character of appeals to vision, grasping, and the like. The real problem is that, in most cases, it is not easy, and, in many cases, it is not possible, to see what is (or is not) the case. More often

[33] Cf., for instance, Hawthorne 2013: 129–30.
[34] Aristotle, *Metaphysics*, Book 4 (1006a/Ross 737).
[35] On literal and metaphorical seeing see Ayers 2019.

than not, we have to guess, suspect, opine . . . rather than see. Those who at every turn take themselves to see clearly and distinctly what is what are often shown to be mistaken. But the problem is not the appeal to evidence (that is, the appeal to clearly seeing something). The problem is affirming as seen what is not really seen. One of the outcomes of the account of knowledge advanced in this book is the acknowledgment that genuine evidence of 'what is' is only very sparsely available to individual knowers. Mistakes are part and parcel of our laborious, incessant search for what is what. Yet, the best one can do is to come to see, eventually, that this or that was mistaken. In the end, there is nothing else but try to go back to what presents or shows itself to a sentient or thinking being.

2.3 Locke and Leibniz: Perception, Degrees of Knowledge, and Belief

2.3.1 Knowledge as Perception

While Descartes shares the Platonic distrust towards the senses, Locke belongs to the epistemic tradition that identifies sense-perception as the primary and fundamental form of cognition which puts us in touch with 'what is'—in a word, sense-perception is *knowledge*.[36] In his *Essay Concerning Human Understanding* (Book IV, chap. II, 14), he lists therefore '*three degrees of Knowledge*, viz. *Intuitive, Demonstrative, and Sensitive*: in each of which, there are different degrees and ways of Evidence and Certainty'. It is true that the main definition of knowledge in the *Essay* focuses on the perception of relations among ideas rather than on the perception of external objects afforded by the senses. In fact, Locke even tries to subsume sensitive knowledge under the general scheme of relations of ideas,[37] presumably in order to provide a unified account. In my view, however, what unifies his account is not this problematic attempt, but the adoption of a *perceptual* model across the board.[38] Knowledge is a kind of perception, and this perception (akin to vision) compels assent:

> When the Agreement of any two *Ideas* appears to our Minds, whether immediately, or by the Assistance of Reason, I can no more refuse to perceive, no more

[36] Draft A of Locke's *Essay Concerning Human Understanding* (echoing a passage in the earlier so-called *Essays on the Law of Nature*) starts: 'I imagin that all knowledg is founded on and ultimately derives its self from sense, or something analogous to it & may be cald sensation which is donne by our senses conversant about particular objects which give us the simple Ideas or Images of things' (Locke, *Drafts for the Essay*, p. 1). I am grateful to Michael Ayers for drawing my attention to this passage.

[37] Cf., for instance, Locke, *Essay*, Book IV, chap. I, 7.

[38] Cf. Bengson 2015, arguing for 'a quasi-perceptualist view of intuition'. Interestingly, Bengson caps his paper with a citation from Locke, *Essay*, Book IV, chap. I, 1.

> avoid knowing it, than I can avoid seeing those Objects, which I turn my Eyes to, and look on in day-light. (Book IV, chap. XX, 16)

To be sure, Locke's definition of knowledge in Book IV, chap. I, 2 of the *Essay* ends up being remarkably in line with the Cartesian notion of a clear and distinct vision ('evidence') of the connection between objects of thought. The deepest common element in the Cartesian and Lockean accounts is not, however, the stress on relations of ideas but the stress on knowledge as *seeing* (either literally in sense-perception or metaphorically in intellectual perception). 'Knowledge', Locke writes, 'seems to me to be nothing but *the perception of the connexion and agreement, or disagreement and repugnancy of any of our Ideas.* In this alone it consists. Where this Perception is, there is Knowledge, and where it is not, there, though we may fancy, guess, or believe, yet we always come short of Knowledge' (*Essay*, Book IV, chap. I, 2).

From this very definition of knowledge onward Locke draws a sharp distinction between knowledge and belief: the domain of knowledge is the domain in which we perceive the connection between ideas; the domain of belief is the domain in which we are unable to perceive such connection. There is no talk of justifying beliefs to turn them into knowledge, or of conditions or criteria by which beliefs can count as knowledge. As we will see, believing, for Locke, is quite simply another kind of epistemic state than knowing.

Finally, Locke's conception of knowledge as 'evidence'—in its primary sense of seeing (*videre*) the connection between objects of thought—is underscored by the striking number of sight metaphors in the first paragraph of the chapter of the *Essay* devoted to the degrees of knowledge (*Essay*, Book IV, chap. II, 1): 'All our Knowledge', he writes, consists

> in the view the Mind has of its own *Ideas*, which is the utmost Light... The different clearness of our Knowledge seems to me to lie in the different way of perception, the Mind has of the agreement, or Disagreement of any of its *Ideas*. For if we will reflect on our own ways of Thinking, we shall find, that sometimes the Mind perceives the Agreement or Disagreement of two *Ideas* immediately by themselves, without the intervention of any other: And this, I think, we may call *intuitive Knowledge*. For in this, the Mind is at no pains of proving or examining, but perceives the Truth, as the Eye doth the light, only by being directed toward it. Thus the Mind perceives, that *White* is not *Black*, That a *Circle* is not a *Triangle*, That *Three* are more than *Two*, and equal to *One* and *Two*. Such kind of Truths, the Mind perceives at the first sight of the *Ideas* together by bare *Intuition*... This part of Knowledge is irresistible, and like the bright Sun-shine, forces it self immediately to be perceived, as soon as ever the Mind turns its view that way... the Mind is presently filled with the clear Light of it. 'Tis on this *Intuition*, that depends all the Certainty and Evidence of all our Knowledge.

The 'intuition' described by Locke in this passage aligns with Descartes's *intuitus* and with Aquinas's *intellectus*. It is notable, among other things, for its irresistibility. Furthermore, as Descartes ultimately reduces *deductio* to *intuitus* (that is, to a 'perception' of what follows from what), so Locke ultimately reduces 'demonstration' to 'intuition':

> The next degree of Knowledge is, where the Mind perceives the Agreement or Disagreement of any *Ideas*, but not immediately.... Now, *in every step Reason makes in demonstrative Knowledge, there is an intuitive Knowledge* of that Agreement and Disagreement, it seeks, with the next intermediate *Idea*... So that to make any thing a *Demonstration*, it is necessary to perceive the immediate Agreement of the intervening *Ideas*. (*Essay*, Book IV, chap. II, 2, 7).[39]

2.3.2 Degrees of Knowledge

Locke's reference, in the passage just quoted, to 'degrees of knowledge' may seem at first sight inconsistent with the conception of knowledge explored in this book. If knowledge, at its most basic, is a primitive, irresistible, direct, and certain perception or intuition of what is the case, then how can it admit of degrees? In answer to this question, Locke devotes an entire chapter of his *Essay* to the different degrees of knowledge.[40] But for an even more penetrating and valuable analysis of the degrees to which we know, or can know, something, it is better still to turn to Leibniz.

Before doing so however, a potential confusion must be removed: namely, the possibility that, in considering degrees of *knowledge*, Locke and Leibniz actually mean degrees of *probability*. According to Pasnau (2017), the fundamental shift between pre- and post-Cartesian epistemology is the shift from certainty to probability, which follows the successful challenge of scepticism to claims of certainty. This view may seem to invite the thought that, for all their talk of compelling vision and clear sight, early modern authors begin to realize that knowledge is a matter of degrees of *probability* that something is true.[41] The higher the degree of probability, the higher the permissibility or justification of belief. Could one argue that early modern philosophers finally begin to move towards the approach to knowledge espoused by present-day formal epistemology, that is, the exploration of knowledge through the formal tools of maths, logic, and calculations of probability?

[39] See also in the Table of Contents, Book IV, chap. II, 7: 'Each step must have intuitive Evidence'.
[40] See Locke, *Essay*, Book IV, chap. II.
[41] For further discussion of Pasnau's position see Chap. 5, sect. 5.1.

The verdict on this historiographical thesis is clear: this is *not* what is implied by Locke or Leibniz's claims that there are degrees of knowledge. In Locke's work, discussion of degrees of knowledge is explicitly and self-consciously distinguished sharply from his account of probability and belief.[42] Leibniz, as a leading mathematician, was particularly well aware of the possibility of calculating the degrees of probability of a *belief*; but this was something sharply distinct from his discussion of degrees of knowledge, to which we now turn.

Leibniz's discussion of degrees of knowledge builds on that of his philosophical predecessors. In his view, Descartes and Locke noticed the distinction between what is 'clear' and what is 'distinct', but did not develop it fully in their accounts of knowledge.[43] 'Cognition', Leibniz explains in *De Cognitione, Veritate et Ideis* (November 1684) with exceptional concision, 'is either obscure or *clear*; and clear cognition is in turn either confused or *distinct*; and distinct cognition is either inadequate or *adequate*, moreover either symbolic or *intuitive*: and indeed if it is both adequate and intuitive, it is most perfect [perfectissima est]' (A VI, 4, 585–6). For Leibniz truth is the inclusion of the predicate in the subject of a proposition. Knowledge is, basically, seeing (immediately or by a process of discovery) this inclusion. Degrees of knowledge reflect the degree to which we can see or discover the inclusion of predicates in a subject, or (to put it in other words) the extent to which we are able to enumerate the properties or requisites which enter into the notion of something. When 'all that enters into a distinct notion is in turn known distinctly, that is when the analysis is carried through to the end [ad finem usque], knowledge is *adequate*'. But, Leibniz adds, 'I don't know whether human beings can give a perfect example of it although our knowledge [notitia] of numbers comes close.' In most cases, and 'especially in a longer Analysis, we do not gaze simultaneously at the entire nature of a thing [non totam simul naturam rei intuemur], but use signs instead of things' (A VI, 4, 587). For present purposes, it is particularly interesting to note that the latter mode of cognition is called by Leibniz *blind* or symbolic, and it is opposed to intuitive knowledge (A VI, 4, 587–8). 'Of distinct primitive notions'—that is, notions which are 'non resolvable' or 'non definable' because are not composed and can therefore be understood only through themselves—[44] 'there is no other knowledge than intuitive knowledge'; on the other hand, 'of composite notions there is for the most part only symbolic thought' (A VI, 4, 588).

Leibniz's conclusion is that this shows that in distinct knowledge no ideas are perceived except by intuition.[45] Once again, the bedrock of knowledge is *intuitus* (that is, literally, 'a look' or 'gaze')—an immediate mental perception which in

[42] Cf. Locke, *Essay*, Book IV, chapters II, XIV, XV.

[43] Cf. A I, 16, 510–11.

[44] See A VI, 4, 587.

[45] A VI, 4, 588: 'Ex his jam patet, nos eorum quoque quae distincte cognoscimus, ideas non percipere, nisi quatenus cogitatione intuitive utimur.'

complex notions are often not possible and is therefore substituted by '*blind* or *symbolic* thought' which uses 'signs instead of things' (A VI, 4, 587). To the extent that one sees (immediately or mediately) the inclusion of a certain predicate in the subject one cannot err about such inclusion ('who knows, to the extent in which he knows, does not err');[46] but to the extent in which the analysis of the subject is not complete, our knowledge of the subject is confused and fallible *despite including infallible elements.* 'It is possible', in other words, 'to have perfect knowledge [scientia] of several truths about objects of which we do not have adequate knowledge [notitia]').[47]

In brief, the core claim is that in most cases we can know some aspects of the object of cognition but our knowledge of this object is not adequate, that is, we are unable (even in principle) to achieve a complete analysis, distinctly enumerating all the predicates which can be attributed with truth to the object of cognition. The fact that our knowledge of the object is inadequate, however, does not prevent it from being knowledge in the strict sense of the term. That is, we do not know everything about the object, but what we do know (to wit: those predicates of which we do see the inclusion in the logical subject of a proposition) is perfectly known.

Given the framework of Leibniz's philosophy and, in particular, his theory of truth and his doctrine of complete concepts, it is not surprising that Leibniz approaches the problem from the point of view of the logical analysis of concepts. His point, however, is the logical version of a broader traditional point, namely, that the finite cognitive abilities of human beings do not stretch to an adequate (that is, perfect, exhaustive) knowledge of individuals. This limitation does not mean that there is no knowledge (in the strict sense of the term) but only belief or probability. There may be little that we can know, but what we do know (because we see, grasp, perceive it, literally or intellectually) is still distinct in kind from what we do not know but suspect, conjecture, or believe with different (from low to very high) degrees of probability.

To conclude—for Leibniz, knowing is, most of the time, a process of progressive determination of what is initially indeterminately apprehended (that is, in early modern terminology, confusedly cognized). There are increasing degrees to which I come to know something, not because it is only probable that this or that property belongs to the object of cognition, but because what I have grasped of the object is only a very limited aspect of what the object is in its fully determinate individuality. It may be perfectly clear, as opposed to merely probable, that what I am seeing is a person coming towards me; but only when the person is much

[46] Leibniz to Johann Friedrich Leibniz, 5 October 1669, in Leibniz 1934: 68–9.

[47] A VI, 4, 590: 'Caeterum memorabile hic discrimen est inter Notiones et Veritates; nam ad perfectam analysin *Veritatis* non opus est perfecta analysi notionis, quia saepe demonstratio rigorosa veritatis cujusdam occurrit notione aliquousque tantum resoluta, possumus ergo perfecta habere scientiam nonnullarum veritatum circa objecta de quibus adaequatam notitiam non habemus.'

closer may I be able to determine that it is my neighbour, as opposed to a stranger; and yet what I know about her (that she is a person, a neighbour, and so on) is only a minimal fraction of what can, in principle, be known.[48] Far from contradicting it, Leibniz's analysis of degrees of knowledge provides a powerful and important refinement of the traditional conception of knowledge rehabilitated and advocated in this book.

2.3.3 Belief

Turning from knowledge to belief, 'to believe', for Leibniz, is not to *see* that something is true: it is 'verum putare', 'to suppose [that something is] true'.[49] Locke, similarly, defines belief or opinion as 'admitting, or receiving any Proposition for true, upon Arguments or Proofs that are found to perswade us to receive it as true, without certain Knowledge that it is so' (*Essay*, Book IX, chap. XV, 3). Such belief has degrees which range 'from full *Assurance* and Confidence, quite down to *Conjecture, Doubt*, and *Distrust*.'[50] Locke is perhaps the most explicit among early modern authors in conceiving belief not as a more generic epistemic category which, with the addition of appropriate conditions, can be turned into knowledge, but as a qualitatively different epistemic state in which precisely that which defines knowledge—the perception of the agreement or disagreement between ideas—is absent (see for instance *Essay*, Book IV, chap. I, 2). I disagree, therefore, with a widespread interpretation of Locke as an 'evidentialist' for whom we should firmly believe only what has evidence sufficient to turn this belief (if true) into knowledge.[51] Of course, one could move from not perceiving the agreement or disagreement between ideas (and therefore guessing, opining, or trusting that there is agreement or disagreement) to perceiving it. In other words, one could move from belief to knowledge; but this movement would be a passage

[48] On cognition as a process of progressive determination of what is initially indeterminately apprehended see also Chap. 10, esp. sect. 10.4.

[49] Leibniz, *Commentatiuncula de Judice Controversiarum*, §20; A VI, I, 550: 'Credere est verum putare'.

[50] It should be noted that, in Locke's terminology, 'certainty' is reserved exclusively to knowledge; in the case of belief or faith Locke speaks of 'assurance' or 'confidence'. Furthermore, Locke (unlike Aquinas) uses the terms 'assent' and 'judgement' to refer only to the cognitive mode identified as belief as opposed to knowledge. Once again, the issue is not what words are used but what cognitive modes are identified as distinct in kind.

[51] Cf. the *Stanford Encyclopedia*'s entry on the ethics of belief (Chignell 2018: sect. 4.1): within evidentialist ethics of belief, 'many Evidentialists (Locke, Hume, and Clifford, for example) add the condition that the amount of evidence in one's possession must be proportioned to one's degree of belief, and that one should only *firmly* believe on the basis of "sufficient" evidence (where "sufficient" involves the evidence being strong enough for the belief to count as knowledge if true)'. See also Wolterstorff 1996 and 2005: 249–53. Wolterstorff's reading of Locke and 'Enlightenment Evidentialism' is discussed in Chap. 14.

from one mental state to another qualitatively different mental state, rather than a passage to a special case of a more generic state.

The watershed between knowledge and this qualitatively different mental state is explicitly identified by Locke by what he calls 'intuition', that is, the vision or presence to the mind which characterizes knowledge:

> herein lies the *difference between Probability* and *Certainty, Faith* and *Knowledge*, that is in all the parts of Knowledge, there is intuition; each immediate *Idea*, each step has its visible and certain connexion; in belief not so. That which makes me believe, is something extraneous to the thing I believe; something not evidently joined on both sides to, and so not manifestly shewing the Agreement, or Disagreement of those *Ideas*, that are under consideration. (*Essay*, Book IV, chap. XV, 3)

It is striking how this position agrees with some scholastic views drawing on Aquinas. Of course, Locke's epistemology is very different from Aquinas's—but not insofar as it identifies the defining feature of knowledge in a primitive and irreducible presence to the mind which distinguishes such a mental state from other cognitive modes, and makes knowledge (*quoad se* if not always *quoad nos*) the primitive and most fundamental cognitive mode. It is not knowledge which is built up from beliefs but beliefs which are justified by knowledge—that is, belief in what we cannot see is justified by what we can see. To put it in scholastic terms, in knowledge assent is determined by the object itself, as in the case of the immediate intellectual perception of principles (*intellectus principiorum*) or of the mediate knowledge of conclusions (*scientia conclusionum*). These are instances in which the connection between the subject and the predicate of a proposition is either immediately seen by intuition or mediately seen by demonstration. There are cases, however, in which the connection between subject and predicate of a proposition is not seen either immediately or mediately. In such cases, the object itself does not sufficiently move the intellect to assent and other reasons (notably the strength of testimony) are therefore needed (in Locke's words, 'That which makes me believe, is something extraneous to the thing I believe').[52]

To summarize—belief is different in kind from knowledge in that it lacks the evidence *a parte rei*, that is, a perception by the mind or a presence to the mind of the relevant aspects of the object of cognition which by itself compels our implicit mental 'yes', 'this is how things are'. On the one hand, this is a limitation of belief, exposed as it is to the only too familiar cases of misplaced trust, fanciful guesses, and so on. On the other hand, belief is a cognitive mode the importance of which

[52] Locke, *Essay*, Book IV, chap. XV, 3. Cf. Aquinas, *Scriptum super Sententiis*, lib. 3 d. 23 q. 2 a. 2, qc. 1, co.: 'credens... ab extrinseco determinatur ad unum'.

is difficult to exaggerate in that it enables us to extend the grip of our cognition beyond our actual, and crucially, possible knowledge.

2.4 Conclusions

The first chapter concluded by observing how the sharp distinction between knowledge and belief as two fundamentally different cognitive states not only recurred in the key series of ancient Greek philosophical schools but was incrementally refined and elaborated over many centuries. As this chapter has shown, this process of recapitulation, refinement, and elaboration continued seamlessly despite the enormous discontinuities between ancient Greek, medieval Christian, and early modern philosophy.

Thomas Aquinas (who represents the medieval scholastic tradition in this brief account) articulated with characteristic clarity the core observation that 'what is known is seen, and what is believed is not seen' and naturalized it by grounding it in a richer analysis of sense-perception. First, he characterized sense-perception as the basic case of a cognitive mode characterized by the presence of the object of cognition to the cognizer who is directly moved by this presence. Although this type of cognition of particulars is achieved without conceptual schemes provided by the human intellect, he then argued that the senses also afford a sort of discursive cognition which Aquinas called *aestimativa* in non-rational beings and *cogitativa* in rational beings. Understanding (*intelligere*), knowing (*scire*), and knowledge (*scientia*) were then situated as the fully-fledged cognitive modes characterized by 'clear sight'. Aquinas continued to regard belief as a very different type of intellectual cognition which requires conceptual thought but in which 'clear sight' is lacking. Unlike the Platonic distrust of *doxa*, however, this Thomist position does not disparage belief, for example, by regarding it as botched knowledge. Finally, Aquinas (like the Stoics, of which he was unaware) grouped all of these cognitive modes together under the general category of 'thinking with assent'.

Contrary to much textbook historiography, the continuity between medieval and early modern thought on this crucial point is almost as striking as that between ancient and medieval thought. His claims to break new ground notwithstanding, Descartes shared with the Scholastics the conceptions of knowledge as an immediate mental apprehension, a primitive grasping or seeing, and of the irreducible presence of the object of knowledge to the knower. In key texts of Descartes's philosophical maturity, this conception of knowledge is fully expressed as 'evidence', taken in its primary sense, derived from the Latin *ex videre*. The seemingly fundamental epistemological divide between Descartes and Locke—as standard-bearers of 'rationalism' and 'empiricism' respectively—did not prevent them from sharing the basic distinction between knowledge as directly perceiving and belief as *not* directly perceiving (in Locke's case the connection between ideas). There is no talk in Locke of justifying beliefs or adding conditions which turn them into knowledge. On the contrary: Locke was perhaps the most explicit among early modern authors in *not* conceiving belief as a more generic epistemic category which, with the addition of appropriate conditions, can be turned into knowledge. Belief, for Locke, is an epistemic state in which the defining characteristic of knowledge—namely, the direct perception of the agreement or disagreement between ideas—is lacking.

Similarly, the fact that Leibniz devoted one of his most extensive philosophical works to a sustained critique of Locke's *Essay* was no barrier to the two men sharing this fundamental conception of knowledge and belief. Leibniz's chief contribution was to enhance this tradition with an analysis of degrees of knowledge. In our knowledge, he argued, we normally grasp only some aspects of fully determinate objects of cognition. We are unable (even in principle) to distinctly enumerate all the predicates which can be attributed with truth to the object of cognition, and therefore our knowledge is inadequate, imperfect, incomplete. But although we do not know everything about the object, what we do know is perfectly known. To believe, on the other hand, for Leibniz, is not to *see* that something is true: it is 'verum putare', 'to suppose [that something is] true'. Medieval and early modern philosophy therefore provides abundant further material from which a restatement of this classic conception of knowledge and belief can be reconstructed.

3
The Gap between Mind and World

In discussing Greek epistemology in Chapter 1, one very important ancient philosophical school was left out: Scepticism. The reason that Scepticism needs to be discussed separately is not that it departs from the 'traditional' or 'standard' view revealed in the first two chapters. Like their contemporaries, ancient Greek Sceptics distinguished sharply between knowledge and belief, and characterized knowledge not as a form of belief, but as a direct 'seeing' or 'grasping' of 'what is'. Where they differed is in denying that human beings have the capacity to see or grasp 'what is' in a reliable way. Scepticism, I suggest, therefore either concludes that human beings at best achieve belief or remains noncommittal on whether knowledge is, or is not, attainable for human beings.[1] This chapter highlights some features of the long and complex history of these views in antiquity and the eighteenth century in order to locate the chief epistemological fault line running through the history of Western philosophy.

3.1 Ancient Scepticism

Arcesilaus (the leader of Plato's Academy in its middle period, chiefly responsible for its sceptical turn) mounts a frontal attack on Stoicism by denying that there are any cognitive impressions, that is, impressions which 'manifest, in a certain particular way, those objects which make the impressions'.[2] He does so by listing 'many and varied considerations' showing 'why no true impression is to be found of such a kind that it could not turn out to be false'.[3] In other words: either impressions are infallible in accurately revealing their source or there is no certainty that they do so. As Cicero summarizes: 'Arcesilaus was the first who from various of Plato's books and from Socratic discourses seized with the greatest force the moral: nothing which the mind or the senses can grasp is certain.'[4]

[1] Scholarship on ancient Scepticism, especially in its Pyrrhonian version, typically regards the position that knowledge is unattainable for human beings as 'negative dogmatism' rather than 'scepticism'.

[2] Cicero, *Academica* I.41 (trans. Frede 1999: 297).

[3] Sextus Empiricus, *Adversus Mathematicos* VII. 154 (trans. Schofield 1999: 326). Schofield notes that although Sextus gives no details, this kind of argument became the standard line of attack against Stoicism.

[4] Cicero, *De Oratore*, III. 67 (trans. Schofield 1999: 327).

Thinking with Assent: Renewing a Traditional Account of Knowledge and Belief. Maria Rosa Antognazza, Oxford University Press. DOI: 10.1093/oso/9780198831518.003.0004

Arcesilaus was, however, not the first to take a general sceptical stand. Arguably, views which raise sceptical worries or have sceptical implications go as far back as Xenophanes's fragment B34 or Protagoras's famous motto 'Man is the measure of all things'.[5] Explicit scepticism is normally traced to Pyrrho of Elis, although it is controversial whether Pyrrho himself had a specific interest in epistemological (as opposed to moral) issues, and whether the source of Pyrrhonian scepticism was actually Pyrrho's immediate pupil, Timon of Phlius.[6] At any rate, the kind of thorough-going scepticism attributed to Pyrrho was revived and systematized in the first century BCE by Aenesidemus and the neo-Pyrrhonians as a reaction to what they regarded as a progressive betrayal of Scepticism in the third phase of the Academy led by Carneades and Philo of Larissa.

3.1.1 Suspending Assent

According to the report by Aristocles preserved by Eusebius of Caesarea:

> [Timon] says that [Pyrrho] declares that things are equally indifferent [*adiaphora*] and unmeasurable [*astathmēta*] and undecidable [*anepikrita*], and that for this reason neither our sense-perception nor our beliefs tell the truth or lie, and so we ought not to put our trust [*pisteuein*] in them but ought instead to be without beliefs [*adoxastous*] and uncommitted and unswayed, saying of each and every thing that it no more is this than it is not [*ou mallon*], or both is and is not, or neither is nor is not. Timon says that the result for those who are in this disposition will be first speechlessness, and then freedom from disturbance [*ataraxia*].[7]

In brief, in response to the apparent radical untrustworthiness of our cognitive faculties, Pyrrhonists recommend to suspend judgement [*epochē*] or to decline to assent [*aprosthetein*].[8]

A similar recommendation, aimed specifically at Stoicism, is found in Academic Sceptics. 'Given that everything is incognitive', they argue, according to Stoicism's own principles, 'the wise person... will have to withhold assent about everything. But to withhold assent [*asugkatathein*] is no different from

[5] Cf. Plato, *Theaetetus* 151e and Sextus Empiricus, *Adversus Mathematicos* VII. 60. Protagoras's views are criticized by Plato in the first part of the *Theaetetus*. Cf. Brunschwig 1999: 231–2.

[6] According to Brunschwig 1999: 241–51, it was Timon 'who first gave Pyrrho's ideas an epistemological complexion'.

[7] Eusebius, *Praeparatio Evangelica* 14.18.758c–d (trans. by Gerson 2009: 112–13, slightly modified). Cf. the first chapters of Sextus Empiricus, *Pyrrhoniae Hypotyposes*.

[8] Diogenes Laertius, *Vitae Philosophorum* (*Lives of Eminent Philosophers*) 9.61–2; 76. Quoted by Gerson 2009: 115.

suspending judgement [*epochē*]. Therefore the wise person will suspend judgement about everything.'[9]

To sustain such a radical suspension of judgement is, of course, very hard. It commits the sceptic to having no position at all.[10] In fact, to maintain (for instance) that 'neither our sense-perception nor our beliefs tell the truth or lie' or that 'nothing which the mind or the senses can grasp is certain' is already to hold a position. A consistent, radical sceptic of Sextan–Pyrrhonist inclination would need to remain noncommittal on any such claims. Such a sceptic seems to be cornered in the same tight spot as the denier of the principle of non-contradiction: 'our discussion with him is evidently about nothing at all; for he says nothing.... for otherwise there would already be something determinate'.[11] The usual lines of defence include arguing that the position of the like of Arcesilaus should be read as purely dialectical, that is, as putting on the hypotheses for discussion on which the sceptic himself does not have a position one way or the other. It is, however, at best doubtful that the body of textual evidence supports such an interpretation.[12]

3.1.2 Believing but Not Knowing

In any case, the kind of scepticism which is most relevant for present purposes is a more easily defensible, mitigated variety, namely the sceptical position that acknowledges the need of holding beliefs but stresses that no commitment to the truth of such beliefs can be made. Carneades, for instance, seems to have held that it is sometimes permissible for the wise person to hold mere opinions.[13] The key point is that the wise person will be aware that such opinions do not have the status of knowledge. Later Academics such as Philo of Larissa have no qualms in endorsing a moderate brand of scepticism which allows holding beliefs as long as there is no claim to certainty. Catulus, a spokesman for this position, is reported as saying:

> I think nothing can be grasped cognitively. Yet I also think that the wise person will assent to what is not grasped cognitively, i.e. he will hold opinions—but in such a way that he understands he is holding opinions and knows [*sciat*] that there is nothing which can be grasped cognitively.[14]

[9] Sextus Empiricus, *Adversus Mathematicos* VII. 156–7; trans. Schofield 1999: 326.

[10] For a classic debate on whether ancient Scepticism restricted doubt to 'philosophical' views see Burnyeat and Frede 1998.

[11] Aristotle, *Metaphysics*, Book 4, chap. 4 (1008a30–4/Ross 742; trans. slightly modified).

[12] Cf. Schofield 1999: 324–32.

[13] Cf. Cicero, *Academica* II.78: 'nihil percipere et tamen opinari'. Cicero, however, expresses doubts that this was the position actually held by Carneades as opposed to being merely offered by him for discussion.

[14] Cicero, *Academica* II. 148 (trans. Schofield 1999: 335–6).

Once again, *knowing* 'that there is nothing which can be grasped cognitively' is hardly coherent with the view that no knowledge is possible and that, therefore, we can at best hold opinions. But let us allow this to pass and charitably assume that what is meant is merely that the sceptic's *opinion* is that no knowledge is possible. To hold a coherent position the sceptic will have to grant that she has no claim to the truth of this opinion and that the opposite may be true.

The ancient Sceptics were well aware of this sort of problem. Arcesilaus and Carneades appear to have answered the question: 'is the claim that nothing can be grasped cognitively itself grasped cognitively?' with a resounding: no.[15] To be sure, answering 'no' goes some way towards rescuing the coherence of their position, but does not in itself explain what we should make of a position which, on its own terms, cannot claim any truth or certainty. Cicero tries to sketch an answer on Carneades's behalf, drawing on a sort of 'plausibilism' based on Carneades's notions of 'acceptable' (*probabilia*) or convincing (persuasive, *pithana*) impressions.[16] Schofield insightfully identifies Carneades's crucial move as follows:

> The key feature of Carneades's scheme is the fundamental distinction between truth and falsehood, which obtain with respect to the relation between impression and things or facts they purport to represent, and *apparent* truth and falsehood, which are merely functions of the way the impressions seem to those who experience them. For Carneades there always remains an epistemological as well as a logical gap between the two sorts of assessments of impressions... his chief complaint against Epicurus is effectively that he confuses what the Epicureans call 'evidence' (*energeia*), which as properly understood is apparent truth, with truth.[17]

Thus, it is no longer a matter of assenting to truth but of 'going along with' or 'following' what *appears* to be true (that is, 'acceptable' impressions, 'convincing' presentations) purely as a guide to action.[18] This is, basically, the way in which scepticism counters the common-sense charge of *apraxia* ('inability to act'), as well as the charge of incoherence for holding a definite position while claiming that all assent should be withheld:

> There are two senses in which the wise man is said to suspend judgement. In one sense, he gives assent to nothing at all; in another sense, he suspends judgement by not responding to a query as to whether he approves of something or

[15] See Schofield 1999: 345–6.

[16] See Schofield 1999: 345–50. Burnyeat's unpublished paper 'Carneades Was No Probabilist' stresses that Cicero's use of the word *probabilia* should not suggest a theory of probability. On Cicero's own sceptical outlook see Woolf 2015.

[17] Schofield 1999: 347.

[18] Cf. Gerson 2009: 123; Schofield 1999: 346, 351.

> disapprove of it, so that he is not forced to deny or affirm anything.... Since we believe that he who withholds assent from everything is nevertheless moved and does something, there remain presentations of the sort that excite us to action and also those about which, when questioned, we would be able to respond either way, following only the claim that the presentation was like that, but still without assent.[19]

In short: Carneades's scepticism (and scepticism more broadly) accepts the Platonic distinction between reality and appearance but, unlike Plato, holds that, as cognitive subjects, we have access only to appearances. Between the cognizer and the object of cognition there is, for scepticism, an original, unbridgeable gap.[20] The fundamental dividing line in epistemology is drawn, in my view, at this point: it is the line between those who affirm a primitive cognitive contact between *cognoscens* and *cognitum*, and those who affirm a primitive gap between mind and world.

3.1.3 Fallibility and Certainty

As far as I can see, however, the defence mounted by the Sceptics against charges of incoherence does not allow them to affirm a gap any more than it would allow them to reject it. At best Scepticism could affirm that there *appears* to be a gap.[21] Now, as far as appearances go—that is, as far as the phenomenology of cognition goes—for the most part, we *appear* to be successfully connecting with at least some features of what is the case. Why then is Scepticism arguing against what appears to be the case?

At the root of Scepticism's assumption that—contrary to what is manifested by the phenomenology of cognition—there is an unbridgeable gap between mind and world, is the experience of error in our coming to grips with the world, especially in sense-perception: things sometimes turn out to be in fact different from how they appear to be. It seems to me, however, that from this experience one can infer only the *fallibility* of the cognitive contact between mind and word, and not the lack of any cognitive contact.

The next sceptical move is therefore to say that, due to this fallibility, we can never be certain of when we hit the mark and when we do not. That is, lack of

[19] Cicero, *Academica* II. 104 (trans. Gerson 2009: 123). Arcesilaus had already taken a similar line, claiming that suspending judgement about everything is not incompatible with acting according to reasonableness [*to eulogon*] (cf. Sextus Empiricus, *Adversus Mathematicos* VII. 158).

[20] This claim is not intended to imply idealism, especially when applied to ancient Scepticism. As Burnyeat 1982 magisterially shows, 'the realist assumption' is something which 'Greek thought even at its most radical never quite managed to throw off' (p. 40).

[21] Arguably, Sextan Pyrrhonism would indeed claim nothing stronger.

infallibility is equated to lack of certainty. The answer to this line of argument is, in my view, that infallibility and certainty ought to be kept distinct.[22] What is at issue with the sceptic is not whether we have a general capacity such that, whenever it is exercised, we are safe from error (as fallible beings, we cannot), but whether there can be, in principle, a cognitive contact between mind and world. If there can, whether there is successful cognitive contact on particular occasions can be adjudicated only on a case-by-case basis, and cannot be decided in general and once-and-for-all.[23] In some cases, the answer will be positive, in some cases negative, and in some cases, it will be out of our cognitive reach altogether. The crucial point is whether there is, in principle, an original (albeit limited and imperfect) contact with 'what is', as opposed to there being an original, ultimately unbridgeable, gap between cognizer and cognized. And this is not something the sceptic can decide one way or the other. This being the case, it stands to reason that presumption is on the side of what appears to be mostly (albeit not infallibly) the case, namely, that in cognition we do make contact with 'what is'. The burden of proof falls on who affirms the contrary in particular cases—and whoever it might be who attempts to discharge this burden, it cannot be the sceptic.

3.2 Scepticism redivivus: Hume and Reid

After a long period of relative quiescence, Scepticism revived in the early modern period, thanks especially to the humanist recovery of sceptical texts during the fifteenth and sixteenth centuries.[24] This section traces some aspects of Hume's philosophy—and of Thomas Reid's response to it—that are crucially important for understanding the shift from a distinction in kind between knowledge and belief to counting justified (or reasonable, warranted, entitled, etc.) true belief as knowledge. Needless to say, Hume's views had and continue to have an enormous impact. In particular, one of the most significant ways in which Humean philosophy shaped early modern and modern Western thought is by breathing new life into Protagoras's ancient dictum that 'Man is the measure of all things'. This is not

[22] An illuminating and extended discussion of the distinction between certainty and infallibility is offered by Ayers 2019.

[23] As I argue in Chap. 5, sect. 5.2.2, one of the chief problems with scepticism is that it is an 'all-or-nothing' position: either something is perfectly known or nothing is known. By contrast, I propose that in knowledge we do make successful contact with mind-independent, fully determinate objects but our grasp of these objects is always *inadequate* and *indeterminate*, in the technical sense of never exhausting the *adaequatio intellectus ad rem* or never being able to grasp all the aspects of a fully determinate individual and the fully determinate states of affairs in which individuals are involved. Most importantly, although we only ever grasp some very limited aspects of a concrete object or state of affairs, the aspects with which we *do* connect may be known with certainty even if most aspects of that very object/state of affairs are not known at all (see esp. Chap. 10, sections 2–4).

[24] On the transmission and recovery of Pyrrhonism by Italian and French humanists see Floridi 2002.

at all to claim that Hume's thought can be regarded as a straight case of relativism, subjectivism, or scepticism.[25] There are, however, sceptical aspects to it that have far-reaching consequences and have informed in a significant way the (J)TB+ theory of knowledge.

3.2.1 Hume: 'All Our Knowledge Degenerates into Probability'

Hume devotes only a few pages to knowledge proper.[26] However short and perfunctory his treatment may be, it reveals what counts, for him, as knowledge in the strict sense, what its limits are, and how sharply it should be distinguished from belief.[27] Knowledge is restricted to relations of ideas, that is, to analytic a priori propositions. These propositions 'are either intuitively or demonstratively certain' and 'discoverable by the mere operation of thought, without dependence on what is any where existent in the universe'.[28] Geometry, algebra, and arithmetic are the sciences which have this kind of propositions as their object. These are 'demonstrative sciences' the rules of which 'are certain and infallible'.[29]

The trouble is, Hume hastens to say, that also in these matters we are so prone to error that 'all our knowledge degenerates into probability'.[30] 'Knowledge and probability', however, 'are of such contrary and disagreeing natures, that they cannot well run insensibly into each other, and that because they will not divide, but must be entirely present, or entirely absent.'[31] That is, Hume is perfectly aware that probability, however high, does not turn into knowledge (*pace* much present-day formal epistemology) because knowledge and probability have 'contrary' natures. Hume himself is therefore operating withing a genuinely traditional model which sharply distinguishes belief (however probable) from knowledge.

One may thus be surprised by Hume's claim, a few lines below, that 'therefore knowledge resolves itself into probability, and becomes at last of the same nature with that evidence, which we employ in common life'. What Hume is saying is that, although there is, in principle, a kind of cognition which counts strictly as knowledge, in fact, due to the fallibility of our reason, we achieve only

[25] There is a long-standing debate on whether Hume's philosophy should be interpreted as a version of Scepticism. Early interpreters such as Thomas Reid (1710–1796) attack it as sceptical. N. Kemp Smith (to mention only one classic study) sees the charge of scepticism as a result of underestimating the impact of Francis Hutcheson (1694–1746) and 'moral sense' ethics on Hume (cf. Kemp Smith 1941). However, also according to Kemp Smith, although the existence of external bodies or of causal relations is not rejected by Hume, their existence is, strictly speaking, an object of *belief* and not of *knowledge*. This is the aspect of Hume's doctrine which is of interest in the present discussion.

[26] See Hume, *Treatise*, Book I, Part III, sect. I and Book I, Part IV, sect. I; *Enquiry* sect. 4.

[27] Cf. Kemp Smith 1941: 349–63.

[28] Hume, *Enquiry*, sect. 4. Cf. *Treatise*, Book I, Part IV, sect. I.

[29] Hume, *Treatise*, Book I, Part IV, sect. I.

[30] Hume, *Treatise*, Book I, Part IV, sect. I.

[31] Hume, *Treatise*, Book I, Part IV, sect. I.

probability.[32] This weaker kind of cognition has 'the same nature' of the kind of cognition that 'we employ in common life' or in all matters of fact, namely, belief.

'Matters of fact' (as opposed to 'relations of ideas'),[33] including the existence of external bodies and causal relations (that is, necessary connections between objects), are indeed objects not of *knowledge* but of *belief*.[34] The latter is a *natural* belief, that is, the result of natural psychological features of the human mind, analogous to the instinct which successfully guides also other non-human animals through life.[35] Due to the way in which our mind naturally works, we cannot but believe in the existence of external bodies and causal relations. Whether there *are* (independently of what we irresistibly believe) external bodies or casual relations is, however, beyond the limits of our cognition. Therefore, asking whether bodies do or do not exist is an idle question. 'We may well ask', Hume writes in the *Treatise*, '*What causes induce us to believe in the existence of body?* But tis in vain to ask, *Whether there be body or not?* That is a point, which we must take for granted in all our reasonings. The subject, then, in our present enquiry is concerning the *Causes* which induce us to believe in the existence of body' (Book I, Part IV, sect. II).

Belief in the independent existence of bodies, as well as belief in causal relations and in the existence of a cognitive subject, is not the result of reasoning but of custom or habit,[36] and is attended by 'some sentiment or feeling' which distinguishes it from fiction.[37] Thus what rescues us from scepticism is not reason but 'nature', that is, a 'species of instinct' by which we naturally believe certain things.[38] In this sense, man is the measure of all things and wondering whether things really are as we believe them to be is simply absurd.[39]

[32] This seems to me another instance of conflating infallibility and certainty, i.e., another instance of the ancient sceptical thought that, since we are fallible, nothing is certain. Although Hume refuses to be associated with 'those sceptics, who hold that all is uncertain' (*Treatise*, Book I, Part IV, sect. I), what rescues us from scepticism is that our nature necessitates us to *believe* certain things.

[33] 'All the objects of human reason or enquiry' divide for Hume 'into two kinds, to wit, *Relations of Ideas*, and *Matters of Fact*' (*Enquiry*, Part 1, sect. 4,).

[34] I disagree that Hume can be counted as an 'evidentialist' for whom we should only firmly believe on the basis of evidence 'strong enough for the belief to count as knowledge if true' (Chignell 2018: sect. 4.1). Hume is very well aware of the distinction in kind between knowledge and belief.

[35] Cf. Hume, *Treatise*, Book I, Part III, sect. xiv and *Enquiry*, sect. 9.

[36] Hume, *Treatise*, Book I, Part IV, sect. i: '*all our reasoning concerning causes and effects are deriv'd from nothing but custom;... belief is more properly an act of the sensitive, than of the cogitative part of our natures.*' See also Book I, Part III, sect. vii and sect. xiv.

[37] Cf. Hume, *Enquiry*, Part 2, sect. 5: 'the difference between *fiction* and *belief* lies in some sentiment or feeling, which is annexed to the latter, not to the former, and which depends not on the will, nor can be commanded at pleasure. It must be excited by nature, like all other sentiments... In this consists the whole nature of belief.'

[38] Cf. Hume, *Treatise*, Book I, Part IV, sect. I and *Enquiry*, sects. 5 and 9.

[39] Hume, *Treatise*, Book I, Part IV, sect. I: 'whether it be the *senses*, *reason*, or the *imagination*, that produces the opinion of a *continu'd* or of a *distinct* existence [of objects]. These are the only questions, that are intelligible on the present subject. For as to the notion of external existence, when taken for something specifically different from our perceptions, we have already shewn its absurdity.'

3.2.2 Reid: Sensation and Perception

Against Hume's views, Thomas Reid (1710–1796) mounts a penetrating critique which has received a great deal of attention in recent decades, not least due to the inspiration found in Reidian epistemology by the founding fathers of the so-called 'Reformed Epistemology' movement.[40] Reid reads Hume's philosophy as the fully-fledged scepticism resulting from the way of ideas inaugurated by Descartes and followed by Locke, Malebranche, Berkeley, and, finally, Hume.[41] As long as the immediate objects of our cognition are ideas—that is, mental entities which are supposed to mediate between our mind and the world—we are trapped in our mind and its modifications. Whether these modifications are what Hume calls 'impressions', or what he calls 'ideas', Reid argues, does not really matter, since the distinction between these two categories of mental items (or Humean 'perceptions') is merely one of degrees of liveliness.[42]

For Reid, we should instead distinguish between 'sensation' and 'perception'.[43] That is, unlike Hume, Reid draws attention to the difference between act and object of cognition, noting that sensations (such as feeling pain) are modifications of a sentient being in which there is no real (as opposed to grammatical) distinction between mental act and felt object: 'when we attend to sensation by itself... it appears to be something which can have no existence but in a sentient mind, no distinction from the act of the mind by which it is felt'.[44] By contrast:

> perception, as we understand it, hath always an object distinct from the act by which it is perceived; an object which may exist whether it be perceived or not. I perceive a tree that grows before my window; there is an object which is perceived, and an act of the mind by which it is perceived; and these two are not only distinguishable, but they are extremely unlike in their natures. The object is made up of a trunk, branches and leaves; but the act of the mind by which it is perceived, hath neither trunk, branches, nor leaves.[45]

In my view, Reid underestimates the extent to which this difference in nature between the act of the mind and the object of cognition is preserved by the scholastic distinction between formal and objective reality still endorsed by early modern authors such as Descartes.[46] But be that as it may, Reid has the merit of

[40] On Reformed Epistemology and its link to Reidian philosophy see Chap. 14 below.

[41] Cf. Reid, *Inquiry*, esp. chap. 1; chap. 2, sect. iv–v; chap. 5, sect. vii; chap. 6, sect. xx and xiv; chap. 7.

[42] As Hume explains at the very beginning of the *Treatise* (Book I, Part I, sect. i), 'all the perceptions of the human mind resolve themselves into two distinct kinds, which I shall call impressions and ideas'.

[43] Reid, *Inquiry*, chap. 6, sect. xx: 'Sensation, and the perception of external objects by the senses, though very different in their nature, have commonly been considered as one and the same thing.' See also Reid, *Inquiry*, chap. 6, sect. xx, pp. 167–8.

[44] Reid, *Inquiry*, chap. 6, sect. xx, p. 168.

[45] Reid, *Inquiry*, chap. 6, sect. xx, p. 168.

[46] On the significance of this distinction see Chap. 7, sections 7.2.3 and 7.3.1.

distinguishing between two fundamentally different ways in which something is present to a subject—for example, pain as opposed to a tree—and of pointing out that perception already implies a judgement of existence.[47] In perception we perceived a tree as something existing independently from the mental act by which we perceive it. In sensation, on the other hand, the felt pain is not distinct from the act of feeling pain.

3.2.3 Incorrigible Belief and Natural Credulity

Given this position one might have expected an account of the existence of external objects and of causal relations sharply different from that offered by Hume. Instead, Reid seems to me much closer to Hume than he appears to realize. In fact, he goes on to explain the existence of the tree as a *belief* that 'is not the effect of argumentation and reasoning' but an 'immediate effect of my constitution'.[48] Next, he acknowledges that such a view—not so different, after all, from the natural instinct which, according to Hume, leads to the natural belief in the existence of external objects[49]—is exposed to scepticism (the main point of Reid's own critique of Hume to start with).[50]

Reid, however, brushes aside in the name of 'common sense' the envisioned sceptical attack:

> The sceptic asks me, Why do you believe the existence of the external objects which you perceive? This belief, Sir, is none of my manufacture; it came from the mint of Nature; it bears her image and superscription; and, if it is not right, the fault is not mine: I even took it upon trust, and without suspicion. Reason, says the sceptic, is the only judge of truth, and ought to throw off every opinion and every belief that is not grounded on reason. Why, Sir, should I believe the faculty of reason more than that of perception; they both came out of the same shop, were made by the same artist; and if he puts one piece of false ware into my hands, what should hinder him from putting another?[51]

[47] On the importance of distinguishing between two fundamentally different ways in which something is present to a subject, see Chap. 6, sections 6.1 and 6.2. On the importance of the judgment of existence already implicit in simple apprehension see Chap. 9, sect. 9.1.1.

[48] See further Chap. 9, sect. 9.1.1.

[49] Cf. Reid, *Inquiry*, chap. 6, sect. xx, p. 172: 'The belief which is implied in [perception] is the effect of instinct.'

[50] Reid, *Inquiry*, chap. 6, sect. xx, p. 172: 'I am aware, that this belief which I have in perception, stands exposed to the strongest batteries of scepticism.'

[51] Reid, *Inquiry*, chap. 6, sect. xx, p. 169. As we will see in Chap. 14, sect. 14.2, Reid's metaphor regarding cognitive mechanisms as all 'coming out of the same shop' provides a key inspiration for one of William Alston's distinctive theses, namely the rejection of epistemic double standards in the evaluation of doxastic practices. Plantinga too draws inspiration from this passage by Reid.

Reid is of course aware that this line of reasoning can result in a broadening of scepticism to reason and intellectual cognition, in addition to sense-perception, rather than in a successful defeat of the sceptical attack.[52] As an answer, Reid offers the following reasons why he 'will never attempt' 'to with-hold assent, and to throw off this belief of external objects' which, according to the sceptic, 'may be all delusion': first, it is not in our power (that is, this is an incorrigible, irresistible belief which results from our natural constitution);[53] second, even if it were in our power, 'it would not be prudent to throw off this belief' (shall we really resolve not to believe our senses, and break our nose against a post, step into a dirty kennel, and so on, until we are 'clapt into a mad-house'?); third, 'this instinctive belief' is 'one of the best gifts of Nature' which kept us safe from 'a thousand accidents' well before we started doubting about anything.[54]

In brief, Reid's reasons for holding on to the independent existence of bodies are not grounded in the claim of a direct contact with an external reality but, once again, in an appeal to our natural constitution which instinctively leads us to believe what is conducive to our survival. Now, to be fair, neither Descartes nor Spinoza (nor any other early modern philosopher I am aware of) ever advocated disbelieving the senses for what concerns practical matters of our day-to-day navigation of posts and dirty kennels. If the reasons for holding on to the belief in external objects are merely of a pragmatic and prudential kind, surely they can be accommodated by Descartes's and Spinoza's provisional moral codes.[55]

Furthermore, that belief in the external world is conceived by Reid as a kind of 'faith' or credence is also shown by his extensive analogy between this instinctive belief and the instinctive belief, at a young age, in 'whatever [parents and tutors] told me'.[56] For Reid, our belief in the external world and in causal relations is the result of the same 'natural credulity' by which we trust human testimony.[57] Such 'principle of credulity' serves us well since it is coupled by another principle of our natural constitution, namely, the 'natural principle of veracity' by which people have 'a natural impulse' or 'a propensity to speak truth'.[58] Thus, 'in matter of testimony, the balance of human judgement is by nature inclined to the side of belief'.[59] Finally, not unlike the harshly criticized Descartes, Reid thinks that the

[52] Reid, *Inquiry*, chap. 6, sect. xx, p. 169: 'Perhaps the sceptic will agree to distrust reason, rather than give any credit to perception.'

[53] Cf. Reid, *Inquiry*, chap. 6, sect. xx, p. 172.

[54] Reid, *Inquiry*, chap. 6, sect. xx, pp. 169–70.

[55] Descartes, *Discourse on Method*: AT 6:22–8; CSM 1:122–5. Editor's note: it is unclear what passage from Spinoza the author had in mind, but see *Tractatus de Intellectus Emendatione*, §17, in *Opera*, ed. Gebhardt, vol. ii, p. 9; *Complete Works*, trans. Shirley, 6.

[56] Reid, *Inquiry*, chap. 6, sect. xx, p. 170. See also sect. xxiv, devoted to 'the analogy between perception and the credit we give to human testimony'.

[57] Reid, *Inquiry*, chap. 6, sect. xx, pp. 170–1. Specifically on belief in causal relations see Reid, *Inquiry*, chap. 6, sect. xxiv, p. 197, quoted below.

[58] Reid, *Inquiry*, chap. 6, sect. xxiv, pp. 193–4.

[59] Reid, *Inquiry*, chap. 6, sect. xxiv, p. 194. For further discussion of Reid's principles of credulity and veracity in relation to the issue of testimony, see Chap. 12, sect. 12.3.2.

veracity of these instinctive beliefs is guaranteed by God, the author of our nature who:

> hath implanted in human minds an original principle by which we believe and expect the continuance of the course of nature, and the continuance of those connections which we have observed in time past. It is by this general principle of our nature, that when two things have been found connected in time past, the appearance of the one produces the belief of the other.[60]

To conclude, Reid's bone of contention with Hume is not that the existence of the external world or of causal relations is a kind of belief—that is, a faith or credence resulting from a natural 'credulity' which trusts the testimony of the senses in a way analogous to our native trust in human testimony. What he strongly disapproves of is Hume's conception of belief as 'a certain degree of vivacity in the idea of the thing believed' rather than as 'an original principle of the mind'.[61] Reid has been rightly hailed, in recent times, for his denunciation of the sceptical consequences of conceiving ideas as intermediaries between mind and world. His overall position, however, seems to me closer in relevant respects to Hume than to the classical direct realism of the Aristotelian–Scholastic tradition, or, for that matter, to the direct realism of early modern authors such as Arnauld.[62] All in all, it seems to me that Reid's outlook is more open to sceptical and neo-Cartesian implications than Reid himself would like it to be.[63]

3.3 Conclusions

Even the ancient and modern Sceptics discussed in this chapter maintain the *genuinely* 'standard' or 'traditional' sharp distinction between knowledge and belief as cognitive states different in kind. Where they differ from the figures discussed in the previous two chapters is in denying our capacity to attain knowledge. Ancient Sceptics of the moderate variety (who allow the holding of beliefs as long as they make no claim to certainty) typically accept the Platonic distinction between reality and appearance; but, unlike Plato, they hold that we have access only to appearances. Hume sharply distinguishes belief (however probable) from knowledge; but he follows the ancient Sceptics in concluding that, although there is, in principle, a kind of cognition which counts strictly as knowledge, in fact, due to the fallibility of our reason, we achieve only probability,

[60] Reid, *Inquiry*, chap. 6, sect. xxiv, p. 197. [61] Reid, *Inquiry*, chap. 6, sect. xxiv, p. 197.

[62] On Arnauld's position see Chap. 7, sections 7.3.2 and 7.3.3.

[63] Cf. Chap. 14 for an account of how possible sceptical and neo-Cartesian implications play out in Reformed Epistemology.

which has 'the same nature' as the kind of cognition that 'we employ in common life' and in all matters of fact: namely, belief. This (I submit) is the fundamental dividing line in epistemology: between those who affirm and those who deny a primitive cognitive contact between *cognoscens* and *cognitum*. The way to escape this trap, it has been suggested, is to avoid conflating two things that ought to be kept separate: infallibility and certainty. The fact that cognitive contact between mind and world is subject to error does not imply that there is no such contact.

Going forward, once cognition has been reduced, de facto, to belief and probability, it may seem that the only way to avoid scepticism is to redefine knowledge as a special kind of belief. This is precisely what (J)TB+ theories of knowledge—including their many variants as warranted belief, strongly warranted belief, belief which tracks truth, belief with a sufficiently high degree of probability, belief which could not easily have been wrong, and so on—have tried and (now according to many) failed to do. While their intention is to keep scepticism at bay, their recurrent failure to do so is rooted in their being, ultimately, the offspring of scepticism. The crux of the matter is not whether we are content to call (or have become accustomed to call) 'knowledge' some kind of belief (however probable, or entitled, or permissible, or incorrigible such belief may be): it is whether our cognition puts us in touch with 'what is' as opposed to 'what appears to be'.

4
The Distinction in Kind after Hume

Hume's revival of the sceptical denial of the ability of the mind to make contact with 'what is' marks a major departure in the philosophical tradition especially of the English-speaking world; but it does not spell the end of the defence and further development of the traditional conception of knowledge and belief outlined in Chapters 1 and 2. Kant's critical philosophy maintained but also radically reconceptualized how the classic distinction between knowledge and belief applies to human cognition. Far from disappearing during the early twentieth century, the distinction in kind between knowledge and belief was also reaffirmed in uncompromising terms even within the English-speaking world by such diverse philosophical movements as Oxford Realism and neo-Scholasticism. These modern restatements generated further fresh insights which can contribute to a reintroduction of this epistemological approach into the contemporary debate.

4.1 Kant: *Wissen*, *Glauben*, and *Fürwahrhalten*

After being awakened from his 'dogmatic slumber' by Hume,[1] Kant does not develop a conception of knowledge as justified true belief (JTB) , as the designation of this conception as 'standard' might lead one to expect. On the contrary, this section argues that, like Plato, Kant thinks of knowledge and belief as two kinds of cognition that have, in some important cases, different objects, and cannot one be a species of the other. One key difference from Plato is that Kant inverts what we can know and what we can only believe. Knowledge is only of what falls within the confines of our possible experience bounded by space and time, the a priori forms of our sensible intuition.[2] That is, knowledge is only of the sensible. Physical objects as we know them are not 'things in themselves' (noumena, things as they really are) but phenomena constructed, in important respects, by our mind; we know and conceive of them only as they appear to us.[3] Crucially, it is precisely because they are, to some extent, mental constructions that there is no gap between mind and phenomenal world, and knowledge is, therefore, possible. Conversely, there can be no knowledge of what is separated from us by an ontological and epistemological gap. In this respect, Kant too

[1] Cf. Kant, *Prolegomena to Any Future Metaphysics* (Ak 4:260).
[2] Cf. Kant, *Critique of Pure Reason* (A26/B42, A33/B49).
[3] Cf. Robert Adams 1987: 5.

Thinking with Assent: Renewing a Traditional Account of Knowledge and Belief. Maria Rosa Antognazza, Oxford University Press. © Maria Rosa Antognazza 2024. DOI: 10.1093/oso/9780198831518.003.0005

endorses the view that a *conditio sine qua non* of *knowledge* is the absence of a gap between cognizer and cognized. Where there is such a gap, we have to turn to types of cognition other than knowledge.[4]

In a famous passage in the Preface to the second edition of the *Critique of Pure Reason*, Kant in fact concludes: 'Thus I had to deny [aufheben] *knowledge* [*Wissen*] [of things-in-themselves] in order to make room for *belief* [*Glaube*]' (Bxxx). Noumena lie beyond the limits of possible experience.[5] Speculative reason should abandon

> its pretension to extravagant insights; because in order to attain such insights, speculative reason would have to help itself to principles that in fact reach only to objects of possible experience, and which, if they were to be applied to what cannot be an object of experience, then they would always actually transform it into an appearance, and thus declare all *practical extension* of pure reason to be impossible. (Bxxx)

The aspiration to a theoretical knowledge of the noumenal world should be abandoned not only because such knowledge is impossible (due to our structural limitations) but also because it distorts its alleged object, conceiving it as part of the world of appearances or phenomenal world. Belief (*Glaube*), however, can extend in a *sui generis* way our cognitive grip beyond what can be known.

4.1.1 Assenting as '*Fürwahrhalten*'

In his insightful paper, 'Belief in Kant', Andrew Chignell stresses that the genus under which Kant groups more specific cognitive modes is *Fürwahrhalten*, 'that is, "assent" or, more literally, "holding-for-true"'.[6] Kant's nominalization of holding-for-true as 'das Fürwahrhalten'—a nominalization mirrored by Chignell's translation as 'an assent' or 'assents'—may give the impression that we are dealing with mental items or mental tokens.[7] It seems to me, however, that Kant's use of a verb (*halten*, 'holding') indicates that *Fürwahrhalten* is essentially a mental act ('assenting' rather than 'an assent') which corresponds quite closely to what I have called

[4] Cognition is taken here not as *Erkenntnis* but rather in the broad sense of any mental act of judgement which is concerned with holding-for-true, whether this judgement implies a cognitive mistake or not. In this broad sense, cognition embraces also instances of what Kant calls 'thinking' (*denken*) (cf. Chignell 2007: 348).

[5] I remain neutral here, as in the case of Plato, on whether this position should be interpreted as a two-world view or a one-world view. Cf. Robert Adams 1987: 5.

[6] Chignell 2007: 324. My discussion is greatly indebted to this splendid paper, although I have a different take on some of the issues discussed. On belief in Kant see also Stevenson 2003.

[7] This nominalization could lead to an 'objectification' of 'assenting' as 'assent', to use Cook Wilson's phrase (cf. Cook Wilson 1926: 796 denouncing the 'objectification' of 'appearing' as 'appearance'). On Cook Wilson see below, sect. 4.2.

'thinking with assent'.[8] More precisely, in the key section of the *Critique of Pure Reason* in which Kant discusses these matters, the Canon of Pure Reason, *Fürwahrhalten* is treated as the mental act of judgement by which we assent to something.[9]

In the Canon, Kant offers a fine-grained taxonomy of the modes of our cognition according to which persuasion (*Überredung*), conviction (*Überzeugung*), opinion (*Meinung*), belief (*Glaube*), and knowledge (*Wissen*) are all regarded as different species of the genus *Fürwahrhalten*. In general, there is some form of assenting when we have *sufficient* (*zureichend*) grounds for it (something is *zureichend für wahr gehalten*, sufficiently assented to).[10] What distinguishes the different species of assenting from one another is the combination of two different kinds of grounds, namely, objective grounds and subjective grounds. Objective grounds are valid for any rational being and are, therefore, at least in principle communicable.[11] Typically, they not only make assent rationally permissible but compel or necessitate assent. Subjective grounds, on the other hand, lay 'solely in the subject', that is, 'in the particular constitution' of a certain individual (A820/B848).

Persuasion (*Überredung*) is a kind of thinking with assent based purely on subjective grounds of assent. In Kant's words, it is 'a judgement' which 'has only private validity'. Therefore, 'this holding something to be true cannot be communicated'. Most importantly, persuasion has an additional feature, namely, these grounds are 'held to be objective' when in truth they are merely subjective (A820/B849).

By contrast, conviction (*Überzeugung*) is assenting to something on sufficient objective grounds, that is, grounds 'valid for the reason of every human being to take it to be true' (A820/B849). As such, these grounds are in principle communicable, and communication is indeed a test of whether a judgement should count as mere persuasion or as conviction. Crucially, however, there may be conviction without ability to communicate its objective grounds. As Chignell rightly notes, 'what children and animals have by way of objectively sufficient assent' may well fall under this category (Chignell 2007: 332). More generally, according to Chignell, conviction is for Kant 'an involuntary response to the presence of perceived evidence' (Chignell 2007: 356).

[8] Note that 'das Fürwahrhalten' is literally translated as 'the holding-for-true' or 'the assenting' (that is, the act of assenting) rather than 'an assent'. I suspect that a translation of *Fürwahrhalten* as 'an assent' is driven by an implicit interpretation of Kant's account in the framework of the twentieth-century JTB orthodoxy, where 'an assent' holds the place of 'a belief'.

[9] See A820/B848–A831/B859.

[10] Assenting (*Fürwahrhalten*) is 'an occurrence in our understanding that may rest on objective grounds [*Gründe*], but that also requires subjective grounds [*Ursachen*] in the mind of him who judges' (A820/B848). (Cf. Chignell 2007: 325. The Cambridge edition translates *Ursachen* as 'causes'; I follow Chignell's translation as 'grounds'.)

[11] On the issue of communicability see Fonnesu 2015.

In turn, 'having an opinion [*meinen*] is holding something to be true with the consciousness that it is subjectively as well as objectively insufficient'. Believing [*glauben*], on the other hand, is holding something to be true with the consciousness that it is subjectively sufficient but objectively insufficient (A822/B850; trans. slightly modified).[12] Both opinion and belief have an element of voluntariness which, in the absence (by definition) of objectively sufficiently grounds, plays a role in determining assent either on subjectively insufficient grounds (opinion) or on subjectively sufficient grounds (belief). Furthermore, unlike persuasion, neither opinion nor belief implies a cognitive mistake; rather, they are both imperfect kinds of cognition which, despite this imperfection, make important contributions to our cognitive life.[13] Finally, 'when holding something to be true is both subjectively and objectively sufficient it is called knowing' (A822/B850; trans. slightly modified).

4.1.2 Assenting and the (J)TB+ analysis

Having outlined Kant's taxonomy of varieties of *Fürwahrhalten*, let us now consider its relationship to the (J)TB+ analysis. The first thing to note is that knowing (*wissen*), for Kant, cannot be a species of being persuaded, of having an opinion (*meinen*), or (most importantly) of believing (*glauben*): objectively sufficient grounds are in fact required by knowledge (and by conviction) whereas the other three mental acts are partially defined by the absence of objectively sufficient grounds. That is, as Le Morvan explains, knowledge cannot be a species of belief because 'knowledge (essentially) has what belief (essentially) lacks (namely, objective sufficiency)'.[14]

One could wonder, nevertheless, whether the structure of Kant's proposal is that of the (J)TB+ analysis, with *Fürwahrhalten* or 'assent' playing the functional role of what in the twentieth century is called 'belief'.[15] My reply is as follows. If by 'belief' is meant the mental act of judgement or the mental act by which something is acknowledged or affirmed, then the structure of Kant's proposal does take the structure of a generic act of affirming (or assenting) of which there are different species depending on the combination of two main families of conditions: objectively sufficient grounds and subjectively sufficient grounds. But this is manifestly not what Kant means by 'belief/*Glaube*'. Instead, this is what he means

[12] A822/B850: 'If taking something to be true is only subjectively sufficient and is at the same time held to be objectively insufficient, then it is called believing.' Belief (*Glaube*) is in turn divided by Kant into sub-categories. I discuss this further Kantian taxonomy in Chap. 13, sect. 13.1.

[13] Cf. Ak 24:218: 'Opinion is not really a mistake, but only an imperfect cognition [Unvollkommene Erkenntniß], a lack, since something in our judgment does not have sufficient grounds.'

[14] Le Morvan 2017: 1225–7, esp. p. 1227.

[15] Chignell appears implicitly to assume throughout his paper that this is indeed the case.

by *Fürwahrhalten* or assenting. If (like Kant himself) we mean by 'belief' a cognitive mode in which there is an ontological and/or an epistemic gap between cognizer and cognized, subject and object, then on Kant's proposal there is no way that knowledge could be a species of such a cognitive mode because the ontological and/or epistemic gap simply excludes objectively sufficient grounds, that is, excludes a 'cognition of grounds in the object' (Ak 16:371–2).

Kantian *Meinung* and *Glaube* are precisely cases of such a cognitive mode, the nature of which excludes knowledge. If the gap is merely epistemological, that is, if it can, in principle, be filled, and is, in fact, eventually filled, then we will no longer have opinion or pragmatic belief but another, specifically different, cognitive mode, namely knowledge. If the gap is, however, ontological (that is, it is the gap between appearances and things-in-themselves), then the gap cannot be filled and there cannot be knowledge. The best we can do is theoretic or moral belief.[16]

In conclusion: if one wishes to call 'belief' what the tradition has called 'assenting' or 'thinking with assent', and what Kant has called *Fürwahrhalten*, this is technically acceptable but historically inaccurate and needlessly confusing. The issue is not ultimately which word we use, but which mental act is referred to by that word. What is crucial is that the mental act at stake here is a generic act of affirmation or acknowledgment which must not be conflated with what Hume called 'belief'. As far as I can see, historically, the latter is the sense of belief which has underpinned (J)TB+ theories. Insofar as this is the case, both the letter and the spirit of Kant's proposal is very different from the (J)TB+ analysis of knowledge.

At the core of the Kantian proposal there is the (frankly Platonic) idea of cognitive modes which are sharply distinguished by their objects and by the function they play in relation to those objects. Knowledge (*Wissen*) has phenomena as its objects; belief (*Glaube*) may be concerned, instead, with the noumenal world. In the phenomenal world, knowledge is possible because physical objects, as we know them, are constituted through the a priori forms of our sensible intuition, that is, they are in some sense mental constructions. Therefore, there is no irreducible epistemic and ontological gap between mind and world. By contrast, knowledge of things-in-themselves is not possible owing to the ontological gap between the noumenal world and the world of our possible experience bounded by space and time. We can, however, turn to a different cognitive mode: 'rational Belief, in which the act of assenting has the same degree as in Knowledge [das Fürwahrhalten eben den Grad hat als beym Wissen)], but is of *another kind*' (Ak 16:371–2; trans. modified and my emphasis).[17] This is a cognitive mode which cannot and does not bridge the ontological gap (that is, it

[16] Cf. A830/B858. On the difference between pragmatic, theoretic, and moral belief in Kant see Chap. 13, sect. 13.1.

[17] Attention to this passage is drawn by Chignell 2007: 349, footnote 32.

is not and cannot be 'the cognition of grounds in the object' Ak 16:371–2) but still responds to the needs of reason, opening thereby rationally grounded 'prospects beyond the bounds of experience' (A830/B858).

On the massively controversial question of whether we can relate at all to things-in-themselves, I side here with Chignell's proposal of 'Liberalism'. For 'Hardliners', human reason can have no access whatsoever to fully uncognizable things-in-themselves. For 'Moderates', theoretical reason can at most entertain as 'regulative' or heuristic notions ideas of unconditioned entities beyond the realm of appearances, acting 'as if' they were true on purely moral considerations. For 'Liberals', 'theoretical reason itself can provide grounds on which to form assertoric rather than merely problematic assents about certain things-in-themselves' (Chignell 2007: 357–9). That is, I take, some type of belief can open theoretical prospects on things-in-themselves.[18]

4.2 Knowledge and Apprehension in the Twentieth Century

4.2.1 Oxford Realism: 'Knowing and believing differ in kind'

Kant was not the only major philosopher after Hume to maintain the distinction in kind between knowledge and belief, nor is the further development of this distinction confined to the European continent. On the contrary: this traditional distinction is reaffirmed in uncompromisingly strong terms by the philosophical movement that flourished in Oxford in the early twentieth century and which is known as Oxford Realism.[19] Although its inspirator, John Cook Wilson (1849–1915),[20] did not publish a great deal during his life, his philosophical positions influenced Oxford philosophy for several generations,[21] grounding a tradition of Oxford realism which stretches, arguably, as far as the current philosophical work of leading philosophers as diverse as John McDowell and Timothy Williamson.

Cook Wilson opposes any attempt to define knowledge in terms of belief plus additional conditions such as truth and justification. Most emphatically, for him, knowledge is *not* a species of belief. In the words of his student, and subsequently White's Professor of Moral Philosophy at Oxford, H. A. Prichard:

[18] This type of belief is theoretical belief, discussed in more detail in Chap. 13, sect. 13.1.

[19] On Cook Wilson and Oxford Realism see the excellent accounts offered by Marion 2000a, 2000b, 2016, and by Travis and Kalderon 2013, from which I am drawing.

[20] Cook Wilson read classics and mathematics at Balliol College, Oxford. He was elected fellow of Oriel College in 1873, and Wykeham Professor of Logic in 1889.

[21] Among others, H. A. Prichard (1871–1947), Gilbert Ryle (1900–1976), and J. L. Austin (1911–1960). On the connection between Austin and the Oxford Realism tradition see Longworth 2018.

> Knowing is absolutely different from what is called indifferently believing or being convinced or being persuaded or having an opinion... Knowing and believing differ in kind as do desiring and feeling... Their difference in kind is not that of species and genus, like that of a red colour and a colour. To know is not to have a belief of a special kind, differing from beliefs of other kinds; and no improvement in a belief and no increase in the feeling of conviction which it implies will convert it into knowledge. (Prichard 1950: 87)[22]

Indeed, for Cook Wilson, 'Belief is not knowledge and the man who knows does not believe at all what he knows; he knows it' (Cook Wilson (1926): 100). That is, believing is a different mental state, which is not entailed by knowing.

At the root of this position is the view that knowledge cannot be reductively analysed or defined in terms of something more basic,[23] because knowledge is a *sui generis*, non-derivative 'frame of mind'.[24] In modern parlance, knowledge is a primitive mental state.[25] From 1906 onwards, Cook Wilson calls this primitive mental state 'apprehension'. As he puts it, 'we cannot *construct* knowing—the act of apprehending—out of any elements' (Cook Wilson 1926: 803). Although undefined, for Cook Wilson, apprehension appears to be close to Aristotle's 'noēsis' or to Russell's knowledge by 'acquaintance' (provided one does not assume, in the latter case, any kind of sense-data or *tertium quid* mediating between subject and object).[26] That is, 'apprehension' is a direct grasp of the object of cognition, a direct seeing 'what is'. As this primitive apprehension, knowledge is presupposed by other activities of thinking, such as judging, believing, opining.[27] One of the crucial features which distinguishes it from these other acts of thinking is its being a state of mind which is not preceded by any doubt. By contrast, judging, believing, opining are 'decisions':

> A judgement is a decision. To judge is to decide. It implies previous indecision; a previous thinking process, in which we are doubting. Those verbal statements,

[22] Cf. also Urmson 1988: 15: 'I do have much sympathy with the view of Cook Wilson and Prichard that... knowledge has to be contrasted with belief and opinion rather than being treated as a special case of belief.'

[23] Cf. Williamson's unanalysability hypothesis: 'the concept knows cannot be analysed into more basic concepts' (2000: 33).

[24] Cf. Cook Wilson 1926: 100: 'our experience of knowing then being the presupposition of any inquiry we can undertake, we cannot make knowing itself a subject of inquiry in the sense of asking what knowledge is'.

[25] Cf. Travis and Kalderon 2013: 499.

[26] Oxford Realists reject sense-data as direct objects of perception or apprehension. Their key objection is that sense-data theories, as other indirect realist theories, introduce a medium or a *tertium quid* between subject and object, leading either to idealism or to scepticism. See in particular Prichard's attacks against Cambridge philosophy as chiefly represented by his Cantabrigian contemporary, Bertrand Russell (1872–1970) (cf. Marion 2000b: 489–90).

[27] Cf. Cook Wilson 1926: 86–7, 92–3, 96; Marion 2016: sect. 3.

> therefore, which result from a state of mind not preceded by such doubt, statements which are not decisions, are not judgements, though they may have the same verbal form as judgements. (Cook Wilson 1926: 93)[28]

In turn, according to a highly original Oxford Realist of the second generation, Gilbert Ryle, propositional knowledge and belief belong to radically different logical types.[29] Although they are both dispositional, knowledge, for Ryle, is a capacity, while belief is a tendency. 'Epistemologists', he writes:

> are apt to perplex themselves and their readers over the distinction between knowledge and belief... even when it is seen that both are dispositional verbs, it has still to be seen that they are dispositional verbs of quite disparate types. 'Know' is a capacity verb, and a capacity verb of that special sort that is used for signifying that the person described can bring things off, or get things right. 'Believe', on the other hand, is a tendency verb and one which does not connote that anything is brought off or got right.[30]

Interestingly, in their discussion of cases of 'knowing that P without believing that P', Myers-Schulz and Schwitzgebel (2013) offer Ryle's capacity-tendency account as a possible alternative to standard, present-day views according to which knowledge requires or entails belief.

Other Oxford Realists are keen to stress that knowledge is not a matter of having 'evidence' for a certain opinion, belief, or judgement,[31] but of being aware of some fact of nature.[32] Helen Wodehouse (1880–1964), a British philosopher who studied mathematics and 'morals sciences' at Cambridge and went on to complete a DPhil at Birmingham University (1906), argues in *Mind* that 'knowledge consists of the presentation of reality in consciousness': 'presentation is of the essence of knowledge', she claims, 'there can be no knowledge, even the highest, without presentation, and presentation is all that is necessary'.[33] On his part, Austin writes in a famous passage of *Sense and Sensibilia*:

[28] Cf. also Cook Wilson 1926: 96: 'There will be something else besides judgement to be recognized in the formation of opinion, that is to say knowledge, as manifested in such activities as occur in ordinary perception; activities, in other words, which are not properly speaking *decisions*.'

[29] See Kremer 2016: 31.

[30] Ryle 1949: 133–4. Cf. Myers-Schulz and Schwitzgebel 2013: 380–1, drawing attention to this passage.

[31] 'Evidence' is taken here in its secondary sense, that is, as the reasons or arguments which support a belief or judgement, as opposed to its primary sense as a perspicuous presentation of something which is clearly seen or understood. On the senses of evidence cf. Ayers 2019: 34, 66–7, 115–16, 118–19, 194. For a discussion of evidence see Chap. 2, sect. 2.2.2.

[32] Cf. Travis and Kalderon 2013: 500. I take it that 'fact' is understood here as a concrete (as opposed to an abstract) entity. On the importance of keeping these two conceptions of facts distinct, see Hyman's illuminating discussion (Hyman 2017).

[33] Wodehouse 1909: 391, 396, 399. See also Wodehouse 1910.

> The situation in which I would properly be said to have *evidence* for the statement that some animal is a pig is that, for example, in which the beast itself is not actually on view, but I can see plenty of pig-like marks on the ground outside its retreat. If I find a few buckets of pig-food, that's a bit more evidence, and the noises and the smell may provide better evidence still. But if the animal then emerges and stands there plainly in view, there is no longer any question of collecting evidence; its coming into view doesn't provide me with more *evidence* that it's a pig, I can now just *see* that it is, the question is settled. (Austin 1962: 115)[34]

Of course, as it has been noted, seeing that what is standing there in plain view is a pig presupposes the ability of recognizing pigs by sight. More generally, assent is given, in this case, to whatever one is able to recognize by sight as standing there in plain view: if one is already acquainted in the relevant way with pigs, it will be a pig; if one has never encountered a pig before, but can recognize, say, quadrupedal animals, it will be a quadrupedal animal. The specific point here is that the viewer will have latched on to a bit of reality (albeit more or less confusedly apprehended) instead of having to reach a decision, on the basis of various signs, as to whether something one could recognize by sight is, or is not, there.

One cannot but note the structural similarity between Cook Wilson and Prichard's account of knowledge and belief/judgement and Aquinas's two manners in which we assent to something. The Oxford Realists contrast two mental states which are different in kind: on the one hand, knowledge, that is, the direct apprehension of an object/the awareness of a fact of nature, characterized by no doubt and requiring no decision; on the other hand, belief/opinion/judgement, that is, the mental state in which the object of cognition (the pig of Austin's example) is not presented and, therefore, reasons other than the presence of the object of cognition itself are needed in order to take a decision (is the pig there or not?). Aquinas contrasts two manners in which we are moved to assent: on the one hand, understanding/knowledge (*intellectus*/*scientia*) in which assent is compelled by the object itself ('ab ipso objecto') of which there is clear sight ('manifesta visio'); on the other hand, belief/opinion in which there is no clear sight of the object of cognition which sufficiently moves assent, and external reasons are therefore needed in order to take a decision ('through a certain voluntary choice turning toward one side rather than the other').[35]

[34] Cf. Cook Wilson 1926: 100: 'In knowing, we can have nothing to do with the so-called "greater strength" of the evidence on which the opinion is grounded; simply because we know that this "greater strength" of evidence of A's being B is compatible with A's not being B after all.'

[35] ST IIa IIae, q. 1, a. 4. On Aquinas's account see Chap. 2, sect. 2.1. Cf. also Aquinas's views on 'unformed' cognitive acts and Cook Wilson's theory of judgement as a process of decision which involves previous indecision.

4.2.2 Neo-Scholasticism: Knowledge as Consciousness of an Object—Different Motives of Assent

Drawing especially on Aquinas, the neo-Scholastic movement, which thrived in Catholic circles in a period roughly contemporary to Oxford Realism, recovers and institutionalizes this and other key insights of the thirteenth-century theory of cognition.[36] Neo-Scholastic thinkers typically agree that 'knowing, cognition, knowledge, is *sui generis*, that therefore it cannot properly speaking be defined, or explained in terms of anything other than itself' since 'nothing is more intimate to us than knowing'.[37] To put it another way, knowledge cannot be reductively analysed into concepts which are explanatorily more basic, or clearer, or less in need themselves of explanation. The extent to which this view becomes institutionalized is shown by its reception in the *Catholic Encyclopedia* composed between 1905 and 1914. The entry 'knowledge' begins by stating: 'Knowledge, being a primitive fact of consciousness, cannot, strictly speaking, be defined; but the direct and spontaneous consciousness of knowing may be made clearer by pointing out its essential and distinctive characteristics.' That is, although there is no reductive analysis of knowledge, one can still describe what knowledge essentially or paradigmatically is; and according to neo-Scholastic views, 'Knowledge is essentially the consciousness of an object.'[38]

'Belief', in turn, is described in the same source as 'that state of the mind by which it assents to propositions, not by reason of their intrinsic evidence'.[39] This state of mind, the entry laments, 'is often used indiscriminatingly . . . for other states of mind'; in particular, it should be distinguished 'from the assent of knowledge'.[40] Following a line clearly inspired by Aquinas, the entry's author,

[36] Neo-Scholasticism flourished between the late nineteenth century and the first half of the twentieth century. The impetus for the rediscovery of Aquinas and scholastic philosophy of the later Middle Age came from the Encyclical *Aeterni Patris* of Pope Leo XIII (1879). This process of recovery continues nowadays and extends to the so-called Second Scholastics (or Early Modern Scholasticism) which flourished in the Iberian peninsula in the sixteenth and seventeenth centuries and included influential thinkers such as Francisco Suárez (1548–617). Leo XIII's *Aeterni Patris* had the effect of raising Aquinas to the quasi-official norm of Catholic theology, an effect tempered in more recent times by the sustained study of other traditions, notably the strand of Franciscan thought represented in the thirteen–fourteenth centuries by the *Summa Halensis*, Bonaventure, Duns Scotus, and Ockham.

[37] Coffey 1917: 25. Peter Coffey (1876–1943) studied at the University of Leuven (one of the chief centres of nineteenth–twentieth century neo-Scholasticism) and was Professor of Logic and Metaphysics at Maynooth College (Ireland). His manuals of Thomistic philosophy were used as the standard textbooks.

[38] Dubray 1910. On the indefinability of the most fundamental mental acts/states via a reduction to more basic notions, cf. Reid, *Inquiry*, chap. 6, sect. xx, p. 167: 'The most simple operations of the mind, admit not of a logical definition: all we can do is to describe them, so as to lead those who are conscious of them in themselves, to attend to them, and reflect upon them.' More generally, it is crucial to distinguish between reductive analyses and analyses which explain non-reducible fundamental concepts by relating them to concepts at the same level (i.e., concepts which are not supposed to be more basic) (cf. Strawson 1992: chap. 2).

[39] On the difference between intrinsic and extrinsic evidence see Chap. 12, sect. 12.2.

[40] Aveling 1907.

Francis Aveling,[41] identifies the difference between the kind of assent involved in knowledge and in belief, not as a difference in the nature of the assent, but as a difference in its motive: unlike the assent of knowledge, the motive of which is a clear vision of the relevant object of cognition, the assent of belief is chiefly motivated by testimony and 'partial evidence'. 'Probable opinions, conjectures, obscured or partially recalled memories, or any truths or facts of which we have not a consciously evidential grasp,' the entry explains:

> are the main objects of a belief resultant upon partial evidence. In this its distinction from knowledge lies. We are said to know intuitional truths as well as all those that are indirectly evident in their principles. We know all facts and truths of our own personal experience, whether of consciousness or of objective nature. Similarly, we know the truth of the reports of memory that come clearly and distinctly into consciousness. (Aveling, 1907)

Against the Reidian view (as reproposed by the editor of Reid's works, Sir William Hamilton) that knowledge implies 'an initial belief or trust', Aveling maintains that 'we do not believe evident truth'[42]—a claim remarkably close to Cook Wilson's dictum 'that the man who knows does not believe at all what he knows' (Cook Wilson 1926: 100).

Furthermore, neo-Scholastic textbooks identify 'apprehension' or 'simple apprehension' (*apprehensio simplex*) as the starting-point of all knowledge insofar as it is 'the act of mind' which 'places an object before consciousness'.[43] 'To *apprehend*', they explain, 'is to take hold of a thing as if with the hand; an *apprehension*, as an act of the mind, is an intellectual grasping of an object.'[44] Although apprehension is typically treated as an intellectual act of mind, the neo-Scholastics acknowledge an analogous process of cognitive apprehension in sense-perception, enabling 'the animal in different ways to acquire cognition of the material objects with which it comes into immediate or mediate contact'.[45]

4.2.3 Commonalities: Ancient Roots

These striking similarities between two philosophical movements as far apart as Oxford Realism and neo-Scholasticism are not so surprising if one considers their

[41] Francis Aveling (1875–1941) was a pioneering Canadian professor of psychology who taught at University College London and at King's College London. Educated at McGill University, Keble College, Oxford, the Canadian College in Rome, the University of Leuven, and the University of London, he held a Doctor of Divinity from Rome, a PhD in Philosophy from Leuven, and a Doctorate of Science from UCL.

[42] Aveling 1907: 'Nor is it necessary, with Hamilton, to have recourse to an initial belief or trust as implied in all knowledge. We cannot properly be said to trust our faculties. We do not believe evident truth.'

[43] Rickaby 1889: Part I, chap. II, sect. 1.

[44] Coppens 1891: *Logic*, Book I, chap. I, sect. 9.

[45] Coppens 1891: *Mental Philosophy*, Book III, chap. II, sect. 161. Cf. also Rickaby 1889: Part II, chap. II.

common source in Aristotle and other aspects of ancient philosophy. Cook Wilson and his contemporaries at Oxford typically emerged into philosophy from the intensive study of Aristotle (it is certainly no accident that Cook Wilson, having read classics and mathematics at Balliol, contributed regularly to the study of ancient philosophy). For their part, the neo-Scholastics knew their Aristotle chapter and verse through the mediation of Aquinas. Most importantly for the matter at hand, the view of knowledge as a primitive, undefinable mental state by which we are in conscious cognitive contact with an object, and which is distinct in kind from belief—a view held by both Oxford Realism and neo-Scholasticism—indicates the strength and pervasiveness of a tradition of non-sceptical philosophy of cognition going back to ancient philosophy and its medieval developments, and finding its expression in philosophical contexts with very different intellectual agendas.

More generally, it turns out that even in the first half of the twentieth century, the so-called standard analysis of knowledge is not so standard after all. Surprisingly, the only clear-cut (as opposed to 'in the ballpark') example of a definition of knowledge as justified true belief to be found in the decades immediately preceding Gettier's paper of 1963 appears to be the leading Harvard philosopher C. I. Lewis's definition in *An Analysis of Knowledge* (1946: 9): 'Knowledge is belief which not only is true but is also justified in its believing attitude.'[46] Even Ayer's definition of knowledge ('first that what one is said to know be true, secondly that one be sure of it, and thirdly that one should have the right to be sure')[47] is, on closer inspection, a 'ballpark' case rather than a clear-cut example of conceiving knowledge as justified true belief.[48]

4.2.4 Disagreement: Assent and Belief

Three years before Gettier's paper was published, an interesting disagreement flared up between leading figures associated with these two movements. A discussion of this disagreement shines the spotlight on a further conflation between elements of cognition which, I claim, should be distinguished: namely, assent and belief.

The key text is the Gifford Lectures given by H. H. Price at the University of Aberdeen in 1960.[49] Price belongs to the generation of Oxford Realists between the older Cook Wilson and Prichard, and the younger Austin and Ayer.[50] The

[46] This is the conclusion reached by Le Morvan 2017 in his illuminating discussion. On Lewis, see Hunter 2021.

[47] Ayer 1956: 34. [48] Cf. Gettier 1963: 121 and Le Morvan 2017: 1223–4.

[49] H. H. Price (1899–1984) was Wykeham Professor of Logic at Oxford from 1935 to 1959. After reading *Literae Humaniores* at Oxford, he completed his post-graduate studies at Cambridge. His work shows the influence both of Cook Wilson's views and of the rival sense-datum theories of Cantabrigian philosophy. Cf. Marion 2000b: 490–501.

[50] Cf. Marion 2000b: 490–501; Flew 1970.

central topic of his Gifford Lectures (published in 1969 under the title of *Belief*) is 'two very different ways of analysing belief', namely, 'the traditional way', according to which 'believing is a special sort of mental occurrence (sometimes described as a 'mental act')', and 'the modern way' (favoured by Price), according to which believing is a disposition.[51] Before tackling 'Occurrence' versus 'Dispositional' analysis of belief, however, Price discusses some preliminary questions, including the issue of the 'Degrees of Assent'.[52]

Price's target was another erstwhile Oxford academic whom although not normally associated with the neo-Scholastic movement per se, was one of the giants of Catholic thought in an older generation who drew directly (on the question of assent) on the medieval philosophical inheritance: John Henry Newman. In chapter VI of his *Grammar of Assent* (1870), Newman objects to the claim that assent has degrees.[53] To be sure, Newman notes, 'we often speak of giving a modified and qualified, or a presumptive and *primâ facie* assent, or . . . a half-assent',[54] as we do speak, loosely, of half-truths. When we consider the matter in philosophical rigour, however, we have to grant that, as truth is in itself indivisible, so 'assent is in its nature absolute and unconditional'.[55]

Price is bewildered. The conclusion of his criticism is worth citing at some length since it makes his bafflement with Newman's position wonderfully clear:

> If Newman were right . . . our human condition would be at once more miserable and more intellectually-disreputable than we commonly suppose. It would be more miserable, because we so often need to be able to assent to propositions on evidence which is far less than conclusive; and therefore we need to be able to assent to them with something far less than total or unreserved self-commitment, if we are to have any guidance for our subsequent thoughts and actions. But Newman tells us that we cannot do it. According to him, the very nature of assent makes it impossible for anyone to assent in this conditional and tentative way. If Newman were right, our situation would also be more intellectually-disreputable than we commonly suppose. In such circumstances, where we have evidence which is less than conclusive, only two alternatives would be open to us: either complete suspense of judgement, or else an assent of the all-or-nothing ('unconditional') sort, which would be unreasonable, because nothing short of conclusive evidence could justify it.[56]

[51] Series 1, Lecture 1, Introduction (quoted from https://www.giffordlectures.org/lectures/belief).
[52] Series 1, Lecture 6.
[53] Newman is specifically objecting to Locke's claim that there are degrees of assent (cf. Locke, *Essay*, Book IV, chap. XVI). As far as I can see, what Locke calls 'degrees of assent' are really degrees of belief proportional to the degree of probability that there be agreement or disagreement between ideas (that is, an agreement or disagreement between ideas which we cannot perceive but 'presume' to obtain).
[54] Newman 1870/1895: 181. [55] Newman 1870/1895: 157.
[56] Price 1969: series 1, lecture 6 (quoted from https://www.giffordlectures.org/lectures/belief).

Price's bewilderment is, I suggest, a classic consequence of having conflated assent and belief. Newman is talking of the implicit mental 'yes' which may be either the immediate, spontaneous response to the 'evidentness', 'seeableness' of something, or the mental 'yes' of a 'decision' (to use Cook Wilson's expression) which follows a process of deliberation in which reasons, signs, symptoms, testimony, pros and contra are weighted.[57] In the latter case, our 'unconditional' mental 'yes' is to whatever we have judged to be the case, for example, that it is very unlikely that the train will be in time, or that the recovery of the patient is doubtful, or that it is certain that the future is uncertain. To say that 'assent is in its nature absolute' does *not* mean that assenting is to take the uncertain for certain. Rather, assent is mentally affirming that the matter is as one has judged it to be: for example, uncertain, or doubtful, or fairly likely, or very probable, and so on. As Helen Wodehouse (1908: 361) puts it: 'the typical expression of assent is "Yes, I see"'. The point is that a 'yes'—insofar as it is a 'yes' and not mere entertaining or a suspension of judgement—is in itself *indivisible*, although by no means *irreversible*.

In the encyclopaedia's entry on belief discussed above, Aveling makes the same point: 'assent is of its nature simple and indivisible'; the assent of knowledge and the assent of belief are distinct kinds of assent due to the difference not in their *nature* but in their *motive*.[58] In brief, assent is an on/off state which should be distinguished from states which have degrees (that is, belief, credence, opinion, confidence, persuasion, conviction, suspicion, doubt, and so on).[59]

As Newman explains:

> In truth 'suspicion, conjecture, presumption, persuasion, belief, conclusion, conviction, moral certainty,' are not 'assents' at all... When I assent to a doubtfulness, or to a probability, my assent, as such, is as complete as if I assented to a truth; it is not a certain degree of assent. And, in like manner, I may be certain of an uncertainty[.][60]

For instance, Newman notes, in the case of conditional propositions such as 'If this man is in a consumption, his days are numbered', strictly speaking

> the assent is given neither to antecedent nor consequent of the conditional proposition, but to their connexion, that is, to the enthymematic *inferentia*. If

[57] 'Implicit' in the sense of the Scholastic *in actu exercito* as opposed to *in actu signato*—a terminology which I prefer to the term 'unconscious' used by Newman. Cf. Newman 1870/1895: esp. 188–91, where the 'simple assent' or 'mental assertion' which is 'exercised unconsciously' is contrasted with 'complex or reflex assents' which are 'made consciously and deliberately'.

[58] Aveling 1907.

[59] Newman 1870/1895: 176: 'there is no medium between assenting and not assenting'.

[60] Newman 1870/1895: 175.

we place the condition external to the proposition, then the assent will be given to 'That 'his days are numbered' is conditionally true'; and of course we can assent to the conditionality of a proposition as well as its probability.[61]

4.2.5 Conclusion: On/Off Versus Scalar States

I conclude by recalling some remarks of the Introduction to this part of the book on on/off versus scalar mental states. Post-Humean anglophone epistemology, I suggested, has adopted 'belief' as an overall category covering significantly different elements of cognition. This has led to an equivocal use which manifests itself, among other things, in the tension between treating belief as a binary state and acknowledging that belief has degrees. Likewise, the categorical versus graded conception of belief is reflected in the divide between those who stress the primarily qualitative nature of belief and those following the Bayesian approach, which dominates decision theory and formal epistemology, according to which belief is primarily a quantitative and not a qualitative notion.[62] As I also noted, this problem has recently been tackled in anglophone epistemology through the technical distinction between 'belief' and 'credence', used, respectively, for 'binary' (that is, on/off, categorical) belief and 'scalar' (or 'graded') belief.[63] For the reasons already outlined, my proposal is to abandon the artificial distinction between 'belief' and 'credence' and to recover instead the traditional distinction between 'assent' and 'belief'. This distinction marks, on the one hand, the on/off implicit mental 'yes' which is 'of its nature simple and indivisible'; and, on the other hand, the scalar state which corresponds to perceived degrees of likelihood of such-and-such being true or false on the basis of having weighted pros and contra, signs, symptoms, traces, testimony, and so on.

One could still wonder, however, whether the 'assent' of this earlier tradition maps onto another categorical (on/off) 'attitude' which has received sustained attention in recent literature and which has been contrasted with scalar or graded belief, namely, 'acceptance'.[64] My answer is no, at least insofar as a distinctive feature of acceptance (as understood in most contemporary literature) is its voluntary nature. This voluntariness does not sit well with knowledge and high levels of confidence in belief, although it seems to be related somehow to very low degrees of belief (aka low 'credences'): the latter appear in fact to be responsive to

[61] Newman 1870/1895: 183. [62] Cf. Engel 1998: esp. 144.

[63] On current debates regarding the relationship between belief and credence see, for instance, Jackson 2020, Jackson 2019a, and Buchak 2014: 59–71.

[64] See, among others, Stalnaker 1984: chap. 5; Lehrer 1990; Cohen 1992; Bratman 1992; Alston 1996; Engel 1998, 1999, and 2000. Engel 1998 regards assent as a form of acceptance (cf. esp. pp. 147, 150). The difference between belief and acceptance, on the one hand, and acceptance and assent, on the other hand, is stressed instead by Engel 1999: 220–5, although the way in which the distinction between acceptance and assent is traced is significantly different from my proposal.

the will in ways that knowledge and highly confident belief are not. So important is this voluntary element that in some accounts 'acceptance' is considered to be a non-doxastic mental state altogether, that is, a state which does not entail belief.[65] By contrast, on the account I am offering, assent is the implicit mental 'yes' which applies across the board to knowledge and all degrees of belief; that is, to cases in which this 'yes' is compelled (leaving no role for the will) and to cases in which it is not compelled.[66] In brief, assent is a broader category than acceptance: it covers both voluntary and involuntary aspects of cognition, and, as an indivisible mental 'yes', is relevant to both knowledge and belief.

[65] For a discussion of the relationship between belief and acceptance, and the role of the will in cognition, see Chap. 10.

[66] I take a mental 'yes' to apply also to cases in which what is affirmed is that something is *not* the case (e.g., A is not not-A; London is not Paris; black is not white).

5
Non-Sceptical Philosophy of Cognition

The survey of key milestones in the history of Western epistemology in the previous four chapters is not offered merely to set the historical record straight, however laudable such a project might be in its own right. The deeper purpose of reviewing this history is to provide four things of value to philosophy itself. First, this brief history helps explain why epistemology currently finds itself at a dead end. If justified true belief (JTB) is not in fact the standard or traditional conception of knowledge, and if indeed this conception was considered and rejected at the very outset of the Western philosophical tradition, it is perhaps less surprising that the collective effort to repair it during the past six decades has proved (according to many) so fruitless. Second, this history indicates where the battle must be fought if we are to find our way out of the cul-de-sac of post-Gettier epistemology. Third, the reflections arising from this history suggest the outlines of the strategy needed to win that battle. Finally and most importantly, this history provides some of the philosophical materials with which this perennial conception of knowledge can be reframed and reintroduced into contemporary philosophical discussion (in Part II) and used to address a range of outstanding philosophical issues (in Part III). These four objectives set the agenda of the following chapter.

5.1 The Main Battleline

5.1.1 The Shift from Certainty to Probability

For identifying the crucial battleline in epistemology through the ages, a useful foil is provided by one of the most eminent historians of philosophy currently at work: Robert Pasnau. In his vastly learned *After Certainty: A History of Our Epistemic Ideals and Illusions*, Pasnau endorses and reinforces a familiar historiography which divides the history of Western philosophy into two parts: the ancient and medieval period, and the modern period.[1] Pre-modern (or pre-Cartesian) epistemology (so the story goes) embraced an extremely demanding conception of what should count as knowledge. Aristotle's *epistēmē*, Pasnau argues, constitutes a normative account of our epistemic ideal: it does not offer a theory of knowledge

[1] Pasnau 2017. See also Pasnau 2014. I am indebted to Michael Ayers for stimulating conversations on the interpretation proposed by Pasnau.

Thinking with Assent: Renewing a Traditional Account of Knowledge and Belief. Maria Rosa Antognazza, Oxford University Press. © Maria Rosa Antognazza 2024. DOI: 10.1093/oso/9780198831518.003.0006

but an idealized epistemology which has *scientia*—that is, 'unconditionally or unqualified knowledge'[2]—as its object. Descartes, the story continues, took up the same normative project of accounting for our epistemic ideal: for Pasnau, Descartes offers, like Aristotle, a theory of *scientia* rather than a theory of knowledge, but with one key difference: certainty is now central to the epistemic ideal.

According to this account, it is precisely the failure of this approach that leads to epistemology in its modern shape. Under the pressure of scepticism and its successful challenge to claims of certainty, modern post-Cartesian epistemology fundamentally shifts from certainty to probability. Scepticism's hammer shatters all attempts to find certainty at least in some restricted domains (notably, the domain of the senses; the inward domain of ideas; the intellectual domain of reason). Thus, Pasnau concludes, there is a fundamental shift in the history of epistemology when some early modern authors finally come to realize that we cannot achieve absolute certainty and all we have is probable belief. Crucially, however, belief with an appropriately high probability counts now as *knowledge*, contra the unattainable epistemic ideals and attendant illusions of the previous tradition.[3] John Wilkins (1614–1672) is in particular identified as the early modern author who first lowered the bar for knowledge from certain cognition to probable belief, thereby shaping the programme of modern epistemology.[4]

Modern epistemology is therefore

> a struggle between those who optimistically maintain high epistemic standards and insist that these standards can be met, and those who pessimistically relax their expectations, give up proportionality [that is, the thesis that 'we should give our absolute assent only to what is infallibly certain'], and nevertheless claim that we are entitled to believe. Ultimately such entitled true beliefs are what came to count as knowledge. (Pasnau 2017: 44–5)

In brief, according to Pasnau, the fundamental dividing line in the history of epistemology falls between the (unattainable) Cartesian and pre-Cartesian epistemic ideal of absolute certainty embodied by Aristotelian–Cartesian *epistēmē/ scientia*, and the post-Cartesian 'everyday' conception of knowledge as (J)TB+ sanctioned by Humean scepticism—a conception that Pasnau seems to take for granted as the ordinary, refreshingly non-Panglossian, conception of knowledge which we should endorse.

[2] Pasnau 2017: 5.

[3] Cf., for instance, Pasnau 2017: 43: 'Wilkins . . . rejects the principle of proportionality in favour of a broad scope for absolute belief and identifies the whole range of such belief with *knowledge*. . . . in looking for the boundary between what is and is not morally certain—the threshold for reasonable, warranted, justified belief—we can simply say that we are looking for the boundary between what is and is not known.' (Emphasis in the text.)

[4] For a very interesting discussion see Pasnau 2017: 40–5. Cf. Wilkins 1675.

5.1.2 Sceptical and Non-Sceptical Philosophy of Cognition

I fully agree with Pasnau that the shift to counting 'reasonable, warranted, justified belief' or 'entitled true beliefs' as *knowledge* (Pasnau 2017: 43–4) marks a fundamental watershed in epistemology. This is, in my view, the watershed between non-sceptical and sceptical philosophy of cognition. I disagree, however, on other key points, notably (1) on how to divide the history of epistemology according to this fundamental shift; (2) on what the account of knowledge as 'reasonable, warranted, justified belief' is shifting away from; (3) and most importantly, on whether counting 'reasonable, warranted, justified belief' as knowledge is a more satisfactory account than the account of knowledge offered by the rival tradition. My reasons for disagreement are as follows.

First, what is being rejected by 'justified true belief' theorists is not an idealized, lamentably illusory epistemology. Pasnau's focus is on *epistēmē/scientia* understood as the (ultimately unattainable) aim of an idealized epistemology which admits as knowledge only an articulate, systematized 'science', as opposed to 'everyday' knowledge. This focus, however, misses the key point that *epistēmē/scientia* is grounded in a more fundamental cognitive mode, variously described as *nous* (Aristotle), *intellectus* (Aquinas), and *intuitus* (Descartes). *Epistēmē/scientia* is a discursive mode of intellectual cognition which is grounded in a non-discursive mode: the irreducible grasp or primitive intellectual seeing/apprehending of something. This 'seeing' is nothing else than the 'evidentness' (*ex parte objecti* and *ex parte subjecti*) which compels assent (rightly emphasized by Pasnau as a key aspect of this earlier tradition).[5] For Plato, Aristotle, Aquinas, Descartes, and Locke (among others) this primitive seeing/grasping/apprehending 'what is' is what knowledge most fundamentally is. In brief, *epistēmē/scientia* is grounded in something more fundamental: a primitive contact between mind and 'what is'. Moreover, the empiricist tradition acknowledges an even more basic and literal contact between the cognizer and 'what is', namely sense-perception.[6] For this tradition, the primitive contact between a cognitive subject and the world afforded by sense-perception not only counts as knowledge but is the foundation of all knowledge and of all other cognitive modes. The crucial point is that this is no idealized epistemology. On the contrary, this is what gets all our cognition going—in the pre-modern and early modern period, today, everyday, and for everyone.

Second, it is true, as Pasnau shows, that much traditional epistemology regarded infallibility as an epistemic ideal, but infallibility should not be confused

[5] Cf. Pasnau 2017: 31–5.

[6] See Brewer 2011 for a recent defence of the early modern empiricist insight that perceptual experience is most fundamentally to be construed as a relation of conscious acquaintance with physical direct objects.

with certainty.[7] Although infallibility is beyond our ken, the limitation of our cognitive abilities does not imply that there cannot be certainty of both a subjective and an objective kind. If one starts from the certainty which comes with the primitive, natural contact between senses and environment which we share with other perceiving beings and which constitutes the most basic case of 'seeing' or 'grasping' characteristic of knowledge, scepticism does not take hold.[8]

Third, as Pasnau rightly notes, Descartes saw knowledge (*scientia*) and belief as sharply distinct. Moreover, as he also acknowledges, philosophers from Aristotle to Descartes 'plainly did not take themselves to be fashioning a theory of what we should firmly believe' (Pasnau 2017: 43–4). The fact that Pasnau seems to regard this Aristotelian–Cartesian (and, I add, Platonic and Lockean) distinction between knowledge and belief as lamentable (cf. p. 25) is explained by the assumption (shared by Pasnau contra this earlier tradition) that knowledge is a kind of belief which meets certain criteria.

To be sure, as Pasnau 'keeps arguing', when it comes to all 'the fuss over what counts as knowledge', 'the word itself is not really that important' (p. 127). Indeed, *pace* Pasnau (p. 219), this is not about which *word* we use. This is about identifying our most fundamental cognitive modes and how they are distinct from one another. Call them what you like. What matters is that state α, in which assent is compelled by the presence of the object of cognition to the cognizer, is not a species of state ß, in which there is no such presence. What matters is whether one endorses or rejects the basically sceptical conclusion that there is no state α and all our cognition reduces to forms of ß.

In my view, if there is a fundamental dividing line in the history of epistemology this line is not a vertical one between pre-Cartesian idealized epistemology and post-Cartesian naturalized, everyday epistemology. As I hope has emerged from Chapters 1 to 4, there is a much greater continuity between ancient, medieval, and modern philosophy than Pasnau's account would allow. Rather, the division is horizontal and runs throughout the entire history of philosophy: as claimed above, it is the division between sceptical and non-sceptical philosophy of cognition. That is, according to the interpretation I offer, the main battleline in the history of epistemology is drawn between the affirmation of a natural mental state in which there is a contact between *cognoscens* and *cognitum*, 'mind' and 'reality' (whatever the ontological nature of this 'reality'), and the rejection of such a natural mental state. For the former position there is a mental state which is different in kind from belief, and which is constituted by the presence of the object of cognition to the cognitive subject with no epistemic gap between them—in the

[7] On the distinction between infallibility and certainty see Ayers 2019: 144–52 (esp. 145–7). I discuss this distinction in Chap. 3, sect. 3.1.3.

[8] For further discussion, see sect. 5.2 below. I offer an account of the most basic cognitive relation and of its anti-sceptical import in Chap. 6 (see esp. sect. 6.2).

act of cognition they are one ('*sunt unum*') although their ontological distinction remains. As I tried to show in Chapters 1 to 4, this view tracks a large swath of epistemology from ancient times to present days. For the latter position, all our cognition is belief, and the question becomes how and when belief is permissible.

These two broad traditions face one another from the beginning: one starting, roughly, with Parmenides and Plato, the other starting, roughly, with Xenophanes, Protagoras, and ancient scepticism. Although in different historical periods one strand may seem to gain the upper hand over the other, each is remarkably resilient in its capacity to take new forms adapted to the spirit of the time. Under the pressure of Humean-type scepticism, however, sceptical philosophy of cognition achieved a new prominence and led eventually to the (J)TB+ conception of knowledge dominant in the second half of twentieth-century anglophone analytical epistemology. In sum, the shift to counting 'reasonable, warranted, justified belief' or 'entitled true beliefs' as *knowledge* (Pasnau 2017: 43–4) constitutes a deviation from the competing tradition (embraced by sceptics and non-sceptics alike) which saw a distinction in kind between knowledge and belief (with the sceptics denying and the non-sceptics asserting the possibility of attaining knowledge of some things).

5.2 How the Battle Is Won

5.2.1 Naturalism

One of the main theses of this book is that the battle of non-sceptical philosophy of cognition against scepticism is won at the very beginning by maintaining that there is a primitive, effective contact between cognizer and cognized. Much of the tradition I have been discussing in previous chapters has resisted scepticism, not by arguing that the gap between cognizer and cognized can be bridged, but by arguing that there is no gap to start with.[9] If it is conceded instead that there is an original gap, the battle is lost for ever even before it has been fought. This is also the fate, I contend, of epistemic externalism, taken as the thesis that a subject cannot be aware of some of the necessary and sufficient conditions for a belief to count as knowledge.[10] Insofar as this position grants a gap between mind and world, it has already lost the battle against scepticism.[11]

[9] See Ayers and Antognazza 2019: 29. [10] See Ayers 2019: 164–85.

[11] For an illuminating, extensive discussion of scepticism and externalism see Ayers 2019: 164–93. 'Externalism' may of course mean quite different things. If it means that there are mental states whose 'essence involves the world' (Williamson 1995: 563), this book supports it. Helpful surveys on internalism/externalism in epistemology are offered by Poston 2023; Pappas 2023; Steup and Neta 2020 (esp. 3.3).

The reason for maintaining that there *is* such a primitive contact is what I call *naturalism*: human beings are, first of all, simply a species of sentient beings which share with other sentient beings capable of perception the natural ability to connect with, and respond to, their physical environment.[12] The most primitive of such beings do not have anything like mental representations or beliefs about putative state of affairs not currently perceived.[13] Therefore, the question does not arise of whether reality is as they represent it to be. The most basic cognitive abilities of human beings are simply more evolved versions of this natural ability of perceiving beings to relate to their surroundings here and now. As with some other types of perceiving beings, their immediate environment is simply present to human beings as something *other* than they are, and with which they interact for the preservation of their life.[14] Of course, depending on their stage of evolution, their physiology, the kind of sense organs they have, and so on, there will be vast differences between the way in which these surroundings are perceived by different kinds of perceiving beings. A bat or a bloodhound or an eagle will perceive its environment in ways which are in some respect richer and in some respect poorer than mine.[15] But it does not follow that no perceiver can be sure of having made contact with its environment on account of the vast diversity of perceptions among perceivers. Likewise, from the fact that in the dark Peter can become aware of objects only by bumping into them, whereas in broad day light Jane perceives by sight many more objects in the room than Peter did, it does not follow that neither Peter nor Jane had a successful cognitive contact with their surroundings on account of disagreements in their perception. What follows is that no perceiver has a perfect grasp of its surroundings in all its fully determinate particularity.[16]

In brief, on my account, a successful non-sceptical philosophy of cognition starts with the *natural* assumption that sentient beings capable of perception make effective cognitive contact with their environment, shifting the burden of proof onto the sceptical claim that there are sufficiently cogent reasons to think otherwise.

[12] See Chap. 6, sect. 6.1.2 for a discussion of the distinction between sensation and perception.

[13] I do not enter here into the controversial question of which species of beings are capable of perception. I am happy to endorse whatever the constantly developing scientific consensus sees as most likely. What matters in this context is that there are plenty of perceiving beings (that is, beings capable of some awareness of their environment as other than they are) which are vastly more primitive in all respects than human beings. On 'believing' as a cognitive mode belonging to more evolved stages of cognition, see Chap. 10, sect. 10.2.2.

[14] See Chap. 6 for further discussion.

[15] Cf. the ten modes (or tropes) of Scepticism (esp. modes 1–3) attributed to Aenesidemus, the reviver and systematizer of Pyrrhonian scepticism in the first century BCE (Sextus Empiricus, *Pyrrhoniae Hypotyposes* I). Arguably, the appearance of disagreement (*diaphōnia*) between different perspectives, classified in Sextus's ten modes, provides a main motivation for much ancient scepticism.

[16] See Chap. 10, sections 10.2–10.4, and Chap. 8, sections 8.1 and 8.2, for further discussion of the indeterminacy of human cognition and the importance of acknowledging this indeterminacy.

5.2.2 All-or-Nothing

In fact, as I see it, one of the chief problems with scepticism is that it is an 'all-or-nothing' position which runs in outline as follows:[17]

1. *either* there is an infallible mental state with no possibility of error *or* nothing is certain;
2. the experience of error easily shows that there is no such infallible state;
3. therefore, nothing is certain and no knowledge is possible.

This position is underpinned by at least three assumptions: (1) knowledge requires certainty; (2) certainty requires infallibility; (3) certainty requires a perfect grasp of the object of cognition in all its fully determinate particularity. One way to address the sceptical challenge is to deny (1)—an option which has gained and is gaining increasing traction in current epistemological debates in the form of so-called 'fallibilism' (that is, the idea that high probability, as opposed to certainty, is enough for knowledge).[18] This is, I propose, a self-defeating move because it concedes too much to a distinctive key claim of scepticism, namely, that nothing is certain. At best, 'knowledge' is rescued only in name. What is at stake, however, is not whether we are content to label as 'knowledge' a cognitive mode which falls short of certainty, but whether there is a cognitive mode which entails certainty, whatever that cognitive mode is called.

On the other hand, assumptions (2) and (3) can and should be rejected. Let's grant that I have a daughter who has lived with me since her birth and whom I see every day. The question of whether I am able to know with certainty that a given person is my daughter is obviously different from the question of whether I am able to *infallibly* know that a certain person is my daughter. The answer to the first question is yes, the answer to the second question is no. From the fact that I don't know that the person playing the Tin Man in the theatrical performance of *The Wizard of Oz* I am watching is my daughter does not follow that I am not able to know with certainty that a given person is my daughter. It only follows that I cannot do so infallibly because, in this case, sight is insufficient. Like any other sense or combinations of senses, sight puts us in contact with 'what is' only in a limited and approximate way.

[17] Cf. Vanni Rovighi 1963–1979: 37. An example of this all-or-nothing approach is sketched by Cicero in *Academica* II. 76–8, where both the Stoic notion of a cataleptic impression, that is, an impression which perfectly conforms to 'what is' ('ex eo quod esset, sicut esset, impressum et signatum et effictum') and Arcesilaus's sceptical response are considered. I am grateful to Raphael Woolf for drawing my attention to this passage.

[18] For criticism of fallibilism, including a discussion of its relation to scepticism, see Ayers 2019: 145–6, 151–2.

The same is true of intellectual cognition. According to a long and dominant tradition traced in Chapters 1 and 2, we are never able to grasp any individual thing in its fully determinate particularity. We only grasp some very limited aspects. The aspects with which we *do* connect, however, are known with certainty even if other aspects are not known at all. As Leibniz teaches, this explains, for instance, why it is easier to achieve certainty in mathematics: the objects of mathematics are abstract objects which, as such, have a finite number of features. In principle, all those features could be discovered by a finite mind which would thereby achieve a perfect, adequate knowledge of that object. This level of adequacy is not possible, even in principle, for existing, concrete individual things. One of the mistakes of scepticism is to demand that our knowledge be able to exhaust the object of cognition in order to achieve certainty. Another mistake is to demand that we are infallibly able to do so.

In brief, if it is granted at the outset that there is an original contact between cognizer and cognized, as shown for instance by primitive perceiving beings which successfully relate to their surroundings, there is no reason to deny such contact to human perceivers. That is, cognition starts in the same way for humans as for other perceiving beings: as animal sense-perception which imperfectly and gradually apprehends those features of the environment which are in principle open to the exploration of that particular kind of perceiving being. If this initial contact is granted, higher kinds of cognition can then be evaluated in a framework which does not start by assuming a gap.

To conclude: my contention is that the (J)TB+ analysis is the offspring of scepticism.[19] It is not merely an innocent historical mistake to assume uncritically that the standard Western conception is that knowledge is a kind of belief which meets certain criteria. On the contrary, this basic historical mistake implies a substantive philosophical position that dismisses without a hearing a historically prominent and vastly important alternative account. The twentieth-century (J)TB+ orthodoxy is rooted in the epistemological strand which rejects an original contact or direct presence of reality to the mind. Once a gap is introduced, there is no way to bridge it. I agree with Pasnau that much pre-modern epistemology was not primarily concerned with permissible belief but disagree that this is to be lamented as a Panglossian illusion from which modern times eventually liberate us. The hero of Pasnau's story is Hume. The heroes of my story are the many thinkers who conceived knowledge as a natural mental state in which there is no gap between knower and known, and saw a distinction in kind between a mental state in which the object of cognition is directly present (seen, grasped) and a

[19] Black concludes her brief paper on 'Knowledge without Belief' by noting: 'Are there any good philosophical reasons for conflating knowledge and belief? I suggest that there are some reasons that will do quite nicely for the sceptic, but not for anyone else' (1971: 158).

mental state in which assent to the object of cognition is not moved by its presence but a variety of reasons with different degrees of force.

5.3 Knowledge First, but Give Belief Its Due

5.3.1 A High Bar for Knowledge

A key implication of my proposal is that, as in the best early modern tradition, it sets the bar for knowledge high. There could be no successful cognition without a primitive contact between mind and reality, but what one knows (and can know) is limited because, primarily or paradigmatically, knowledge is akin to acquaintance and, in intellectual cognition, involves understanding.[20] Its primitive mode is non-discursive and non-propositional: it is a perception which takes the form both of sense-perception, which grounds further modalities of sensitive knowledge, and of intellectual perception, which grounds further modalities of intellectual knowledge.[21] On this primitive perception of 'what is', in other words, are based discursive modes of knowledge in which the evidence of 'what is' is followed step-by-step by inference, as well as other cognitive modes such as memory and recognition, in which the original cognitive contact with 'what is' can be preserved (albeit with varying degrees of success).[22] This is, I surmise, what Wodehouse means by her striking claim that 'all kinds of knowledge are equally immediate' because 'presentation is of the essence of knowledge'.[23] Knowing, on her account, is a type of consciousness that presents one with reality[24] and 'reality is presented in consciousness...in all the presentation fields we have', including sense, memory, expectation, intuition. If and when these faculties issue in knowing, our cognitive contact with reality 'is just as close, just as immediate, in every field;...the past, for instance, is as really and directly presented to us as the present is'.[25] That is, what makes memory, recognition, inferential seeing of

[20] Aristotle's *epistēmē* corresponds to understanding rather than justified true belief (see Burnyeat 1984). In his insightful discussion of early modern epistemology, Carriero 2013 stresses that Descartes, Spinoza, Leibniz, and Locke are primarily interested in understanding. On the notion of 'primary knowledge' see Ayers 2019, esp. pp. vi, 27, 61–4, 115, 185, 195.

[21] The conception of rational intuition as a sort of perception analogous to sense-perception has ancient roots and plenty of early modern accolades (see Chapters 1 and 2). For a recent defence of this conception see Bengson 2015.

[22] The distinction between non-discursive and discursive knowledge is traced esp. in Chapters 1 and 2. I make a case for the primacy of non-propositional knowledge in Chap. 10, sect. 10.1.1. A brief discussion of cognitive modes which can preserve the contact with 'what is' (including memory, recognition, and some types of inference) is offered in Chap. 9, sect. 9.1.2.

[23] Wodehouse 1909: 395–6.

[24] Longworth and Wimmer 2022. I am grateful to Wimmer and Longworth for drawing my attention to the work of Wodehouse in the unpublished version of this paper.

[25] Wodehouse 1909: 392, 394.

what follows from what, and so on, types of knowing is their all being types of presentations in consciousness of 'what is'.

On the other hand, even if extended to memory as well as to recognitional and inferential abilities, this kind of primitive perception of 'what is' is possible only in limited cases. This is why belief, I contend, is by far the most common mode of our individual cognition. Most of one's cognitive activity relies in fact on assent given for reasons 'extrinsic' or 'extraneous' to the object itself.[26] No amount of reasons or justification supporting such belief will turn this mode of cognition into the 'cognition of grounds in the object', to use Kant's phrase, which characterizes knowledge. *Justified* belief, however, is mostly very reliable in tracking truth, and constitutes an indispensable mode of successful cognition, with enormous power of extending one's cognitive grip beyond what (strictly speaking) can be known.

5.3.2 Is the Bar too High? Individual and Collective Knowing

An obvious objection is that the bar for knowledge is set too high and that most of what 'we' normally take as knowledge will not qualify, including the enormous amount of cognition based on testimony.[27] While I have no problem in granting that the bar for knowledge is set high (claims to knowledge are a serious matter), I reject the charge that it is set *too* high.

My first reply to this objection is ad hominem: those who think that knowledge is a kind of belief are hardly in a position to complain that, on my account, too much of our cognition counts as belief. As in their accounts, I fully acknowledge the difference between mere belief and belief which meets conditions of justification, entitlement, and so on. Only the latter is reliable in tracking truth. Furthermore, I acknowledge the force of the shared intuitions which point to the key epistemological difference between Gettiered and not-Gettiered cases of justified true belief (JTB).[28] But, unlike their accounts, I argue for a mental state which is ontologically distinct from *any* sort of belief, whereas for them all our cognition is, at bottom, *some* sort of belief.

Second, there is a crucial social dimension to knowledge that allows us to count as *known by the community* those aspects of 'what is' with which some group and/or individual in the community has, or has had, the kind of cognitive contact required for knowledge. As persuasively argued by Bird, this is a type of knowing

[26] Aquinas, *Scriptum super Sententiis*, lib. 3 d. 23 q. 2 a. 2, qc. 1, co.: 'credens . . . ab extrinseco determinatur ad unum'; Locke, *Essay*, Book IV, chap. XV, 3.

[27] For a specific discussion of testimony see Chap. 12, where I defend the claim that testimony does not, on its own, produce individual knowledge although it can (and often does) lead to individual knowledge.

[28] By 'Gettiered and not-Gettiered cases of JTB' I mean the debate started by Gettier 1963 about cases of justified true belief which intuitively do not qualify as knowledge.

which is neither reducible to individual knowing nor simply supervenient on facts about what individuals know. It has its own distinctive characteristics which make it analogous to individual knowing while exhibiting irreducibly different features.[29]

A prime example of this is science. The level of sophistication and specialization in any of the natural, mathematical, and social sciences is such that no individual scientist can claim to have done, or be able to do by herself, all the experiments, demonstrations, gathering and analyses of data, and so on, presupposed by her own scientific work. Much of what a scientist does is based on authority and testimony. Furthermore, division of labour is such that, especially in large and complex scientific projects, no single team of researchers (let alone a single scientist) has knowledge of all the aspects which contribute to the successful completion of that project. Indeed, in enterprises such as the development of the atomic bomb or the CERN Large Hadron Collider, not even the project leaders can be said to have a detailed knowledge of each and every element of the project. And yet, it is perfectly fine to say that not only the Manhattan project team but also the USA (as collective entities) knew how to construct the atomic bomb, even if no individual in this community had individual knowledge of it.[30]

In brief, insofar as there is someone or some group in the scientific community which does have, or has had, the relevant cognitive contact with 'what is' (as checked and certified by the relevant peer-reviewing processes) that aspect is *known* by the scientific community collectively although not distributively by each individual member. At the same time, there is a vast amount of scientific work that the scientific community itself regards as driven by hypotheses—that is, epistemically, by justified belief, rather than knowledge—and which plays an indispensable and ineliminable role in scientific progress.

Something analogous applies to our everyday cognition. Say, I am upstairs in my study, and you are downstairs looking in the fridge. If after a thorough and competent inspection of the fridge you see that there is a full bottle of milk there,[31] and shout to me: 'There is a full bottle of milk in the fridge!' does this count as knowledge? Well, it depends. On my account, *you* know that there is a bottle of milk in the fridge while *I* have a justified true belief based on your reliable testimony. For all practical purposes (for example, my continuing to sit comfortably in my study as opposed to dashing out to buy milk) it makes no difference. The latter claim raises, of course, the well-known issue mooted by Plato in the

[29] Bird 2010, 2020: 70-107. Cf. also Hyman 1999: 433; 2015: 159. The nature of social knowledge as *analogous* to individual knowing explains why not all key features of individual knowing are relevant to social knowing (e.g., in endorsing social knowing, I am not forced to allow collective agents who *see*. I am grateful to Simon-Pierre Chevarie-Cossette for pressing me on this point).

[30] These are examples discussed by Bird in his illuminating paper of 2010.

[31] Competent also in the sense that you are able to recognize milk containers and their content by sight. Furthermore, the example assumes that it is indeed the case that there is a full bottle of milk in the fridge.

Meno: namely, why it is then better to know the road to Larissa rather than merely having a true belief about it? On this issue, I agree with Hyman that, ultimately, the reason why we value knowledge over true belief is that we value truth, and only knowledge (as opposed to belief) *essentially* entails truth.[32] That is, even in the case of beliefs which are de facto true, truth is not a feature of belief *de jure*, the way it is of knowledge. As regards specifically the case at hand, I will just say that, although knowledge and true belief may result in the same behaviour in many (but by no means all) cases, in this case my ability to track 'what is' for practical purposes is explained by the fact that someone in the community has or has had an effective cognitive contact with 'what is'. The latter mode of cognition has therefore ontological and epistemic priority over the former. Most importantly, however, as a family community, we collectively *know* of the presence of a bottle of milk in the fridge, even if not every individual knows of it distributively. My focus in this book is on individual knowledge, and my point here is that individual knowing is a tiny fraction of what may still strictly count as collectively or socially known.[33]

Finally, one of the key aims of my proposal is to stress the crucial contribution to our cognition of a cognitive mode which, I argue, is irreducibly different from knowledge as a different mental state not entailed by it: namely, belief. Belief is not something sub-standard in relation to knowledge because belief has its own standards, namely justification, degrees of probability, level of support by reasons, and so on. It is a distinct, essential, and complementary way to engage cognitively with reality and/or the world. It seems to me that adult individual cognition is a closely knit fabric of knowledge and of belief with different degrees of justification. Acknowledging that much of one's cognition relies on belief rather than knowledge makes it even more crucial for belief to meet certain criteria, since no belief is rationally justified without there being reasons which can be given in its support. Conversely, an inflated use of the notion of knowledge often goes hand-in-hand with fundamentalism and dogmatism (including, but not only, in religious contexts).[34] Indeed, historically, fundamentalism is not uncommonly wedded to the assumption that each individual can have his own access to knowledge on all sort of matters, and that therefore reliance on experts, authorities, and collective tradition should be shunned.[35]

The practical and political consequence of the position defended here is the following: genuine claims to knowledge by individuals are very limited; this is why we must massively rely on collective knowing—that is, on a kind of knowing

[32] For an insightful, detailed discussion see Hyman 2015: 191–210.

[33] For further discussion see Chap. 12.

[34] The contribution of belief (including religious belief) to cognition is specifically discussed in Part III of this book.

[35] In a brilliant discussion of authority and belief in the medieval Islamic world, Peter Adamson notes that, in the Islamic tradition, it has often been fundamentalists who polemicized against authority (*taqlīd*) and rejected legal and religious learning in favour of a direct engagement with the revelation (Adamson 2022: chap. 1).

which is analogous but crucially different from individual knowing. As individuals, most of our successful cognition is justified belief based on the authority of those who are most likely, collectively, to know due to their training, the means at their disposal, their methodology in studying hugely complex matters, and so on. Namely, if one wishes to track truth, one has to identify and trust appropriate *communities* of *experts*—scientists, medical doctors, pharmacists, teachers, professional historians, biblical scholars, and so on.[36] Those who, in the name of an inflated pretence to individual knowledge, reject reliance on the authority of experts, and do not take on board that there is a distinction in kind between what one individually knows and what one (more or less justifiably) believes, may often be those who deny what is collectively known in order to embrace with the utmost conviction the wildest conspiracy theories fuelled by fake news. In sum: 'knowledge first' but 'give belief its due'—a clear sense of why and how extensively one has a claim to (more or less justified) belief rather than to individual knowing fosters a Socratic epistemic humility which helps in countering gullibility and fundamentalism.

[36] The focus of my discussion in this book is on *individual* knowing and/or believing. Collective knowing and communities of experts are huge issues central to epistemology in general and social epistemology in particular which require a much deeper and broader discussion. Nevertheless, they cannot but figure to some extent also in my discussion due to their crucial importance, in my view, to epistemology.

PART II
KNOWLEDGE AND BELIEF
Phenomenology and Ontology

Introduction to Part II

II.1 Individual Knowledge as Essentially First-Person

One way to summarize the account of individual knowledge proposed in the first part of this book is to say that knowledge is essentially—that is, primarily, fundamentally, paradigmatically—first-person.[1] Strictly speaking and at its most fundamental, knowledge is not a bundle of information that can be passed on to an individual as a parcel,[2] because each one of us has to see, grasp, perceive for herself (either literally in sense-perception or metaphorically in intellectual perception) the object of knowledge. In this regard, sense-perception and understanding are knowledge's paradigmatic manifestations.

As Part I tried to show, the view that each one of us has to do her/his own knowing is firmly attested in the tradition and shared, for instance, by thinkers as diverse as Plato, Descartes, and Locke.[3] Roughly, knowing is a first-personal apprehension of 'what is', or a cognitive contact with the object of cognition which is present to the cognizer and directly moves assent. Believing is a mental state different in kind in which the object of cognition is not present to the cognizer, and assent is moved by reasons extrinsic to the object itself.[4] In the final chapter of Part I, I have argued that a genuinely non-sceptical philosophy of cognition acknowledges this difference in kind between knowledge and belief, and that (J)TB+ theories of knowledge are historically and theoretically the offspring of a sceptical outlook.

[1] I draw inspiration from Michael Ayers's notion of 'primary knowledge' in rejecting the widespread assumption that the best way to illuminate the notion of knowledge is to provide a definition that fits every case of what is commonly regarded as knowledge. As convincingly argued by Ayers, we should instead start with the identification of the essential core of knowledge, that is, with the identification of what is central to knowledge in its primary sense. This notion of 'primary knowledge' was first introduced by Ayers 1991: 139–44 and then further developed and defended in Ayers 2019: esp. vi, 27, 61–4, 115, 185, 195.

[2] This is not to deny the crucial importance of testimony (see Chap. 12) or of the social dimension of knowledge (see Chap. 5, sect. 5.3.2, where I address also the question of whether, on my account, the bar for knowledge is set too high).

[3] Cf. Ayers and Antognazza 2019: 3–33 (see esp. pp. 22, 26–9). As Locke famously wrote, transferred information is not really knowledge but 'borrowed Wealth, like Fairy-money, though it were Gold in the hand from which he received it, will be but Leaves and Dust when it comes to use' (*Essay*, Book I, chap. IV, 23).

[4] Cf. Aquinas, *Scriptum super Sententiis*, lib. 3 d. 23 q. 2 a. 2, qc. 1, co.: 'credens... ab extrinseco determinatur ad unum'; Locke, *Essay*, Book IV, chap. XV, 3: 'That which makes me believe, is something extraneous to the thing I believe.'

With this historical and theoretical framework in place, Part II delves deeper into the phenomenology and ontology of knowledge and belief. Its overall aim is to offer a positive model of cognition which renews some traditional insights.

II.2 'Subject', 'Object', and Their Relation

If (as argued throughout the Western tradition surveyed in Part I) knowing is a primitive cognitive contact of a cognizer with an object of cognition, then the natural starting point for a thoroughgoing analysis of knowledge (Chapter 6) is an account of how we arrive, in the first place, at the distinction between 'subject' and 'object'. This distinction is often simply presupposed without explanation. By contrast, I aim to show that focusing on why and how subject and object are distinct is of key importance for understanding the nature of knowledge itself. I will claim that, as regards a study of cognition, the first phenomenological datum is the presence of something (whatever that is), and that this presence manifests itself in two phenomenologically distinct ways: some aspects are experienced (that is, lived, *erlebt*) as 'mine', others are experienced as 'other' (*aliud*) than me. The distinction between subject and object is grounded in this phenomenology: something is phenomenologically present to me as 'other' than me, whatever the ontological nature of this 'other' might be (at this point, we are still on the cis-side of idealism and realism, intended as further metaphysical claims regarding the nature of what manifests itself as *aliud*).

A first result is that there are beings capable not only of awareness of the presence of something but also of awareness of the presence of something other than oneself. Call them 'perceiving' (as opposed to merely 'sentient') beings. In familiar terms, at least some sentient beings are beings capable of awareness of themselves *and* of their environment, *as* their environment. After this groundwork, I will return to the nature of knowledge. Knowledge, it will be claimed, is the result of a natural relationship between a perceiving being (the subject or 'I') and a 'not-I' (the object). On this account, the conditions *sine qua non* of a *cognitive* relation (as opposed to other types of relation) are a subject capable of this type of awareness and an object. That is, a cognitive relation requires an awareness (consciousness) directed towards an *aliud* (intentionality). In this framework, knowledge is the intentional presence of an object to a subject—a presence characterized by a *sui generis* unification between knower and known, in the act of knowing. This is an account, it will be argued, which supports the view of individual knowledge as essentially and paradigmatically first-person that has already emerged in the first part of the book.

The second chapter of Part II (Chapter 7) focuses on intentionality itself, that is, on the nature of the contact between subject and object. It explores and commends a tradition which construes intentionality as intrinsically relational, contra some present-day views which understand intentionality as a non-relational mental representation. Starting from the discussion of the Aristotelian roots and the medieval developments of the doctrine of intentionality, it will point at the importance of the medieval distinction between formal and objective reality for a proper understanding of this doctrine. This distinction is further developed in early modern thought, and, especially, in Antoine Arnaud's argument against a 'representative being' which mediates between subject and object. After discussing the modern rejuvenation of the doctrine of intentionality by Franz Brentano and later thinkers influenced by him, the chapter will conclude that the doctrine of intentionality explains knowledge in terms of a *sui generis* assimilation of cognizer and cognized, namely, a *sui generis* presence of an *aliud* to a subject.

II.3 The Ontology of Cognition

Further to the phenomenological exploration of Chapters 6 and 7, Chapters 8 and 9 turn to the ontology of cognition, that is, to an investigation of which kind of entities are involved in cognition. My proposal will revisit a prominent strand of the ancient–medieval tradition which explains this ontology in terms of objects (Chapter 8), acts, and faculties (Chapter 9). Starting from sensible objects and the cognitive process by which they can be grasped, Chapter 8 discusses sense-perceptual cognition and intellectual cognition of mind-independent things. All really existing, mind-independent things, it will be claimed, are fully determinate individuals: it is with these individuals that cognition begins via sense-perception. Most importantly, I contend, this first cognitive contact is already knowledge—that is, a *sui generis* presence of an *aliud* to a subject which, in its most primitive forms, does not involve universals or generalities. According to this proposal, the most basic or primitive type of knowledge is therefore pre-conceptual and, a fortiori, pre-propositional.

In order to discover the stable core (the 'whatness' or quiddity) of the object which impinges on the senses, however, a higher capacity is required: the capacity for abstraction and universalization, that is, the ability to discover what can be attributed to a plurality of individuals through abstraction from the *singularity* of individual sensible objects. In what follows, intellectual cognition of really existing, extra-mental things will be presented as this discovery of 'whatness', that is, as the discovery of what kind of thing an individual is. More generally, cognition will be construed as a process of progressive determination of what is apprehended in an indeterminate way first by the sense and then by the intellect—a process which, no matter how advanced, can never fully exhaust the richness of fully determinate individuals. The upshot of this account is that, although senses and intellect latch on to reality, human knowledge does not stretch to a perfectly adequate (that is, complete) knowledge of *any* of the concrete individuals which really exist.

The second section of Chapter 8 turns to the discussion of ideal objects and imaginary objects. These are, it will be claimed, abstract entities which, as such, do not qualify for extra-mental existence. The latter claim does not imply, however, that their natures depend on human thought or on psychological features of the human mind. In fact, it will be argued, one should not conflate two orders of questions: (1) what are the conditions under which an ideal object or an imaginary object can have some being or reality (that is, it must be thought by some mind); and, (2) what is the nature of those objects. It will be proposed that these objects are logical possibilities either with necessary natures (ideal objects, for example, the objects of mathematics) or with contingent natures (imaginary objects). Most importantly for the matter at hand, it will be maintained that these natures—whatever their more precise ontological status—are what constitute the relatum of an intentional relation. The bottom line is that so-called non-existing things do not force us either to abandon the relationality of intentionality or to introduce relations without a relatum. The chapter will conclude that there are two ways of considering the objects of cognition: either as they are in themselves—that is, according to their formal reality, whatever that is (extra-mental, ideal, imaginary)—or insofar as they are cognized. Most importantly, the latter amounts to a *mode of being* of objects themselves, and not to some additional category of objects (intentional objects, mental contents, mental representations, and the like).

Chapter 9 focuses, respectively, on the nature of acts of cognition and on the nature of faculties, tracking, in turn, the occurrent and the dispositional aspects of cognition. After a discussion of the three main types of mental acts characterizing developed human cognition—apprehension, judgement, and reasoning—the ontological status of acts of cognition is tackled. Mental acts, it will be proposed, are actions of a certain type, namely, immanent actions (actions which do not produce something distinct from, or external to, the agent). It is this immanent action (that is, a property, mode, or modification of the cognitive subject) that grounds the relation of the cognitive subject to what is knowable or perceptible. In turn, cognition can be understood as having the nature of a relation between mind and world, thereby providing the basis of the immensely influential Aristotelian account of truth in terms of conformity of mind to reality or of correspondence between mind and reality. In this regard, the importance of distinguishing between ontological truth and logical truth (taken in their older sense) will be noted—the former being a property of things; the latter being a property of thought. Truth, it will be concluded, is a non-mental element only if one is considering ontological truth as opposed to logical truth. It is the latter, however, which is the specific concern of a cognitive relation—that is, truth as a property of *thought* to conform to how things are.

Turning now to faculties, on the account proposed by Chapter 9, faculties are potentialities of a specific kind: they are capacities, powers to actively do certainly things. Although they fall under the broader genus of dispositions, they will be treated as abilities, capacities, or powers rather than, generically, as dispositions, since not all dispositions are powers. Their ontological status, I will suggest, is that of being natural properties or qualities of the mind in which the nature of the mind is manifested. As powers, I will maintain, faculties have an aspect of actuality, that is, they are principles of operation actually present in a cognitive subject. On the other hand, faculties have also a crucial aspect of potentiality insofar as they are powers which are not always exercised. This important duality of actuality and potentiality is captured, I will note, by the Aristotelian-medieval distinction between *actus primus* and *actus secundus*—a distinction which, for the purpose of providing an ontology of cognition, has the advantage of approaching dispositional versus occurrent cognition from a metaphysical angle.

Finally, Chapter 9 will stress that cognitive powers are complemented by a different kind of powers which are equally important in order to understand the activity of cognitive beings: namely, conative powers. As a consequence, the cognitive model proposed by this book is built on a philosophical anthropology in which these two complementary kinds of powers—cognitive and conative—play crucial, distinct, but fundamentally integrated roles, as shown by the account of the distinction between subject and object offered in Chapter 6, and as will emerge from the relationship between belief and will suggested by Chapter 11.

II.4 The Object of Knowledge and the Object of Belief

The phenomenology and ontology outlined in Chapters 6 to 9, provide the basis for answering the questions addressed by the concluding chapter of Part II (Chapter 10), namely, what is the object of knowledge and what is the object of belief. The discussion of rival views on these matters will lead to a positive alternative account. The immediate object of knowledge, I will argue, are objects in themselves, that is, objects as they are according to their formal reality, whatever that is (extra-mental, ideal, imaginary). If this nature is that of mind-independent, fully determinate concrete individuals, our grasp of such objects is always *indeterminate* and *inadequate*, in the technical sense of never being able to exhaust the *adequatio intellectus ad rem* in which logical truth consists. On the other hand, if their nature is that of an ideal or imaginary object, our knowledge of these objects, I will suggest, can be in principle adequate in virtue of their very abstractness. In turn, I will suggest that belief may or may not have the same object as knowledge depending on whether the sort of cognitive contact required by knowledge is or is not in principle available. More generally, the object of belief will be (imagined or conceived) putative entities or states of affairs which may or may not correspond to 'what is'. Finally, the view that 'representational content' is the immediate object of knowledge will be rejected. 'Representational content', I will argue, still fails to explain what is most in need of explaining, namely, the very phenomenon of an original presentation—be it the original presentation of an extra-mental thing or of a mental 'representational content'.

In conclusion, it will be suggested that cognition is a process of progressive determination of what is initially indeterminately (that is, confusedly) apprehended. In this progressive determination, most of what contribute to fully determining what an individual (or state of affair) is, is not (and, in many cases, cannot be) present. This is why, in our successful cognition, we need to rely on a massive scale on a mode of cognition complementary to knowledge—a mode of cognition in which something which is not present, is nevertheless affirmed on the basis of reasons, symptoms, traces, signs. In a word, we need to rely on belief.

6
Phenomenology
Subject and Object

This chapter offers an account of how we arrive at the distinction between 'subject' and 'object'. Instead of simply presupposing this distinction, as it often done, I aim to show that explaining why and how subject and object are distinct is of key importance for understanding the nature of knowledge itself.

As regards a study of cognition, I will suggest, the first phenomenological datum is the presence of something (whatever that is). In turn, this presence manifests itself in two phenomenologically distinct ways: some aspects are experienced (that is, lived, *erlebt*) as 'mine', others are experienced as 'other' (*aliud*) than me. The distinction between subject and object is grounded (I will contend) in this phenomenology. On this basis, I will argue that: (1) cognition starts with an *aliud* which is present to a *felt* self in a way fundamentally different from one's own modes of being; (2) individual human knowledge in its paradigmatic form is essentially first-personal, that is, its object-directedness requires a built-in, implicit awareness of a 'self' that provides the unifying perspective from which the *aliud* is apprehended; (3) this is a first-order awareness which is crucially distinct from the second-order awareness which requires a reflexive cognitive act—a distinction which I propose to cash out in terms of 'first-person knowledge' versus 'self-knowledge'.[1] My proposal is capacious enough, therefore, to embrace self-knowledge; but it is crucial to it to acknowledge that self-knowledge is *sui generis* insofar as, normally or generally, the object of knowledge is a not-I, and its being a not-I or an *aliud* is central to explaining how cognition generally works. Although, as I will discuss below (in section 6.3.2), in the case of self-knowledge, the self becomes the object too, self-knowledge is not the basic knowledge on which I am focusing here, but a higher-order type of cognition.[2]

[1] I take this proposal to be in line with the subjective character of experience as described by Nagel 1974: 436–7.

[2] I am very grateful to an anonymous OUP adviser for pressing me on this point. As I elaborate further in the course of this chapter, my proposal is that individual knowing in its paradigmatic form is essentially first-personal, that is, its object-directedness requires a built-in awareness of the self as the unifying perspective from which the *aliud* is apprehended. By contrast, self-knowledge is a higher, second-order, reflective cognitive act in which the cognitive *subject* is capable of reflecting on herself and her actual states, standing attitudes, and dispositional properties in a unique way which makes of herself the *object* of cognition. This being said, self-knowledge is such a large, rich topic of its own that it would be overambitious to try to discuss it in detail in this book.

Thinking with Assent: Renewing a Traditional Account of Knowledge and Belief. Maria Rosa Antognazza, Oxford University Press. © Maria Rosa Antognazza 2024. DOI: 10.1093/oso/9780198831518.003.0007

6.1 The Distinction between Subject and Object, I and Not-I

6.1.1 Is the Subject Just Another Object?

For Franz Brentano, the object-directedness of every mental act involves two objects: the intentional object and the act itself.[3] Mental acts are therefore directed on themselves as well as other objects. Crucially, however, for Brentano, '*perceiving x* and *awareness of perceiving x* are the same act under different descriptions'.[4] Furthermore, there is never a single perception at a time, or multiple simultaneous mental acts each with its own object (say, distinct mental acts by which we simultaneously consciously see, hear, smell, feel, and so on) but a single mental act that simultaneously presents itself and many physical objects.[5]

This is, in my view, an attractive proposal but several questions remain open. First of all, speaking of an object or objects towards which mental acts are directed seems to presuppose a distinction between a subject of the mental act and an object towards which this mental act is directed. But how do we reach the distinction between subject and object in the first place? How are subject and object different? If it is the case that the object-directedness or intentionality of the mental also has the mental act itself as its object, is this mental act just another object?

Moreover, Hume seems right in his phenomenological remark that in perception we never have an impression of the 'self':

> self or person is not any one impression, but that to which our several impressions and ideas are suppos'd to have reference.... For my part, when I enter most intimately into what I call *myself*, I always stumble on some particular perception or other... I never can catch *myself* at any time without a perception... I may venture to affirm of the rest of mankind, that they are nothing but a bundle or collection of different perceptions. (*Treatise*, Part IV, Book I, Section VI; Selby-Bigge, pp. 251–2)

I interpret Hume's view as denying that we have an immediate grasp, or an immediate experience, of the 'self' as a *cognitive* subject. What is phenomenologically given are perceptions (to use Hume's vocabulary) or intentional objects (to use Brentano's terms) but not the subject as another object along with other intentional objects (or, in Hume's terms, another impression along with other impressions). It seems to me that Berkeley's view that we have no idea of mind

[3] See Textor 2017a: 1–4.

[4] Textor 2017a: 6. See also p. 4: 'perceiving and awareness of perceiving are in fact the same activity... conscious perceiving cannot be factorized into ontologically independent mental acts'.

[5] Textor 2017a: 9–10.

tracks an objection in the same ballpark—that is, an objection to construing the subject as a special type of object. For Berkeley, the only objects of perception are ideas, and the *esse* of ideas is exhausted by their being perceived. The perceiver (or mind/spirit, or 'that which acts') belongs to another category altogether: its *esse* is not *percipi*; being essentially active, it cannot be constituted by a passive and inert entity such as an idea.[6]

In turn, Brentano's own student, Edmund Husserl, objects that the mental has no appearance, no 'adumbration' (*Abschattung*), that is, roughly, no mode of presentation under which it appears, unlike a 'thing' which is always perceived under a mode of presentation, a perspective from which it appears:[7]

> We perceive the Thing through 'adumbrations' [dadurch, dass es sich 'abschattet'] of all its possibly 'real' determinates that properly [eigentlich] 'fall' into our perception. An experience [that is, following Brentano, a mental phenomenon] has no adumbrations [Ein Erlebnis schattet sich nicht ab].[8]

More generally, I agree with Brentano that consciously perceiving is a single act which does not factorize into two distinct acts—consciousness/awareness *and* perceiving—but this very claim seems to indicate that, in perception, the conscious subject is not an additional object towards which intentionality is directed. It seems to me that this is the implication of Elizabeth Anscombe's paper on 'The First Person' (1975).[9] As far as I can see, Anscombe's famous claim that 'I' does not refer, or is not a referring expression, draws attention to the fact that 'I' is not a kind of object at all, namely, it is not an object which happens to be myself as opposed to some other object, with the only difference of being reachable through some kind of internal perception. In other words, if reference implies the same mechanism by which, according to Frege, a proper name picks out an object among other objects, then 'I' does not refer.[10] A broadly similar point is made by Anscombe's 'The Subjectivity of Sensation' (1976): sensory reports have an essentially first-person character. As Adrian Haddock explains in his discussion of the

[6] Berkeley, *Principles of Human Knowledge*, Part I, sec. 27: 'A spirit is one simple, undivided, active being: as it perceives ideas, it is called the *understanding*, and as it produces or otherwise operates about them, it is called the *will*. Hence there can be no idea formed of a soul or spirit: for all ideas whatever, being passive and inert, *vide Sect.* 25, they cannot represent unto us, by way of image or likeness, that which acts.'

[7] Cf. Stumpf 1939: 342; quoted by Textor 2017a: 9.

[8] Husserl 1933, 79 [77]. Trans. modified by Textor 2017a: 179 (cf. also pp. 175–80).

[9] Anscombe 1975: 21–36.

[10] For a discussion of Anscombe's paper see especially Harcourt 2000 and chap. 2 of O'Brien 2007. Harcourt argues that 'the force of Anscombe's argument is . . . to show that one cannot both have a full-dress Fregean account of the relation between "I" and the thing it stands for and hold that "I" stands for the human being who utters it'. O'Brien shows that an internal perception model of self-presentation leads to the conclusion that, if 'I' refers, it refers to a Cartesian Ego. It is because Anscombe took the internal perceptual model of first-person reference as the only available model—O'Brien concludes—that Anscombe came to the inacceptable claim that 'I' does not refer.

paper, 'this insight is distorted when this character is taken to introduce a certain kind of object—'the subject'—for this has the effect of turning the sensible properties into private objects. The remedy is to acknowledge that this character 'does not introduce any *thing* at all, precisely because "I" is not any kind of name'.'[11]

In what follows, I try to unpack the insight that the subject is *not* another object by offering a phenomenological account of the origin of the distinction between subject and object, I and not-I.

6.1.2 Two Different Ways of Being Present

I follow Husserl in thinking that in an inquiry on knowledge one should go back *zu den Sachen selbst*, that is, to things themselves as they show or manifest themselves. In other words, the starting point is phenomenological.[12] In such an inquiry, I suggest, the first phenomenological datum is the following: something is present. Note that no claim is made as to the *nature* of what is present. Likewise, no reference is made to a subject and/or an object, or (a fortiori) to their being or not being distinct. So far, this remark—something is present (whatever that is)—is merely a phenomenological observation which comes before any further metaphysical claim. This observation is nothing else than the indubitable core of the Augustinian and the Cartesian *cogito*. That is, what is first and foremost really indubitable in Augustine and Descartes's *cogito* is that *aliquid est* (rather than *ergo sum*).[13]

The second phenomenological observation is that this presence manifests itself in two, fundamentally distinct ways. Some aspects of what is present—for example, being tired, feeling cold, wishing to warm up—are phenomenologically experienced as modes of being of whatever it is that keeps together or unifies these modes of being. Such aspects of what is present are the affective and conative/appetitive states which are experienced (that is, lived, *erlebt*) as 'what is it like' to *be* what keeps together or unifies these modes of being.[14]

Other aspects of what is present are not phenomenologically experienced in this way. In the phenomenology of the same unitary experience in which cold and white (the white of snow) are both present, feeling cold is experienced as what is it like to *be* cold, while the white of snow is experienced as something *other* than a mode of being of whatever it is that is feeling cold and is wishing to warm up.

[11] Haddock (unpublished draft), citing Anscombe 1976/1981: 56 (emphasis in Anscombe's paper). I am very grateful to Adrian Haddock for sharing his draft paper with me. The remarks which follow are inspired by the writings of Sofia Vanni Rovighi, in particular Vanni Rovighi 1962: 109–132 (esp. pp. 109–18); 1963–79: 347–74 (esp. pp. 350–6); 1982: 19–24. I am greatly indebted to her insights.

[12] This is the approach taken by Ayers 2019: chap. 2.

[13] Vanni Rovighi 1962: 112; cf. Maritain 1948: 148.

[14] Cf. Nagel 1974; Frey 2013.

Of course, a snowball can also be felt as cold, but there is still a phenomenal difference between feeling what it is like to *be* cold and feeling cold as the mode of being of something *other*. Likewise, in holding a heavy wooden box, one may feel tired, but not cubic or wooden. Both tiredness and cubicalness are present, but the first is experienced as what it is like to be tired, the second as a mode of being of something other.

These two different types of presence correspond, as far as I can see, to Thomas Reid's key distinction between 'sensation' and 'perception'.[15] As Reid notes:

> The same mode of expression is used to denote sensation and perception; and therefore, we are apt to look upon them as things of the same nature. Thus, *I feel a pain; I see a tree*: the first denoteth a sensation, the last a perception. The grammatical analysis of both expressions is the same: for both consists of an active verb and an object. But, if we attend to the things signified by these expressions, we shall find, that in the first, the distinction between the act and the object is not real but grammatical; in the second, the distinction is not only grammatical but real. (Reid, *Inquiry*, chap. 6, sect. xx, pp. 167–8)

That is, 'sensations' are given, at least phenomenologically, as what it is like to be in a certain way (in Reid's terms, there is no real distinction between the act—feeling—and the object—pain), whereas 'perceptions' are phenomenologically given as referring to something other (in Reid's terms, there is a real distinction between the act—seeing -and the object—a tree).

It seems to me that the fundamentally different way in which an affective or an appetitive state, as opposed to something else, is present, was clear also to Hume. Hume is often taken to deny that the 'self' or 'subject' is phenomenologically given because (as we saw above) he denies that we find an impression of the self in the bundle of perceptions which constitutes what is present.[16] In fact, even Hume grants that the subject is primitively given but in a *sui generis* way, that is, as the subject of affective states (the 'passions'), as opposed to being given as an impression on a par with other impressions. After introducing in Book I of the *Treatise* (devoted to 'the Understanding') the famous metaphors of the bundle of perceptions and of the mind as 'a kind of theatre' constituted only by 'successive perceptions', Hume explicitly says that 'we must distinguish betwixt personal identity, as it regards our thought and imagination, and as it regards our passions or the concern we take in ourselves. The first is our present subject' (*Treatise* I, IV, VI, ed. Selby-Bigge p. 253). That is, the 'bundle' and the 'theatre' metaphors regard

[15] Reid, *Inquiry*, chap. 6, sect. xx: 'Sensation, and the perception of external objects by the senses, though very different in their nature, have commonly been considered as one and the same thing.' On the introduction of this distinction by Reid in his polemic against Hume, see Chap. 3, sect. 3.2.2.

[16] Cf. *Treatise* I, IV, VI, ed. Selby-Bigge, pp. 251–3.

the self as a *cognitive* subject (discussed in Book I of the *Treatise*), not as the subject of affective states. The latter is the subject of Book II of the *Treatise*, devoted to 'the Passions'—and it is indeed through 'the passions', and not via an 'impression', that the 'self, or that individual person, of whose actions and sentiments each of us is intimately conscious' is primitively given.[17]

I suggest that the distinction between subject and object originates from these two fundamentally distinct ways in which something is present. In traditional scholastics terms, these different types of presence correspond to the distinction between two different kinds of unity: the *real* (or, we could say, 'ontological') unity of the complex of affective and conative/appetitive states which we could label 'I',[18] and the *intentional* unity between 'I' and something which is phenomenologically present as *other* (*aliud*) than 'I'.[19]

6.1.3 '*Gaudeo, doleo, volo, ergo sum*': The Awareness of One's Own Body

In sum, instead of *cogito ergo sum*, we should say '*Gaudeo, doleo, volo, ergo sum*: I feel pleasure, pain, desire, therefore I am.'[20] The 'self' is first given through the affective and the conative/appetitive states of a sentient being—that is, through what 'it is like' for a sentient organism to *be* that organism.[21] These affective and conative/appetitive states are qualitatively different from the kind of mental states in which something is phenomenologically given as 'other' than one's own embodied self, whatever the ontological status of this 'other'.

I take this also to mean that a sense of 'self' is first established as awareness of one's own body as one's own body.[22] This is not at all to deny that, in sense-perception, one's body can be itself an object of perception, but to point out that self-related sensations are still crucially different from other-related perceptions,

[17] Hume, *Treatise*, Book II, Part I, Section V (ed. Selby-Bigge, p. 286); cf. also *Treatise*, Book II, Part I, Section XI (ed. Selby-Bigge, p. 317): 'our consciousness gives us so lively a conception of our own person, that 'tis not possible to imagine, that any thing can in this particular go beyond it'. See further Inoue (2018), with thanks to Mark Textor for this reference.

[18] Scholastic terminology would call this kind of unity also 'physical', in the sense of pertaining to the *physis*, that is, to the nature of the subject.

[19] On intentionality (understood as a quality of mental states which are directed toward some object) see Chap. 7.

[20] I take this point from Vanni Rovighi 1962: 112, where the Latin expressions are used.

[21] Cf. Nagel 1974: 436. I note that what is distinctive of a sentient being is not only its capacity to register and track changes in its environment (a thermometer can do that), or to react to its environment (a piece of iron which becomes hot in fire can do that), or even its capacity to represent (also a mirror or a picture represent). None of these capacities are sufficient conditions of sensation, either individually or jointly: what is also needed is awareness. In Nagel's words, 'there is something that it is like to *be* that organism'.

[22] On my account, one's own body is not something 'other' somehow opposed to the 'self'—quite the contrary (*pace* Osorio-Kupferblum, and Sickinger 2021: 491 and Ayers 2021: 624–6).

as Spinoza, for instance, clearly acknowledged.[23] Indeed, I take this account to be in line with Spinoza's view that one's own mind is first of all awareness of one's own body,[24] and that any perception of external things is accompanied by some sort of awareness of the affective states of one's body. Furthermore, Spinoza's doctrine of *conatus*, central to his metaphysics in general and to his philosophical anthropology in particular, points (it seems to me) in the same direction, namely to the claim that an individual is primitively identified by its appetitive states, that is, in Spinoza's terms, by its *conatus* (that is, tendency, striving) towards self-preservation.[25]

In other words, in sharp contrast to Descartes's disembodied *cogito*, the subject which is aware of something 'other' (that is, of an 'object') impinging, as it were, on the self is precisely the *embodied* 'self' that is; and this awareness is primitively *felt* as the subject of a range of appetites, drives, affects: first of all, according to our generic animal nature, as the drive or *conatus* towards self-preservation, and the attendant drives towards avoiding pain, seeking pleasure, and so on; and only then, according to our specifically rational animal nature, as the higher affects and volitions.

6.2 Knowledge as Intentional Presence

These preliminary observations, I suggest, provide the basis on which an account of knowledge can be built.

6.2.1 Cognitive and Non-Cognitive Aspects of Mental Life

On this proposal, experiencing affects and appetites is the original and primitive way in which a sense of self is established. This embodied feeling of oneself is a condition of possibility of a cognitive relation but does not yet establish a cognitive relation. It is only with the awareness of an *aliud* that cognition proper begins—that is, cognition starts with something which is present to a *felt* self in a way fundamentally different from the way in which one's own mode of being is present.

The tendency to focus on the cognitive element of our mental life without sufficiently acknowledging the distinctiveness of affects and appetites is rooted (I contend) in the Cartesian inheritance and ultimately leads to the Cartesian fear

[23] See Renz 2019, 19 and Renz 2018, 161–7.

[24] I find the spirit, if not the letter, of Spinoza's position to be not all that distant from the Aristotelian view that the mind is the form of the body.

[25] For Spinoza, this appetite for self-preservation is constitutive of any individual thing: 'Each thing, as far as it can by its own power, strives to persevere in its being' (E IIIp6); 'the striving [*conatus*] by which each thing strives to persevere in its being is nothing but the actual essence of the thing' (E IIIp7).

that we may be victims of an extraordinarily comprehensive illusion because the objects we think we are perceiving may just be our own modes of being. In Descartes, affective and appetitive mental states such as feeling warm or wishing to warm up are construed as cognitive mental states:[26] that is, it is assumed that affective and appetitive states are the same kind of mental states which present some type of object, in this case a 'subject' feeling warm or wishing to warm up, reached through an internal perception. By contrast, the present proposal emphasizes the difference in kind between cognitive and non-cognitive mental states,[27] and suggests that this difference is crucial to an understanding of the nature of knowledge itself.

Furthermore, although my proposal is consistent with the 'direction of fit' explanation of the difference between cognitive and non-cognitive states prevalent nowadays,[28] it approaches this difference from another perspective: namely, from the difference between mental states which present my own mode of being (my feeling cold, my desiring to warm up) and mental states which present something 'other' than me (that is, a 'not-I' or an object). One could object that my desire to eat an apple is also presenting something other than me, and that desires are indeed typically directed to an object. The point is, however, that desiring an apple is still distinct in kind from perceiving, imagining, remembering, conceiving or, generally, thinking of an apple: it is true that in order to desire an apple, I have to be in a mental state in which something other than me is presented, but *desiring* this 'other' than me is *my* mode of being as opposed to a mode of being of the world presenting itself to me.

As my modes of being, affective and appetitive mental states are transparent in a *sui generis* way which does not yet involve a cognitive relation. To be sure, in introspection, we have the ability to turn to states such as feeling cold and wishing to warm up as the intentional object of an act of cognition. One is therefore able, in many cases, to *know* that one is feeling cold, or to *know* that one is hoping for such and such. That is, one is able, in many case, to be in a cognitive relation to one's own affective and appetitive mental states; but insofar as one is not *always* in a position to do so, these mental states are not cognitively 'transparent'.[29] The

[26] See Descartes's *Second Meditation*, where feeling heat or growing warm (*calescere*) are reduced to thinking (AT VII 29): 'this is properly what in me is called to feel [sentire]; and which taken in its strict sense is nothing other than thinking [nihil aliud est quam cogitare]'.

[27] Against prevalent tendencies in contemporary philosophy to associate belief and desire as two varieties of propositional attitudes, Alvarez 2010: 65–89 stresses their difference, as well as the often overlooked distinction between non-rational desires (such as bodily appetites) and rational desires.

[28] While cognitive states such as beliefs aim at fitting the world, non-cognitive states such as desires aim at realization, and 'their realization is the world fitting with them' (Platts 1979: 257).

[29] Cf. Williamson's attack on the luminosity of mental states. Williamson demonstrates that one is not always in a position to know that one feels cold whenever one feels cold (see Williamson 2000: 24, 96–8 and esp. the 'luminosity' premise 2*i*: 'If in α*i* one feels cold, then in α*i* one knows that one feels cold'). This point is consistent, however, with the one I am making—namely, that there is another, *sui generis* way in which certain mental states are transparent.

point I am trying to advance, however, is that a cognitive act of internal perception does not constitute the primitive way in which conative/affective states are present or experienced, 'lived', '*erlebt*', and that it is by this primitive *Erlebnis* that these mental states are transparent in their own *sui generis* way: they are constitutive of a felt/sensed self.

The difference between affective/conative states and cognitive states tracks also the difference between a merely sentient being—that is, a being capable of awareness of the presence of something—and a *perceiving* being—that is, a being capable of awareness not only of something present but also of something 'other' than itself being present. It is only through this perception of an *aliud* that the subject of affects and appetites also becomes a *cognitive* subject.

6.2.2 The Most Fundamental Cognitive Mode

I propose that cognition is, most fundamentally, this primitive presence of something other than the self or subject to a perceiving subject.[30] I also propose that this kind of presence of an *aliud* (or object) to a subject is the most fundamental cognitive mode without which no other mode of successful cognition would be possible, and that this most fundamental cognitive mode is also what human knowing essentially is. By the latter claim I mean the following: (1) notwithstanding the existence of vastly more evolved and sophisticated forms of knowledge with their own distinctive features (notably, propositional knowledge), all other forms of individual knowing and of successful individual cognition are ultimately grounded in this most primitive form of knowing; (2) any embodied being capable of knowledge must be capable of this most basic form of knowing; (3) the most primitive and fundamental form of knowing is a form of perceiving; (4) all forms of individual knowing ultimately involve some form of perceiving, in the form either of sense-perception or (in rational cognitive subjects) of intellectual perceiving/seeing/grasping.[31]

Knowledge, I suggest, is therefore the result of a natural relationship between a perceiving being (the subject or I) and an object, merely understood here as not-I.[32] There is a primitive openness of a perceiving being (precisely qua perceiving being) to the object which, in its most basic form, impinges in some way or

[30] Gerson (2022: sect. 2) notes that 'Plotinus draws on both Plato and Aristotle to argue that knowledge must meet two basic conditions: (a) the knowable item (whatever that may turn out to be) must be present to the intellect or knower and (b) that intellect or knower must be aware of its presence.' Most importantly, however, 'the knowledge of the subject in (b) is not a new piece of knowledge': all knowledge in the paradigmatic sense 'is self-knowledge or self-consciousness'. Or—as I propose to put it to distinguish this built-in consciousness from any reflexive, psychologically second-order knowledge of the self—all individual knowledge in its primary sense is 'first-person'.

[31] For further discussion see the next four chapters (esp. Chaps. 8 and 9).

[32] On the relevant sense of 'natural', see especially sect. 5.2.1 above.

another on the perceiver.[33] What is distinctive of this relationship is that, *in the act* of perceiving/knowing, there is a *sui generis* unification between perceiver and perceived, knower and known, with no gap between them. This *sui generis* contact is captured in a non-metaphorical way by the notion of intentional identity,[34] that is, by a kind of identity between subject and object which is sharply different from a real or ontological identity. In this framework, human individual knowledge is the intentional presence of an object to a subject.[35]

More generally, if the most basic form of perception is construed as having a certain feature of the objective environment present to one's awareness, and the most basic form of knowing is identified with this perception, then all beings capable of this perception are capable of the most basic form of knowing. It is a feature of the present account that there cannot be awareness of an *aliud* without some *felt* sense, however primitive and inarticulate, of distinction from this 'other'. It need hardly be said that the latter claim does not imply that all beings capable of such awareness have a *concept* of 'self', or 'I', or 'subject'. Still, they must sense or feel themselves as distinct in order to perceive the presence of something other as 'other'.

Wherever the (constantly evolving) scientific account of animal perception and of infant development places the first primitive instances of awareness of an *aliud*, there I would locate the most basic instances of knowing. This awareness is manifested in the behaviour of many non-human animals and of very young children in pre-linguistic stages of their development, arguably marking one of the very first steps of infant development. Insofar as this is the case, they manifest the first, most primitive forms of knowing. A consequence of this account is that knowing is not essentially conceptual and does not require linguistic abilities, although there are more evolved and sophisticated forms of knowing which are, both, essentially conceptual and language-based.

6.2.3 Naturalism and Scepticism

Why does it matter to establish that much more primitive animals than *Homo sapiens* are also capable of knowing? One could object that even if we call the most

[33] This proposal is crucially different from McDowell's neo-Kantian account of experience as rational openness to independent reality. At the centre of my account is the claim that, as in the case of other animals capable of perception, the most basic human cognition is non-conceptual. Cf. McDowell 1994, 1995, 2011 and Sellars 1956/1963. For a sustained criticism of McDowell from the point of view of a new empiricism see Ayers 2019: 74–85.

[34] See the introduction of the notion of intentional identity in Chap. 1, sect. 1.2.1, in the context of the discussion of Aristotle's account of cognition. Intentionality is discussed in detail in Chap. 7.

[35] See Vanni Rovighi 1982: 19–30. Cf. Moore 1903, where the nature of knowing is identified in the 'unique relation' of intentional identity which holds between knower and known, and which consists in '"being aware of" or "experiencing" something'; a relation which is in turn 'perfectly distinct' from the relation of real identity which holds between a thing and its constituents (in Moore's example of a blue bead, the relation between me and blue as seen, as opposed to the relation between blue and the blue bead).

primitive forms of perceptual awareness 'knowledge', the distance between inarticulate animal awareness and human knowledge is such that very little is gained, and much is lost, in classifying both under the same general cognitive category. I disagree. What we gain is an antidote against scepticism.

As I argued in the concluding chapter of Part I, the reason for maintaining that there *is* a primitive contact between mind and 'world' is naturalism: human beings are, first of all, simply a species of perceiving beings which share with other perceiving beings the natural ability to connect with, and respond to, their physical environment as their physical environment. By this I mean that their behaviour manifests awareness that something other than them is impinging on them here and now.[36] In the most primitive beings capable of perceiving their environment, such perception does not entail imagining states of affairs not currently perceived, let alone the formation of beliefs about imagined states of affairs or conceptual thought.[37] The question of whether reality is as these beings imagine or conceive it to be does not, therefore, arise. The most basic cognitive abilities of human beings are simply more evolved versions of this basic, natural perceptual ability (their cognitive and memorative powers, for instance, are regarded by Aquinas as 'not different powers, but the same powers albeit more perfect than in other animals' ST I, Q. 78, a. 4, *ad quintum*). As with other perceiving beings, the immediate environment of human beings is simply present to them here and now as something 'other' with which they interact for the preservation of their life.

If it is granted that primitive sentient beings successfully perceive and respond to their surroundings, thereby showing a primitive contact between perceiver and world, there is no reason for denying such contact to human perceivers. And in this case, scepticism loses its initial and all-important foothold. Going forward, it will be a matter of making a case for higher, vastly more sophisticated types of apprehension of 'what is', but the starting point of these cases will be a cognitive contact between mind and world, as opposed to a gap which needs to be bridged. The continuity between human and animal sense-perceptual knowledge is therefore a key aspect of a non-sceptical philosophy of cognition insofar as it supports the claim that the natural starting point of an inquiry on cognition is that perceiving beings do make contact with their environment. It is the sceptic who has the burden of proving that they don't.[38] It is difficult to see, however, how s/he can successfully discharge this *onus probandi*, given that a coherent sceptical

[36] This is a lower requirement than being able to *think* of their environment as their environment or being able to think *that* their environment is their environment. As Ayers 2019: 114 puts it: 'Knowledge of the world is a natural relation to what is known just as perception—conscious awareness of one's environment *as* one's environment—is a natural relation to what is perceived.'

[37] Cf. Phillips et al. (2021).

[38] On the importance of burden of proof considerations in relation to scepticism see Ayers 2019: 157–63.

position cannot really speak of how things are, but only of how they *appear* to be—and even under a sceptical light perceiving beings *do appear* to make contact with the world for the most part. As already argued in the last chapter of Part I, at the very least, non-sceptical philosophy of cognition has the presumption of truth on its side and can legitimately maintain this presumption until convincing arguments to the contrary are forthcoming.[39]

6.3 First-Person and Self-Knowledge

6.3.1 Human Knowledge as First-Person

Continuity does not of course imply lack of significant difference. Knowing differs not only as regards the conceptual and propositional knowledge of which only rational beings are capable but also as regards purely sense-perceptual knowing. Notably, I take it that the 'felt' distinction from something 'other' of which also primitive perceivers are capable becomes increasingly rich in more evolved animals and has unique and distinctive features in human beings. What follows concerns specifically individual human cognition.

I suggest that the account proposed above supports the view that human knowing is essentially or paradigmatically first-personal,[40] in the sense that it possesses the subjective character of experience qua conscious awareness of a not-I (the object). 'Not-I' is obviously different in kind from 'I': indeed, it is identified by its being *not* 'I'. The awareness of '*not*-I' which characterizes human perception entails a first-person which is aware of doing the perceiving, that is, is aware (however primitively, inarticulately, or implicitly) of being presented with an *aliud*. If epistemic externalism is the view that knowledge does not essentially—that is, primarily, fundamentally, paradigmatically[41]—require awareness or consciousness of knowing in the sense outlined above, then this account is a rejection of externalism.[42]

It is crucial to stress, however, that this primitive awareness or consciousness of perceiving an object—in the terms of the KK principle, this knowing that one knows—may be logically second-order but is not an ontologically distinct factor in the act of knowing, produced by a psychologically second-order act of reflection.

[39] See Chap. 5 above, and also Chap. 3. [40] Cf. Introduction to Part II.

[41] The notion of 'primary knowledge', introduced by Ayers, is meant to identify what is central to knowledge in its basic, primary sense, without claiming that all instances of knowledge must exhibit all these features in order to qualify as knowledge in a secondary and derivative sense. See Ayers 2019: esp. vi, 27, 61–4, 115, 185, 195.

[42] If by 'externalism' is meant instead that there are mental states whose 'essence involves the world' (Williamson 1995: 563), then this proposal supports it. Here, however, externalism is taken as the thesis that a subject cannot be aware of some of the necessary and sufficient conditions of knowing (see Ayers 2019: 164–85).

As one could put it, following Brentano, perceiving x is not distinct from awareness of perceiving x.[43] Or, as Ayers notes in his insightful phenomenological analysis of what it is like to be in direct cognitive contact with one's environment, 'conscious perceptual knowledge is such that those that have it not only have perceptual knowledge of their environment, but also perceptual knowledge that and how they have that knowledge. They have that logically second-order knowledge without second-order reflection. They have what I have called "primary knowledge", knowledge gained by being evidently, self-consciously, in direct cognitive contact with the object of knowledge.'[44]

In sum, the claim is not that one is always in a position to know that one knows, but that being in a position to know that one knows is central to knowledge in its primary sense. Furthermore, the claim is that the luminosity of 'primary knowledge' does not imply an act of psychological reflection. In traditional scholastic terms, human conscious perceptual knowledge entails an implicit 'I know, I perceive' *in actu exercito* (that is, in the very act by which one knows or perceives) and not *in actu signato* (that is, by a new mental act). Insofar as the KK principle requires that one is always in a position to know that one knows,[45] or insofar as it implies a psychologically second-order act of reflection, the present proposal is compatible with a rejection of that principle. What the present proposal stresses, however, is that any rejection of the KK principle should not obscure that *some* knowledge is luminous and that without it there would be no knowledge at all.

6.3.2 First-Person Knowledge Versus Self-Knowledge

Does 'I' therefore immediately know itself in knowing 'not-I'? Yes and no. 'Yes' if by knowing itself is meant the first-personal account of knowledge which I have proposed, and which entails (at least in its paradigmatic form) a subject consciously presented with an object. I agree, once again, with Ayers that in conscious perceptual experience, our 'total experience is such that we are aware of the source of our knowledge' and such awareness 'is central to what it is for the object to be directly "presented" to the knower, rather than being merely "represented" in thought or imagination'.[46]

[43] Textor 2017a: 6.

[44] Ayers 2019: 63. For a detailed defence of the thesis that 'when we have (at least, pure or basic) perceptual knowledge, in general we know immediately that and how we have it' see esp. Ayers 2019: 34–69.

[45] The KK principle 'says that, if a subject knows that *p*, then that subject is in a position to know that one knows that *p*' (Greenough and Pritchard 2009: 3). Cf. Williamson 2000.

[46] Ayers 2019: 62. By 'source of our knowledge' is meant here the object known.

'No', if by knowing itself is meant a reflective act of knowledge in which the subject reflects on her act of cognition. This kind of self-knowledge is a higher, second-order kind of cognition. While being first-personal, the first acts of cognition immediately reveal the *other* rather than the cognitive self, precisely because the self (qua cognitive subject) is not an intentional object but the actualization of a primitive capacity of conscious awareness of an object.[47] I agree therefore with Aquinas that the first acts of cognition are directed not at ourselves but at external things.[48] It seems to me, however, that Aquinas's restriction of the knowledge of our acts of thinking to higher, second-order cognition in which the self becomes an intentional object of a reflective cognitive act, does not sufficiently acknowledge the essentially first-person character of the first acts of cognition directed towards external things. The very character of 'otherness' or 'externality' of these things implies that built into the first, object-directed acts of cognition is the awareness of a self which constitutes the unifying perspective from which things phenomenologically given as 'other' are apprehended—a unifying perspective which, in turn, determines the mode of presentation under which this *aliud* is apprehended.[49]

I would like to draw inspiration, at this point, from another highly original (if lesser known) thirteenth-century thinker, namely the Franciscan Peter John Olivi. According to Olivi, there is a first-order knowledge which 'comprises (i) knowledge of one's own activities and (ii) knowledge of oneself as the subject of these activities'.[50] This first-order knowledge can be construed as an '*experiential* self-knowledge'[51] which only tells us 'about the *existence* of one's own activities and the underlying subject'.[52] This is the kind of first-order knowledge which maps onto what I have called the essentially first-personal character of knowledge. There is then also for Olivi a higher, second-order self-knowledge which is 'theoretical self-knowledge' and which is 'about the *essence* [that is, the metaphysical nature] of one's own activities and the underlying subject'.[53]

This distinction between first-order and second-order knowledge of the self seems to me an important, fruitful distinction, which I propose to cash out in

[47] This claim follows from the view, outlined above, that there is a properly cognitive activity, and a cognitive self, only when a felt self becomes aware of an *aliud* (an object) which is present in a way fundamentally different from the way in which the self's modes of being are present.

[48] Cf. Perler 2017: 116–21. Cf. ST I, q. 87, art. 3, ad 2.

[49] See Brewer 2011 and 2021 for the thesis that a person's position and orientation, and her particular perceptual circumstances are essential to the metaphysics of conscious perceptual experience itself.

[50] Perler 2019: 2 (handout).

[51] See Olivi, *Quaestiones in II librum Sententiarum*, q. 76: 'The first is by way of an experiential sense and, as it were, tactile [quasi tactualis]' (trans. Perler).

[52] Perler 2019: 3 (my emphasis).

[53] Perler 2019: 3 (the square parenthesis is my addition). See Olivi, *Quaestiones in II librum Sententiarum*, q. 76: 'The second way of knowing oneself is gained through discursive reasoning by which one investigates the genera and the [specific] differences which one does not know in the first way of knowing' (trans. Perler).

terms of a distinction between 'first-person knowledge' and 'self-knowledge'. My proposal is that individual knowing in its paradigmatic form is essentially first-personal, that is, its object-directedness requires a built-in awareness of the self as the unifying perspective from which the *aliud* is apprehended. This proposal is therefore crucially different from Sosa's distinction between first-order 'animal knowledge' and second-order 'reflective knowledge', according to which any knowing that one knows requires psychologically second-order reflection.[54] As noted by Ayers, Sosa's 'knowing that we know' is 'available only to sufficiently reflective human beings, rather than an absolutely characteristic, built-in feature of ordinary, conscious, "animal" perceptual knowledge'.[55] In a way similar to Ayers's basic perceptual knowledge, on my account, there is a sense in which knowing that one knows (in the form of a primitive, 'animal' awareness of the self which is confronted with an *aliud*) is a built-in feature of first-order knowledge as essentially first-personal—or, in another words, is a built-in feature of the subjective character of experience.[56] There is then a higher, second-order, reflective cognitive act in which the cognitive subject is capable of knowing herself, that is, is able to reflect on herself and her actual states, standing attitudes, and dispositional properties, or even on her 'being subject to the human condition'.[57] This second-order kind of cognition—or, generally, any metacognition which is cognition of one's cognition—is not a constituent of cognitive acts which, as it were, comes for free; it is an achievement of which the highest kind is arguably the Socratic self-knowledge which represents a morally significant, but always limited, achievement.[58] In particular, it is certainly a limitation of our capacity for self-knowledge that the human mind will never be completely transparent to itself,[59] but this acknowledgment of self-knowledge's limitation should not cause us to overlook the essentially first-personal character of knowing. The self or subject provides the unity of experience by determining and unifying the mode of presentation under which objects are apprehended.

[54] See Sosa 2001, 2007, and 2009. See Ayers 2019: 181–3. [55] Ayers 2019: 183.

[56] Cf. Nagel 1974. [57] Renz 2017a: esp. 9–12 (here p. 11).

[58] Renz 2017b. The character of this second-order cognition as an achievement (or a 'cognitive ascent') is stressed for instance by Aquinas. Cf. Perler 2017: 118 (as noted by Perler, the expression 'cognitive ascent' is borrowed from Pasnau 2002: 336–47).

[59] Leibniz, for instance, provides one of the most compelling early examples of a philosophy of mind which takes fully on board the pervasiveness of unconscious thought.

7

Intentionality

The Nature of the Contact between Subject and Object

The expression 'cognitive contact' between subject and object is of course metaphorical and calls for an explanation of the nature of this 'contact'.[1] This chapter explores an historical tradition which explains the cognitive contact between subject and object in terms of intentionality.

7.1 Relational Versus Non-Relational Intentionality

As is now well known, the notion of intentionality (from the Latin *intentio* and *intendere*: *tendere in aliud*, to stretch out toward another) was recovered by Franz Brentano (1838–1917) in the late nineteenth century. In an often-quoted paragraph from his *Psychologie vom empirischen Standpunkt* (1874), Brentano explicitly acknowledges the origins of the doctrine of intentionality in medieval Scholastic thought,[2] before proceeding to offer his own version:

> Every mental phenomenon is characterized by what the Scholastics of the Middle Ages called the intentional (or mental) inexistence of an object, and what we might call, though not wholly unambiguously, reference to a content, direction toward an object (which is not to be understood here as meaning a thing), or immanent objectivity. Every mental phenomenon includes something as object within itself, although they do not do so in the same way. In presentation, something is presented, in judgment something is affirmed or denied, in love loved, in hate hated, in desire desired and so on. (Brentano 1874)

[1] This and similar metaphors are found in a number of contributions, including Ayers 2019: 63–4; Millar 2019 (see, for instance, p. 5: 'knowing is having a grip on reality, being in cognitive contact with a fact') and Millar 2007; Putnam 1994: 454. Zagzebski supplements her definition of knowledge as 'belief arising out of acts of intellectual virtue' (cf. 1996: 271; 1999: 109), with 'a more comprehensive definition' as 'cognitive contact with reality arising out of acts of intellectual virtue' (Zagzebski 1999: 109).

[2] Interestingly, Brentano too looked to the tradition for inspiration in tackling a contemporary philosophical problem.

Thinking with Assent: Renewing a Traditional Account of Knowledge and Belief. Maria Rosa Antognazza, Oxford University Press. DOI: 10.1093/oso/9780198831518.003.0008

In the last few decades, interest in intentionality especially in its Brentanian version has multiplied, making of intentionality one of the most debated topics in philosophy of mind and epistemology. As defined by Searle (1983: 1), 'Intentionality is that property of many mental states and events by which they are directed at or about or of objects and states of affairs in the world.'[3] Thus, 'an intentional mental state is normally understood . . . as one which is about, or represents, something in the world' (Crane and French 2015: sect. 3.3.1).

As regards, in particular, the approach of most present-day intentionalists to the problem of perception, Crane and French (2015) place intentionality in the broad family of direct realism.[4] According to Crane and French's interpretation, for intentionalists, perceptual experience is a *non-relational* mental representation. It is non-relational because 'aboutness'—namely, the property of mental activities of being 'about' some object—does not essentially imply a relation to something really existing.[5] We routinely think about non-existing objects such as imaginary entities (a golden mountain, a centaur, the god Jupiter) or even impossible entities (a square circle). There are, therefore, mental representations of something as being *F*, without there actually being something which is *F*, as shown also by the case of illusions. Even veridical experiences, it is argued, are not fundamentally cases of perceptual awareness of ordinary objects. Thus, for the intentionalist, 'experience does not genuinely have an act-object structure'.[6]

To put it another way, in his study of relational intentionality in Brentano and the Aristotelian tradition, Hamid Taieb notes that philosophers are faced with a dilemma: on the one hand, they are willing to understand intentionality in relational terms when the focus is on how to ensure our access to reality; on the other hand, the case of non-existing objects appears to force philosophers to acknowledge its non-relationality (Taieb 2018a: v). But, Taieb argues, Brentano follows Aristotle and some medieval interpreters in distinguishing three kinds of relations: intentionality, causality, and reference (the latter understood as the

[3] See also the definition given in the *Stanford Encyclopedia* (Jacob 2019): 'intentionality is the power of minds and mental states to be about, to represent, or to stand for, things, properties and states of affairs'.

[4] Crane and French 2017: sect. 3.1.2.

[5] Crane 2001 argues that intentionality (understood as mental representation or as thought's representational power) is not a relation to its objects, because of the phenomenon of thought about the non-existent. Crane 2013 is devoted to the latter problem. It argues that what we think about are intentional objects, and that some of these intentional objects exist and some do not; what make certain truths about non-existing objects of thought (or intentional objects) true are certain facts about mental representation and its irreducible reality.

[6] Crane and French 2017: sect. 3.1.1. According to the interpretation of Brentano's early position on intentional inexistence in Crane (2006), from the point of view of intentionality, even real, physical objects are phenomena which have the same ontological nature of imaginary objects, although they indicate something real but inaccessible to our consciousness. In turn, according to Kriegel 2016, for the mature Brentano intentionality is a non-relational, intrinsic property of subjects.

conformity or *Übereinstimmung* of cognitive acts to reality).[7] A possible solution to the dilemma would be to regard intentionality as relational but to keep this relation distinct from the relations of causality and reference. Thus, an intentional relation would imply, strictly speaking, only aboutness, pure aiming at an object, as opposed to causality and/or reference.[8] Another solution would be to introduce a new ontological class of objects—intentional objects or immanent objects—embracing *all* objects of thought, including imaginary entities (for example, the god Jupiter), ideal objects (for example, an ideal triangle), and even impossible entities (for example, a square circle).[9] This special kind of objects existing only in the mind would be the objects towards which the mind's intentionality is directed. Relationality would, thereby, be rescued but at the cost of adding a new class of objects to our ontology. Many present-day authors, however, (1) reject the introduction of a class of intentional objects as ontologically mysterious, and (2) resist the idea that there can be a relation without a reference. According to them, if intentionality is merely aboutness, and this is distinct from a relation of reference, then intentionality is non-relational (a relation, they argue, requires two *relata*; if there is no second term of the alleged relation, then there is no relation).[10]

This non-relational nature, however, is not supposed to preclude that, in veridical experience, we can be directly perceptually aware of an ordinary object. Following this account, veridical experiences can be occasions for such awareness of an ordinary object because they represent ordinary objects. That is, their very nature is to be about, to be directed towards, the mind-independent world, as opposed to being about some mind-dependent entities such as sense-data, or some mentally constructed phenomenal appearances. When 'the world plays its part', that is, when things in the world are as we represent them to be in perceptual experience, we have perceptual awareness of these mind-independent things by having such experiences.[11] In short, contrary to naïve direct realism, according to which perceptual experiences are *non-representational relations* to ordinary objects, for intentionalists, perceptual experiences are *non-relational representations* of ordinary objects.[12]

[7] Cf. Aristotle, *Metaphysics*, Book 5, chap. 15, 1020b26–1021b11 and Brentano 1930: 117: '[Aristotle] divided relations into three classes: comparative [*die komparativen*], causal [*die kausalen*], and intentional [*die intentionalen*].' Trans. Chisholm 1966: 70. Cited by Taieb 2018a: 5–6.

[8] See Taieb 2018a.

[9] Versions of this solution range from forms of medieval Platonism to the views of Brentano's student, Alexius Meinong (1853–1920).

[10] Cf. Crane 2001: 23. Taieb 2018a: 97–102, 172–3 argues, however, that the late Brentano develops a theory of relations without two *relata*, and that this theory has an important precedent in Francisco Suarez's theory of transcendental relations (*respectus transcendentalis*). In Chap. 8, sections. 8.2 and 8.3, I propose a different solution.

[11] Crane and French 2017: sect. 3.1.1.

[12] Crane and French 2017: sect. 4. Cf. the non-relational, adverbial theory of intentionality first proposed by Duchasse 1968: 232–3, and then embraced and developed by Chisholm 1957 and Kriegel 2007.

Thus, according to this account, intentionality does not imply a relation between things as they are in the world and mental representations, although our mental representations may correspond to things in the world. I suggest that, if this account is right, intentionality may well appear to be a version of occasionalism rather than a version of direct realism. That is, when the world (rather than God, as in classical occasionalism) 'plays its part'—or 'does one the favour of being so arranged that what one takes to be so is so'[13]—mental representations are the occasion of awareness of things as they are in the world. Insofar as externalism allows a similar epistemic gap between mind and world, it seems also liable to sliding into a form of occasionalism.[14]

By contrast, the understanding of intentionality tracked in the following sections is an attempt to account for a cognitive contact between knower and known which excludes such a gap. Most importantly, medieval philosophers, from whom the theory of intentionality originated, would strongly reject views according to which intentionality concerns a type of objects existing only in the mind—that is, an additional ontological realm of 'intentional objects' having mental 'inexistence'—as opposed to ordinary physical objects, having ordinary extra-mental existence.[15] Broadly speaking, for this earlier tradition, cognitive intentionality[16] concerns the receiving and processing of information by a cognitive subject about something which is other (*aliud*) than the subject, whatever the ontological nature of this *aliud* might be, and whatever the exact physical/physiological mechanism underpinning such information-carrying process might be.[17] Whether the 'other' (the object) is an externally existing entity, an ideal entity (say, a mathematical entity), or an imagined entity, the key point is that intentionality implies a relation of a cognitive subject to something *other* than the subject, in a mental act characterized by a *sui generis* identification between subject and object.[18] Conceived in this way, cognitive intentionality is intrinsically relational: the very

[13] McDowell 1995: 881. McDowell criticizes both full-blown externalism (in which standing appropriately in the space of reasons plays no role and a thermometer may as well be said to know the temperature in the room) and the hybrid conception according to which knowledge has internal conditions (justification; reasons) and external conditions (truth).

[14] Externalism is taken here as the thesis that a subject cannot be aware of some of the necessary and sufficient conditions of knowing.

[15] Klima 2013: 359–60.

[16] The qualification 'cognitive' is important. For medieval authors such as Aquinas, intentionality does not apply only to cognition. For Aquinas, for instance, 'intentionality or aboutness is the property of any form of information carried by anything about anything' (Klima 2013: 360; cf. more generally Klima 2014). As noted by Klima, medieval authors would therefore disagree with the so-called Brentano thesis, namely, the thesis that intentionality is 'the mark of the mental' because all and *only* mental phenomena exhibit intentionality.

[17] Cf. Klima 2013: esp. 370–3.

[18] Even one of the champions of the non-relational, adverbial theory of intentionality, Kriegel 2011: 158, asserts that the 'signature' of the experience of 'being intentionally directed F-wise' is to present something as 'foreign' or 'other' to the possessor of this property. As noted by Orlando 2012 and Taieb 2018a: 4, however, if F is reduced to a way of being of the thinking subject, one cannot make sense of F's phenomenological dimension of foreignness or otherness.

idea at its core—the presence to a subject of some information about some object—implies a relation between a subject and an object. In the next chapter, devoted to objects and the ontology of cognition, I will discuss how this approach can tackle the issue of non-existing objects. In this chapter, I will focus on presenting an understanding of intentionality significantly different from some current (and even prevalent) non-relational views of what intentionality amounts to.

7.2 Aristotelian Roots and Medieval Developments

7.2.1 The Assimilation of Cognizer and Cognized

Aristotle's explanation of the cognitive contact between perceiving subject and world, knower and known, is underpinned by his metaphysical hylomorphism and the metaphysical pair of potentiality and actuality: the faculty of sense is the capacity (potentiality) to receive sensible forms without matter; analogously, the intellectual faculty is the capacity to receive intelligible forms. Empedocles and Democritus had already maintained that cognition requires some sort of similarity between cognizer and cognized. Aristotle agrees: to be capable of cognition means to have the potentiality of becoming similar, in some sense, to the cognized. In other words, cognition is a process of 'assimilation' between cognizer and cognized. This process differs however from other types of assimilation characteristic of natural processes (for example, the assimilation of food in nutrition) due to the fact that it concerns the form of the thing to be assimilated and not the matter. Thus, before the start of a cognitive process, the cognizer is different from the thing to be cognized but has the potentiality of becoming similar to it by receiving its form. Cognition is the actualization of this potentiality. Sense-perception, as the first and most basic form of cognition, is explained in these terms:

> By a 'sense' is meant what has the power of receiving into itself the sensible forms of things without matter. This must be conceived of as taking place in the way in which a piece of wax takes on the impress of a signet-ring without the iron or gold[.] (*De Anima*, Book II, chap. 12, 424a; Smith trans.)[19]

Intellectual cognition is understood as analogous to perception insofar as it is also a capacity to become similar to the cognized by abstracting the intelligible, universal form from particulars:

[19] Cf. Augustine, *De Trinitate*, XI, chap. 2, sect. 3: 'we could not have sensation at all, unless some similitude of the body seen was wrought in our own sense'. Augustine uses the same Aristotelian analogy with a ring impressing its form in wax.

> If thinking is like perceiving, it must be either a process in which the soul is acted upon by what is capable of being thought, or a process different from but analogous to that. *The thinking part of the soul* must therefore be . . . capable of receiving the form of an object; that is, *must be potentially identical in character with its object without being the object.* Mind must be related to what is thinkable, as sense is to what is sensible. (*De Anima*, III, chap. 3, 429a; Smith trans., my emphasis)

Indeed, for Aristotle, the intellect is a capacity to become all forms since 'everything is a possible object of thought' (*De Anima*, III, chap. 3, 429a; Smith trans.).

For present purposes, it is particularly important to stress Aristotle's claim that there is a potential *identification* between mind and object which is actualized in the act of cognition.[20] That is, as we have seen in Chap. 1, a cognitive act consists in a peculiar kind of identity between perceiver and perceived, or between knower and known, in which, in *occurrent* cognition, perceiver and perceived are unified while maintaining their ontological distinction ('The actuality of the object of perception and of the senses are one and the same, but their being is different' *De Anima*, Book III, chap. 2, 425b; Shields, 52). In the metaphysical framework of his hylomorphism, Aristotle understands this unification in terms of the intellect becoming 'identical in character' with the object (the same form is both in the intellect and in the object, but in different senses of 'in'). In modern parlance, we could understand this process as a capacity by senses and intellect to receive and process information from the external world as regards those aspects of the external world which are, respectively, potentially sensible or potentially knowable.[21] In the case of intellectual knowledge, this is a capacity to extract the 'whatness' of individual things (that is, a capacity to grasp what makes an individual thing that kind of thing) by leaving aside (*abstracting* from) the fully particular sensible features (or accidents) with which an individual thing presents itself in sense-perception.

7.2.2 '*Non latere*' and '*intentio*'

Medieval authors tend to think of cognition in similar terms, that is, as a process of unification between cognizer and cognized through the reception of the form of an external thing.[22] At the same time, they develop Aristotle's proposal in original ways by introducing the notions of cognitive *species* and of intentionality.

By the Latin term *species* is normally meant the essential information associated with the form instantiated by a given individual.[23] That is, *species*—literally,

[20] See esp. Aristotle, *De Anima*, Γ 4, 429b8, 6, 430b25–6, 7, 431b17.
[21] See Amerini 2013: 20–2. [22] See Amerini 2013: 44. [23] Amerini 2013: 21.

'something presented to view' –are those *aspects* of individual things which can be cognized.[24] It is important to note that there are, even in principle, plenty of aspects of individual beings which are neither sensible nor knowable. Sensible or intelligible *species* are, by contrast, those aspects of individual beings open to view, as it were, and therefore graspable, respectively, by the senses or by the intellect in an act of sensitive or intellectual knowledge. It seems to me that the gist of this medieval doctrine (greatly developed, for instance, by Aquinas) is already present in Augustine's account of sensitive cognition as *non latere* ('not being hidden'). In *De quantitate animae* (XXV, 48), Augustine defines sensation as 'a modification of the body which is not hidden to the soul' ('passio corporis per se ipsam non latens animam'), that is, as a corporeal modification of which the mind is immediately or directly aware.[25] The key point is that, in perception, the mind is aware of something which is manifesting itself (is 'not hidden') to the mind.

In Augustine we find also a first account of the mind's *intentio*, that is, of its 'stretching out' or its being directed towards something (from the Latin verb *intendere*).[26] At the same time, the term *intentio* is used by Augustine interchangeably with the term *attentio* ('attention'), to indicate the mind's attending to or focusing on something.[27] In *De Trinitate* XI, II.2, he notes that in a cognitive process such as vision are normally involved three different elements, each of a different nature: (1) 'the thing which is seen' (for example, a stone), and which 'certainly might exist also already before it was seen'; (2) 'vision or the act of seeing, which did not exist before we perceived the object itself which is presented to the sense'; and (3) 'that which keeps the sense of the eye in the object seen, so long as it is seen, *viz.* the attention of the mind [id est animi intentio]'. Augustine distinguishes therefore: (1) a mind-independent object; (2) a cognitive act; (3) the mind's *intentio*. In the latter are combined two aspects: aboutness and attention. That is, the mind's *intentio* can be taken in two manners: from the point of view of the cognized thing, it is the intentional presence of a mind-independent object to the mind as long as the mind is attending to it, and as long as the object is visible;

[24] Note that *spicere* (or *specere*), the Latin verb associated with *species*, means to see, observe. The so-called species-theory, as developed in particular by Aquinas and Scotus, is extremely complex. It is well beyond the scope of this book to attempt an in-depth evaluation. On the notion of species in medieval optics, see Tachau 1988. On the theory of intelligible species, and on Ockham's reasons for rejecting it, see the insightful discussion by Panaccio 2004: 27–31.

[25] The immediacy or directedness of this awareness is captured by the words 'per se ipsam'. Cf. Vanni Rovighi 1963–1979: 44–5.

[26] This is one of the senses of *intentio*. As noted by Trego 2016, the polysemy of *intentio* originates from the two main sources of the medieval reflection on this notion: on the one hand, Augustine, who stresses the meaning of *intentio* as the mental activity of stretching out towards another; on the other hand, Avicenna, for whom *intentio* (*ma'nâ*) designates that which is thought (namely, an intelligible or a concept by which the mind grasps some aspect or another of a thing).

[27] Cf. Amerini 2013: 33. These two aspects—aboutness combined with attention—are found also in Brentano, as noted by Taieb 2018a: 2.

from the point of view of the cognitive subject, the mind's *intentio* is the mental state of attending to a present object of perception.

7.2.3 Immateriality and Intentionality: Formal Versus Objective Being

Following Aristotle, Aquinas conceives the soul as the form of a hylomorphic composite. Cognition starts already with living beings whose souls have sensitive powers: 'sense is cognitive', Aquinas explains, 'because it can receive *species* without matter' (ST I, Q. 14, a. 1). Unlike other activities of a living being (such as growing or becoming hot), cognition is therefore 'immaterial' in the sense of being an activity in which the cognitive subject is able to assimilate aspects (*species*) of the cognized object without its 'matter': the cognitive subject becomes similar in some sense to the cognized object without becoming that cognized object. In seeing red, Aquinas notes, the eye's pupil does not become red:[28] the change which happens in a cognizer that sees red is qualitatively different from the change in a piece of wood which 'assimilates' fire by catching fire. On the other hand, although 'immaterial' in Aquinas's sense, sense-perceptual cognition is still limited by the material conditions of particular individuals. That is, the senses grasp only this particular individual, *hic et nunc*, through its accidental features, without being able to abstract its stable, universal 'whatness'. The latter is the distinctive achievement of intellectual knowledge, as the natural continuation of the cognitive process started by the senses.[29] Intellectual knowledge achieves, therefore, a more perfect kind of 'immateriality' constituted by its grasping the intelligible form of a thing (its 'whatness').[30]

One may object that in some cases of sensitive cognition, the sensitive subject seems to assimilate also material features of the sensed body, as in the case, for instance, of a hand warming up in hot water. Aquinas notes, however, that becoming warm due to exposure to a warmer body is not yet in itself cognition, otherwise a piece of iron which becomes hot in fire would be a sentient body. That is, for sensation, and, a fortiori, for perception and cognition, a physical change (*immutatio naturalis* or *physica*) is not sufficient: a different, psychological change (*immutatio spiritualis*) is also needed.[31]

[28] Cf. ST, I, q. 78, a. 3; Aquinas, *Compendium theologiae*, I, c. 177.

[29] Amerini 2013: 56, drawing attention to Aquinas, *Quaestiones disputatae de veritate*, q. 26, a. 3, ad 12; and Aquinas, *Scriptum super Sententiis*, II, d. 3, q. 1, a. 6, ad 2; d. 24, q. 2, a. 3.

[30] See Aquinas, *Quaestiones disputatae de anima*, art 13 (cited by Vanni, *Antropologia*, p. 64) and Aquinas, *Quaestiones disputatae de veritate*, q. 1, a. 12, vol. 1, fasc. 2, p. 35, lin. 24–9: 'Dicendum quod nomen intellectus sumitur ex hoc quod intima rei cognoscit: est enim intelligere quasi intus legere. Sensus enim et imaginatio sola accidentia exteriora cognoscunt; solus autem intellectus ad interiora et essentiam rei pertingit.'

[31] ST I, q. 78, a. 2.

On the other hand, the 'immaterial' or 'spiritual' aspect of cognition does not imply that cognition can happen without natural or physical changes—whatever the precise physiology of seeing red or feeling a hot body, it is obvious that complex physical changes in the sentient being are involved. The study of what these changes are, and how exactly they happen, however, is the task of physics and biology, rather than of the philosophy of mind. No doubt much of ancient and medieval physiology is way out of kilter with current natural science but the enduring value of Aquinas (and Aristotle's) insights regard the metaphysics of cognition rather than its physiology. The key point is that, for cognition, a qualitatively different type of modification is needed, a modification which can also be described in terms of the intentional, as opposed to physical, presence of a cognized object in a cognizer, entailing some kind of awareness. In other words, what Aquinas calls the 'immateriality' of cognition is what we may label its 'intentionality'. For Aquinas, to exist 'spiritually' in something else means in fact existing in it *per modum intentionis*, namely, intentionally.[32]

Furthermore, Aquinas is clear that

> cognition is brought about by the presence of the cognized object in the cognizer. But the cognized object is in the cognizer according to the mode of the cognizer. Hence, the cognition of any cognizer is according to the mode of the cognizer's own nature [Cognitio enim contingit secundum quod cognitum est in cognoscente. Cognitum autem est in cognoscente secundum modum cognoscentis. Unde cujuslibet cognoscentis cognitio est secundum modum suae naturae]. (ST Ia, Q. 12, a. 4)[33]

That is to say: the mode of being of a cognized thing qua *cognized* is not the same mode of being of that thing in its extra-mental existence, although the cognized thing is numerically one and the same. A mind-independent thing (say, a tree) has its own nature (for example, it is a material object made of wood, leaves, and so on). Obviously, when a tree is present to the mind, there are no wood or leaves in the mind. In scholastic terms, the tree cannot be *formally* (that is, according to its own nature) in the mind. It can only be in the mind according to the *mind*'s own nature.

In *Quodlibetum*, VII, q. I, art. 4, Aquinas explains this distinction between the 'real' or 'physical' aspect of cognition and its 'intentional' aspect—in scholastic vocabulary, the distinction between its 'formal' and 'objective' being—in the following terms:

[32] See Vanni Rovighi 1965: 65 and Amerini 2013: 73.

[33] Cf. also ST I, q. 84, a. 1: 'intellectus species corporum, quae sunt materiales et mobiles, recipit immaterialiter secundum modum suum: nam receptum est in recipiente ad modum recipientis'.

> Knowledge [notitia] can be considered under two aspects: either in relation to the knower—and considered in this way it inheres in the knower as an accident in the subject, and thus does not transcend the subject, because it can never be found in anything but the mind—or in relation to the knowable, and in this regard it does not inhere in someone but refers to something. Now that which is said to relate to something does not have the property of being an accident on account of its relating to something, but only on account of its being in a subject...and therefore knowledge [notitia] considered in relation to the knowable is not in the mind as an accident in the subject, but transcends the mind[.]

In sum, for Aquinas, the nature of knowledge consists in a *sui generis* identification of what is known ('quod intellectum') with the knower ('cum intelligente').[34] In Aquinas's hylomorphic terms, knowledge is to have in oneself the form, but not the matter, of what is known.[35] Moreover, according to its formal being, knowing is a modification of the subject (that is, a cognitive act is an accident of the mind); according to its objective being, however, its nature is not that of being a modification of the mind but of referring to something other than the mind.

7.2.4 Latching on to Reality

Although the notions of *intentio* and *intendere* (*tendere in aliud*, to stretch out towards another) are already found in Augustine and Aquinas, it is in the generation after Aquinas that an explicit theory of intentionality takes shape. The first substantial treatise on intentionality is by the Dominican master, Hervaeus Natalis (d. 1323). Notably, in his *Tractatus de secundis intentionibus* (1310–1316), Hervaeus seems to have been the first to use in a technical sense the Latin term *intentionalitas* (intentionality). Hervaeus clarifies that *intentio* is 'a stretching out' towards another (*tentio in aliquid aliud*) which applies not only to the will (as previous medieval authors, including Aquinas, stressed) but also to the intellect.[36] For present purposes, it is particularly significant to note Hervaeus's account of *intentio* from two complementary points of view. From the point of view of the knower, an *intentio* is whatever directs the mind to something other than the mind; from the point of view of what is known, the term *intentio*

[34] 'Ex hoc enim quod intellectum fit unum cum intelligente, consequitur intelligere' ST Ia, Q. 44, a. 1 ad tertium.

[35] '...Cognoscentia a non cognoscentibus in hoc distinguuntur, quia non cognoscentia nihil habent nisi formam suam tantum, sed cognoscens natum est habere formam etiam rei alterius' ST Ia, Q. 14, a. 1. See Vanni Rovighi 1963–1979: 75.

[36] Cf. Hervaeus Natalis, *Tractatus de secundis intentionibus*, d. 1, q. 1, ed. Dijs, p. 116.

can signify both the thing itself which is known (*illud quod intelligitur*), and the relation between known thing and knower.[37]

At the beginning of the fourteenth century, Hervaeus engages in a debate with another key medieval player in the history of the theory of intentionality, the Franciscan Peter Auriol (*c.*1280–1322).[38] Despite significant differences, Hervaeus and Auriol agree on a crucial issue, namely, that a thing qua cognized is the same extra-mental thing. Likewise, an *intentio* is the extra-mental thing qua cognized and not some additional item existing only in the mind.[39] In turn, the mature, considered view of Duns Scotus (*c.*1266–1308) is that *esse cognitum/esse intelligibile* is reducible to the cognitive act. That is to say, *esse cognitum/esse intelligibile* is 'nothing in reality' (*nihil secundum rem*) over and above the cognitive act.[40] Although in the *Ordinatio* (Book I, distinction 36), Scotus seems to suggest that God's cognitive act produces a mental item with its own positive (albeit weak) ontological status (*esse deminutum*, 'diminished being'), in the *Reportatio* he abandons this characterization, arguably due to its misleading suggestion of some kind of mental item with its own existence.[41]

At any rate, William Ockham (*c.*1288–1348) is the author who most explicitly denies the existence of a tertium quid ('some third thing') supposed to mediate between cognizer and cognized.[42] As M. M. Adams notes in her monumental study, Ockham tenaciously defends direct realism in epistemology, insisting 'that our mental life *begins* with an immediate awareness of mind-independent particular physical objects'.[43] In order to account for this intuitive grasp of an object, Ockham reasons, there is no need for any intervening representation between the act and the object; and if this applies to intuitive cognition, there is no reason why it should not apply also to the following abstractive cognition.[44] In his mature theory, he explains therefore the ontology of intellectual cognition as requiring only two entities: the mental act and the extra-mental thing. Both act and thing are singular and are related in an immediate way. The cognized thing *is* the

[37] Cf. Hervaeus Natalis, *Tractatus de secundis intentionibus*, d. 1, q. 1, ed. Dijs, p. 116, lin. 15–28. Quoted by Amerini 2013: 31, from which I am drawing. On Hervaeus, see also Perler 2004: 294–317.

[38] In recent years, Auriol has attracted sustained attention. For an overview see Friedman 2016. See also Friedman 1999, 2000; Taieb 2018b.

[39] Amerini 2009: 248, 259. I find the interpretation of Auriol's texts on intentionality offered by Vanni Rovighi 1978a, 1978b still very persuasive.

[40] See Cross 2014: esp. 191–5, quoting Scotus, *Reportatio* 1.36.1.1–2, n. 65 (Wolter and Bychkov, ii. 402–3).

[41] Cross 2014: 189–90, 192, from which I am drawing.

[42] On Ockham see M. M. Adams 1987 (esp. vol. I, 73–107; 495–550). It should be noted that there is a change from Ockham's earlier theory of the *fictum* to his mature theory. This change, discussed in detail by M. M. Adams and Panaccio 2004: 23–7, is clearly summarized by Cross 2014: 200. In *Quodlibeta* IV, q. 53 (OTh IX, 473), Ockham criticizes is his own earlier theory in no uncertain terms: 'such a *fictum* hinders the cognition of a thing. Therefore, *ficta* should not be assumed to explain cognition. Proof of the premise: The *fictum* is... some third thing that is a mean between the cognition and the thing. Therefore, if the *fictum* is understood, the mind-independent thing is not understood' (quoted from M. M. Adams 1987: vol. I, 85).

[43] M. M. Adams 1987: vol. I, 84.

[44] Panaccio 2004: 29, from which I am drawing.

extra-mental thing, with no distinction between them and no different mode of being or mode of existence of the extra-mental thing bestowed by an act of cognition.

The crucial point is that no third thing (mental content, mental object, immanent object, and so on) is needed to explain the presence of a cognized thing to the cognizer, although the same, singular act of cognition can be understood in two ways: (1) metaphysically (or ontologically), as a singular, real modification or quality of the intellect (inhering, as such, in the cognitive subject); (2) intentionally, as making present to the cognizer an extra-mental thing. That is, a cognitive act, by its own nature (*ex natura sua*), is capable of signifying extra-mental things.[45] In brief, for Ockham the intellect latches on directly to reality.[46]

7.2.5 Real Distinction Versus Distinction of Reason

Overall, it seems to me that the key conceptual tools to be employed here are the notions of 'distinction of reason' and of 'real distinction'.[47] There are only two really distinct *res* involved in cognition: the mind (of which cognitive acts are modifications or qualities), and some thing other than the mind (the object of cognition).[48] The object of cognition (say, the large tree I am seeing and touching in broad daylight) can be considered in two ways: in itself (that is, formally, according to its own nature) or qua cognized. What is crucial is that there is only one object considered in two ways, not two objects (one mind-independent and outside the mind, and one mind-dependent and immanent). The distinction between the extra-mental object and the object qua cognized is a mere distinction of reason. Assuming we are considering a mind-independent object, the object qua cognized is a mode of being of the extra-mental object.[49]

In turn, what exists as a real, ontological constituent of the cognitive subject (as a 'quality' inhering in the subject) is only the act of cognition, the nature of which is to manifest or make present to the subject something other than the subject. As Ockham's radical position has the merit of stressing, there is no spooky mental object, with its own ontologically positive status, 'inexisting' in the subject in addition to, or even as result of, a cognitive act.

[45] Cf. Ockham, I *Sent.* Dist. II, q. VIII. As explained by Panaccio 2004: 26, the crucial turning point in Ockham's move from his early *fictum*-theory to his mature *act*-theory, is his 'realization that some intellectual acts can serve as *mental signs*, be endowed, that is, with significations of their own and be capable of referential functions'.

[46] Cf. Amerini 2009: 240–2; Vanni Rovighi 1963–1679: 82–9.

[47] Ockham reduces the distinction of reason to a distinction between ways of conceiving the same thing; between things (*res*) he grants only real distinctions. Cf. Marenbon 2007: 297.

[48] In the primary case, the 'thing other than the mind' is a mind-independent thing; as we will see in the next chapters, however, there are also other cases.

[49] Auriol is clear that a thing in itself and a thing qua cognized 'sunt unum, et ideam realiter, quamvis differant in modo essendi' (I *Sent.*, d. 9, a. 1, p. 320 a D).

7.3 Formal and Objective Being in Early Modern Thought

7.3.1 Formal and Objective Being

The scholastic distinction, introduced above, between formal/real being and objective being (or formal reality and objective reality)—that is, in the case of the mind's cognitive activities, the distinction between the psychological/ontological aspect and the intentional aspect of mental events/states—plays a greater role in early modern conceptions of ideas than is often acknowledged by early modern critics of the way of ideas and present-day interpreters alike.[50] Early modern thinkers (including Descartes) typically hold that ontologically, or formally, mental phenomena or 'ideas' have a psychological nature, that is, they are modes of the mind. Their intentional aspect (in early modern terms, their objective reality), however, does not manifest or present modifications or qualities of the mind but something other than the mind (the idea of the sun, whatever its ontological status, presents the sun, not a quality of the mind).Thus, the early modern focus on ideas, as well as the view that ideas are modifications of the mind, does not in itself endanger realism (and even direct realism) any more than Aquinas's remark that 'the cognized thing is in the cognizer according to the mode of the cognizer'.[51]

The point on which early modern thinkers crucially differ—both among themselves and from the medieval champions of direct realism—is on whether the distinction between extra-mental objects in their formal reality (that is, objects as they are in themselves) and objects qua cognized, is a real distinction or a distinction of reason. Descartes comes down on the side of a real distinction. Malebranche, as a highly original heterodox Cartesian, stretches Descartes's position further, and sees not only a real distinction between the idea of the object and the object; he conceives also the distinction between idea and act of thought as a real distinction. Another highly original heterodox 'Cartesian'—Spinoza—goes in the opposite direction and sees only a distinction of reason between act of thought, idea, and object: for him, all three are, really, only one thing.[52]

7.3.2 True and False Ideas

For present purposes, the most interesting thinker is, however, yet another highly original 'Cartesian'—Antoine Arnauld. Arnauld may be considered a Cartesian at

[50] For an insightful discussion of ideas and objective being in the seventeenth century see Ayers 1998b. An alternative narrative is offered by Pasnau 2017 (cf. esp. p. 254).

[51] ST I, q. 12, a. 4: 'Cognitio enim contingit secundum quod cognitum est in cognoscente. Cognitum autem est in cognoscente secundum modum cognoscentis.'

[52] See Ayers 1998b: 1080.

least insofar as, in attacking Malebranche's theory of ideas, he took himself to be defending what Descartes had really meant with his doctrine of ideas. In so doing, he offers one of the most insightful discussions of intentionality in early modern philosophy. As in the case of other thinkers,[53] interpretations of his theory of cognition divide between those who hail him as a direct realist, according to whom there is a direct contact with reality with no need for intermediaries between subject and object, and those who see him as a representationalist.[54] Both camps can point to relevant textual evidence. My purpose here is not to defend one or the other interpretation, or to adjudicate whether Arnauld slides between alternatives, but to highlight some texts in which an insightful critique of ideas as a tertium quid is presented.

In his *Des vrais et des fausses idées* (1683), Arnauld claims that by 'idea' one may mean either the mental act of apprehending something (that is, '*la perception*') or a 'representative being' (*être représentatif*) in the mind that is supposed to mediate between mind and things. True ideas are ideas taken in the first sense: that is, ideas are simply our perceptions of things. As maintained by Descartes in the *Third Meditation*,[55] Arnauld notes, an idea has a formal reality and an objective reality: its formal reality is to be a modification of the mind; its objective reality is to be representative of an object. We are dealing, however, with only one entity, of which the first aspect is best indicated by the term 'perception' and the second aspect by the term 'idea'.[56] In other words, there is only a distinction of reason between mental act and content of the mental act: the mental act of apprehending a thing, and the apprehended thing as it is present to the mind are really the same mental phenomenon considered under two respects: ontologically, as a mode of the mind, and intentionally, as manifesting an object.

By contrast, false ideas are ideas taken in the second sense, as a 'representative being' which mediates between mind and object. Taken in this way, they are 'superfluous entities'.[57] It would be useless, Arnauld argues, to have these 'representative beings' in the mind if they were not somehow apprehended by the mind. In fact, a local presence 'inside' as opposed to 'outside' has nothing to do with the

[53] Another prominent case is Aquinas. Kretzmann 1993: 138–42 and Perler 2000, 2004 attribute direct realism to Aquinas (qualified by Perler 2004: 83 as 'modified direct realism'). Pasnau 1997, 2008 champions instead an interpretation of Aquinas as a representational realist (the position according to which 'we come to apprehend external things—to perceive them and think about them—in virtue of grasping an internal representation of those things' Pasnau 2008: 131). Amerini 2013: 205–19 charts a 'middle way' according to which Aquinas's direct realism is compatible with representationalism. On the main 'arguments against direct realism and how to counter them' see the admirably clear Le Morvan 2004.

[54] The direct realist interpretation is defended, for instance, by Nadler 1989. Pasnau 2017: 269–71 sides instead with a reading of Arnauld's theory of cognition as still requiring a tertium quid, a reading already proposed by Malebranche and Thomas Reid (cf. Reid, *Essays on the Intellectual Powers of Man*, II.13).

[55] See esp. AT VII 41–2/CSM 28–9.

[56] See Arnauld, *Des vrais et des fausses idées*, p. 366.

[57] Cf. Arnauld, *Des vrais et des fausses idées*, pp. 365–80.

kind of presence which is relevant to cognition: otherwise we should perceive our kidneys or our brain better than we perceive a tree in the garden. Suppose then that, at some point, the mind becomes aware ('s'aperçoit') of this represented being—call it B—which is in the mind. Will this perception of B be also a perception of the body—call it A—which B is supposed to represent? If it is, and both B and A are thereby immediately perceived, what is the point of postulating B? One may retort that only B is immediately perceived, and that A is mediately perceived through B. But if the mind needs to perceive B in order to perceive A, thereby showing a primitive capacity for awareness (the ability '*de s'apercevoir*'), why should the mind not be able to perceive A directly? A standard reply is that a spiritual, immaterial mind cannot directly apprehend something as gross and imperfect as a material body. This is a strange view, Arnauld replies: the imperfection of bodies would be an obstacle to attributing to *them* what is undoubtedly a great perfection—that is, the ability of knowing—but it cannot have anything to do with their being knowable by the mind.[58]

7.3.3 Efficient and Formal Causation

What is exposed by the objection countered by Arnauld is, at bottom, the confusion between two different problems. The first problem is what are the physical and psychological conditions and mechanisms which make knowledge possible. This is the issue of the efficient causes of cognition. The second problem is how best to understand and describe the primitive experience we all have of perceiving/being aware of things/having objects intentionally present. This is the issue of the nature, or formal cause, of cognition.[59] The first issue is the subject-matter of the natural sciences (physics, biology, neuroscience, empiric psychology, and so on); the second issue is the proper subject-matter of epistemology and philosophy of mind. In Brentano's distinctive terminology, the first issue is the concern of genetic psychology, the second is the concern of descriptive psychology.[60] In Dominik Perler's present-day terms, an adequate investigation

[58] Cf. Arnauld, *Des vrais et des fausses idées*, pp. 390–1. As far as I can see, a similar line of reasoning is present in Ockham's rejection of intelligible species (see Panaccio 2004: 27–31, here esp. 30): if it were really impossible for material things to casually affect the mind, introducing intelligible species as intermediary between material things and mind would be useless and could only lead to an infinite regress; if, on the other hand, the causal impact of material things on the mind has to be acknowledged at some point, then the relevant causal role should be assigned to material things themselves, without superfluous intermediaries.

[59] See Arnauld, *Des vrais et des fausses idées*, p. 365 and Vanni Rovighi 1963–1979: 150–2, where key passages from Arnauld's *Des vrais et des fausses idées* are identified and the distinction between efficient and formal causation is noted.

[60] Cf. Taieb 2018a: 2–3. Mulligan and Smith 1985 see Brentano's descriptive psychology as 'an ontology of mind'.

of intentionality requires two complementary insights which cannot be reduced one to the other: a genetic insight and a structural insight.[61]

All this amounts to saying that cognition in general, and cognitive intentionality in particular, are primitive and *sui generis* phenomena which, as such, cannot be explained in terms of something else (brain states, electrical impulses, waves, chemical reactions, or whatever the best physics, chemistry, and neurology of cognition currently is). Even if we had a perfect account of these physical conditions and mechanisms, we would still not have an account of our being aware of, or knowing, things. This is the gist of Arnauld's point—a point made in present-day philosophy by Jackson's famous article 'What Mary Didn't Know'.[62] This is not to say that the physical conditions and mechanisms of cognition are irrelevant to a philosophical inquiry on cognition (or vice versa). Rather, the point is that natural sciences and epistemology/philosophy of mind ask and answer different questions. Being aware—*s'apercevoir*—is something more than its material conditions. To think that it can be reduced to them is to fail to understand the difference between an *immutatio naturalis* (the iron becoming hot) and an *immutatio spiritualis* (being aware of the hand becoming hot; seeing red without becoming red). It is failing to recognize the difference between local presence (of brain waves, electrical impulses, and so on) and cognitive presence. This is also the lesson of the Aristotelian doctrine that what is distinctive of cognition is the reception of the form of the cognized object without a reception of its material constituents.[63] Neither the material conditions of the subject nor the material conditions of the object are sufficient to explain the intentional presence of objects to a subject. In brief, the distinction between efficient and formal causes of cognition seems to me as up-to-date as it has ever been.

7.4 Modern Rejuvenation

7.4.1 Relational Nature of Intentionality

In reintroducing the scholastic notion of intentionality, Brentano presents intentionality in relational terms. In *Psychologie vom empirischen Standpunkt* (1874), he describes it as a 'relation to an object' (*Beziehung auf ein Object*), 'a relation to a content' (*Beziehung auf einen Inhalt*), a 'relation to something as an object'

[61] Perler 2004: 409–10. [62] Jackson 1986.

[63] On Aquinas's distinction between *immutatio naturalis* and *immutatio spiritualis* and its grounding in the Aristotelian doctrine that perception/cognition is a reception of the form without matter, see above sect. 7.2.3.

(*Beziehung auf etwas als Object*).[64] In 1890–1891, he speaks of an 'intentional' or 'psychic' relation (*intentionale Relation*; *psychische Relation*).[65] As late as 29 March 1916 (less than one year before his death on 17 March 1917), he still describes it as a relation:

> Whoever presents *in recto* a thinking being as a thinking being also presents *in obliquo* something to which the thinking being is related as the object of his thinking. This is called an intentional relation.[66]

His understanding of what counts as the 'object' or the 'content' to which the mind relates develops, however, over time.[67] According to some interpretations, the early Brentano suggests that the objects towards which intentionality is directed are a special category of immanent, mental objects or 'intentional objects'.[68] The introduction of this category of objects would both rescue the relationality of intentionality and solve the problem of non-existing objects (imaginary objects like a centaur, ideal objects like a mathematical triangle, impossible objects like a square circle) but at the heavy ontological cost of introducing an additional category of mental *res*. Other interpreters deny that Brentano ever thought of internal, intentional objects as the objects towards which intentionality is directed.[69] At any rate, it is, in my view, at best unclear that the early Brentano was making ontological claims as opposed to merely *phenomenological* claims. Phenomenologically, cognition presents itself as a relation between a cognitive subject and something other (*aliud*) than the subject,[70] whatever the ontological status of this *aliud* might be. In my view, this is in itself a crucial point.[71] As long as one makes no ontological claims about the nature of the object, the phenomenological point remains valid.

In any case, after 1900, Brentano explicitly rejects the existence of any *entia rationis*. In his so-called 'reist' phase, he maintains that only concrete, fully

[64] Brentano 1874, ed. Kraus: vi, 124, 137; ed. Chrudzimski and Binder: 9, 106, 115. Trans. Rancurello et al., in *Psychology from an Empirical Standpoint*, vii, 88, 97 (modified by Taieb). These passages are identified by Taieb 2018a: 1–2, from which I am drawing.

[65] Brentano 1982: 22. Quoted by Taieb 2018a: 2.

[66] (Brentano 1968: 282). Taieb 2018a: 102. See also Brentano 1911: 145–58.

[67] There are two opposing interpretations on this issue, namely a 'discontinuist' school (according to which Brentano changes his position) and a 'continuist' school (according to which there is continuity in Brentano's views). On this debate, see Taieb 2018a: 83–96. Rather than endorsing one or the other interpretation, I limit myself to observing that there is at least a development in Brentano's position.

[68] Cf. Crane 2006.

[69] Rollinger 2009 argues that Brentano has an act/content/object distinction already in 1874. The distinction between content and object is further articulated later in Twardowski 1894 who in turn refers to Höfler 1890 §6. I am grateful to Mark Textor for drawing my attention to this contribution.

[70] Cf. note 18 above.

[71] The crucial significance of this phenomenological observation is explored in Chap. 6.

determined individuals exist, and that the object of a mental act must always be a real entity.[72] Thus:

> a centaur, or the being or not being of a centaur, cannot be made the object of thought, but only one who acknowledges or denies a centaur, in which case the centaur becomes, at the same time, an object in a distinctive modus obliquus. And thus it is true in general that nothing else can provide an object of psychical relations but things [*Dinge*], all of which fall under the concept of real.[73]

It seems to me that this passage is making the following claims: in the case of fictional or non-existing entities, (1) there is still an object of the intentional relation, (2) this object must be a real entity, (3) ontologically, the real entity towards which intentionality is directed is a psychical activity (in this case, the psychical activity of a subject affirming or denying a centaur); (4) in so doing, the centaur becomes an object of thought *in obliquo*, that is, indirectly, without implying any kind of existence distinct from the existence of the cognitive act.[74] At least as regards this key text of 1911, I see no need either to introduce relations without two *relata* (as proposed by Taieb 2018a) or to deny that Brentano continues to think of intentionality as relational (as proposed by the 'adverbial' interpretation of the late Brentano).[75]

7.4.2 Cognitive Intentionality as the *sui generis* Presence of an *aliud* to a Subject

The most successful of an impressive cohort of Brentano's students—Edmund Husserl—distinguishes two aspects of consciousness: a real aspect, that is, any psychical event (*Ereignis*) belonging to the complex reality we call 'I', and an intentional aspect by which states of consciousness present (*meinen*) an object.[76] The relation of one's consciousness to the intentionally present object, Husserl notes, is different from the relation that consciousness has to its own real ontological constituents (its psychical events). The object, even if it is a merely imagined entity such as the god Jupiter, is not a real constituent of the subject who is imagining Jupiter (I am imagining Jupiter but I am neither Jupiter nor

[72] Cf. Brentano 1911: 145.

[73] 'Von den wahren und fiktiven Objekten' in Brentano 1911: 149. My trans.

[74] Brentano appears to be referring here to the medieval/early modern notions of *in recto*/*in obliquo*. Oblique grammatical cases (such as the dative and genitive cases) are cases other than the nominative. They mark the indirect object of a verb. Thus, the centaur is 'an object in a distinctive oblique way [*modus obliquus*]' because it is an object of thought only qua thought *by* a subject, or only qua thought *of* a subject. In brief, it is an object of thought only indirectly, via a thinking subject who thinks it.

[75] Throughout this essay Brentano speaks of *Beziehung*.

[76] This is analogous to the traditional distinction between formal and objective aspects of ideas.

imagining to be Jupiter); it is not a 'content' (*Inhalt*) of consciousness in the same way in which psychical events are 'contained' in the 'I'.[77] For Husserl, the distinction between subject and object is, therefore, immediately given as the distinction between the complex of psychical events which constitutes the subject, and what is manifested by these events (the 'object'). What is *known* is what is manifested (what 'appears'); the consciousness of this manifestation is not known but *lived* (*erlebt*).[78]

Most importantly, the aim of this phenomenological investigation is not to make ontological claims regarding the nature of what is manifested (for example, about its independent or non-independent existence) but simply to note that in any fact of consciousness there is a difference between the act of consciousness (*noesis*) and that of which one is conscious (*noema*).[79] This distinction is experienced (*erlebt*) as a cognitive presence to a subject of something other (*aliud*) than the subject.

To summarize: individual knowledge is this intentional presence of an *aliud*. Or as one of Husserl's early followers, Max Scheler (1874–1928), puts it, knowledge is, first of all, 'consciousness of something [Bewußtsein von Etwas]' founded upon the immediate 'presence and self-givenness of things [Selbstdasein und Selbstgegebensein von Sachen]'.[80] Cognitive intentionality, as the stretching out of the mind towards another (*tendere in aliud*), is intrinsically relational: it implies a subject stretching out towards an object, where the latter is identified precisely by its not being the subject (its being *aliud*). The cognitive contact between subject and object is understood non-metaphorically as a distinctive type of identification, in the act of cognition, of subject and object. As the Scholastics put it: *cognoscens in actu et cognitum in actu sunt unum* ('the knower in the act of knowing, and what is known in its being known, are one'). This identification is *sui generis* because the ontological distinction between subject and object remains: the subject becomes one with the object by assimilating its 'form' (that is, by assimilating essential information about the object) without becoming the object itself. In short, this is 'intentional' identity, as opposed to real or ontological identity.

[77] Cf. Husserl's fifth Logical Investigation (*Über intentionale Erlebnisse and ihre 'Inhalte'*), devoted to an investigation of intentional mental states and their 'contents', and Husserl, *Ideen* I, §97: 'marvellous consciousness of something determinate and determinable, given thus and so, which is something over against consciousness itself, something fundamentally other, non-really inherent, transcendent' (trans. 1982: 239).

[78] Husserl 1900: *Logische Untersuchungen* II, 5, §2: 'Die Erscheinungen selbst erscheinen nicht, sie werden erlebt.'

[79] See Husserl, *Ideen* I, §§87–96.

[80] Scheler 1957: 397.

8
Ontology I
Objects

The next two chapters investigate which kinds of entities are involved in cognition, and which kind of entity is knowledge itself. Is knowledge a disposition, a capacity, an ability? If so, is it on the potentiality side?[1] Or is it something on the actuality side, such as a mental act? In the famous Aviary analogy of the *Theaetetus* (196d1–200c6), Plato (via Socrates) already wonders whether 'know' is a potentiality word or an actuality word.[2] In his terminology, is knowledge 'possessed' as one possesses a bird flying around in an aviary, or does it require actually catching the flying bird ('having' or actively 'holding' it)? Alternatively, is knowledge a relation (say, the relation between subject and object, or the relation between mind and some feature of the world)?[3] Ditto for belief.

These different characterizations of knowledge and/or belief are all attested in contemporary literature. In fact, it is not unusual to see accounts sliding between knowledge/belief as an ability or a disposition, to knowledge/belief as a mental act, to knowledge/belief as a relation. Abilities, dispositions, acts, states, relations are not, however, the same kind of things. Moreover, as it is widely acknowledged in theory but not always reflected in the way discussions are framed in practice, knowledge/belief taken as the *object* of knowledge or belief (that is, as what is known or believed) is not the same kind of thing as knowledge/belief taken as the *act* or mental state of knowing or believing.

The ontology of cognition I propose in the next two chapters revisits and renews the ancient–medieval tradition which explains this ontology in terms of objects, acts, and faculties. Like a good Aristotelian,[4] Aquinas sees the order of investigation as starting from kinds of objects which require certain kinds of

[1] In particular, Hyman 1999, 2014, 2015 (esp. pp. 159–90), and 2017 argue for the equation of knowledge with an ability—the ability to be guided by the facts. According to Hyman, knowing that A is being able to do things for the reason that A (being able to do things because A). See Chap. 9, sect. 9.2.3 for a brief discussion. On the question of whether cognitive abilities are potentialities or actualities see Chap. 9, sect. 9.2.

[2] See Sedley/Long 2011: 140–1.

[3] One of the characteristic theses of Williamson 2000 is that knowledge is a mental state, although Williamson also refers to knowing as a relation (more precisely, a mental relation to a proposition; see Williamson 2000: 21). Zagzesbki 1999: 92 summarizes her account of what knowledge is as follows: 'Knowledge is a highly valued *state* in which a person is in cognitive contact with reality. It is, therefore, a *relation*' (my emphasis).

[4] Cf. for instance *De Anima* 415a.

Thinking with Assent: Renewing a Traditional Account of Knowledge and Belief. Maria Rosa Antognazza, Oxford University Press. © Maria Rosa Antognazza 2024. DOI: 10.1093/oso/9780198831518.003.0009

activities and which, in turn, manifest certain kinds of abilities/capacities/powers. Metaphysically, abilities/capacities/powers are potentialities. 'A potentiality [potentia]', Aquinas notes, 'is as such directed toward an act.' It follows, that 'we learn what is the nature [ratio] of a potentiality from the act to which it is ordered'. That is, we can discover the existence and nature of a potentiality only when that potentiality is actualized.[5] In turn, 'the nature [ratio] of an act is diversified according to the different nature of the object'. That is, we discover what are the different kinds of activities of which we are capable by looking at the different kinds of objects with which these activities deal.[6]

Towards which kinds of objects, then, are our activities directed? Needless to say, any answer to this question is hugely controversial. While acknowledging the controversial nature of claims in this area, I will begin by adopting a framework which many have found plausible, and which is traceable back to the Aristotelian tradition. According to this tradition, there are activities of living beings which have as their object the animated body, such as the activities of nutrition and growth. These activities manifest the 'vegetative' powers of living beings—a set of powers which already marks a fundamental distinction between living and non-living beings. A further set of activities has as its object what can be sensed. These activities manifest sensible powers, and it is from this set of powers that cognition begins. Finally, there is a set of activities which has as its object the whole being (*omne ens*) insofar as it can be thought.[7] These activities manifest intellectual powers.[8]

8.1 Sensible Objects

Let us first focus on what can be sensed, and the cognitive process by which it can be grasped. A key traditional metaphysical claim, which I endorse, is the following: all that has real, mind-independent existence is individual. That is to say, all really existing, extra-mental things are fully determinate: there is no metaphysical vagueness or indeterminacy about what they are at any given moment, whatever that is. To put it another way, as Leibniz saw especially clearly, the full determinacy of individuals is the metaphysical expression of the principle of identity. For the Aristotelian–Thomist tradition, cognition begins from an encounter with fully determinate, bodily individuals which can be sensed. Similarly, in the nominalist strand of medieval philosophy championed by Ockham and John Buridan

[5] In line with this tradition, Hyman 2015: 164–6 stresses that, in order to give an account of an ability, we have to ask how this ability is exercised or expressed. That is, abilities or powers are defined in terms of their exercise.

[6] Cf. ST I q. 77, a. 3; q. 78, a. 1 and a. 4.

[7] Cf. ST I, q. 78, a. 1.

[8] Cf. Aristotle, *De Anima* 415a, 15–20.

(*c*.1300–*c*.1360), the stress on the ontological priority of particular, individual things is, if anything, even stronger.

8.1.1 Sense-Perceptual Cognition

Sense-perception is therefore what puts us originally in touch (literally or metaphorically) with really existing things, no matter how primitively and inarticulately. Particular, corporeal things are of course sensed by perceiving beings according to different sensory modalities, depending on the nature of those perceiving beings; but since what is sensed is always some particular individual, it is always some particular quality or feature which is sensed.[9] This initial contact with the bodily objects which impinge on the senses is then deepened and extended by further abilities. The Aristotelian tradition already adds four internal senses to the five external senses: (1) the 'common sense' (*koine aesthesis*, *sensus communis*), a sort of higher-order perceptual capacity which coordinates the five senses and allows the performance of complex perceptual activities not explainable in terms of the mere collection of the individual operations of the five senses; (2) the imagination (*phantasia*, *imaginatio*), thanks to which images of currently absent objects are preserved; (3) the *aestimativa* (in non-rational animals)/*cogitativa* (in human beings), a cognitive power analogous to judgement and capable of discriminating between the beneficial and the harmful (albeit without universals, as required in proper judgement); and,(4) sensitive memory, thanks to which animals are able to remember past experiences.[10]

No doubt this list is in many ways out of date, but its enduring value rests, in my view, in the acknowledgement of the richness and complexity of purely sensitive cognition (shared by human beings with other animals), before the introduction of any concepts, conceptual schemes, or linguistic expression. As already mentioned,[11] according to Aristotle and Aquinas, sensitive cognition (including the *aestimativa/cogitativa*) does not involve universals, generalities, or concepts. Moreover, as far as Aquinas is concerned, individuals are grasped directly *only* by the senses. To be sure, this is, in Aquinas's view, a kind of cognition inferior to intellectual cognition due to its relying on the accidental features through which individuals are apprehended by the senses. It is nevertheless highly significant that the senses are assigned a unique role in establishing the direct primitive contact

[9] Cf. Aristotle, *De Anima*, Book II, chap. 5, 417b (Shields, 34): 'actual perception is of particulars'. Medieval authors such as Abelard, Ockham, and John Buridan are most emphatic in taking the view that all real things are particular. Cf. Ghisalberti 1975; Zupko 2018.

[10] ST I, q. 78, a. 4. Cf. also Aquinas, *Quaestiones disputatae de anima*, art. 13.

[11] See Chap. 1, sect. 1.2.1 and Chap. 2, sections 2.1.1 and 2.1.2.

between a cognitive subject and what really exists in a mind-independent way (that is, particular individuals).[12]

8.1.2 Intellectual Cognition

In order to discover what is (*quid sit*) the object which impinges on the senses—that is, in order to discover its stable core over and above the accidental features with which the object presents itself to the senses—a higher capacity is required: the capacity for abstraction and universalization. This capacity is the faculty of intellect.[13] According to the Aristotelian–Thomist tradition, intellectual knowledge rests on the ability to form universals (intended as what can be predicated of a plurality of individuals) through abstraction from the singularity of individual sensible objects.

Abstraction, as an intellectual operation, is the separation in thought of certain features from other features. One way to abstract is to separate individual aspects of things from other individual aspects (say, the red of an apple from its taste). The abstraction which leads to universals, however, is of a different kind: it consists in leaving aside the very singularity with which anything exists in its extra-mental mode of existence.[14] Universals are the way in which the intellect thinks of that very individual, fully *determinate* reality, but in an *indeterminate* way. Furthermore, this ability to abstract and universalize is not only a capacity to leave aside singularity and accidental features of individuals: it is a capacity to grasp aspects of individuals which are *not* sensible. In this sense, the intellect has as its object *omne ens*, the whole being, including its intelligible, as opposed to its merely sensible aspects.

On the other hand, it is important to stress that, for this tradition, 'universal forms' (or the intelligible essences of things) are not as such *in re*, although they have a foundation *in re*. In other words, universals are not found by the mind in things, as if they were already there as universals, albeit incapable of exiting on their own outside individual things. Universality and universals are 'made' (or 'actualized') by the intellect.[15] That is, the intellect produces a mode of being of

[12] Cf. Aristotle, *De Anima*, Book II, chap. 5, 417b (Shields, 34): 'Actually perceiving is spoken of in a way similar to contemplation. But there is a difference: what is capable of producing this actuality, the object of sight and hearing and so on for the remaining objects of perception, is external. The reason is that actual perception is of particulars, whereas knowledge is of universals, which are in a sense in the soul itself.'

[13] A beautiful summary of the process which led to Aristotle's view that 'in sensibilibus esse aliquid stabile', graspable not by the senses but the intellect, is found in Aquinas, *De Spiritualibus Creaturis*, a. 10 ad 8.

[14] Vanni Rovighi 1962: 144–5. See also Vanni Rovighi 1982: 31–41 to which I am indebted.

[15] Aquinas, *De Ente et Essentia*, chap. 4: 'The intellect is what makes [agit] universality in things' (Aquinas adopts this phrase from Averroes, *De Anima* I, com. 8; attention to this passage is drawn by Vanni Rovighi 1982: 36); ST I, q. 79, a. 4: 'the soul makes [facit] the intelligibility of things actual . . . we

things which is different from the mode of being those very things have in extra-mental reality—this is the mode of being things have as thought or conceived. In extra-mental reality, everything is singular, individual (including all properties things have: no individual apple has some generic, or universal redness as a property). In brief, universality is the way in which the intellect grasps what things are by abstracting from the singular mode of being things have in their extra-mental existence.

This mode of cognition is conceived by the Thomist tradition as both a sign of the greatness of the intellect, insofar as the intellect is capable of grasping the 'whatness' of things, and of its limitation, insofar as the human intellect is incapable of an adequate knowledge of things in their full individuality (God, this tradition teaches, has no use for universals since He immediately sees the *individual* essences of things in all their singularity).[16] Thus, cognition in general, and intellectual knowledge in particular, is a process of progressive determination of what is apprehended in an indeterminate way first by the senses and then by the intellect—a process which can never fully exhaust the richness of a fully determinate individual. Thinkers as diverse as Aquinas, Locke, and Leibniz all acknowledge that the finite human intellect does not stretch to an adequate knowledge of individuals—that is, it does not stretch to an adequate knowledge of *any* of the concrete things which really exist. Denying adequate knowledge of individuals is different, however, from denying knowledge. Although not *all* aspects of an individual can be known, *some* can be and are known. That is, senses and intellect do latch on to 'what is', although they cannot exhaust its richness. This structural indeterminacy of human cognition is, in my view, of paramount importance, as I will argue in the concluding chapter of this part (Chap. 10).

8.2 Ideal Objects and Imaginary Objects

8.2.1 *Entia rationis*

Another way to say that the intellect is what *produces* universality in things is to say that universals (or concepts) are mental entities or *entia rationis*.[17] As Aquinas writes:

> *Ens rationis* is properly said of those concepts [intentiones] which reason discovers in the things considered, such as the concept [intentio] of genus,

perceive ourselves abstracting universal forms from their particular conditions, which is to make the intelligibility of things actual [quod est facere actu intelligibilia]'. Cf. also Aquinas, *De Spiritualibus Creaturis*, a. 10 ad 8.

[16] There are, however, Franciscan medieval authors who go much further than Thomist Aristotelianism in extending human intuitive cognition to individuals.

[17] See Vanni Rovighi 1982: 35–6.

> species, and the like which indeed are not found in reality but result from the investigation of reason. And of this kind, namely, *ens rationis*, is properly the subject of logic. (*Sententia Libri Metaphysicae*, lib. 4 lectio 4 n. 5)

For this tradition, *entia rationis* are not mental things (*res*) existing in the mind as if the mind were a container with a special ontological kind of things in it. Concepts are mental entities in the sense that concepts need a mind thinking them. They are the way in which the mind groups things, abstracting some essential traits (I leave aside here the hugely controversial issue, brought to the forefront of modern discussion by Locke's *Essay*, of whether these traits may ever amount to the real, as opposed to the nominal, essence of those things). Thus understood, an *ens rationis* is not a *res*, a thing, but a *mode of being* that really existing extra-mental things (*res*) have as thought by the mind. It is called (perhaps misleadingly) *ens rationis* or mental entity because it is a mode of being that things would not have without a mind thinking them.[18]

8.2.2 Ideal Abstract Objects

There are, however, at least some *entia rationis* which seem to have their own fixed natures and properties independently of our thought: these are *abstract* logical objects, such as the ideal objects of mathematics. In the scholastic tradition reaching as far as Leibniz and beyond, *concretum* and *abstractum* are technical terms which track the distinction between 'determinate' and 'indeterminate'.[19] That is, we think of concrete, fully determinate mind-independent things in an abstract, indeterminate way, that is, through concepts (where concepts are universal in the sense of being predicable of a plurality of individuals).

In the ontological framework in which mind-independent existence is the only concrete, fully determinate existence, abstract objects do not qualify for extra-mental existence. And yet, as Leibniz notes, even if no human being ever thought of it, 'there would still exist the impossibility of a square larger than an isoperimetric circle' (A VI, 4, 17). This raises the question of the ontological status of ideal mathematical objects and of necessary truths about them. 'It is true, and even necessary', Leibniz argues, 'that the circle is the largest of isoperimetric figures. Even if no circle really existed. Likewise even if neither I nor you nor anyone else

[18] It can be misleading especially in contexts in which *res* and *ens* are taken as synonymous (as, for instance, by Scotus; cf. Cross 2014: 195).

[19] In Leibniz's terms, abstract objects have 'incomplete' concepts, in the sense that their concepts have a finite number of properties (as opposed to the infinitely many properties of 'complete' concepts corresponding to individual substances). This explains why a finite mind as the human mind can have adequate knowledge of mathematical objects but not of individual substances. Cf. for instance Leibniz to Antoine Arnauld, 14 July 1686 (A VI, 2, 75).

ever existed... Since, therefore, this truth does not depend on our thought, there must be something real in it' (A VI, 4, 18). I think Leibniz has a good answer to the question of the ontological status of ideal abstract objects—an answer which involves a modified version of Platonism.[20] This is not, however, the place to outline and defend that answer or to attempt an ontology of logic and mathematics. I limit myself to note that there is a robust tradition which explains the ontology of ideal objects neither by postulating a thought-independent intelligible world nor by reducing ideal objects to human psychology.

For present purposes it is enough to say that numbers or ideal geometrical figures are objects of thought which have a different nature than imaginary objects such as the older brother I never had and who secretly exists only in my thought. Although both an ideal triangle and my imaginary older brother do not have an extra-mental existence, I can gradually discover the properties of an ideal triangle but not create them in the same way in which I can add properties to my imagined brother. An ideal triangle, although it exists only as thought, has its own necessary nature wholly independent of what I, you, or a student who is getting its properties wrong, think of it. This nature is the object towards which intentionality is directed when ideal mathematical objects are thought. Thus, the fact that abstract, ideal mathematical entities have no extra-mental existence does not eliminate their status as the object of an intentional relation, nor does it make that object a property, accident, modification, or psychological feature of individual human minds. Whatever else my mind is, it does not have a triangular nature. By contrast, it is that triangular nature (whatever its more precise ontological status) which is the object of my thought. In brief, it seems to me that, if the circle would still be the largest of isoperimetric figures, even if no concrete circle really existed and no human being ever thought of it,[21] then a non-psychologist account of logical and mathematical entities as ideal objects is called for.[22]

8.2.3 Imaginary Objects and Logical Possibility

What about the ontology of imaginary objects (the god Jupiter, a centaur, a golden mountain)? In thinking these imaginary objects, people are normally perfectly aware (at least nowadays) that they do not have an extra-mental existence. Does this mean that they are nothing at all? Here it may be helpful to recall some views

[20] For magisterial discussions, see Adams 1994: esp. 177–213 and Mugnai 2018: 11–26.

[21] Cf. A VI, 4, 18, quoted above.

[22] Cf. Husserl's move in his philosophy of mathematics from an early psychologistic phase to a firm rejection of psychologism. This move reflects his acknowledgement that there is a mode of being which is the mode of being of ideal entities such as numbers (see esp. *Prolegomena zur reinen Logik*, the first volume of Husserl's *Logische Untersuchungen*).

of Duns Scotus regarding the extension of the term *ens* (being).[23] Scotus (as other medieval thinkers)[24] divides *ens* (being) into two main categories—*ens reale* and *ens rationis*—including under *ens* all that is 'not nothing'. 'Nothing' 'is that and only that which includes a contradiction, for this excludes every existence both outside the intellect and in the intellect'.[25] Accordingly:

> 'being' or 'thing'... is taken entirely most generally, and includes anything which does not include a contradiction, whether this be a being of reason [ens rationis]—that is, having being only in the thinking [considerante] intellect—or a real being [ens reale], having some entity apart from the intellect's thought.[26]

The domain of being is co-extensive with the domain of logical possibility; anything which is not contradictory has some degree of being, even if that is the being of a mere logical possibility requiring a mind thinking it.

Thus, insofar as it is non-contradictory, a merely imagined entity is not nothing. What is it then? Since, *ex hypothesi*, it is not an *ens reale* (a really existing extra-mental being), it will be an *ens rationis*. With respect to the mind, ontologically or formally there is nothing else 'in' the mind but its own modifications, its acts of thinking. However, what a psychological act of imaging a centaur presents is not a modification of the mind but a logical possibility. One should not conflate here two different orders of questions: one question concerns the conditions under which a mere logical possibility can have some being or reality (that is, it must be thought by some mind); another question concerns the nature of logical possibility. The fact that my imaginary older brother would not have any degree of being unless I (or someone) thought of him does not make the logical possibility of having an older brother a feature or a modification of my mind. This logical possibility (and not a modification of the mind) is the object of intentionality. Once again, lack of extra-mental existence does not eliminate the object of an intentional relation.

Finally, I side with Duns Scotus and Leibniz, against Alexius Meinong, in taking the view that there are no impossible (that is, contradictory) objects or concepts of impossible things.[27] When we think of a square circle we do not think at all of a square circle nature because there is no such logically possible nature: a square circle cannot be conceived (let alone imagined). Apart from a *flatus vocis*, a square

[23] See the illuminating discussion by Cross 2014: 195–6, quoting Scotus, *Quodlibetum* 3, n. 2.

[24] E.g., Aquinas, *Sententia Libri Metaphysicae* lib. 4 lectio 4 n. 5: 'ens est duplex: ens scilicet rationis et ens naturae'.

[25] Scotus, *Quodlibetum* 3, n. 2 (Wadding, xii. 67); trans. Cross 2014: 195.

[26] Scotus, *Quodlibetum* 3, n. 2 (Wadding, xii. 67); trans. Cross 2014: 195.

[27] For a present-day modal version of Meinongianism see Priest 2016. The view that we cannot believe an impossibility has been strongly defended, for instance, by Marcus (1983, 1990).

circle is nothing at all. What we think or conceive is a square *and* a circle, and we refer then to them together by using the label 'square-circle'.[28] The square and the circle are the objects which an intentional relation requires, without any need of postulating a new ontological realm of *impossibilia*.

8.3 Objects in Themselves and Objects as Cognized

To summarize—there are two ways of considering the objects of cognition (where 'object' is anything which a cognitive subject perceives as other than the subject):[29] objects as they are in themselves (that is, according to their formal reality, whatever that is), and insofar as they are cognized. Regarding the first way of consideration, according to realist views of sensible objects, the formal reality of particular dogs, trees, and other sensible things is that of being really existing, fully determinate individuals which exist independently of thought. For metaphysical views which combine this kind of realism with some version of Platonism, there are (more controversially) also some objects of cognition which do not have extra-mental existence (that is, they need a mind thinking them) but which are not reducible to psychological features of the human mind (for example, ideal mathematical objects).[30] Furthermore, there are some objects of human cognition which are purely imaginary albeit logically possible (centaurs, golden mountains). The ontological status of logical possibility is, of course, highly controversial. Without entering into the ontology of logic, and focusing instead on phenomenological considerations, I note and commend a tradition which has drawn attention to the following: the phenomenology of thinking about the god Jupiter is not that of thinking about a feature of the mind, but that of thinking of something 'other' than mind, whatever its more precise ontological status.

Regarding the second way of considering the objects of cognition (that is, insofar as objects—whatever their formal reality—are cognized), I endorse a tradition according to which objects as cognized are whatever they are in their own ontological kind, under the *mode of being* of being cognized given to them by the mind. In the case of imaginary objects, objects have no other mode of being but that of being thought. By contrast, in the case of extra-mental, really existing objects (particular dogs, trees, and the like), objects do have another mode of being, although 'being cognized' is, also in their case, a mode of being they would

[28] Cf. Leibniz, *Meditationes de Cognitione, Veritate et Ideis*, November 1684 (A VI, 4, 588–9).

[29] On the distinction between subject and object see Chap. 6, sect. 6.1. Self-knowledge is a special case, requiring second-order cognition in which the subject becomes the object of psychological reflection (see Chap. 6, sect. 6.3.2).

[30] Of course, not all versions of Platonism envisage the need for ideal objects to be eternally thought by some mind.

not have without a mind thinking them. What the mind thinks, however, are those very extra-mental things.

In general, the result of this thinking (the result of cognition) is not a new ontological category of objects (intentional objects, mental contents, mental representations, and the like) but merely a *mode of being* of objects which, in themselves, have their own formal reality, their own ontological status (sensible or not-sensible; mind-independent or mind-dependent; sensible, or ideal, or imaginary...), whatever that is more precisely. These objects in themselves are the objects of cognition.

This account also allows us to offer a different solution to the problem raised in the first section of Chapter 7: does thought about non-existing objects require one of the following three alternatives: (1) either intentionality is non-relational, (2) or there can be relations without referent, (3) or there is an additional class of objects to be added to our ontology, namely intentional objects (embracing all objects of thought)? On my account, intentionality is relational (1) but we should neither grant relations without referent (2) nor introduce a new ontological class of intentional objects (3).

On the one hand, although relations require a referent, the ontological status of this referent can vary. In fact, also for Frege, reference is not limited to objects (*Gegenstände*), that is, self-standing, complete entities (corresponding, roughly to the fully determinate individuals of the scholastic tradition). The reference of an incomplete expression ('( ) is a planet') is a concept (*Begriff*).[31] In oblique contexts (such as 'John knows that the morning star is a planet'; 'John knows that the evening star is a planet'), the reference of a complete expression is not its customary (or primary) reference (the planet Venus) but its customary sense (that is, its secondary reference, picking out a 'mode of presentation', rather than the primary reference itself).[32] There is a way to conceive reference, therefore, that does not limit it to picking out individual things but embraces also different kinds of entities. As proposed above in sections 8.2.2 and 8.2.3, these different kinds of entities comprise logical possibilities with necessary natures (for example, the ideal objects of mathematics) or contingent natures (such as merely imaginary entities).

On the other hand, although objects may belong to different ontological categories, there is no need for an *additional* ontological category of intentional objects. Objects in themselves, with their own formal reality (sensible, or ideal, or imaginary...), are the objects towards which a cognitive intentional relation is directed.[33]

[31] See, for example, Frege (1914): 243.

[32] As Leibniz had already noted, these are contexts in which the principle of substitutivity *salva veritate* is violated because 'we are not concerned with the thing itself but with the way of conceiving it [non de re sed modo concipiendi agitur]' (*Notationes Generales*; A VI, 4, 552).

[33] For further development of this claim see Chap. 10, sect. 10.2.

Their being the object of cognition does not make them, however, fully known or even fully knowable. Arguably, as far as human beings are concerned, the only fully knowable objects in themselves are abstract objects (such as mathematical ideal entities). Many aspects of concrete, fully determinate individuals are neither known nor knowable, especially in their full individuality. To get some grip on some of these unknown or unknowable aspects we often have to rely on a different cognitive mode, namely, belief.[34]

[34] For further discussion of belief as a different cognitive mode see Part III.

9
Ontology II
Acts and Faculties

Chapter 8 has discussed the first element in the ancient–medieval tradition which explains the ontology of cognition in terms of objects, acts, and faculties. This chapter focuses on the other two elements: acts and faculties. Metaphysically, acts of cognition (perceiving, knowing, remembering, believing, and so on) are on the side of actuality. The focus of the following section is, therefore, on cognition as it is exercised, that is, on occurrent cognition. The second section of this chapter, devoted to our cognitive faculties, will discuss the dispositional aspect of cognition, that is, cognition as a set of abilities, capacities, powers.

9.1 Acts

9.1.1 Apprehension and Judgement

In *De Anima*, Book III, chap. 6, 430a–b, Aristotle distinguishes two operations of the intellect: intellection of simple objects of thought (or indivisibles) and judgement.[1] Medieval interpreters, probably influenced by Averroes, add a third operation, namely, reasoning (*ratio, ratiocinatio*).[2] As a result, the scholastic tradition distinguished three main types of cognitive mental acts: apprehension, judgement, and reasoning. Although in fully developed rational beings the mental acts of apprehension, judgement, and reasoning are logically expressed (respectively) by concepts, propositions, and propositional argumentation, it is important to note that the relevant mental acts should not be identified with the logical entities which express them. That is, a proposition is a logical entity and, as such, is not a judgement, but the expression of an act of judgement. Likewise, a concept is a logical entity; apprehension is a mental act. As pointed out, among others, by Bolzano and Frege, failure to distinguish between these two categories leads to a conflation between logic and psychology (the latter including what used to be

[1] Cf. Aquinas, *Scriptum super Sententiis*, lib. 3, d. 23, q. 2, a. 2, qc. 1 co.

[2] Cf. Aquinas, *Sentencia Libri de Anima*, Book III, chap. 11. See Amerini 2013: 54–5. These scholastic distinctions between the acts of the mind were still common ground in the eighteenth century, as shown by Hume's attack in *Treatise*, Book I, Part III, sect. vii, footnote 1.

Thinking with Assent: Renewing a Traditional Account of Knowledge and Belief. Maria Rosa Antognazza, Oxford University Press. © Maria Rosa Antognazza 2024. DOI: 10.1093/oso/9780198831518.003.0010

called 'rational psychology' or 'mental philosophy'—roughly, philosophy of mind—to distinguish it from empirical psychology).[3]

This distinction between mental acts and their logical expression provides the space, in my view, for the acknowledgment of pre-conceptual and pre-propositional versions of apprehension and judgement manifested, for instance, in the behaviour of pre-verbal children and non-rational animals. To be sure, according to the Aristotelian tradition, proper judgement requires a grasp of universals (that is, broadly speaking, conceptual thought). However, the Aristotelian tradition also recognizes cognitive processes of discrimination which do not involve concepts or universals, and which are analogous to judgement (notably, Aquinas's *aestimativa/cogitativa*).[4] In fact, the early twentieth-century neo-Scholastic revisitation of Aristotelianism goes as far as describing the cognitive processes of comparing, identifying, discriminating, and connecting, found implicitly in ordinary sense-perception, as *equivalent* to judgments.[5] My contention is that there is therefore a sufficient basis for a present-day renewal of this traditional account of the main acts of cognition in which pre-conceptual and pre-propositional stages of cognition are fully taken on board. In what follows, I will refer to these pre-propositional or non-propositional cognitive processes as acts of discrimination (rather than acts of judgement) or as proto-judgements. In so doing, I am not claiming that *all* discriminating, comparing, identifying, connecting is non-propositional but that at least *some* is non-propositional, and that being articulated in logical entities such as propositions is not, therefore, essential to these processes.

Turning to an account of what apprehension and judgement amount to, I propose to recover a broadly Aristotelian tradition according to which simple apprehension is the act of perceiving an object 'without affirming or denying anything concerning it', or 'the act of the mind' that 'merely places an object before consciousness' or considers a 'present object'.[6] As Aristotle already points out, there can be no error in simple apprehension because at this stage nothing is yet affirmed or denied. Error originates in judgement, that is, in the process of affirming or denying, *componere et dividere*, in which things may be mistakenly combined or divided, for example, affirming 'the chair is made of wood', or combining 'chair' and 'wood', when the chair is in fact made of plastic).[7]

[3] Bernhard Bolzano (1781–1848) stresses that the concern of logic is 'truth in itself' expressed in true propositions and that this study is strictly distinct from the study of the acts of thought. The latter is the concern of psychology. In turn, in his opposition to late nineteenth- to early twentieth-century psychologism, Frege points out that the task of logic is to find the laws of what it is to be true ('die Gesetze des Wahrseins') as opposed to the laws of thinking ('die des Fürwahrhaltens oder Denkens'), Frege 1918–1919: 59.

[4] See Chap. 2, sections 2.1.1 and 2.1.2.

[5] See Dubray 1910, quoted below.

[6] Coppens 1891: *Logic*, book I; Rickaby 1889: Part I, chap. II, sect. 1; Dubray 1910.

[7] Cf. Aristotle, *De Anima*, Book III, chap. 6, 430b and Aquinas, *Scriptum super Sententiis*, lib. 3, d. 23, q. 2, a. 2, qc. 1 co. It should be noted, however, that for Aristotle sensation is always unerring only regarding its proper sensible.

Notably, this notion of 'judgement ' (*iudicium*), found in medieval, early modern, and modern Scholastics, is different from Locke and/or the Oxford Realists's notion of 'judgement' as a mental process to be contrasted with knowledge.[8] In fact, the older notion tracks more closely the original Aristotelian account of judgement (*hupolēpsis*) as the generic cognitive mode under which Aristotle's *De Anima* groups more specific cognitive modes, including knowledge (*epistēmē*) and belief (*doxa*).[9] In broad outline, it seems to me to correspond to the general mental act called 'thinking with assent' by Aquinas, *Fürwahrhalten* by Kant, and 'the acknowledgement of the truth of a thought [*Gedanke*]' by Frege.[10] This act of judgement ('das Urteilen') is distinguished by Frege from a mere act of thinking ('das Denken') in which a thought is simply grasped. As I interpret it, this means that an act of judgement is not merely thinking (entertaining a thought) but thinking with assent. Or as Rickaby (1889) puts it: 'every judgement consists in judging something to be true'.[11] Finally, the neo-Scholastic notions of *apprehensio* and *iudicium* as, respectively, the act of considering a present object 'without affirming or denying anything concerning it' and the act of affirming or denying, resonate in a striking way in the roughly contemporary notions of *Vorstellung* (presentation) and *Urtheil* (the mental act of acknowledgement/rejection) by Franz Brentano.[12]

Now, does knowledge proper start from the simple presentation of the object to the mind (as Oxford Realists seem to think), or from the mental act of affirming or denying something of this object present to the mind (as proposed by the neo-Scholastics)? In this regard, it may be helpful to go back to Thomas Reid. For Reid, the most primitive mental act already implies a judgement of existence of what is perceived (say, a tree in front of me in clear day-light).[13] Thus cognition starts from judgement but this judgement is not really distinct from the act of apprehending, at least as regards the judgement of existence of what presents itself clearly and directly to the mind or to the senses. Interestingly, Helen Wodehouse explicitly argues for the identification of judgement and apprehension. The reason for this identification is that, on her account, judgement is 'the act of apprehending the real' and 'to judge is simply to allow ourselves to see'.[14] In fact, even neo-Scholastic textbooks stress that one should not draw 'a very hard and fast line between apprehension and judgment, as between quite different acts of mind. The

[8] See Chap. 4, sect. 4.2 on Oxford Realism.

[9] *De Anima*, Book III, chap. 3, 427b, trans. Smith: 'within the field of judgement itself we find varieties—knowledge [*epistēmē*], opinion [*doxa*], understanding [*phronēsis*], and their opposites'.

[10] Frege 1918–1919: 62, defining 'das Urteilen' (the act of judgement) as 'die Anerkennung der Wahrheit eines Gedankens'.

[11] Rickaby (1889): Part I, chap. II, sect. 3 (c).

[12] Cf. Brentano (1874 [1973]): vol. II, chap. 3.

[13] Reid, *Inquiry*, chap. 2, sect. iv.

[14] Respectively, Wodehouse 1909: 392 and Wodehouse 1908: 367. On Wodehouse and her conception of knowledge as consisting in presentation of reality in consciousness (Wodehouse 1909 and 1910), see also Chap. 4, sect. 4.2.

Scholastics are prepared to recognize in the two a certain identity of act.'[15] In other words, in some cases for example, in paradigmatic cases of immediate assent to a present object) the distinction between apprehension and judgement is a mere distinction of reason. Or, as Francisco Suarez explains, 'since apprehension is a certain cognition of a thing, it is also some kind of judgement by which it is implicitly judged that the thing is that which we know of it'.[16] Similarly, Brentano, in his late work, regards the distinction between presentation (*Vorstellung*) and judgement (*Urtheil*) as a distinction of reason insofar as all presentations are parts of judgements.[17]

In agreement with the latter views, I conclude that in the case of assent to present objects or states of affairs—a case which is central to the conception of knowledge defended in this book—the distinction between the apprehension of what is presenting itself and the mental act of acknowledgement of this presentation (that is, judgement) is merely a distinction of reason. In short, as noted by Reid, the most primitive mental acts of apprehension have already implicit a judgement of existence of what is apprehended.

9.1.2 Judging, Reasoning, and Preserving the Cognitive Contact with 'What Is'

Reasoning is, in turn, the discursive or inferential process by which our initial cognitive grip on 'what is' is gradually extended to other things (some present, some absent, some remembered, some imagined, some believed, and so on) through the 'joining and dividing' (*componere et dividere*) of judgements. Reasoning and judging, or (generally speaking) the mental activity of thinking with assent, therefore span knowing, believing, and their cognates. Whether an act of judgement (an act of thinking with assent) is an act of knowing as opposed to an act of believing depends (I suggest) on whether assent is compelled by an original cognitive contact with 'what is' and/or by the *preservation* or retention of this cognitive contact.

A key feature of the present proposal is that it acknowledges that the cognitive contact which is required for knowledge may be preserved. The most basic and crucial way in which this contact is retained (with different degrees of success) is by remembering, that is, through the exercise of a capacity of cognitive beings which has long been regarded as central to cognition: memory.[18] Plato, Aristotle, and Augustine—to mention just three obvious authors—all provide distinctive

[15] Rickaby 1889: Part I, chap. II, addenda 10.

[16] Suarez, *Disputatio* VIII, sect. 4.

[17] See Brentano 1903/1987, 26ff.

[18] Cassam 2009 notes that although 'seeing that A' and 'remembering that A' are both ways of 'knowing that A', they are also very different insofar as the former but not the latter is a way of *coming*

theories about the place of memory in cognition with far-reaching metaphysical and epistemological consequences. Closer to our time, the study of memory is one of the most fertile and fast-developing interdisciplinary fields. It is well beyond the scope of this project to attempt to account for the currently recognized distinctions between procedural and declarative memory, and their subdivisions (notably, the subdivision of declarative memory into semantic and episodic memory, or factual and episodic memory). For present purposes it is enough to say that, insofar as memory allows a successful retention of an original cognitive contact with 'what is', memory extends and expands knowing, and indeed it is crucial to it. Ditto for a capacity closely connected to memory, namely, the capacity for recognition: insofar as it is grounded in a successful retention of an original cognitive contact with 'what is', recognition builds on memory and expands knowing.[19] A fuller account of our cognitive abilities may list other capacities similarly grounded in a successful retention of an original apprehension of 'what is'. Once again, on the present proposal, insofar as they preserve and extend this original cognitive contact, they preserve and extend knowledge.

On the other hand, these same capacities have a role to play also in a different cognitive mode, namely, believing. Take the case of believing that one remembers locking the car but not being sure; or of doubting that one remembers when your aunt's birthday is; or of suspecting that the person walking towards you is your neighbour but not being sure. In all these (and many other analogous) cases, the capacities of memory and recognition play a role in a judgement in which the object of cognition (locking the car; your aunt's birthday; your neighbour) is not clearly grasped, and assent to a certain state of affairs is not compelled.

Another crucial way in which a cognitive contact with 'what is' may be retained and extended is by inference. It is generally uncontroversial that valid deductive inferences starting from true premises (for example, mathematical demonstrations) deliver knowledge. As we have seen in Part I, while many thinkers agree that this discursive, demonstrative knowledge depends on the immediate intellectual apprehension indicated by terms such as *nous*, *intellectus*, *intuitus*, or *intuition*, they also agree that, notwithstanding their derivative nature, deductive demonstrations are strictly knowledge. But what about the cases of inductive inference and of inference to the best explanation? I propose that, in a philosophical context, one must be careful in distinguishing in these types of inference what is (strictly speaking) known and what is instead believed. Induction infers a general conclusion from the observation of particular instances. As Hume and many others rightly point out, it results in probability, and probability (however high) lies on

to know that A. In my view, this observation supports the point that also among ways of *knowing* there is an ontological and epistemic order of priority, and that 'seeing' (broadly taken) is prior to other ways of knowing (as already suggested by Aristotle at the beginning of the *Metaphysics*).

[19] On recognitional abilities and their relation to perceptual knowledge see in particular Millar 2014 and 2019: 73–96.

the side of belief and not of knowledge.[20] Of course, one could say that we may *know* the exact probability of something but such a piece of knowledge will be a matter of mathematical calculation and not of induction. As regards inference to the best explanation, having seen and smelled pig-droppings, and having heard plenty of pig-noises coming from the pigsty, do we know that there is a pig in the pigsty? Strictly speaking, on my account, the abductive inference that there is a pig is a case of justified belief rather than knowledge. There are, however, plenty of aspects of this situation which would count (on my account) as knowing (for example, the presence of pig-droppings and pig-noises), and what we know about this situation justifies a judgement about what we do not (strictly) know. Once again, judging, reasoning, or, more generally, thinking with assent, span knowing and believing.

9.1.3 Cognitive Acts as Actions

After this review of the three main types of cognitive mental acts identified by a long tradition originating in Aristotle, we can now tackle the question of the ontological status of these acts. For medieval thinkers, answering this question basically means identifying the Aristotelian category to which acts of cognition belong. In what follows I will discuss the categorization which seems to me most promising, namely, the view that mental acts are *actions* of a certain type. According to this tradition, a mental act, as any action, inheres in a subject[21]—that is, in this case, in the mind. Since mental acts do not exist per se but in a subject, they are, ontologically, accidents—that is, in this case, modes or modifications of the mind. Furthermore, they are a specific type of action. Following the Aristotelian distinction between 'transitive' actions (actions which produce something distinct from, or external to the agent, such as, for instance, the illumination of an external body by a source of light), and 'immanent' actions (actions which do not produce somethings distinct from, or external to the agent, such as the shining of a luminous body), Aquinas classifies cognitive acts as *immanent* actions,[22] labelling them, in turn, 'operations'.[23] 'Seeing' is a classic example of operation: when we see an external body (say, a stone), the cognizer performs an action (that of seeing), but this action does not produce any real property in the seen body

[20] Cf. Chap. 3, sect. 3.2.

[21] According to a scholastic formula which Leibniz still endorses, *actiones sunt suppositorum* (actions belong to *supposita*).

[22] ST I, q. 34, a. 1 ad secundum: 'understanding [intelligere] does not signify an action exiting the cognizer but an action remaining in the cognizer [in intelligente manentem]'. See also *Quaestiones disputatae de veritate*, q. 8, a. 6. Cf. Cross 2014: 107–8.

[23] *Quaestiones disputatae de veritate*, q. 8, a. 6.

(the stone does not change, as opposed to the change which would be produced in an external body as the result of a transitive action, such as warming).[24]

In this framework, a mental state seems to correspond to what Aquinas calls a 'perfection' of the mind, that is, the immanent action that 'remains in the agent itself as a perfection of the agent'.[25] Thus, a mental state is a way of considering a mental action which has fulfilled its aim (say, that of seeing an external body), actualizing a capacity or potentiality of the mind (that is, 'perfecting' the mind), rather than being something distinct from the mental action itself. Actual (that is, occurrent) cognition is, for Aquinas, a mental state with the natural capacity of referring to external reality.[26] To the question of whether knowing/knowledge is a state or a process, I propose to answer in similar terms: knowing/knowledge is a mental state fulfilling a mental action.

At this point, the pressing question is whether this conception of mental acts/states as *immanent* actions suggests that the mind is closed into itself. As we will see in the following sub-section, the answer is 'no'.

9.1.4 Cognition as Relation: Ontological Truth and Logical Truth

Although Aquinas thinks that the nature of cognition (that is, its ontological status) is that of being a mental action, he acknowledges that Aristotle describes cognition as a relation. More precisely, Aristotle places knowable and knowledge, perceptible and perception, in the third class of relatives, that is, relatives which stand in a relation of measurable to measure (*Metaphysics*, Book 5, chap. 15; 1020b30).

Aquinas is happy to accept this Aristotelian doctrine insofar as the action of the mind grounds a relation between the cognitive subject and what is knowable or perceptible. Now, in the framework of medieval theories of relations, relations need to be grounded in properties of the relata. That is, there must be a *fundamentum relationis* (a foundation of the relation), as there must be (more generally) a *fundamentum veritatis* (a foundation of truth which grounds the truth of what is stated in a proposition). Thus, in a relation of similarity between two black men, Plato and Socrates, the properties of being black which inhere, respectively, in Plato and in Socrates, ground a real relation of similarity between them.

In the case of cognition, the property which grounds the relation between mind and what is knowable/perceptible is the cognitive act which (as a mode or modification of the mind) inheres in the mind. There is, however, no quality or property which grounds the cognitive relation in the known/perceived thing (for example, the 'being seen' of a stone is not a real or, in modern parlance, 'ontic'

[24] Cf. Amerini 2013: 111–12.

[25] *Quaestiones disputatae de veritate*, q. 8, a. 6.

[26] Cf. Amerini 2013: 114–16.

property of the stone which could ground a converse relation between perceived and perceiver; it is instead, in technical terms, a purely extrinsic denomination).[27] The converse relation is, therefore, a mere relation of reason (*relatio rationis*). Thus, while there is a real relation (*relatio realis*) between mind and world, grounded in a real property of the mind (that is, the act of cognition), there is no real converse relation between known thing and mind, although we think of it as a relation.[28] The outcome is that there is a way in which the view that cognition is a relation between mind and world fits comfortably with the view that cognitive acts (qua immanent actions) are, ontologically, modifications of the mind that naturally refer to things other than the mind (typically, extra-mental, really existing things).[29]

More precisely, as anticipated above, the relation of knowable to knowledge, perceptible to perception is, according to Aristotle, the relation of measurable to measure. This type of relation brings us to the issue of truth. In *Metaphysics*, Book 4, chap. 7 (1011b/Ross 749), Aristotle states: 'to say of what is that it is, or of what is not that it is not, is true'. From this Aristotelian view develops the immensely influential tradition according to which truth is the conformity of mind to reality (*adaequatio intellectus ad rem*) or the correspondence between mind and reality (*adaequatio intellectus et rei*). The correspondence theory of truth has of course been the target of powerful attacks, not least in the influential work of Frege in the early twentieth century and in present-day deflationism.[30] This ancient theory, however, is far from dead. Provided it is underpinned by an appropriate ontology, it still offers, I suggest, the most natural explanation of truth.

In its original version, conformity or correspondence is taken in two different ways, leading to the scholastic distinction between ontological truth and logical truth (the latter having a broader meaning than is usual nowadays).[31] The roots of this distinction are already found in Plato's *Republic*, where the intelligibility given by the Good to the Forms (analogous to the visibility given by the sun to things) constitutes ontological truth, while the expression or representation of what is intelligible through a proposition with the property 'true' constitutes semantic truth.[32] Similarly, in the scholastic tradition, ontological truth is the truth of things themselves, in the sense of things being what they are supposed to be (for example, a true horse is a horse which conforms to what a horse properly is—a living being

[27] Cf. Aquinas, *De Spiritualibus Creaturis*, a. 10, ad 12. Famously, Leibniz denies the existence of purely extrinsic denominations. This is not the place, however, for a proper evaluation of this distinctive Leibnizian view.

[28] Cf. Aquinas, *Scriptum super Sententiis*, I, d. 8, q. 4, a. 1, ad 3, vol. 1, p. 220 and Amerini 2013: 115–23.

[29] Cf. Ockham's view that some intellectual acts are themselves capable of referential functions and by their own nature are capable of signifying extra-mental things (Panaccio 2004: 26).

[30] See Frege 1918–1919.

[31] Cf. ST I, q. 21, a. 2. A discussion of ontological and logical truth, and of truth as transcendental in Aquinas is offered by Aertsen 1992.

[32] See Plato, *Republic*, 6.508e1–4; 509b6; 7.517b–c and Gerson 2022: sect. 1.

with four legs and so on, as opposed to being, say, a wooden model). Following a Christianized version of Platonism, the scholastic tradition reads this as conformity of things to their ideas or essences in God's mind. Thus, things are measured by thought in a way analogous to the conception of an artist or an architect that sets the standard of the work which will be created. Broadly speaking, however, ontological truth is proper of all things insofar as, owing to the principle of identity, everything is what it is and not something else. Hence the medieval doctrine that 'truth' is one of the transcendentals, that is, one of the common notions that transcend the categories and apply to everything, such as 'being' and 'one'.

In semantic or logical truth (*veritas logica*), on the other hand, thought is measured by things. 'Logical' is taken here in the classic sense of concerning the properties of what is thought insofar as it is thought (technically, concerning the *intentio secunda*, as opposed to the *intentio prima*, of what is thought). Accordingly, logical truth has a greater extension than the notion of logical truth as necessary (analytical, a priori) truth (or as a proposition true purely in virtue of its logical form) commonly used in present-day analytical philosophy.[33] In this older sense, logical truth is the kind of truth which concerns human cognition, and which is expressed in propositions and propositional argumentation. Thought is measured by things insofar as what we think is true if it corresponds to how things are. Logical truth is, therefore, a property of thought, not of things,[34] and when thought is expressed in propositions, is a property of propositions. As explained in Burgersdijk's *Institutionum logicarum libri duo* (one of the most widely used logic textbooks of the early modern period), logical truth 'is not in things, but in mental judgement [non est in rebus, sed in judicio mentis], or in a proposition.[35] A mental judgement is said to be true when it joins [componit] things which are in fact conjoined, or divides [dividit] things which are in fact different. A proposition is said to be true when it conforms to things [cum rebus convenit].'[36]

To be sure, the conformity of thought to things is *grounded* in things. In traditional terms, the foundation of the truth of a proposition (*fundamentum veritatis*) is the relevant proprieties of things.[37] But one should not conflate the

[33] Cf. Gómez-Torrente 2019 for an overview of the notion of logical truth in contemporary debates.

[34] Cf. Aristotle, *Metaphysics*, Book 4, chap. 4, 1027b (trans. Ross, 782): 'falsity and truth are not in things...but in thought'; Aquinas ST I, q. 16, a. 1: 'terminus appetitus, quod est bonus, est in re appetibili, sed terminus cognitionis, quod est verum, est in ipso intellectu'.

[35] The word used here by Burgersdijk is *oratio* (discourse, sentence), but the type of *oratio* relevant in this context is the *enunciatio* (enunciation, statement), that is, the verbal expression of a mental proposition (*propositio*).

[36] Burgersdijk 1660: 118–19.

[37] I agree with Ayers (2019: 121, note 39) that the traditional notion of *fundamentum veritatis* is preferable to the 'intrinsically rather absurd notion of a "truth-maker", or what "makes" a proposition true. True statements are true because they match the world, not because the world obligingly "makes" them true.'

foundation of logical truth with logical truth itself. By the same token, logical truth should not be hypostasized, as if there were abstract 'truths' existing somewhere without a mind thinking them. As discussed in Chapter 8, the present proposal follows the tradition according to which mind-independent existence is proper only of concrete individuals with their properties. All other types of entities, qua abstract entities, need a mind thinking them, although their 'quiddity' (*quid sint*) does not depend on the mind thinking them. In this sense, the type of truth which *specifically* concerns cognition—that is, logical truth or what is thought insofar as it is thought—is never and can never be a 'non-mental' component of knowledge.[38] What is non-mental is ontological truth—that is, things being what they are and not otherwise, independently of their being cognized.

9.2 Faculties

In an Aristotelian framework, a cognitive process may be seen as a passage from potentiality to actuality. Having considered mental acts or occurrent cognition, it is time to turn to the potential or dispositional side of cognition and to an account of the ontological status of faculties.

9.2.1 Powers, Potentialities, and Dispositions

In this regard, medieval philosophy is, once again, particularly rich in insights. Cognitive faculties are typically called, by medieval authors, *potentiae animae*—a notion which already raises important questions given that *potentia* can be taken in two different ways: (1) as a power; (2) as a potentiality.[39] The first thing to be noted is that not all potentialities are powers. Some medieval authors distinguish in fact two different types of potentiality: passive potentiality (or *possibilitas*) and active potentiality (or *potestas*).[40] This is, in my view, an important distinction which is sometimes overlooked, with the unfortunate consequence that two different notions—disposition and power—are sometimes conflated. Passive potentiality (*potentia passiva*), I contend, is a disposition but not, properly, a power.[41]

[38] Present-day discussions of knowledge are often framed in terms of truth being the non-mental component of knowing.

[39] See Adams 2022: 58.

[40] See Henry of Ghent, *Summa*, art. 35, q. 4 (ed. G. Wilson, p. 34, 2–10). Cf. also Plotinus, *Ennead* VI.8 and Aquinas, *Quaestiones disputatae de potentia*, q. 1, a.; Aquinas, *Sententia Libri Metaphysicae*, lib. 5 I, 14 n.1–23.

[41] Hyman 2015: 179 rightly stresses the important difference between 'power' and 'possibility' ('An ability is a power, and therefore an actual property of the substance that possesses it, and not merely the possibility that the kind of act or event that manifests it should occur'). On my account, however, it is not the case that 'dispositions, abilities, and liabilities are all powers' (Hyman 2015: 166).

A disposition (for example, fragility) may be, in fact, no more than a potentiality that something could happen to a certain thing. A power, on the other hand, is a capacity or ability to do something. One should think of fragility and of other similar passive potentialities as 'liabilities' rather than abilities or powers (for example, in philosophical rigour, a glass is liable rather than able to break).[42] More generally, as I have argued elsewhere, all powers, insofar as they are powers, are active. There are, therefore, passive potentialities or passive dispositions but there are not, strictly speaking, passive powers.[43]

Active potentiality (*potentia activa*), on the other hand, is a capacity, an ability, or an active principle. As such, it qualifies as a power. The upshot is that faculties are potentialities of this second type: they are capacities, powers to actively do certain things. I will refer to them therefore as abilities, capacities, or powers rather than, generically, as dispositions or potentialities, since not all dispositions and potentialities are powers.[44]

9.2.2 Faculties as Principles of Operation and as Properties of the Mind

Although there was no unified doctrine, Scholastic authors tended to agree that faculties are the 'principles of operation' of human beings and that by giving an account of these principles one could grasp what is distinctive of human beings as a particular kind of living beings.[45] On the other hand, they disagreed on whether the faculties of the soul are merely roles or ways of acting of the soul, conceptually distinct but metaphysically identical to the essence of the soul (William of Auvergne and Ockham), or are necessary qualities of the soul distinct from its essence (Aquinas), or are really distinct entities (Suarez).[46] On balance, it seems to me that a promising account of the ontological status of faculties is to consider them natural properties or qualities of the mind through which the nature of the mind is manifested.[47] That is, in medieval and early modern terms, faculties are

[42] The distinction between powers and liabilities is stressed by Richard Swinburne (cf. Swinburne 1996: 21–5). Among other things, this distinction has important consequences for philosophical theology.

[43] Cf. Antognazza 2014.

[44] Bird 2016 notes that, although a power is (on his account) an ontic property which is essentially dispositional in character and has modal fixity (i.e., it is individuated as having that dispositional character in all possible worlds/has that character necessarily and not contingently), power does not equate to disposition since there are dispositions which are not powers.

[45] See Perler 2013 and 2015. Cf. Aquinas, *Quaestiones disputatae de anima*, q. 12; ST I, q. 77, a. 1; Suarez, *De anima*, disp. 3, q. 1. Attention to these texts is drawn by Perler 2013: 9 and 2015: 98.

[46] I am drawing from the excellent discussions of these theories by Perler 2015 and Adams 2022: 45–50 (Aquinas), 69–76 (Ockham).

[47] See Perler 2015: 105–14 and Adams 2022: 49.

propria:[48] qualities or properties of the soul which manifest its essence while being distinct from it.[49] The reason for preferring a distinction between soul/mind's essence and faculties over their straightforward identification is, in my view, important: this distinction, I suggest, allows us to acknowledge the full integrity of human nature also in the absence of some of the manifestations of this nature (as in the case, for instance, of severe disabilities).[50]

Now, are these principles of operation or powers of the mind actual or merely potential properties of the mind? Following the Aristotelian tradition, a power or faculty has actuality (*actus primus*) insofar as a power is an actual propriety of a cognitive subject which enables the subject to perform certain actions in appropriate circumstances. In other words, a power is a principle of operation (*principium operandi*) which is already present in a cognitive subject. As Duns Scotus stresses, it is actually something as opposed to pure potentiality (that is, as opposed to falling, ontologically, under the heading of non-being)—a view that Scotus takes to be in line with Aristotle and Aquinas's considered position according to which cognitive powers are affections or properties of the soul.[51]

On the other hand, there is in a power/faculty also a crucial aspect of potentiality insofar as a power is not always exercised. A power's *actus secundus* marks the cognitive process by which an ability is actualized—a process, Francisco Suarez notes, which is conditional upon the 'conjunction' of a cognitive power with an object ('A cognitive power [potentia cognoscitiva] is in a state of indetermination as regards its operating in respect to this or that object; hence, to be determined to a particular cognitive act, it needs some sort of conjunction with the object itself [indiget conjunctione aliqua ad ipsum objectum]').[52] In sum, the notions of *actus primus* and *actus secundus* elegantly express a key insight, namely, that a faculty or power has both an aspect of actuality (it is a property

[48] According to the classification given by Porphyry (*c.*234–305 CE) in his *Isagoge*, there are five modes of predication (or five types of predicable). A predicate can be predicated of a subject (e.g., Socrates) as genus (e.g., animal), as species (e.g., human being), and as difference (that is, as the property which marks the difference between genus and species, e.g., rational). Genus, species, and difference are essential predicates which directly express the essence of something either indeterminately (genus), determinately (species), or in its determining feature (difference). In addition, there are two types of predicable which do not directly express the essence of a subject but either are or are not manifestations of its essence. The first type is the *proprium* (the typical medieval example is, for human beings, the capacity to laugh as manifesting their rational nature); the second type is the accident (e.g., white). Cf. Vanni Rovighi 1962: 62 and Burgersdijk 1660: liber I, cap. XIII (as noted above, a standard early modern logic textbook).

[49] ST I, q. 77, a. 1, ad 5: 'A proprium does not belong to the essence of a thing. But it is caused by the essential principles of the species. That is why it stands between the essence and the accident... And in this way the faculties of the soul can be said to stand between substance and accident, somewhat like natural properties of the soul.' Trans. Perler 2015: 109 (slightly modified). For Aquinas's arguments in support of the metaphysical distinction between soul and faculties see Adams 2022: 45–8 and Perler 2015: 105–14.

[50] The reason for rejecting a conception of faculties as real distinct entities is briefly outlined below.

[51] Scotus, *Opus Oxoniense*, II, d.16, q.u, n. 7 (Wadding, vi.2.763). See Adams 2022: 60 which draws attention to this passage.

[52] Suarez, *De Anima*, 1. iii. c. i.

already actually possessed by the mind) and an aspect of potentiality (a faculty or power is not always exercised).

9.2.3 Abilities and Habits

There is, however, a further important distinction. One thing is to have a natural capacity (potentiality), say, to read and write; another is to have the actual ability or power to do so: pre-school children, for instance, have the potential capacity to read but not yet the actual ability. Moreover, this ability is not always exercised (that is, when one is sleeping)—there is, therefore, a potential aspect to it—but it is readily available to be exercised (actualized) when appropriate circumstances arise. Understood in this way, actual abilities such as reading and writing correspond to the traditional, technical notion of *habitus* ('habit'). As *habitus*, an ability involves having already actualized a capacity which is merely potential (the potential capacity to speak French, to solve quadradic equations, or to play the piano).[53] Going back to Plato's aviary analogy in the *Theaetetus* (196d1–200c6), one could say that for knowledge it is sufficient to be able to catch the birds in your aviary without needing to actually catch them (occurrent cognition or *actus secundus*).[54] To have this ability, however, the birds must already be in the aviary—they must already have been caught, at some point, and put there. Thus, abilities taken as *habitus* or skills are a further stage of cognition in a which a potential capacity has already been actualized (*actus primus*), already resulting in cognition in the first place. As far as I can see, this is the sense in which Gilbert Ryle can treat knowledge both as a capacity and as an achievement without incurring the charge of inconsistency levelled by some interpreters against this dual classification.[55]

Drawing on an illustrious tradition going back to Plato and renewed in the twentieth century by Ludwig Wittgenstein, Gilbert Ryle, and Anthony Kenny,[56] John Hyman has mounted, in recent years, a powerful and sophisticated case for equating knowledge itself with an ability. On his account, knowledge, rather than being a species of belief, is a species of ability. More precisely, it is the ability to be guided by the facts.[57] This proposal has, among others, the merits of arguing in a

[53] See Panaccio 2004: 21–3 on the importance of the notion of *habitus* in Ockham's theory of cognition. In Ockham, *habitus* is an acquired disposition (*actus primus*) while a mental act is a psychological episode of occurrent cognition (*actus secundus*).

[54] This dispositional character of much of our cognition also helps explain the experience of tacit or implicit knowledge expressed by remarks such as 'oh, I see—I think I knew it all along'. Thanks are due to Peter Adamson for this example.

[55] Cf. Kremer 2016: 33–5 for an insightful defence of Ryle against this charge.

[56] Cf. Plato, *Republic* 477d; Wittgenstein 1953: §150; Ryle 1949: 33–5; Kenny 1989: 108f.

[57] See Hyman 1999, 2014, 2015 (esp. pp. 159–90), and 2017. Kremer 2016 argues that Ryle held a unified conception of knowledge as a 'capacity to get things right', covering both knowledge-how and knowledge-that.

compelling way against the identification of knowledge with a kind of belief, and of stressing the need to look at how knowledge is exercised or expressed in order to understand what knowledge is. The *identification* of knowledge with an ability seems to me, however, too strong. As noted above in relation to *habitus*, an ability is often a manifestation of knowledge rather than being knowledge *tout court*. As regards the specific ability to be guided by the facts, it seems to me that also this ability falls under the category of being a manifestation of knowledge (specifically, knowledge of facts) rather than simply equating to knowledge itself. In other words, it is knowledge of facts which explains the ability to be guided by them. Similarly, it is knowledge of the rules of quadradic equations which explains the ability to solve quadradic equations in a maths exam; it is knowledge of French which explains the ability to speak in French to the waiter during the school trip to Paris. If this is right, it seems to me that knowledge of facts is presupposed by the ability to be guided by them, rather than being identical to it.[58]

Still, as Hyman also maintains, knowledge is *not* a species of belief. The reason 'it can be difficult to tell them apart', he rightly notes, is that 'belief mimics knowledge' (Hyman 2015: 173). As he puts it, 'to believe that p is to be disposed to act (think, feel) as one would if one knew that p, or as one would if one were guided by the fact that p . . . one can do or think or feel something that the facts would justify one in doing or thinking or feeling if one knew them, without being guided by the facts' (Hyman 2015: 174). In conclusion, however:

> the fact that it can be difficult to distinguish between belief and knowledge in practice is not an obstacle to explaining the difference between them in theory, and the root of the difference is that one cannot be guided by a fact one does not know. Of course it does not follow that an act that expresses belief and not knowledge is done aimlessly, or for no reason. (Hyman 2015: 173)

9.2.4 Cognitive and Conative Powers: Intellect and Will

So far, I have focused on cognitive powers. There are, however, powers of a different sort which (I claim) are complementary and equally important in order to understand the activity of cognitive beings. According to the classic Aristotelian account of faculties, sensory faculties are strictly connected with appetition. This means that appetitive or conative tendencies characterize the whole life of sensitive beings:

[58] Hyman discusses this type of objection in Hyman 2015: 171, 181–8. For a reply, cf. Williamson 2018.

> If any order of living things has the sensory [power], it must also have the appetitive; for appetite is the genus of which desire, passion, and wish are the species; ... whatever has a sense has the capacity for pleasure and pain and therefore has pleasant and painful objects present to it, and wherever these are present, there is desire, for desire is just the appetition of what is pleasant. (*De Anima* 414b; Smith trans.)

Movement, in particular, originates from the appetitive faculty, and, more specifically, from desire—namely, from 'a form of appetite' that moves sensitive beings towards what is or appears good to them.[59]

If we turn from sensitive to rational faculties, two faculties are commonly identified as the key features which account for the rational nature of human beings: intellect and will. Interestingly, even the Cartesians hold on to these two faculties. When it comes to vegetative and perceptual processes in bodies, Descartes and other early modern proposers of a mechanist philosophy of nature abandon the Scholastic ontology of faculties: nutrition and growth in living beings, and perception in animals, are explained as a mechanical arrangement of material parts which need no powers (including sensory powers) in bodies. It is significant, however, that Descartes and his followers do not go as far as eliminating faculties altogether. On the contrary, intellect and will continue to have a key place also in their philosophical anthropology.[60]

What is the ontological status of these two rational faculties? Are they really distinct entities? Despite the use of reifying language and the associated tendency to take 'the' intellect and 'the' will as some sort of self-standing things (*res*), it is only in the late sixteenth century, and, in particular, in the account of Francisco Suarez, that faculties come to be understood as really distinct entities. Those who, like Ockham, regard faculties as metaphysically identical to the essence of the soul, think that intellect and will are merely ways of acting of the rational soul.[61] And even those who, like Aquinas, admit a distinction between faculties and the essence of the soul, conceive intellect and will as qualities or properties of the soul and not as distinct entities.

The conception of intellect and will proposed by this book is in line with this pre-Suarezean account. Like other faculties, intellect and will are not to be understood as really distinct entities but as natural capacities, qualities or properties of the mind. They are not concrete *res* but principles of operation in which the nature of embodied beings such as human beings is manifested. Their reification is, in fact, one of the key reasons for the early modern onslaught against

[59] Cf. Aristotle, *De Anima*, 433a 21–433b 1.

[60] See Perler 2015: 6. One way to read extreme forms of present-day physicalism is to see it as a continuation and radicalization of the Cartesian programme of reducing all processes to material arrangements of parts, chemical reactions, and so on.

[61] See Perler 2013 and 2015.

an ontology of faculties and powers, dismissed by early modern authors as mysterious entities operating in a human being 'as so many distinct Agents' or homunculi.[62] Once reification is avoided, however, thinking in terms of faculties is far from explanatorily otiose, as the current comeback of powers and abilities in metaphysical inquiries shows.[63]

As regards the will in particular, one fruitful way of conceiving it is as the higher, rationally guided version of the appetitive faculty, that is, as a version of the drive towards real or apparent good which characterizes all sensitive beings. In Aquinas's terms, the faculty of will is an 'intellectual appetite' (*appetitus intellectivus*). Like any appetite, intellectual appetite has the good as its object but, unlike sensitive appetite, the good towards which it is directed is apprehended by the intellect under the aspect of the common good (*sub communi ratione boni*).[64] This model commends itself, I suggest, both for its naturalism and for offering a unified account of the conative/appetitive tendencies which permeate the life of sensitive and rational beings.

Following this tradition, my positive proposal builds on a conception in which cognitive and conative/appetitive aspects of sensitive and rational beings play distinct but complementary roles. On my account, both roles are crucial and fundamentally integrated also as regards, in particular, our cognitive life.[65]

[62] Locke, *Essay*, Book II, chap. XXI, 20. See Perler 2015: esp. 97–100, 138–9.

[63] A major example is the project on human abilities led by Dominik Perler and Barbara Vetter (https://www.human-abilities.de). Cf. also Vetter 2015.

[64] Cf. ST IIa IIae, q. 24, art. 1.

[65] The case for the fundamental integration of cognitive and conative aspects of human life is made, in particular, in Chap. 6. For the role of will (and, more generally, of appetite) in belief see Chap. 10.

10
The Object of Knowledge and the Object of Belief

The discussion of the ontology of cognition in terms of objects, acts, and faculties, spanning the last two chapters, allows me to tackle, at this point, the following key questions. What is the object of knowledge? What is the object of belief? Do knowledge and belief have, or can they have, the same object?

10.1 Propositions, Facts, Truths, and Concrete Individuals

10.1.1 Epistemological Alternatives

It follows from (J)TB+ accounts of knowledge as a species of belief that all objects of knowledge are objects of belief, although not all objects of belief are objects of knowledge. Moreover, for a typical (J)TB+ analysis, the object of knowledge is a true proposition (*p*): S knows that *p* iff (i.) *p* is true; (ii.) S believes that *p*; (iii.) S is justified [warranted/entitled ...] in believing that *p* [S's belief tracks truth/tracks the facts/is non-accidentally true/arises out of acts of intellectual virtue ...].[1] In short, for (J)TB+ analyses, both knowledge and belief have propositions as their object—a view routinely presented as the claim that knowledge and belief are 'propositional attitudes', that is, to know and/or believe something is to have an attitude to a proposition (say, the attitude of holding the proposition to be true).[2]

Williamson (2000) strongly rejects analyses of knowledge in terms of true belief plus other conditions, but maintains the focus on knowing and believing as propositional attitudes.[3] According to him, 'believing that something is so, conceiving that it is so, hoping that or fearing that it is so, wondering whether it is so,

[1] There are of course many significant variations of (iii), the most important strand of which is constituted by the family of reliabilist theories according to which knowledge is true belief formed in a reliable or truth-conducive way.

[2] See, for instance, the entry 'Belief' in the *Stanford Encyclopedia* (Schwitzgebel 2019): 'Much of epistemology revolves around questions about when and how our beliefs are justified or qualify as knowledge. Most contemporary philosophers characterize belief as a "propositional attitude".'

[3] Williamson 2000: 21: 'Paradigmatic mental states ... include attitudes to propositions: believing that something is so, conceiving that it is so, hoping or fearing that it is so, wondering whether it is so, intending or desiring it to be so. One can also know that something is so. This book concerns such propositional knowledge.'

Thinking with Assent: Renewing a Traditional Account of Knowledge and Belief. Maria Rosa Antognazza, Oxford University Press. © Maria Rosa Antognazza 2024. DOI: 10.1093/oso/9780198831518.003.0011

intending or desiring it to be so', are all attitudes to propositions—that is, 'relations of subjects to propositions' which should be distinguished from merely entertaining a proposition without having some 'attitude' towards it.[4] Likewise, on Williamson's account, knowing that something is so is a propositional attitude. More precisely, knowing is a mental relation to a proposition 'such that, for every proposition *p*, having that relation to *p* is a mental state'. So construed, the object of knowledge (what one knows) are true propositions.[5] Of course a focus on propositional knowledge (explicitly identified by Williamson as the concern of his inquiry) does not per se exclude the existence or importance of non-propositional knowledge. It seems fair to say, however, that the centrality accorded to 'knowing *that p*' agrees with the common tendency in analytical philosophy to consider propositional knowledge as the proper and principal focus of epistemology.[6] Thus, although the distinctions between knowledge by acquaintance and knowledge by description,[7] and between objectual knowledge ('knowing John', 'knowing Rome') and propositional knowledge are widely recognized, the idea that 'the 'know that P' construction is the more fundamental and perspicuous' remains 'popular with analytic philosophers'.[8] As for believing, for Williamson, the object of belief (what one believes) are also propositions (although, of course, such propositions may or may not be true).

To summarize: contra (J)TB+ accounts, Williamson argues that 'knowing is *merely* a state of mind' (no non-mental components need to be added to the relevant mental state in order for that state to be knowledge);[9] he agrees however with (J)TB+ theorists in focusing on knowing and believing as propositional attitudes which have propositions as their objects. If these believed propositions are true, I take that also for Williamson the object of belief will be exactly the same as the object of knowledge, that is, a true proposition.[10]

[4] For an insightful criticism of the common characterization of desiring as a propositional attitude, see Alvarez 2010: 66–7. I agree that desiring is not an attitude to a proposition. Ditto for intending, fearing, and hoping.

[5] Williamson 2000: 21–2: knowing is 'a *factive* attitude; one knows *p* only if *p* is true'.

[6] For a compelling criticism of this tendency see Ayers 2019, chap. 4.

[7] Russell 1910–11 and 1912: chap. 5.

[8] Ayers 2019: 128. Benton 2017: 814–15 notes that while the distinction between objectual and propositional knowledge is marked in English only by grammar ('S knows NP' versus 'S knows that ϕ'), in many other languages it is marked also lexically (cf., for instance, the distinction in German between *kennen* and *wissen*, and in Romance languages between *conoscere* and *sapere*, *connaître* and *savoir*, *conocer* and *saber*; the same applies, Benton notes, to widely spoken Sino-Tibetan and Semitic languages, such as Mandarin, Cantonese, modern Hebrew). It seems to me that this very fact may make native speakers of those languages less amenable to accepting without much questioning the priority accorded by anglophone epistemology to propositional knowledge.

[9] Williamson 2000: 21. See also Williamson 2009: 293–301.

[10] Ayers 2019: 103–4 argues that Williamson's characterization of knowledge as 'a (factive) 'propositional attitude'... looks like an implicit endorsement of the very idea that he explicitly rejects, that knowledge simply *is* belief that is true, provided that it is also non-accidentally or reliably engendered (and so on and so forth)'.

Other prominent present-day philosophers disagree with the latter claim. Vendler and Holton distinguish facts from propositions, and claim that we believe propositions but know facts.[11] 'The world of facts', Vendler explains, 'is the objective realm.' A proposition 'is somebody's creation'. It is true if it conforms with the facts, whereas facts 'are not true or false at all'; they 'are "there", objectively given, to be found or discovered'.[12] Hyman agrees that facts are not propositions, argues that a fact is the truth *of* a proposition (as opposed to being a true proposition),[13] and concludes that the object of knowledge is the *truth of* a proposition while the object of belief is a proposition.[14]

For his part, Ayers maintains that the objects of knowledge and belief are different but is critical of regarding the object of knowledge as either propositions or facts. A proposition, Ayers argues, is far too abstract an entity to serve as the object of knowledge (as opposed to being instead an eminently suitable entity for the purposes of logic).[15] On his account, knowledge 'is essentially a natural relation between knower and object known. As Plato pointed out in distinguishing knowledge from belief, the object of knowledge is "*to on*", what *is*, reality.'[16] On his view, facts, as discriminated by propositions, are also far too close to propositions and far too infected, as it were, by the same atemporality and abstractness to serve as the objects of knowledge.[17] 'The first or fundamental objects of knowledge', Ayers concludes, 'are the objects with which we are in immediate cognitive contact and that are directly presented to us in perception, objects of which we have direct knowledge or "acquaintance", and these, unlike propositions or facts, are "thick" particulars, concrete ingredients or elements in the passing scene'.[18] In short, the objects of knowledge are concrete individuals and the particular events and states of affairs in which these individuals are involved.[19]

If we look back at the traditional views discussed in Part I, we are reminded that, according to famous passages of Plato's *Republic*, knowledge and belief are directed to two different kinds of objects: 'what is' versus 'what both is and is not'

[11] Vendler 1972; Holton 2017: 251–2. For a recent criticism of Vendler's position from the point of view of the relationship between knowledge and truth in Plato, see Rowett 2018: 34–40.

[12] Vendler 1972: 82–4; see also 112–14.

[13] See also Slote 1974: 98–100 (to whom, Hyman notes, the proposal that a fact is the truth of a proposition is originally due) and Fine 1982: 52. Other philosophers equate facts, truths, and true propositions (e.g., Alvarez 2010: 3).

[14] Hyman 2017: esp. 281–3. I will return to this issue in sect. 10.1.3 below: 'Facts and Truths'.

[15] Cf. Ayers 2019: 95–129 (here esp. p. 117).

[16] Ayers 2019: 129.

[17] Ayers 2019: 123: as 'timeless or eternal entities, existing nowhere in particular', facts (like propositions) 'are not convincing candidate denizens of the physical, natural, concrete world'.

[18] Ayers 2019: 125.

[19] Ayers 2019: 124: 'Particular events and states of affairs are therefore significantly better candidates for being what in the world we have in the end 'latched onto' or apprehended when we have knowledge of the world.' Cf. Brewer 2011: 139–40, arguing that conscious acquaintance is 'a fundamental perceptual relation between subjects and mind-independent physical objects from a given point of view... which is more basic than any relation with facts, propositions or contents concerning the particular physical objects in question'.

(*Republic* 478a3–b2). *Mutatis* some important *mutandis*, Kant also held that, at least in some important cases, knowledge and belief have different objects: knowledge can be only of phenomena while noumena can be the object of belief. On the other hand, Aquinas agrees with Plato in drawing a sharp distinction in kind between knowledge and belief but leaves open the possibility that the object of knowledge may be, in some cases, the same as the object of belief ('it may happen', Aquinas writes, 'that what is seen or known [visum vel scitum] by one, is believed by another' ST IIa IIae, Q. 1, a. 5). Furthermore, there is a sense in which Plato too allows that knowledge and belief may have the same object: after all, some people know the road to Larissa, while others merely have a true belief about it. It seems that, in this case, the object of knowledge and true belief is the same.

What to make of all this? We have at least four candidate objects of knowing and/or believing: propositions, facts, truths, and concrete, particular individuals (with the attendant concrete, particular events and states of affairs in which these individuals are involved).[20] Furthermore, among those who embrace a distinction in kind between knowledge and belief, there seem to be a disagreement and/or oscillation on whether knowledge and belief may or may not have the same object.

10.1.2 Propositions

In the search for a resolution of these questions, I propose to start with a clarification of what propositions, facts, and truths are supposed to be. According to contemporary usage (as summarized by the *Stanford Encyclopedia*), propositions 'are the sharable objects of [propositional] attitudes [that is, they are what is believed, doubted, and so on] and the primary bearers of truth and falsity. This stipulation rules out certain candidates for propositions, including thought- and utterance-tokens, which presumably are not sharable, and concrete events or facts, which presumably cannot be false.'[21] I follow the long tradition which shaped medieval and early modern teaching (including at Oxford and Cambridge) in thinking that propositions are the logical expression of a mental act of judgement. In turn, a judgement is the mental act by which

[20] In a more ancient/medieval vein, one could add also intelligible Forms and/or universals. However, on the one hand, Platonic Forms can be understood as concrete, determinate individuals. If, on the other hand, they are understood as universals, on my account, universals do not exist as such either in concrete individuals or by themselves. That is, 'universal forms' (or the intelligible essences of things) are not found *in re* as universals, although they have a foundation *in re*. In brief, universality is the way in which the intellect grasps what things are by abstracting from the singular mode of being things have in their extra-mental existence (see Chap. 8, sect. 8.1.2). Universality so understood, as well as ideal and imaginary entities, will be covered by my positive proposal on the objects of knowledge and belief in sect. 8.2 below.

[21] McGrath and Frank 2018.

something is affirmed or denied. It is a property of this affirmation or negation to be true or false.[22]

Now, as the logical expression of judgements, propositions are more fundamental, and at least conceptually distinct from their linguistic expression in sentences and, a fortiori, from the verbal expression of the latter in utterances, speech acts, or in writing (for example, different sentences in two different natural languages may express the same proposition).[23] If we take truth as the conformity of thought to how things are, however, truth is already relevant to something more primitive than propositions, namely, to the mental act of judgement of which the proposition is the logical expression. It follows that the primary bearer of truth and falsity is thought itself and the relevant mental acts of judgement, rather than propositions.[24] Furthermore, truth and falsity seem also relevant to non-propositional or pre-propositional basic forms of proto-judgement and discrimination.[25] Aquinas notes, for instance, that 'truth and falsity are said to be in the sense, as in the intellect, inasmuch sense clearly judges [iudicat] the being of what is, or is not'.[26] Interestingly, a long-running controversy in Aristotelian studies is whether Aristotle himself, in *Metaphysics*, Book 9, 10 (*Θ* 10), commits to the view that episodes of intuition which consist in an immediate and non-propositional grasp of entities may be regarded as true. Traditional interpretations read this text as claiming that also simple thoughts lacking the complexity of judgements involve truth: namely, a simple thought is true insofar as it 'touches', that is, grasps, the corresponding entity.[27] Other interpretations read instead the claims in *Metaphysics Θ*10 as implicitly involving existential judgements, thereby bringing back also mental acts of simple apprehension under the general Aristotelian doctrine that truth and falsehood depend on composition and division.[28] On either interpretation, the key point, however, still stands: truth and falsehood is first of all relevant to the mental acts themselves and only derivatively to the abstract, sharable logical entities which express them.

[22] See Burgersdijk 1660: 118–19; Vanni Rovighi 1962: 71.

[23] As Marcus remarks (1995a: 238), for Frege, propositions (*Gedanken*) are 'the abstract nonmental contents of sentences toward which we have mental attitudes'; for Jerry Fodor (1975, 1981), 'attitudes toward propositions are in fact attitudes towards formulas in "mentalese", the language of thought, formulas that are internally codified and are correlated with the external sentences of a given language'.

[24] See Crivelli 2022: 599–600 and Crivelli 2004: 45 for a list of passages indicating that, according to Aristotle, truth and falsehood apply not only to linguistic expressions but also to mental states or acts such as thoughts, perceptions, and episodes of *phantasia*. More generally, Aristotle famously states that 'falsity and truth are not in things . . . but in *thought*' (1027b 25–7; my emphasis).

[25] I agree in this respect with Brentano that *Urtheil* ('judgment'), understood as the basic mental act of acknowledging or denying the existence of a presented object, is, in itself, non-propositional. Cf. Textor 2017b: 5.

[26] Aquinas, *Quaestiones disputatae de veritate*, q. 1, a. 11 co.

[27] See Crivelli 2022: 603–4.

[28] Cf. Chap. 9, sect. 9.1.1 for Reid's view that the most primitive mental acts already have implicit a judgment of existence of what is perceived.

All of this is not to deny that fully developed human cognition is, typically, propositionally structured, or that a necessary condition of abstract, complex, or higher-order judgements (for example, judgements *about* truth and falsity, validity and logical consequences) is their articulation through logical, quasi-linguistic, and linguistic entities.[29] But my point is that, as sharable logical entities, propositions are at least one step further removed from the most basic bearers of truth and falsity, namely, the mental acts of judgement and proto-judgement. This is most clearly shown by non-human animals, infants, pre-verbal children, and adults with severely limited or virtually non-existing abilities for abstract expression who are nevertheless perfectly capable of judging competently of many particular things, as manifested by their behaviour.

One could object that lack of linguistic expression by these agents does not show that the relevant judgement, manifested in their behaviour, is non-propositional, but only that they make propositionally structured judgements but cannot express them verbally. What matters for propositional structure, one could argue, is internal codification in the language of thought (Fodor's 'mentalese') and not its expression in the sentences of some natural language. My reply is that what matters for propositional structure is the formation of abstract concepts and their combination in abstract logical entities such as propositions. Insofar as cognitive subjects can exercise such abstraction, they can think propositionally whether or not they are able to express verbally their abstract thinking (there is no doubt that a great deal of disabilities concern verbal expression rather than the ability of making propositionally structured judgements). The crucial point is, however, that the capacity for competent judgement and discrimination outstrips the capacity for abstract thinking and hence propositional structuring: severe learning disabilities which impair the capacity for abstract thought still don't impair all capacity for judging competently about particulars, that is, present, concrete states of affairs or present concrete individuals. Similarly, there are stages of human development in which human cognizers start by judging about present, concrete particulars and only later acquire abstract concepts, just as there are non-human animals which are incapable of abstract thinking but are nevertheless capable of cognition.

The upshot is that the most basic judgements and proto-judgements involving truth (qua conformity with how things are) are not, or need not be, expressed propositionally and that, therefore, judgement and proto-judgement is not essentially propositional, irrespective of whether fully developed human cognizers may

[29] Cf. Marcus 1995a: 241–2.

then use propositions to articulate and describe even the most basic judgements and proto-judgements involving only particulars.[30]

10.1.3 Facts and Truths

What about facts? As Hyman notes in his insightful discussion of facts,[31] the first thing to ask is whether facts are concrete or abstract entities. Bertrand Russell's *The Philosophy of Logical Atomism* and Austin, for instance, conceive of facts as distinct from true propositions and thoughts; facts make propositions true. Some propositions, for example, the proposition that Socrates died are made true by 'physiological occurrences', other propositions require facts that 'combine' particulars and universals. On the other hand, Frege and Strawson conceive of facts as a kind of proposition or thought. For them, a fact is a 'thought which is true' (Frege),[32] or a true proposition, or a truth (Strawson).[33] Against the common identification between true propositions and facts, Hyman argues that a fact is an abstract object of a second-order level of abstraction: according to him, a fact is the truth *of* a proposition. In short, 'a fact is a truth', but 'a truth is not the same thing as a true proposition'. More precisely, a fact is 'an abstract particular, a trope or mode, albeit with an abstract bearer, an instance of the property of being true'.[34]

Similarly, when it comes to 'truths', it is important to clarify whether 'a truth' is an abstract or a concrete entity. If 'a truth' is conceived as some property, occurrence, event, situation, or state of affairs out there in the world in virtue of which a proposition is true, then 'a truth' is a concrete entity.[35] We would be looking in this case at ontological or metaphysical truth, or at the foundation of logical truth (or at the so-called truth-maker) rather than at logical truth.[36] If 'a truth' is conceived instead as the property of being true of a proposition, or is simply identified with a true proposition, we would be conceiving 'a truth' as an abstract entity and we would be dealing with logical truth.

In what follows, I will adopt the distinction prevalent today between facts and events/states of affair, where facts are conceived as a-temporal, abstract objects, and events/states of affairs as spatio-temporal concrete particulars. Moreover,

[30] Cf. Rowett 2018: 40, arguing that 'we should not confine truth and falsity to propositions, but should allow that all kinds of representations can be assessed for truth, just insofar as they have intentionality, and that includes pictures and maps as well as linguistic descriptions'.

[31] Hyman 2017.

[32] As already mentioned, according to Frege, a *Gedanke* is the abstract content expressed by a sentence (*Satz*) or the sense (*Sinn*) of a sentence (see Frege 1918–1919: 61).

[33] See Russell 2010: 7, 9–10; Russell 1940: 154, 284–5; Austin 1979: 104; Vendler 1972: 82–4, 112–14; Frege 1977: 25; Strawson 1998: 403. Texts identified and quoted by Hyman 2017: 269, 273–4.

[34] Hyman 2017: 281–2. See pp. 277–81 for a defence of the distinction between true propositions and facts.

[35] See Ayers 2019: 99.

[36] On the distinction between ontological and logical truth, see Chap. 9, sect. 9.1.4.

I will focus on 'truth' as logical truth, that is, as the property of thought, or of judgement, or of a proposition, of being true.

10.2 Knowledge, Belief, and Their Objects

On the basis of these clarifications, I can turn now to what is, on my account, the object of knowledge and the object of belief. Once again tracking 'the standard contemporary usage', the entry on propositions of *The Stanford Encyclopedia* explains that 'object of belief' refers 'to what is believed, rather than to the entity or entities the belief is intuitively *about*. So, for instance, when I believe that Ford pardoned Nixon my belief is about Ford and Nixon but not about the proposition that Ford pardoned Nixon. This proposition, rather, is what I believe.'[37] I suggest, first of all, that this distinction between 'what is believed' (or 'what is known') and the entity or entities the belief (or knowledge) is *about* is a disguised version of a broader position which should be abandoned, namely, the position which posits a tertium quid (in this version, propositions) between cognizer and cognized.[38]

Second, as suggested above, propositions are the logical expression of a mental act of judgement. Now, it seems clear that the object of knowledge (what one knows) and/or the object of belief (what one believes) is not the mental judgement itself, but what the judgement is *about*. Moreover, the judgement may be expressed in a proposition but is not normally about the proposition. A fortiori it is not normally about a second-order abstract object either, such as the truth of a proposition.[39] My proposal is that the immediate object of knowledge (what one knows) are objects in themselves.

10.2.1 Objects in Themselves

In Chapter 8, sect. 8.3, I have concluded that there are two ways of considering an object (defined as anything which a cognitive subject perceives as other than the subject): as the object is in itself (that is, according to its formal reality, whatever that is), and insofar as it is cognized. Regarding the first way of considering an object, I have endorsed a tradition according to which all mind-independent things are concrete, fully determinate individuals. Likewise, all their properties, and all events and states of affairs in which they are involved are particular and fully determinate. In the epistemological cognitive order, these individuals (and the concrete events and states of affairs in which they are involved) are the

[37] McGrath and Frank 2018, note 1. [38] On positing a tertium quid see below, sect. 10.3.

[39] As mentioned above, there are of course special cases (e.g., knowing the properties of categorical propositions).

primary objects of knowledge. When one knows or believes that this iron is hot, the object of one's knowledge or belief is not primarily a logical entity, although what one knows or believes is expressed and communicated through a logical construction constituted by a subject, a copula, and a predicate. The object of one's knowledge or belief is the reference of the term which appears as logical subject in the proposition: that is, a concrete individual bearing the particular, concrete property of being hot.

Our grasp of these individuals (and the attendant events and states of affairs) is, however, *indeterminate*. According to the tradition I follow, purely sensory cognition can grasp only very limited aspects of objects, depending on the different sensory faculties of the different kinds of beings capable of perception, and on their specific circumstances. Another way to put this point is to acknowledge the essential role in perception of the position and perceptual circumstances of the cognizer in determining the mode of presentation of the cognized object.[40] Intellectual cognition also grasps non-sensible aspects of an object but via the abstraction from their singularity, that is, via the formation of concepts which are predicable of a plurality of individuals.[41] This means, in short, that knowledge of mind-independent things is always *inadequate*, in the technical sense of never being able to exhaust the *adaequatio intellectus ad rem* in which logical truth consists.[42] This inadequacy is manifested by the radical partiality of sensory knowledge and, most importantly, by the very *abstractness* (that is, abstraction from the singularity of fully determinate individuals) of intellectual knowledge. Mind-independent, individual objects as cognized are, ontologically, nothing else than the fully determinate objects or states of affairs themselves (apples, trees, explosions, rain showers...) but under the mode of being of being cognized. Despite the partiality and abstractness—in a word, despite the *indeterminacy*—of their mode of being as cognized, the immediate objects of knowledge are still these fully determinate individuals (and the events, states of affairs in which they are involved) and *not* the abstract entities (concepts, propositions, properties of propositions) by which this inadequate knowledge is expressed.

Mind-independent individuals are not, however, the only kind of objects which may be objects of cognition. There are also objects (defined, once again, as anything which a cognitive subject perceives as other than the subject) which exist only as thought: these are, for instance, the abstract objects of mathematics (for example, an ideal triangle) or imaginary objects (a centaur, the god Jupiter). These abstract objects, with their own formal reality (whatever that is), can also be immediate objects of knowledge. When someone grasps the properties of an ideal

[40] Brewer 2011 and 2020–2021 strongly defend the view that enabling conditions (that is, a person's position and orientation and her particular perceptual circumstances) are essential to the metaphysics of conscious perceptual experience itself.

[41] See Chap. 8, sect. 8.2. [42] See Chap. 9, sect. 9.1.

square triangle, the object of knowledge is the ideal square triangle itself with its properties. Ditto for logical principles such as the principle of non-contradiction: when someone understands that A is not not-A, the object of knowledge is the principle itself, in its own formal reality, whatever that is.

In other words, I propose that knowing something implies being appropriately related to the thing itself. In the case of concrete, mind-independent entities, it implies being appropriately related to these entities and the concrete states of affairs in which they are involved. I do not dispute that, in fully developed human cognition, one's relation to these entities is, typically, expressed by propositions. But that does not mean that, therefore, what one is 'appropriately related to' when one knows that *p* is a proposition, as opposed to things themselves. A proposition, I suggest, is analogous to a picture. It represents or expresses a certain aspect of a given individual or state of affairs (for example, that 'Gandhi wears glasses'), analogously to the way in which a portrait of Gandhi is a visual representation of Gandhi. What the portrait represents, what the portrait is a portrait of, is a concrete individual, and not a visual representation of a concrete individual. Likewise, to know that *p* involves the proposition *p*, but what one knows is not a proposition; what one knows is some particular property of the concrete individual Gandhi which *p* represents or expresses.[43]

10.2.2 Putative States of Affairs

What about the object of belief? I propose that belief may or may not have the same object as knowledge depending on whether the sort of cognitive contact required by knowledge is or is not in principle available. The first case is that of objects and states of affairs which are in principle knowable (for example, an apple, an explosion, the road to Larissa, or the properties of an ideal square triangle). Such knowledge, although in principle possible, may be unavailable to a cognitive subject due to subjective reasons (for example, due to some specific circumstances of that subject which may be, in turn, temporary or structural). For instance, although it is in principle possible to know a state of affairs involving the presence of SARS-CoV-2 in the respiratory system of a patient, the doctor may be unable to know due to the lack of appropriate testing facilities; on the other hand, the doctor may hold a true belief, justified by typical Covid-19 symptoms such as high fever and persistent dry cough, that the patient does have the virus. In this case, the object of knowledge and belief will be the same (namely, a certain state of

[43] This paragraph is inspired by Alvarez's insightful discussion of a portrait of Henry VIII and of the propositional content that 'JFK has been shot' (Alvarez 2010: 151). It seems to me that the conclusion of her discussion regarding mental representations ('having the belief that p might involve having a mental representation of "the propositional content that p", but what you believe is not "a mental representation of the content that p"') applies *pari passu* to propositions.

affairs) but the way in which assent to the relevant state of affairs is determined is different.

More generally, the object of belief will be putative entities and states of affairs which may or may not correspond to 'what is'. A dog looking for food in various places does not believe the proposition: 'there is some food somewhere'. Assuming at least the range of cognitive faculties already acknowledged by the Aristotelian–Scholastic tradition in more evolved types of non-human animals,[44] what the dog is doing is exercising a faculty of proto-judgement (the *aestimativa* of the Scholastic tradition), based on past direct sensory experience (that is, based on past cognitive contact with 'what is') which is retained through sensory memory and the faculty of imagination (the *phantasia* or *imaginatio* thanks to which images of currently absent objects are preserved). According to this tradition, none of this involves universals or concepts, and insofar as propositions require concepts, none of this involves propositions either. Moreover, even if advances in the study of animal cognition were to reveal that the most developed non-human animals are capable of conceptual thought, the point is that there will still be less evolved non-human animals incapable of conceptual thought and yet capable of proto-judgement or discrimination about particulars. In such cases, I take the object of belief to be an imagined (as opposed to conceived) states of affairs involving the image/memory of a particular piece of food.

There are, furthermore, also putative objects or states of affairs which are not even in principle knowable (at least by human beings), such as the winner of a future Formula One championship, Kantian Noumena, or, more generally, all cases in which p is true but unknowable due to the structural limits of our discrimination powers or to its being now too late to find out what was the case at a given time in the past (for example, how long was the finger nail on my left index finger one year ago, assuming no one bothered, at the time, to record its measure in any way).[45] Such putative objects or postulated states of affairs, although they cannot be objects of knowledge, may be objects of belief. In many, if not all, such cases, the objects of belief may be conceived (rather than merely imagined) objects and/or states of affairs which, once again, may or may not correspond to 'what is'.[46]

Finally, may imagined and/or conceived entities and states of affairs also be objects of knowledge or are they solely objects of belief? I propose that they may be also objects of knowledge. One may know, for instance, that centaurs are purely imaginary entities although someone else may (falsely) believe that they have mind-independent reality. The one who knows would have latched on to centaurs

[44] Cf. Chap. 8, sect. 8.1.1.

[45] See Williamson's 'unknowable truths' (Williamson 2000: 18–20).

[46] I use 'conceived' here in a broad, non-specifically Kantian sense.

as they are in themselves, according to their own formal reality—that is, as purely imaginary entities which have no other existence than as imagined or thought.

To conclude, it seems to me that imagining or, a fortiori, conceiving putative states of affairs is a more evolved stage of cognition than the most basic ability to make cognitive contact with what is present in one's immediate environment.[47] Therefore, also from a purely evolutionary point of view, believing presupposes knowing (taken here in its most primitive and basic versions as the presence of an *aliud* to a perceiver). By the same token, believing marks an evolutionary step forward in the cognitive abilities of limited, perceiving beings, greatly extending their cognitive grip beyond what they are able, strictly, to know.

10.2.3 An Object-Centred View and Its Naturalism

This proposal agrees in some respects with the 'object-centered account' defended in the 1990s by Ruth Barcan Marcus, according to which believing is not to be understood as an attitude of agents to propositions (or other linguistic or quasi-linguistic entities)—as proposed, for instance, by Donald Davidson—[48] but as a relation between a subject or agent and a possible state of affairs which may or may not be actual, and where the constituents of states of affairs may be ordinary individuals, properties, and relations. This account, I take it, is not inconsistent with saying that in developed human beings these beliefs are propositionally structured. But the point is that believing is not to have an attitude to the propositions in which beliefs are structured but to be related to a possible state of affairs.

Marcus is explicit in noting the naturalistic advantages of her view since it provides a plausible route for attributing beliefs to 'non-lingual' and 'pre-lingual' agents such as animals and infants. Moreover, as she notes, it allows us to account for non-verbal responses among lingual agents which may uncover unconscious beliefs (that is, I take it, actually held beliefs which are not structured in propositions although they could become so structured if they were to become conscious).[49]

She denounces, on the other hand, the anti-naturalism of alternative accounts which construe cognition as the attitude of an agent to linguistic or quasi-linguistic entities. As she points out, invoking a 'mentalese' does not escape the failings of such language-centred proposals: 'These accounts exclude belief attributions to non-language-users or, alternatively, insist that *if* one can make such

[47] Cf. Phillips et al. 2021 for the striking results reached in the field of cognitive science.

[48] For Davidson (1982: 321, 324) thoughts are propositional attitudes, and among these propositional attitudes belief 'plays a central role'.

[49] See Marcus 1990/1995a, 1995b.

attributions and if the manifestations of a public language are absent, the language of thought sententially organized must indeed be there in the nonverbal child or the dumb animal's mind or brain.'[50] Indeed, if one holds (like Davidson 1982) that thoughts and beliefs are propositional attitudes for which language is required, one eventually arrives to the conclusion that non-language users cannot even have thoughts ('only creatures with speech have thoughts' Davidson 1975/2001: 167; 'a creature cannot have a thought unless it has language' Davidson 1982: 322)[51]—a conclusion surely implausible to most people who have had any substantial dealings with infants, pre-verbal toddlers, and persons with severe learning disabilities impairing language acquisition.

10.3 Say No to Representational Content

In Chapters 8 and 9, I answered the question of which kinds of entities are involved in cognition by proposing an ontology which has objects, acts, and faculties as its three main categories. There is no need, I suggest, for an additional ontological category: mental or representational content. Although it may be useful, in certain contexts, to treat the object and the content of cognition as conceptually distinct, this is a mere distinction of reason. This is not to downplay the enormous importance of distinctions of reasons but to warn against the reification of mental content. Mental content, I contend, is ontologically fully reducible to objects and acts.

10.3.1 Being Thought as a Mode of Being of Things

The claim that the immediate or direct object of awareness of the subject are mind-dependent 'internal objects' is nowadays in retreat, at least as a version of the early modern 'way of ideas'.[52] There is, however, another manner in which mental content is central to present-day orthodoxy or near orthodoxy, namely, in the form of representational content. The defining feature of this position—labelled by Brewer 2011 'content view' (CV)—is to account for our experience of mind-independent physical objects directly in terms of its representational content. Rather than maintaining—as in the rival 'object view' (OV) position—that perceptual experience is most fundamentally to be construed as a relation of

[50] Marcus (1990/1995a: esp. 237–8, 1995b). 'Dumb' is defined by Davidson 1982: 323 as 'incapable of interpreting or engaging in linguistic communication'.

[51] Furthermore, according to Davidson, having beliefs and thoughts require having the *concepts* of belief and thought, and having these concepts require language (cf. Davidson 1975/2001: esp. 170; 1982: 324).

[52] See Brewer 2011.

acquaintance with mind-independent physical objects (the direct objects of our perception), CV theorists maintain that perceptual experience is constituted by our *representations* of things, that is, by how things look (appear) to us.[53] In the terms of Sellars's famous 'myth of the given', there is no such thing as acquaintance with a given direct object of perception.[54] Thus, although prevalent representationalist positions reject the existence of 'internal objects', perceived objects are always, in some important sense, mental constructions. There is no such thing as a cognitive contact with things in themselves, simply open ('given') to us in perception (albeit always in a radically partial and incomplete way). As regards the objects of sense-perception, the 'content view' is in its spirit, if not always in its letter, a neo-Kantian outlook.[55]

By my lights, the problem with this account is the following. If perceived objects are, in some deep sense, mental constructions and never 'given', I do not see how the postulation of a tertium quid (the mentally constructed, perceived objects) between cognizer and cognized can be avoided—and such a tertium quid always implies, I contend, a gap between mind and world which cannot ultimately be bridged. By contrast, according to the account I recommend, the fact that our grasp of objects is radically partial and inadequate does not imply that cognized objects are mental constructions—cognized objects are still objects presenting themselves ('given') to us in their own formal reality, but grasped in an indeterminate way (or, as the early modern would say, 'confusedly' cognized). This last remark leads to a crucial claim, namely, the claim that there is a mode of being of things which is that of being perceived or thought. This is a mode of being of things themselves as perceived and not a mental content representing (constructing) a perceived object.

10.3.2 Presentation Versus Re-Presentation

Furthermore, granting (at least for the sake of argument) the existence of mind-independent objects, construing perceptual experience or cognition as representations of these mind-independent objects still misses the key explanatory element, namely the explanation of how the mental content can represent the mind-independent object. A content can represent something to me only if I am already acquainted with this something. If I see the portrait of Gandhi without already being acquainted with what Gandhi looks like, this portrait will not

[53] See Brewer 2011: esp. chap. 4 (here note 2), chap. 5, and chap. 6. Brewer argues for OV against CV.

[54] Sellars 1956/1963 and Brewer 2011: 138–42.

[55] Cf. in particular John McDowell's (1994) conceptualist approach to perception and perceptual knowledge. For a tightly argued critique underpinned by the invitation to reverse the Kantian turn, and look back at Aristotle, see Ayers 2019: chap. 3.

represent Gandhi to me. It will represent to me only what I am already acquainted with (say, men wearing round glasses).[56] The point is that only what has at some point already manifested or presented itself can be *re*-presented, that is, *presented again* via some 'content'. What still needs explaining is this very phenomenon of an original 'presentation'. To take a leaf from Hobbes's *De Corpore*, what still needs explaining is the most admirable (*admirabilissimum*) among of all phenomena, namely the *φαίνεσθαι*, the 'manifesting' or 'showing itself' of something.[57]

One way to reply would be to say that what is originally *presented* to us are only the representational contents. The perceiving subject does not need to match them, as it were, with mind-independent objects—not least because such matching is not only unnecessary but also impossible. As long as representational contents de facto re-present mind-independent objects, the subject is just fine with her representational contents even if she does not know (and cannot know) that they truly re-present.

This line of argument (which is not miles away from externalism broadly conceived)[58] still does not explain the key point, namely: what is this phenomenon of presentation, what is this 'being present' of something, whatever this something is?[59] The explanation of this phenomenon, I suggest, is that there is a primitive openness of the perceiving being or thinking being to something other than itself of which the perceiving or thinking being is phenomenologically aware as other than itself.[60] If a distinctive feature of perceiving beings is their primitive openness to the 'other' than themselves, there is a significant explanatory advantage in starting with the assumption that this 'other' *is* what it is manifesting itself as being.

10.3.3 Broken Sticks and Fake Barns

The assumption that what is presenting itself in a certain way is in fact that way is of course in principle defeasible.[61] The sort of perceiving/thinking being of which we have direct experience—the human being—is aware of the possibility of illusion and hallucination, that is, is aware that what is presenting itself as a

[56] See Frege 1918–1919: 60 and Millar 2019: 78.

[57] Hobbes, *De Corpore* IV, 25, 1. Cf. Vanni Rovighi 1963–1979: 347.

[58] That is, as the view that a subject not only need not but cannot be aware of some of the conditions of knowing.

[59] Cf. Arnauld's objections against the conception of ideas as *être représentatif*, discussed above, Chap. 7, sect. 7.3.2. A very similar point is made by Cook Wilson 1926: 803, cited by Marion 2016.

[60] See above, Chap. 6. McDowell 1994: 111 grants that perceptual experience is a form of 'openness to the world'. For an illuminating discussion of 'the ordinary conception of perceptual experience' in terms of two central aspects—*Openness* and *Awareness*—see Crane and French 2017. Crane and French propose to read the major theories of experience in the last century as responses to the challenge raised by perceptual illusion and hallucination against the ordinary conception of perceptual experience.

[61] Ayers 2019: 176.

broken stick in the water is not in fact broken (illusion), or that the oasis seen in the desert on certain occasions is not there at all (hallucination). The strange thing is that such cases have been used to cast sceptical doubt on human perception (to the point of rejecting perception as a way to put the sentient being into a successful cognitive contact with an external reality) rather than in support of its reliability.

First of all, as convincingly shown by Brewer, the possibility of illusions and hallucinations is consistent with the identification of the direct objects of perception with mind-independent physical objects. It is rather the 'content view' which is put under pressure by illusions and hallucinations.[62] Second, the very ability to identify (and learn) from erroneous judgements regarding what is present seems to me a sign of the remarkable resilience and sophistication of that openness to the 'other' which characterizes the sentient being. The error is not located in what is presenting itself to the sentient being, but in the latter's judgement about what is present. When an experienced and epistemically competent human being is presented with a stick which appears broken in a glass of water, she will judge that what is present is an unbroken stick which appears broken. If she is still unsure, there are additional strings to her cognitive bow, such as taking the stick out of the water to check, or waiting to be closer to the tower before passing judgement on its shape.

The same goes for the Fake-Barn County of Goldman/Ginet example.[63] When Henry, looking at the façade of the only real barn among dozens of mere barn façades dotting the region, forms the view that this is a barn, does he know that this is a barn?[64] On my account, Henry's perceptual encounter with an actual barn qualifies as his knowing that there is a barn there, that is, qualifies as having made cognitive contact with 'what is'. Had he been looking at one of the many fake-barn façades and formed the view that they were barns, he would have formed a justified but false belief. Is this making knowledge the result of chance? I do not think so. Rather, it is to take on board that knowing is, most fundamentally, the presence of 'what is' to a cognitive subject. Crucially, however, 'what is' presents itself to us only under partial and incomplete modes of presentation. Due to this radical incompleteness of its modes of presentation, and to the fact that we are fallible cognitive subjects, it is easy for us to misjudge what is really present and what is not. But we do have ways of confirming whether we know, or merely justifiably but falsely believe, something—and in the case of Fake Barn County, it would indeed be easy enough to find out. (In fact, it would be difficult to drive past a 2-D façade and still think it is a 3-D building....)

[62] See Brewer 2011: esp. chaps. 4 and 5.

[63] Goldman 1976. The original example is due to Carl Ginet (see Goldman 2009: 79). Needless to say, a very large literature has developed in response to this famous discussion.

[64] Thanks are due to Daniel Whiting for pressing me on this point.

What this ingenious example really tells us is that in sense-perception we always make contact with fully determinate individuals (be they real barns, mere barn-façades, or unbroken sticks which appear broken) but apprehend them in a radically incomplete way, and that on the basis of this very partial apprehension, we are normally remarkably successful, but never infallible, in our judgement of what is it that we have made contact with.

10.4 Cognition as the Progressive Determination of What Is Indeterminately Apprehended

To summarize—I contend that neither the objects of knowledge nor the objects of belief are normally or primarily propositions, although fully developed human knowledge and/or belief can be, and typically is, articulated and expressed by propositions. I propose that what one knows are objects in themselves, that is, objects as they are according to their formal reality, whatever that is. If these objects are mind-independent, fully determinate individuals (and the attendant fully determinate events and states of affairs in which these individuals are involved) our knowledge of them will always be *inadequate* and *indeterminate.* If they are abstract entities (such as mathematical or logical entities, or imaginary entities) our knowledge of them can be in principle adequate precisely in virtue of their abstract nature, although most people will still know them inadequately and indeterminately.

Acknowledging the typical indeterminacy of human knowledge of objects is the way to counter the 'problem of deduction' which may be raised against the claim that one knows objects and not propositions.[65] According to the 'problem of deduction', it seems that, if what one knows is an isosceles triangle, one knowing that the triangle has two sides of equal length should also know that the sum of its internal angles is 180°. However, this does not follow if the indeterminacy of human knowledge (which extends in most cases also to abstract objects which can be, in principle, adequately known) is fully taken on board. A consequence of this indeterminacy is also that people who know the *same* object will grasp it in different ways, that is, there will be different modes of presentation of the same object to different knowers (for example, inadequate or not fully determinate knowledge of Venus results in Venus being known by one person as Hesperus and by another person as Phosphorus).

As regards the object of belief, in some cases it may be the same as the object of knowledge, but assent to its being so-and-so will not be determined by a cognitive presence of the objects of cognition themselves but by reasons which are, as it

[65] On the 'problem of deduction', cf., for instance, Engel 1999: 215, 217.

were, extrinsic to the object (for example, the testimony of a trustworthy authority or the symptoms normally associated with an illness). To put it another way, in some cases, the object of knowledge and the object of belief may be the same (for example, the sum of the internal angles of a triangle, or a state of affairs such as the presence of SARS-CoV-2 in a patient); the difference between knowing and believing will be found in *how* one assents to this state of affairs rather than in *what* one assents to. In other cases—and, most importantly, when the putative entities/states of affairs are not even in principle open to the sort of cognitive contact with the object of cognition required by knowledge—the object of belief will be imagined or conceived entities and states of affairs which may or may not correspond to 'what is'.

Furthermore, I have claimed that the most fundamental mode of cognition, knowledge, is essentially the intentional presence or manifestation/presentation of things to a perceiving or thinking being. Assuming a realist metaphysical framework, the first, most basic form of the presence of things to a subject is sense-perception. That is, it seems plausible that the human animal starts its contact with the 'other' with the same kind of things from which all animals start: concrete, mind-independent, individual things. The Aristotelian–Thomist tradition calls this first cognitive contact *apprehensio simplex*, in which something is simply present to a cognitive subject in an indeterminate way. For this tradition, although in cognition we latch on to the only mind-independent, really existing beings—fully determinate individuals—we do not have an intuition of individuals in their determinacy.[66] Drawing inspiration from this account, I propose to construe cognition as a process of progressive determination of what is initially indeterminately (that is, confusedly) apprehended.

The behaviour of animals and pre-verbal children already manifests this process of progressive determination (for example, a cat alerted by almost imperceptible movement far away in the grass, approaching with care, and eventually pouncing on the mouse is manifesting a progressive determination of what is what, starting from the indeterminate apprehension of something moving in the grass, to the determination of it being a mouse; similarly for an infant progressing from an indiscriminate reaction to voices and noises to manifesting in her behaviour a discrimination between her mother's voice and other noises).

One could object, with Davidson, that the behaviour of these agents indicates discriminatory capacities but not belief.[67] And, of course, if one assumes, like

[66] Other medieval thinkers are more optimistic as regards human beings' knowledge of individuals: for the Franciscan tradition, individuals can be intuitively apprehended not only by the senses but also by the intellect.

[67] Davidson 1982: 326: 'A creature may react with the world without entertaining any propositions. It may discriminate among colors, tastes, sounds and shapes. It may "learn" that is, change its behavior in ways that preserve its life or increase its food intake. It may "generalize", in the sense of reacting to new stimuli as it has come to react to similar stimuli. Yet none of this, no matter how successful by my standards, shows that the creature commands the subjective–objective contrast, as required by belief.'

Davidson, that belief is a propositional attitude which requires the *concept* of objective truth, and denies (as I also do) that these agents entertain propositions or have the concept of objective truth, then none of these behaviours indicate belief. As I explained above, however, I do not think that knowing and believing are to be construed as propositional attitudes or require, at their most basic, having concepts (let alone having the concept of objective truth). Hence, by my lights, not entertaining any propositions or not having concepts is no bar to the attribution of knowledge (the awareness by a subject or agent of an actual state of affairs) or belief (the relation between a subject or agent and a possible state of affairs which may or may not be actual).

To be sure, rational beings with a developed capacity for verbal expression take this process of determination to a new level through their intellectual abilities. That is, the object of knowledge—which is present to the mind in the primitive contact between mind and world—is further determined through the affirmation of, or attribution to an individual of certain features which are discovered in different individuals by the intellect's capacity of abstraction. There is no doubt that for human beings who have reached the age of reason, a massive amount of what they know or believe is conceptually organized and propositionally structured. Crucially, however, the most basic knowing starts well before this stage with the confused or indeterminate apprehension of 'what is' in sense-perception.

Finally, in the progressive determination of what is indeterminately apprehended, most of what contributes to fully determining what this individual (or state of affairs) is, is not (and, in many cases, cannot be) present. For instance, if I have a tree in front of me, in my garden, in broad daylight, I may perceive a number of features of this tree (the colour and faint smell of its leaves, the sound of the rustling leaves, the roughness of its trunk when I touch it, and so on). I may also know that this tree was already here, in my garden, ten years ago. There are, however, infinitely more features of this tree which are not open to view, as it were: for example, how far its roots extend right now, how many acorns it has produced to date, or whether it will still be alive in a year's time. I may have very good reasons to suspect that the roots extend now under my neighbour's house over there, good reasons to estimate that it has already produced a million acorns, and good reasons to predict that it will be alive next year—but I do not strictly know any of this, at least not here and now. It is for this kind of questions (covering, in fact, a large swathe of territory one may wish to come to grips with in cognition) that another, specifically distinct mode of cognition is needed, namely, belief.

PART III
BELIEF
The Doxastic Family and Religious Epistemology

Introduction to Part III

III.1 A Crucial and Distinctive Cognitive Mode

As noted in the General Introduction to this book and at the end of Part I, a key aim of my proposal is to stress the crucial and distinctive contribution of belief to our cognition.[1] Belief, on my account, is a cognitive mental state in which a cognizer assents to a certain state of affairs being true or false. Although irreducibly distinct from knowledge, it is not (I claim) a 'botched' cognitive mode. Rather, belief accomplishes something different from knowledge, namely, it can extend our cognitive grip on reality and/or the world when (for objective or subject reasons) we are unable to know. It has its own standards (justification, degrees of probability, level of support by reasons, and so on) and when these standards are applied in a robust way, it enjoys remarkable success in tracking truth. Maintaining that the norm of belief is knowledge (that is, that one should believe *p* only if one knows *p*),[2] or that the norm of belief is 'sufficient' evidence (meaning by 'sufficient' a level of evidence high enough for the belief to count as knowledge if true),[3] misses, in my view, the distinctive and complementary task of belief: namely, aiming at truth when knowledge is not available. Overlooking the distinctiveness of belief's contribution is, I contend, another casualty of the conflation of knowledge and belief—a conflation still in place in versions of knowledge-first epistemology which regard belief as entailed by knowledge and (mere) belief as botched knowledge.[4] To put it another way, my account is an invitation to take fully on board what it means for belief to

[1] This aim, and some of the features of my position mentioned in this paragraph, distinguish my proposal from other present-day versions of knowledge-first epistemology, most importantly Williamson's.

[2] This view is supported by leading epistemologists, notably Williamson (2000: cf., for instance, p. 11). See also Adler (2002); Sutton (2005, 2007); Littlejohn (2013).

[3] The doyen of this position is Clifford (1879), although it has since reappeared under a variety of reincarnations.

[4] Cf. Williamson's version. Unlike Williamson, I claim that knowledge does not entail belief; I claim that the aim of belief is not (at least typically) knowledge; and my position implies a broadly non-externalist thrust. In brief, I take Williamson's position to be still too close to the (J)TB+ orthodoxy in so far as it does not distinguish belief and assent (one of two fundamental distinctions in my proposal), and consequently still conflates knowledge and belief (the other fundamental distinction in my proposal).

be an 'independent psychological phenomenon',[5] as well as for knowledge to be a 'new kind of state'.[6]

Part III is devoted to an exploration, in more detail, of belief and the doxastic family of cognate mental states for which 'belief' has been used as shorthand,[7] before turning, in the last two chapters, to a specific type of belief, namely, religious belief.

III.2 The Doxastic Family and the Epistemology of Testimony

In recent years, a great number of contributions have called attention to the existence of a variety of belief-like attitudes or 'bedfellows' of belief which appear to be close to and yet somehow different from belief.[8] Although several mental states in 'the neighbourhood of beliefs'[9] have been discussed (notably, assent,[10] holding true,[11] endorsement,[12] assertion,[13] commitment,[14] assumption,[15] acquiescence,[16] and alief[17]), two 'bedfellows' of belief have been singled out as especially hot topics: 'acceptance' and 'faith'.[18] Granted that belief is a complex phenomenon rather than one simple category, the problem remains of determining, first of all, what distinctive features belief is supposed to have; second, which mental states exhibit some but not all of these distinctive features; and third, whether these other mental states should be regarded as species of belief or as

[5] Fricker 2009: 58 (n. 59) notes that there is reason to doubt 'that the whole psychological phenomenon of belief can be fully explained, as Williamson suggests, as a "botched attempt at knowledge": instead it is a real, independent psychological phenomenon'.

[6] Williamson 1995: 563 and 2000: 47.

[7] See above, 'General Introduction'.

[8] Cf., for instance, Bayne and Hattiangadi 2013, where the expression 'bedfellows of belief' is used; Rott 2001, esp. chap. 1.1. on the 'menagerie of doxastic states'; and Engel 2012, on 'the doxastic family'.

[9] Cf. Engel 1999: 219: 'Such psychological states as accepting that P, taking it for granted, premising it, committing oneself to it, or postulating it, do not seem to be beliefs proper, although, we could say, they arise in the neighbourhood of beliefs and are belief-like attitudes.'

[10] For a discussion of 'assent' and its relation to 'belief' and 'acceptance', see Chap. 4, sect. 4.2.4-5. The notion of assent has been aired in some fairly recent literature (cf. De Souza 1971; Marcus 1990; Engel 1999; Schellenberg 2005: esp. 134–7) in ways which are significantly different from the way in which I use this notion, and which is chiefly inspired by certain historic traditions. Like all terms which have a long history, it is not surprising that the term 'assent' has been used by different authors to cover different things. Once again, what I am after are the cognitive modes themselves and not which terms have been historically used by this or that author to refer to them.

[11] Cf. Engel 1998.

[12] Cf. Frankish 2007.

[13] Cf. Reynolds 2011; Goldberg 2015; Nes 2016; Rizzier 2017; Scott 2017.

[14] Zamulinski 2008; Shaffer 2013; Tebben 2018.

[15] Swinburne 2005: 143; Howard-Snyder 2013.

[16] Buchak 2012.

[17] 'Alief' is introduced by Gendler (2008a, 2008b) to indicate a cognitive state more primitive 'than either belief or imagination' and which 'directly activates behavioral response patterns' contradicting one's conscious beliefs.

[18] See, for instance, Stalnaker 1984: chap. 5; Lehrer 1990; Cohen 1992; Bratman 1992; Alston 1996; Engel 1998, 1999, 2000; Swinburne 2005; Audi 2008, 2011: esp. chap. 3; Bishop 2007; Buchak 2014, 2017; Malcom and Scott 2017; Jackson 2019b.

some other kind of non-doxastic mental state. Disagreement on all of these questions is rampant.

A first main disagreement concerns the voluntariness versus involuntariness of belief. The involuntariness of belief remains a strong position, but so-called doxastic voluntarism has always had its advocates and is enjoying a notable come-back. Interestingly, much of the literature which argues for the difference between 'belief' and 'acceptance', starts by stating that belief is involuntary while acceptance is voluntary.[19] A doxastic voluntarist would, of course, not take this for granted.[20]

A second major disagreement regards the doxastic versus non-doxastic status of belief's 'bedfellows': being closely connected to one another does not per se answer the question of whether we are dealing with species of the same genus or with mental states which belong to different kinds. The very use of suggestive but vague metaphorical expressions such as 'bedfellows', 'neighbourhood', and 'menagerie' reflects the difficulty of ascertaining the nature of these mental states.

Notably, views divide on whether 'acceptance' is or is not a doxastic state. Those who regard involuntariness as a defining feature of belief, and voluntariness as a defining feature of 'acceptance', seem pushed to conclude that acceptance is not a doxastic state.[21] One encounters, however, more shades of grey in this area than the two combined claims above would seem to allow. In fact, there is an interesting reluctance in giving up the doxastic status of 'acceptance' altogether,[22] not least for the following reason: notwithstanding the voluntariness of acceptance acknowledged by most literature, it has been noted that many forms of acceptance appear to incorporate some degree of belief.[23]

A parallel disagreement regards the notion of 'faith'. In recent years, a sizable literature has been produced arguing that faith in not really a doxastic attitude. Against non-doxastic accounts of faith, defences of the view that faith belongs

[19] See, for instance, Engel 1998: 143, 146: 'I shall simply assume the following, more or less obvious things about beliefs. (1) Beliefs are involuntary... (1′) Acceptance is voluntary or intentional, unlike belief.' It turns out, however, that according to Engel 'although acceptance is distinct from belief, it rests upon it, and is therefore a species of belief' (1998: Abstract). The conclusion that acceptance (a voluntary state) is a species of belief seems hard to square with the 'more or less obvious' assumption, underpinning the paper, that 'beliefs are involuntary'.

[20] See, for instance, the important debate on whether there is an ought to believe *simpliciter*. Booth 2022 argues 'that on a deontological understanding of ought to believe there must be ought to believe *simpliciter* and that it is the violation of this ought that determines whether we are to blame for our beliefs' (Abstract).

[21] For instance, Cohen 1992 and Alston 1996 draw a firm line between belief and acceptance, regarding the former as involuntary and dispositional, and the latter as a voluntary mental act.

[22] A case in point is Engel 1998. See above, note 19.

[23] For instance, according to Vahid 2009, 'one can redescribe the cases that Alston invokes in support of his claim [that acceptance is an alternative to belief] in terms of the standard notion of degrees-of-belief without loss.... [H]is notion of acceptance, if not identical to belief, is at least a species of belief'; Audi 2011: 80 stresses 'a duality in the use of "accept". On one use, acceptance entails belief; on another, it does not.'

squarely in the doxastic family have been mounted.[24] More generally, debate remains buoyant on whether belief is a necessary and/or sufficient condition of faith (granting that faith may entail belief is obviously different from granting that faith must entail belief; and granting that faith must entail belief is obviously different from regarding belief as sufficient for faith).

I start my discussion of these issues by tackling the relationship between belief and will (Chapter 11). Here it will be maintained that satisfactory answers to the vexed question of whether belief is voluntary or involuntary, and, if it is involuntary, to the question of how we can bear moral responsibility for our beliefs, rest on the distinction between assent and belief proposed by this book. On the basis of this distinction, the following threefold account will be proposed: (1) belief is a spontaneous (that is, in this context, involuntary) response to epistemic reasons (reasons which concern the truth or falsity of the putative state of affairs which is the object of belief); (2) notwithstanding the spontaneity of belief, the will has a key role to play in determining assent; (3) acknowledging this role of the will does not amount to doxastic voluntarism. Finally, it will be suggested that, as a result of this account, a shift from an ethics of belief to an ethics of assent would be, in many cases, appropriate.

Chapter 12 turns to the epistemology of testimony. In line with the account of cognition developed in previous chapters, it will defend the view that testimony does not, *on its own*, produce individual knowledge, although it can, and often does, lead to individual knowledge. The importance of distinguishing between what is collectively known by a community of knowers and what is distributively known by each individual in that community will be stressed, as well as the importance of distinguishing between what a given individual, strictly speaking, knows and what the total successful cognition of that individual is. The latter includes not only knowledge but all cognition which reliably tracks truth. In this framework, I will outline the difference between intrinsic and extrinsic evidence. Finally, I will propose a modified global reductionism (inspired by both Hume and Reid) as my answer to the question of when and how testimony provides sufficient justification for belief.

Chapter 13 explores two historical proposals which offer, in my view, illuminating accounts of particularly significant members of the doxastic family, namely, Kant's taxonomy of belief and Aquinas's doxastic faith. Kant's distinction between three main types of belief (pragmatic belief, theoretical belief, and moral belief)—all three subsumed by him under the broader category of 'assenting' (*Fürwahrhalten*)—provides (I will claim) very valuable insights into the distinctive and irreplaceable contribution of belief to human cognition. In turn,

[24] On the debate over doxastic and non-doxastic faith see for instance Pojman 1986; Alston 2007; Jay 2015; Howard-Snyder 2016, 2018a, 2018b; Audi 2011: esp. 52–5, 58–60; Malcolm and Scott 2017; Ahmed 2020.

Aquinas's discussion of faith as a doxastic state has the merit (among others) of offering a unified account of faith in both its secular and its religious expressions. On the one hand, a unified account shows that, as a general phenomenon of human life which involves cognitive and conative aspects, faith may constitute a valuable (and even indispensable) element in the full range of human flourishing (think of faith that justice will prevail, or of faith in your friend, in humanity, and so on). On the other hand, a unified account of faith provides grounds for rejecting epistemic double-standards when it comes to the specific case of religious faith.

III.3 Religious Epistemology

Part III ends with a discussion of religious belief and with the application to religious epistemology of the account of knowledge and belief proposed in this book. I will maintain that a conception of knowing and believing as two irreducibly different cognitive modes is especially important in religious epistemology owing to its accounting for the distinctive epistemological status of religious belief. Conversely, it will be claimed that the project of showing that religious belief, with the addition of certain conditions, counts as knowledge, is misguided.

I will start by offering an interpretation and criticism of two vastly influential proposals that have transformed the landscape of twentieth-century Anglo-American religious epistemology, namely Reformed Epistemology (especially as expounded by its doyen, Alvin Plantinga) (Chapter 14), and William Alston's epistemology of religious experience (Chapter 15). Contrary to its direct realist posturing, I will suggest that Plantinga's Reformed Epistemology is best understood as a version of neo-Cartesianism according to which we can be rescued from a thoroughgoing scepticism about the reliability of our beliefs (including perceptual beliefs and rational intuitions) only in a theistic framework. Plantinga's claim that 'faith is knowledge' and that warranted Christian belief, if true, counts as knowledge, will be criticized as a version of fideism which, first of all, compromises the very notion of faith, and, second, is based on the analysis of knowledge as (J)TB+ that this book advocates rejecting. Chapter 15 turns to an evaluation of William Alston's view that putative perceptions of God can provide justification for certain beliefs about God. Notwithstanding agreement with some key features of Alston's brilliantly original proposal—such as the case made for the rejection of epistemic double standards and of epistemic imperialism—it will be objected that a Christian doxastic practice built on the perceptual model of a direct perception of God faces overriders from both its own internal overrider system and from independent philosophical reasons.

The chapter ends with the proposal of an alternative framework for religious epistemology to which the model of cognition defended in this book is applied. It will be claimed that a distinctive feature of religion is that of being primarily about matters in which the kind of direct cognitive contact required by knowledge is not available, at least as regards our natural cognitive abilities. Accordingly, when the object of cognition is some putative supernatural, noumenal entity, the appropriate cognitive model is belief rather than knowledge. Although some things may be known also in the domain of religion, I will contend that the specific epistemic status of what, in religion, is held by faith is belief, not knowledge. Finally, it will be claimed that, to be rationally held, also religious belief (as any other belief) needs reasons, including reasons of an epistemic kind.

11
Belief and Will

The aim of this chapter is to tackle the vexed question of the relationship between belief and will. Is belief voluntary or involuntary? And if it is involuntary, how can we have moral responsibility for our beliefs? I will endeavour to show that satisfactory answers to these questions require the distinctions between assent and belief, and between assent and acceptance, proposed by this book.[1]

The difference between assent and belief, I have suggested, is the following. Assent is the implicit mental 'yes' which may be either the compelled response to the 'evidentness', 'seeableness' of the object of cognition, or the mental 'yes' of a 'decision' (to use Cook Wilson's expression) which follows a process of deliberation in which reasons, signs, symptoms, testimony, pros and contra are weighted. The crucial point is that a 'yes'—insofar as it is a 'yes' and not mere entertaining or a suspension of judgement—is in itself 'simple and indivisible':[2] it is an indivisible mental affirmation that the matter is as we have judged it to be (for example, manifestly such-and-such, or uncertain, or doubtful, or fairly likely, or very probable, and so on). In brief, assent is an on/off state which should be distinguished from states which have degrees (that is, belief, credence, opinion, confidence, persuasion, conviction, suspicion, doubt, and so on).[3] By contrast, believing is the more specific mental state or mental act in which assent is not compelled by the presence of the object itself (in Austin's famous example, it is not compelled by the pig standing there plainly in view), but is moved by reasons extrinsic, as it were, to the object of cognition. Depending on the strength of these reasons, there will be lower or higher degrees of belief that the relevant state of affairs is such-and-such. In some cases, these reasons may be so strong as to force assent: such is the case in which one 'cannot but believe' that so-and-so is the case even if so-and-so is not directly presented. In many other cases, these reasons will ground degrees of belief not high enough to determine, on their own, assent to a certain state of affairs being so-and-so.

Moreover, I have argued, assent should also be distinguished from another on/off mental state, namely, acceptance, at least insofar as a distinctive feature of acceptance (as understood in most contemporary literature) is its voluntary

[1] For a discussion of these distinctions see in particular Introduction to Part I, sect. I.3, and Chap. 4, sect. 4.2.5.

[2] Aveling 1907.

[3] Newman 1870/1895: 176: 'there is no medium between assenting and not assenting'.

Thinking with Assent: Renewing a Traditional Account of Knowledge and Belief. Maria Rosa Antognazza, Oxford University Press. © Maria Rosa Antognazza 2024. DOI: 10.1093/oso/9780198831518.003.0012

nature. This voluntariness does not sit well with knowledge and high levels of confidence in belief, although (as we will see below) it seems to be related to low degrees of belief (aka low 'credences'). On my account, assent is therefore a broader category than acceptance: it covers both voluntary and involuntary aspects of cognition, and, as an indivisible mental 'yes', is relevant to both knowledge and belief.

On the basis of these distinctions, I will propose the following threefold account: (1) belief is a spontaneous (that is, in this context, involuntary) response to epistemic reasons (reasons which concern the truth or falsity of the putative state of affairs which is the object of belief); (2) notwithstanding the spontaneity of belief, the will has a key role to play in determining assent; (3) acknowledging this role of the will does not amount to doxastic voluntarism. An important consequence of this account, I will contend, is that a shift from an ethics of belief to an ethics of assent is, in many cases, in order.

11.1 The Indirect and the Direct Role of the Will

11.1.1 The Indirect Role of the Will in Determining Assent

Classic examples of philosophers embracing the non-voluntariness of belief include Locke and Leibniz. Both conceive belief as a non-voluntary response to epistemic reasons supporting the likeliness of a certain state of affairs.[4] Glossing Locke, Leibniz states in the *New Essays*: 'we never believe what we want but rather what we see as most likely'.[5] In 1684, he reiterates: 'opinion is not something which depends on the Empire of the will and which can be changed as one pleases'. And, again, in 1711: 'one does not have a belief at will'.[6] And yet, both Locke and Leibniz recognize that the will has a role to play. First of all, the will can influence belief *indirectly*. Locke notes that '*we can hinder both Knowledge and Assent*, by stopping our Enquiry, and not employing our Faculties in the search of any Truth';[7] and Leibniz warns that, despite the non-voluntariness of belief, 'we can make ourselves believe indirectly what we want by turning our attention away from a disagreeable object in order to apply ourselves to another which we find pleasing; so that by looking further at the reasons for the side which we favour, we end up by believing it to be most likely'.[8]

This account of how belief works seems to me very plausible, both in its stressing that one cannot believe things at will 'irrespective of truth

[4] See Locke, *Essay*, Book IV, chap. XX, 15–16; Locke, *Letter Concerning Toleration*, 39; see also Tully's intro. pp. 7–9.

[5] A VI, 6, 517.

[6] Respectively, A I, 4, 320 and GP III, 415. Cf. also GRUA 216.

[7] Locke, *Essay*, Book IV, chap. XX, 16.

[8] Leibniz, *New Essais*, Book IV, chap. XX, 16 (trans. Remnant and Bennett, p. 517, slightly modified).

considerations',[9] and in acknowledging, at the same time, the indirect influence of the will in belief's formation (an indirect influence which, it should be noted, applies also to knowledge). In fact, the thesis that 'agents have power to directly form beliefs for non-epistemic reasons' seems to me largely a strawman.[10] As far as I can see, an educated adult cannot simply start to believe at will that the earth is flat. If he forms such a belief, it will be for reasons which have to do with the alleged truth of this claim (say, some fake photographic 'evidence' posted on social media, or some Twitter conspiracy theory). While the indirect influence of the will can hardly be controversial (the adult in question *could decide* to check the epistemic reliability of his sources), I doubt that a direct voluntary formation of beliefs on purely non-epistemic grounds is even psychologically possible or is what even the most outspoken doxastic voluntarists have been really arguing for. As I understand it, Pascal's wager is not claiming that one can believe at will but that a previously 'dead' hypothesis may become 'live' (that is, may become, for that person, a genuine epistemic possibility) as a result of voluntarily taking up certain practices.[11] For instance, one may start to attend Hindu meditation classes without believing that there is a soul but eventually come to regard the existence of *Ātman* in every living being as a genuine possibility. The idea is that only in situations of rough epistemic parity (as opposed to situations of merely non-zero logical possibility) conative factors may tip the balance in favour of one or the other side.[12]

Nor is strong voluntarism needed for belief to be ethically praiseworthy or blameworthy. As many people (including Locke and Leibniz) recognize, since in the formation of belief the search for epistemically robust reasons is under voluntary control, failure to engage with one's epistemic duties may well be, in many cases, culpable. Furthermore, as Robert Adams has pointed out, 'many cognitive failures, though not voluntary, are ethically blameworthy'[13]—take the case, for instance, of someone sincerely believing, on the basis of his upbringing and of wide consensus in his community, that women are unfit for education or that his ethnic group is superior to all others.

[9] Frankish 2007: 526. Frankish rejects strong voluntarism (understood as the view that we can form beliefs at will, that is, (1) in a causally direct way, (2) in full consciousness, and (3) irrespective of truth considerations) but defends 'direct activism' (i.e., the possibility of direct active belief formation via an action of 'endorsement') and 'weak voluntarism' (i.e., the possibility of forming beliefs directly and for pragmatic reasons).

[10] According to Levy and Mandelbaum 2014: 15, this is the thesis for which the phrase 'doxastic voluntarism' is 'usually used'.

[11] See Pascal, *Pensées*, Fragment 418 and James 1896: 328: 'a live hypothesis is one which appeals as a real possibility to him to whom it is proposed'.

[12] Cf. Morris 1986: 443, and Jordan 2006, especially chap. 2. As far as I can see, this is in line with Frankish's distinction between having (epistemic) reasons sufficient to permit belief and having (epistemic) reasons sufficient to compel belief (Frankish 2007: 541). According to Frankish, in the former (but not in the latter) case, it is possible to form belief directly for pragmatic reasons (an action that he calls 'endorsement').

[13] Adams 1987: 9.

11.1.2 Epistemic Uncertainty and the Direct Role of the Will

The question, however, is still open of whether there is some other role played by the will in determining assent beyond the indirect influence on belief formation envisaged above. Even Locke, the chief 'evidentialist', acknowledges that there is. In the same paragraph in which belief is presented as a spontaneous response to epistemic reasons, he writes: 'in Propositions, where though the Proofs in view are of the most Moment, yet there are sufficient grounds, to suspect that there is either Fallacy in Words, or certain Proofs, as considerable, to be produced on the contrary side, there Assent, Suspense, or Dissent, are often voluntary actions'.[14]

Locke's point is again, very plausible and very important. There are many cases in which belief, as a spontaneous response to epistemic reasons, cannot by itself determine assent, that is, cannot by itself determine the implicit mental 'yes, this is how I judge things to be' which ends the process of judgement.[15] In these cases, both assent and suspension of judgement are voluntary actions. Now, a Cliffordian or neo-Cliffordian might say that, in these situations, the morally laudable action is to suspend judgement. According to Clifford's famous dictum, 'it is wrong always, everywhere, and for anyone, to believe anything upon insufficient evidence'.[16] In the same vein, an increasingly popular view states that the norm of belief is knowledge, and that knowledge just is one's evidence.[17] In brief, according to a Cliffordian or neo-Cliffordian ethics of belief, it is immoral to believe without sufficient evidence.

To this position I have two replies. First, Clifford is conflating belief and assent. Belief is non-voluntary. One cannot voluntarily withhold belief any more than one can believe at will. Belief is a spontaneous reaction to what, rightly or wrongly, one perceives as the available evidence. Of course, as we have just seen, this fact does not per se make belief morally blameless. The point is, however, that it is not belief itself which can be withheld at will. What Clifford is really thinking about is withholding assent in situations of rough epistemic parity or, at least, of genuine epistemic uncertainty.

Second, as William James and others have argued (to my mind, persuasively), withholding assent is, in many cases, neither practically possible nor morally laudable.[18] Provided one is faced with a genuine option—that is, in James's terms, an option which is live (it appeals as a genuine epistemic possibility), forced (one has to decide one way or the other), and momentous (something

[14] Locke, *Essay*, Book IV, chap. XX, 15.

[15] On my account, 'assent' covers also what Locke calls here 'dissent', that is, assent to not being the case that such-and-such state of affairs obtains.

[16] Clifford 1879: 186.

[17] Cf. Williamson 2000 (arguing, among other things, for the E = K thesis); Adler 2002; Sutton 2005, 2007; Littlejohn 2013.

[18] See James 1896.

important is at stake)—suspension of judgement may well be morally blameworthy. The whole policy of giving people the benefit of doubt is an example of a morally praiseworthy practice that is aimed precisely at resolving situations of rough epistemic parity not by withholding assent but by assenting to the state of affairs most favourable to the person involved (a typical situation in which one cannot withhold assent and applies instead the benefit-of-doubt rule is deciding on final marks of exam papers: how many times genuine epistemic uncertainties over borderline pass/fail exam answers are resolved by accepting that the answer is a pass? Examples could be multiplied).

At any rate, what is most important for the matter at hand is that, in situations of epistemic uncertainty, both assent and withholding of assent (that is, suspension of judgement) are determined by the will. What this means is that they are finally determined by conative as opposed to cognitive factors, that is, by factors such as hope, trust, wishes, drives—including the all-important drive towards self-preservation. Thus, although there are reasons to believe that the creaking, Indiana-Jones-style wooden bridge suspended over the gorge is safe (say, all the tourists in front of me have safely reached the other side), given the high stakes, I may still reach the view that it is unsafe to cross it. Likewise, if I hear roaring noises in the dark during my photographic safari, I may judge it imprudent to loiter further in the hotel garden even if I do not believe that there are lions in this particular area.[19] Hope may play a part in assenting to the view that racial discrimination will be defeated; trust in assenting to the innocence of your friend; and so on.

I suggest that a number of these cases map onto the mental act that the literature calls 'acceptance'. Many (although, I surmise, not all) cases of acceptance entail, in my view, some degree of belief, but this degree of belief is insufficient to explain a certain course of action. Take the only too-familiar cases of believing that one has locked the car but not being sure; suspecting that the train has already left the station; strongly doubting one will be able to catch the flight; believing that the patient does not have cancer but sending him to the hospital for a series of cancer tests. When one goes back to check the car, or rushes to the train station or to the airport, or sends the patient for tests, one shows acceptance (as opposed to belief) that the car is not locked, the train is not gone, the flight will not depart, or the patient has cancer. Many other examples are familiar from the literature. What these actions have in common is that they manifest assent to the obtaining of a state of affairs which outstrips purely doxastic considerations.

[19] It seems to me that it is not necessary to introduce the notion of 'alief' as an alternative to 'belief' (Gendler 2008a, 2008b) in order to explain behavioural responses contradicting one's conscious beliefs. Like other mental states in the doxastic family, such responses can be explained by a combination of tacit, inarticulate beliefs which lie below immediate consciousness, and conative/appetitive factors such as drives, likes, dislikes, and so on.

11.1.3 Theoretical Judgement and the Direct Role of the Will

One may wonder, at this point, if the direct role of the will is limited to determining assent for the practical purpose of guiding action in situations of epistemic uncertainty.[20] In what follows I will claim that the will also has a role in determining assent in *theoretical* contexts, and that acknowledging this role does not amount to endorsing doxastic voluntarism.

As the Oxford Realists point out, judgements and opinions—including, most importantly, theoretical judgements and opinions—are in themselves 'decisions'. The most natural sense of 'judging', Cook Wilson maintains, is that of a 'decision on evidence after deliberation' (Cook Wilson (1926): 1:108). Thus, 'a judgement is a decision. To judge is to decide. It implies previous indecision; a previous thinking process, in which we were doubting' (Cook Wilson (1926): 1:92–3). Likewise, opining is a sort of decision:

> It is a peculiar thing—the result of estimate—and we call it by a peculiar name, opinion. For it, taken in its strict and proper sense, we can use no term that belongs to knowing. For the opinion that A is B is founded on evidence we know to be insufficient, whereas it is of the very nature of knowledge not to make its statements at all on grounds recognized to be insufficient, nor to come to any decision except that the grounds are insufficient; for it is here that in the knowing activity we stop. (Cook Wilson (1926): 1:99–100)[21]

Their being 'decisions' indicate, in my view, the presence of a genuine volitional element. This volitional element does not consist in directly influencing belief or opinion, but in ending enquiry and reaching a decision. In many theoretically uncertain matters, one could in fact remain indefinitely in a state of 'unformed' thinking, as Aquinas would put it,[22] or in a state of mere 'entertaining', as we might put it. It is the conative element of our mental life, I suggest, that allows us to move on. This is the drive which explains change, progress, development in our thinking; this is the drive thanks to which we can implicitly say 'yes, this is how I judge this to be'.

Leibniz captures this intimate relationship between the cognitive and conative sides of mental life through his notions of perception and appetite. Appetite is, for Leibniz, 'the striving from one perception to another' (GP III, 575),[23] or 'the action of the internal principle which produces the change or passage from one perception to another' (*Monadology*, GP VI, 609). It is the natural tendency, impulse, or

[20] Accounts of acceptance generally link acceptance to practical deliberation (cf. Engel 1998: 145; Engel 1999: 219).

[21] See Marion 2016: sect. 3, where attention is drawn to these passages by Cook Wilson.

[22] Cf. Chap. 2, sect. 2.1.2.

[23] Cf. also Leibniz, *Principes de la Nature et de la Grace* (GP VI, 598).

striving which impels us to pass not only from one action to another but from one perception to another, from one thought to another, and so on.

For the Aristotelian tradition, it is this appetite (*appetitus*) that drives sensitive beings towards what is good for them, or what (at least) appears good to them.[24] In Aquinas's interpretation of the doctrine, the human, rationally guided brand of this drive is the will (defined as *appetitus intellectivus*).[25] Thus, for Aquinas, assent remains always an act of the *intellect*, but when this act is not compelled by 'clear sight', it is ultimately determined by an appetitive power which moves us to take a stance, end the enquiry, and assent to a certain state of affairs (for example, to it being likely that such-and-such, or it being doubtful, and so on).[26] As we read in the key passage of the *Summa* already quoted in the first section of Chapter 2:

> In another way, the intellect assents to something, not because it is sufficiently moved to this assent by its proper object, but through a certain voluntary choice turning toward one side rather than the other. And if this is done with doubt or fear of the opposite side, there will be opinion [opinio]; if, on the other hand, this is done with certainty [cum certitudine] and without such fear, there will be faith [fides]. (ST IIa IIae, q. 1, a. 4; my trans.)

The very fact that such 'decisions' may be accompanied by 'fear of the opposite side' shows that they are not meant to be irreversible. But the point is that it is the will which provides the drive necessary to decide and move on, as opposed to stagnating in a wholly implausible mental life of endlessly entertaining and not assenting due to the lack of 'clear sight [manifesta visio]' of what is what.

To summarize: the fact that, in highly probable cases or, in a more Humean vein, in cases of natural (incorrigible, instinctive) belief, assent and belief align makes their distinction often invisible. And yet, acknowledging that assent and belief are at least conceptually, if not always really, distinct, is the way to remove a number of pseudo-problems relating to the divide between voluntarism and anti-voluntarism. It is not belief per se which is voluntary. Belief is a spontaneous response to epistemic reasons. It comes in degrees from very low to very high, depending on the perceived strength of reasons, grounds, degree of probability, reliability of testimony, specificity of symptoms, and so on. In cases in which such spontaneous response is insufficient to determine assent, the latter may be determined by voluntary or appetitive factors such as hope, trust, wishes, drives. These are conative, not cognitive, factors that provide non-epistemic reasons for assent. Their being conative as opposed to cognitive, non-epistemic as opposed to

[24] Cf. Chap. 9, sect. 9.2.4. [25] ST IIa IIae, q. 24, a. 1.

[26] Cf. ST IIa IIae, q. 2, a. 2 and ST IIa IIae, q. 4, a. 1 (both quoted above in note 1, Chap. 2); Aquinas, *Scriptum super Sententiis*, lib. 3 d. 23 q. 2 a. 2, qc. 2, co.

epistemic, does not make them, per se, morally reprehensible any more than it makes them morally laudable. As there are good and bad epistemic reasons (that is, reasons which are or are not truth-conducive), so there are good and bad non-epistemic reasons (that is, reasons which advance or do not advance a genuine, as opposed to a merely apparent, good).

Furthermore, the role of the will in determining assent is not limited to practical deliberations but extends to theoretical 'decisions', that is, to our ability to close the process of theoretical (as well as practical) deliberation. Considered as the human version of the appetitive power which is proper of sensitive beings, the will constitutes the principle of movement of our mental life, the conatus moving us from mere entertaining to the implicit mental 'yes' which is essential to the activity of thinking. My claim is that, by recognizing the distinction between belief and assent, this model acknowledges the fundamental integration of the cognitive and conative aspects of mental life without invoking (weak or strong) doxastic voluntarism.

11.2 Belief, the Doxastic Family, and the Ethics of Assent

11.2.1 The Doxastic Family: Mental States Which Entail Belief but Do Not Reduce to Belief

On the basis of this model, I propose an account according to which the 'doxastic family' is constituted by belief and by other mental states which entail belief but do not reduce to belief. The latter are states which have belief as one of their elements in combination with other (typically conative) factors, such as hope, trust, desires, drives, love (love being construed, traditionally, as a form of appetite). Whether a mental state qualifies or does not qualify as a doxastic state will depend on its entailing or not entailing some degree of belief. On this account, notwithstanding their voluntary aspects, forms of acceptance which entail some degree of belief will qualify as doxastic states, while forms of acceptance which do not entail any degree of belief (if there are any such forms) will not qualify as doxastic states.[27] The same goes for faith. I take the view that faith normally entails some degree of belief, although it does not reduce to it. Therefore, on this view, faith is normally a doxastic mental state. However, *if* there are some forms of faith which do not imply any degree of belief whatsoever in the object of faith, then those forms of faith will not belong to the doxastic family of mental states.[28]

[27] I wonder whether the example of a lawyer who defends in court the innocence of his client without any degree of belief whatsoever in his innocence really qualifies as a case of 'acceptance' of his innocence. But if it does then this 'acceptance' is not a doxastic state.

[28] On the doxastic versus non-doxastic debate on faith see also Chap. 13.

11.2.2 Shifting from the Ethics of Belief to the Ethics of Assent

Furthermore, I propose that at least some of the mental states which belong to the doxastic family are, strictly speaking, species of assent rather than species of belief. Notably, this applies to acceptance: if belief is involuntary, and these mental states are at least partially voluntary states, they cannot be species of an involuntary state (that is, belief), although (insofar as they qualify as 'doxastic' as opposed to purely conative) they all entail some degree of belief.[29] A consequence of this claim and, more generally, of the account proposed above, is that what is normally called the 'ethics of belief' would be more appropriately construed in a number of cases as the 'ethics of assent'.

Take a situation of genuine epistemic uncertainty. For instance, the case of a teacher with a very low degree of belief that the student may have colluded with others in writing his essay—say, a mild suspicion which spontaneously arises when reading some sophisticated turns of phrase. This suspicion is not enough to determine the teacher's assent to this being, or not being, a case of collusion. In this situation, her assent will be typically determined by other factors, for example, trust in the honesty of this student, hope that this student has actually improved, fear of undermining confidence in an already insecure young person, as opposed to wishing to finish marking asap or dreading lengthy paperwork on suspected collusion. On the basis of these factors she accepts that this is not a case of collusion.[30] Moral responsibility will rest on these other factors—factors which are intuitively praiseworthy or blameworthy—rather than on the low degree of belief which arises spontaneously on reading the essay.

In sum, a shift from the 'ethics of belief' to the 'ethics of assent' avoids the ever-returning tension between granting, on the one hand, that belief (as a spontaneous response to perceived 'evidence')[31] is in large measure involuntary, and maintaining, on the other hand, that we bear moral responsibility for our beliefs. Strictly speaking, moral responsibility does not rest on believing such-and-such but on assenting to such-and-such in the case of a low degree of belief responding to low levels of reasons, arguments, signs, or symptoms in support of believing such-and-such. Low degrees of belief are often insufficient to determine assent to a certain state of affairs being such-and-such. In these cases, assent is determined (in combination with belief) by other (typically conative/affective) factors and are those factors that are normally the most direct ground of praise or blame.

[29] For the claim that acceptance is a species of belief, see Engel 1998. As mentioned above, Engel's conclusion that acceptance (a voluntary state) is a species of belief seems to me at odds with the assumption, underpinning the paper, that 'beliefs are involuntary'.

[30] On why assent does not equate to acceptance see Chap. 4, sect. 4.2.5.

[31] I take here 'evidence' in its secondary sense of external reasons, arguments, signs, symptoms in support of believing such-and-such.

The overall take-home point is the following: while the account of cognition proposed in this book narrows the domain of individual knowledge by expanding that of belief, at the same time it reassigns a province wrongly attributed to belief by granting it instead to the more general category of assent. Thinking with assent is a complex mental phenomenon which involves involuntary elements (on my account, knowing and believing) as well as legitimate volitional (appetitive, conative) elements without thereby implying doxastic voluntarism.

12
Belief and Testimony

Parts I and II have built, among other things, towards the claim which is at the core of this chapter: testimony plays a crucial role in our epistemic lives but does not, *on its own*, produce *knowledge* in the specific individual who is the recipient of testimony. This claim will no doubt encounter vigorous opposition since it challenges a deeply entrenched orthodoxy. An immediate objection is likely to be that, on my account, much of what we routinely take as one's knowledge will not count as knowledge. Although this conclusion is, in some sense, correct, it is, in other senses, misleading.

12.1 Testimony and Individual Knowing

12.1.1 Individual Knowing and What an Individual Knows

First, it is misleading because it conflates the mental acts/mental states of a specific individual with what some individual or another knows. As I argued in Parts I and II of this book, individual knowing is essentially—that is, primarily, fundamentally, paradigmatically—first-person. It cannot be passed on as a parcel, because one cannot pass on perceptual or intellectual seeing or grasping 'what is' (either in their immediate or in their mediate form via a chain of inference); one cannot pass on understanding; one cannot pass on episodic memory. To put it more generally: mental states are not the sort of thing which can be shared or passed on. Insofar as knowing is a mental state, it cannot be passed on. Ditto for believing, insofar as believing is also a mental state. What can be passed on, and is constantly passed on, is information. That is, what is passed on are reports that such-and-such is the case. The relevant question, then, is not whether knowing can be passed on—as a mental state, it cannot—but whether a testimonial report may cause the individual who receives it to be in a mental state of knowing. My answer is that it depends on whether a testimonial report may or may not lead to the sort of cognitive contact or presence of 'what is' to an individual which is distinctive of the mental state of knowing. If it can, then a testimonial report may *lead* to knowing. It is however much more common, I contend, that a testimonial report *will not* lead to the direct cognitive presence of the object of cognition which is distinctive of knowing, and this explains why testimonial reports typically lead to believing rather than knowing.

Thinking with Assent: Renewing a Traditional Account of Knowledge and Belief. Maria Rosa Antognazza, Oxford University Press. © Maria Rosa Antognazza 2024. DOI: 10.1093/oso/9780198831518.003.0013

12.1.2 Knowing and Reliably Tracking Truth

Indeed, it seems to me that testimony is a pervasive feature of our cognitive lives which is especially relevant to our ability to reliably track truth if and when the cognitive contact with 'what is' which characterizes knowledge is not available. This points to a second way in which the above objection is misleading: it fails to appreciate that restricting what counts, in philosophical rigour and for a given individual, as knowing does not equate to restricting what counts, in philosophical rigour and for that individual, as successful cognition, that is, as cognition which reliably tracks truth. Once again, 'knowledge first, but give belief its due': a crucial part of our successful cognition is constituted by justified belief which tracks truth if and when individual knowing is out of one's cognitive reach.

12.1.3 Testimony Leading to Individual Knowing

Third, the objection is misleading because (as already suggested above) testimony can, and often does, *lead* to individual knowing. This is what happens every time we go and find the train station, the office, the toilet, on the basis of having been told by an informant where they are supposed to be. And this is what happens when scientists, engineers, technicians, and so on, tell other scientists, engineers, technicians that such-and-such is the way to find, observe, calculate, build, or repair this and that. Moreover, even if the relevant testimony was not complete or completely accurate, as long as one does find the train station or repair the machine with the help of an informant's testimony, testimony has played a key role in leading to knowledge. The point is, however, that to achieve individual knowledge of where the train station is, or of the solution of a quadratic equation, it is not sufficient to be told where the train station is supposed to be, or that the solution to a quadratic equation is provided by the quadratic formula. One must be in a position to find the train station or solve a quadratic equation, were one required to do so. This is another way to say, as I have done in Parts I and II, that individual knowledge is essentially first-person.[1]

12.1.4 Individual Knowing Based on Testimony

Fourth, the objection is misleading because, although I claim that testimony does not, on its own, produce individual knowledge, I acknowledge that there is individual knowledge which is *based* on testimony. Indeed, quotidian life as well

[1] See, in particular, Introduction to Part II and Chap. 6.

as science is full of examples. Take the case of a janitor who inspects an unoccupied apartment on the basis of a phone call from a neighbour complaining of strange noises the night before, and who discovers that the apartment has been infested by bats now all soundly asleep in blissful silence. The janitor now knows of this infestation on the basis of testimony about noises he never heard and which no longer occur. Something analogous happens in science. In a mature scientific field, the level of sophistication and technical detail is such that no individual scientist can avoid partially basing her own original work on the authority of others. In this case, this authoritative scientific testimony counts as knowledge for the scientists who have developed such-and-such a mathematical model, clinical trial, experiments, and so on. In most cases, even this sub-set of scientists will know collectively rather than distributively, although individuals will know distributively various aspects of it. On this authoritative scientific testimony, other scientists may base further research that may well lead to new discoveries which strictly count as knowledge.

12.1.5 Collective Knowing and Individual Knowing

This last point leads to a fifth and most important way in which the above objection is misleading. It is misleading because it fails to appreciate the distinction between what is collectively known by a community of knowers and what is distributively known by each individual in that community. My focus here is on individual knowing as opposed to what an individual (justifiably, reliably, etc.) believes. Much of what does not count, strictly speaking, as individual knowing is often known by groups of individuals in that community. By (Socratically) narrowing and sharpening the limits of individual knowing, the present proposal stresses the importance of collective knowing and the need for an individual to base her beliefs on the trustworthy testimony of authoritative communities of experts—be it the testimony of the medical profession, climate change scientists, or the consensus of historians or biblical scholars.[2] That is, a key aspect of my account is the acknowledgment that on many matters there can only ever be a claim to collective (as opposed to individual) knowing—namely, all those matters which, due to their vast complexity, necessarily require collaborative research, peer review, formal training, professional accreditation, institutional structures,

[2] How to distinguish an authoritative community of experts from any random group which claims to know is one of the key issues investigated by a type of inquiry well beyond the scope of this project, namely, an inquiry on collective or social knowing. I take it, however, that a key feature of genuine collective knowing are its institutional aspects. On collective versus distributive knowing (applied also to scientific knowledge), cf. Chap. 5, sect. 5.3.2, where it is stressed that collective knowing is an *analogue* of individual knowing, that is, it is a type of knowing which has its own set of distinctive features which do not apply to individual knowing (see Bird 2010. Cf. also Hyman 1999: 433; 2015: 159).

and so on. As a consequence, honest Joe who goes on Twitter to express his views on any such matters cannot even in principle have a claim to individual knowledge against institutionally recognized communities of experts for the simple reason that these matters are not open to *individual* knowing.

Furthermore, when knowledge is approached from the point of view of its social dimension, the present proposal acknowledges that what is known by an institutionally recognized group of experts in the community may often count as what the community as a whole collectively knows. We collectively know, for instance, that Covid vaccines offer a high level of protection against severe illness caused by the SARS-CoV-2 virus; any knowledge claim to the contrary amounts, therefore, to false belief.

12.1.6 Knowers and Good Informants

More generally, my approach is radically different from that of Edward Craig in *Knowledge and the State of Nature.*[3] In his ground-breaking book, Craig starts from a hypothesis about the social function of knowledge and the needs it fulfils. According to his account, the concept of knowledge was developed in order to mark people as good sources of information, thereby reversing the usual order of explanation: the notion of 'good informant' explains the notion of 'knower', rather than the other way round. There can be little doubt as to the importance of Craig's account in spearheading a new generation of social epistemology. My proposal, however, tackles the issue of knowledge from a different angle. Notwithstanding the importance of the social dimension of knowledge, when approached from the point of view of individual knowing, I contend that knowledge is not equivalent to information which is passed on, and knowing is not to be explained in terms of receiving information from good informants. *Pace* Craig, the usual order of explanation—according to which the notion of 'knower' explains that of 'good informant'—still stands. Ultimately, someone is a good informant *because* she knows such-and-such, that is, has or has had the relevant cognitive contact with such-and-such and is therefore in a position to report truly on such-and-such to others.

12.2 Intrinsic Versus Extrinsic Evidence

12.2.1 Hearsay and Assurance

The claim that, strictly speaking, testimony does not, on its own, produce individual *knowledge* can count on illustrious advocates. Famously, Spinoza takes a

[3] Craig 1990.

dim view of the cognition 'we have from hearsay', that is, from testimony. In his own examples, 'by hearsay alone I know the date of my birth, who my parents were, and things of that sort, which I have never doubted'.[4] Having never doubted these things is clearly, for Spinoza, no indication of their being undoubtable. In his taxonomy, cognition by testimony is in fact the lowest kind of cognition, the kind which can be true or false. Not that Spinoza has any inclination towards scepticism. Rather, his point is that knowledge (the sort of cognition which cannot be false) consists in grasping the essences of things, in connecting with things as they really are, and this is not something one can do from hearsay ('It is self-evident', he writes, 'that from hearsay, beside the considerable degree of uncertainty therein, we perceive nothing of the essence of the thing, as our example makes clear.... any degree of certainty that we have from hearsay must be excluded from the sciences.')[5]

Without sharing Spinoza's extremely demanding notion of what counts, properly, as knowledge, other early modern authors still make the point that testimony grounds a mode of cognition different in kind from the perception of the object of cognition which characterizes knowledge. William Chillingworth (1602–1644), for instance, is clear that the existence of a distant city like Constantinople is believed rather than known by those who have never seen it: 'in propriety of speech I could not say that I knew it, but that I did as undoubtedly believe it as those things which I did know'.[6]

The acknowledged doyen of this position, however, is Locke. In the *Essay*, he does not mince his words. By his lights, transferred information is not really knowledge but 'borrowed Wealth, like Fairy-money, though it were Gold in the hand from which he received it, will be but Leaves and Dust when it comes to use' (*Essay*, Book I, chap. IV, 23). Such a staunch stand must be understood in the context of his firm distinction between knowing and believing: knowing is *perceiving* the agreement or disagreement between ideas; believing is the cognitive mode we rely on when we cannot perceive this agreement or disagreement, and must therefore judge whether there is or there is not agreement/disagreement on the basis of 'something extraneous' to the object of cognition.[7] Testimony, that is, reports from others regarding the agreement or disagreement among ideas, may well lead us to right judgement but will not normally make us *perceive* the relevant agreement or disagreement—that is, it may be (and often is) the source of true belief rather than knowledge. To guide us towards true beliefs, Locke offers a well-known list of criteria for evaluating the *credibility* of testimony.[8] But no matter

[4] Cf. Spinoza, *Tractatus De Intellectus Emendatione*; trans. Shirley, p. 7.

[5] Spinoza, *Tractatus De Intellectus Emendatione*; trans. Shirley, p. 9.

[6] Chillingworth, *Works*, p. 740. Attention to this passage is drawn by Pasnau 2017: 41.

[7] Locke, *Essay*, Book IV, chap. XV, 3: 'That which makes me believe, is something extraneous to the thing I believe.' On Locke's distinction between knowledge and belief see Chap. 2, sect. 2.3.3.

[8] Locke, *Essay*, Book IV, chap. XVI, 4.

how high the probability of there being an agreement/disagreement between ideas, Locke is very clear that this probability will never result in 'certainty': although in some cases '*Probabilities* rise so near to *Certainty*' that 'our Belief thus grounded, rise to *Assurance*' (Locke, Essay, Book IV, chap. XVI, 6): 'certainty' (as opposed to 'assurance') is a notion which Locke reserves only for knowledge.

As mentioned above, this tradition about testimony tends to be summarily dismissed as having too strong requirements for knowledge and therefore leaving out what is, for most people, obviously knowledge. It seems that if the receptionist tells me that the toilet is on the right-hand side at the end of the left corridor of the fifth floor, and this is indeed the case, I come to know where the toilet is. In common cases such as this, it might appear that Locke was too demanding in denying the status of knowledge (strictly taken) to information we acquire by testimony. Locke and Chillingworth's point, however, is not that the ideal knower does not trust anyone and finds out everything by herself.[9] If this were the proposal, our successful cognition would be so drastically reduced as to impair day-to-day life, not to speak of broader human flourishing. Their point is that (in philosophical rigour) we should be careful in distinguishing individual knowing from truly and justifiably believing. Only if I am in a position to find the toilet, should I need to do so, do I know (as an individual) where it is.

But do I know, say, my own name? That I am called Maria Rosa Antognazza, it seems, is a result of testimony: my parents told me so, and it is written on my birth certificate, passport, driving licence, and so on. There are contexts, however, in which I am called Maria Antognazza-Hotson (say, on my NHS record), or Rosa A. Hotson, or even (to my great annoyance, once or twice, many years ago) Mrs Howard Hotson (as opposed to Professor Maria Rosa Antognazza). Moreover, drastic legal changes to one's own name are commonplace. The upshot is that one's own name is a function of that particular sort of collective knowing which is linked to social convention and public record. Testimony may lead (and indeed routinely does lead) to knowing one's own name but knowing one own name is not a matter of testimony but of having (or not having) made contact with 'what is' according to the relevant social convention.

12.2.2 History

What about the past? To go back to Spinoza's example, do I know the date of my birth? Granted that, on my account, there may be individual knowledge of the past insofar as the relevant contact with 'what is' is preserved in episodic memory (although of course not infallibly), can I have any individual knowledge of my own

[9] Cf. Fricker 2006 rightly points out that, given our dependence on testimony, the ideal of an epistemically autonomous knower is practically impossible.

past involving instead semantic memory? More generally, is it even in principle possible, on my account, to have knowledge of any historical event one has not directly witnessed?

Crucially, the question just posed introduces the notion of 'witnessing' an event. It is generally acknowledged that testimony is, in principle, more reliable if it comes from someone who was present, and actually saw or heard what happened,[10] as opposed to someone who did not witness the event in question but is reporting what someone else saw or heard. It is, of course, also widely acknowledged that people who were all present at a certain event may report what happened in different and sometime incompatible ways. This is a consequence, I suggest, of the structural indeterminacy of human knowledge also as regards *present* individuals and states of affairs we latch on to.[11] A fortiori, if and when we latch on through memory to some past event, we always do so in an indeterminate and fallible way which leaves infinitely many aspects of that event unknown and unknowable.

The key point here is that testimony's reliability mirrors a 'knowledge-first' structure: someone was present at some event, and left (intentionally or unintentionally) some sign, some material remains, or some record which bears testimony to some (always radically limited) aspect of that event or that period in history. When this happens, testimony is ultimately anchored in an original contact with 'what is': the testimonial chain ultimately goes back to a foundation—some first-hand acquaintance, or some direct cognitive contact—which is different in kind from any other second-hand testimonial reports.

In many cases, on the other hand, that original contact with 'what is' is lost. Take the case, for instance, of people whose date of birth, or circumstances of death, are unknown. Even more importantly, in *all* cases of past events, infinitely many aspects of those events are irretrievably lost: not only how many hairs Julius Caesar had on his head when he died but also, say, from which precise angles he was stabbed, which internal organs were struck first, and so on. Any such aspects are now well beyond the reach of knowing, although we may still have about them justified beliefs.

Interestingly, neo-Scholastic textbooks of the late nineteenth century use (like Locke and Leibniz)[12] the example of Julius Caesar to point out that what is at issue, in the evaluation of the epistemic status of many claims about the past, is not the level of conviction with which we may rightly hold certain beliefs, but their being

[10] I am assuming that the relevant witness is a generally trustworthy person, has no conflict of interest, was sober at the time, conditions were such that they could see or hear what was happening, and so on. In brief, I am assuming that *nemo gratis mendax*.

[11] On the structural indeterminacy of our knowledge of concrete individuals and of the states of affairs in which these individuals are involved, see Chap. 10, sections 10.2–10.4, and Chap. 8, sections 8.1 and 8.2.

[12] Cf. Locke, *Essay*, Book IV, chap. XVI, 8 and Leibniz, *New Essais*, Book IV, chap. XVI, 8.

grounded in moral certainty. One may feel 'more intensely convinced' of some specific account of Caesar's death 'than of many theses in Mathematics or Philosophy, which rest on metaphysical principles'[13]—and yet this account rests on probability, and enjoys therefore only moral certainly, rather than latching on to the metaphysical structure of reality, and enjoying therefore absolute certainty. This is not at all to deny that there are plenty of things that we collectively know about the past in virtue of the contact with 'what is' that some groups of individuals have or have had with the relevant events—a contact which has been documented, and thereby preserved, by the relevant experts in the field. We do know, for instance, that over one million people were killed in Auschwitz and that Neil Armstrong landed on the moon. Rather, the point is that infinitely more aspects of the past (and, for that matter, of the present) are not known, although we may have (and often do have) justified beliefs about them.

To conclude: without some form of knowledge of the past, in the sense of someone having had the relevant first-hand involvement in some event, testimony would not play the key role that it does play, in fact, in historiography. There is no bar, on my account, to individual knowledge of those aspects of the past with which one has had the relevant cognitive contact, preserved in memory. Something *analogous*, but at the same time significantly different, happens with our *collective* memory. Much of what has been preserved of the past, is preserved collectively thanks to the work of the relevant communities of experts who understand the significance of certain material remains, ancient inscriptions, medieval manuscripts, and so on. In brief, just as there is collective knowing in the natural sciences, there is also collective knowing in historical disciplines. In history as in science, however, much of what we know, we know collectively rather than individually. And in history as in science, a significant proportion of our collective, successful cognition has the epistemic status of justified belief which reliably tracks truth rather than, strictly speaking, knowledge.

12.2.3 Faith

Now, a distinctive feature of some key historical testimony, as well as testimony relating to events one has not witnessed, is its impersonality. Instances include the information provided by buildings and other physical remains about past activities, habits, achievements; or the material evidence produced in court cases, such as a bullet or an arsenic bottle. Arguably, for historical or for judicial purposes, the more impersonal the relevant testimony is, the better it is: as Leibniz does not fail to note, contemporary testimonies about, say, the hidden motives which moved

[13] Coppens 1891: *Logic*, Book II, chap. I, art. iii, § 88.

someone to do something tell us at best 'what various people have believed' rather than providing evidence for some historical fact.[14]

With respect to this feature of impersonality, the relationship between testimony and faith is significantly different.[15] Typically, in the many cases of faith which involve testimony, the ground on which testimony is accepted as credible is not its impersonality, but its coming from a trustworthy person. Furthermore, in the case of historical or judicial testimony, the trustworthiness of a source of information typically needs to be established on a case-by-case basis (a bottle of arsenic may be trustworthy testimony of a murder in certain specific circumstances, but not in general). By contrast, faith in the trustworthiness of a person typically has a holistic character: if I have faith in the trustworthiness of my endocrinologist as an authority on the treatment of my diabetes, I will trust what she says on the matter in general, and not only for one specific type of medication but not the others. If the latter is the case, what it means is that, in fact, I do *not* have faith in her trustworthiness as an authority on the matter.

In brief, faith typically requires holistic trust in a person or group of persons due to the perceived authority of that person or group of persons on the relevant matter. Strictly speaking, what these persons transmit is not knowledge but information which is believed to be true on the basis of their authoritative testimony (there is more to knowing that—or, a fortiori, why—a certain treatment will cure the disease than simply being told that it will, otherwise we would all become medical doctors and pharmacists in no time at all).

At least in theistic religions, religious faith typically involves features to be found in faith more generally, notably, this kind of holistic trust grounded in what is believed to be the exceptionally authoritative status of testimony. Aquinas, for instance, makes clear that faith is based on testimony as opposed to direct vision, the point being that if there were vision there would be no need for faith and its distinctive element of trust.[16] In turn, Locke stresses that the firmness of faith is grounded not in the perception of the agreement between ideas (say, the idea of Jesus and the idea of Messiah) but in the perceived exceptionally authoritative status of the relevant testimony ('*Faith*... is the Assent to any Proposition, not thus made out by the Deduction of Reason; but upon the Credit of the Proposer, as coming from GOD' *Essay*, Book IV, chap. XVIII, 2).[17]

[14] Leibniz, *New Essais*, Book IV, chap. XVI, 10 (NE 466–7).

[15] See Vanni Rovighi 1962: 191–2, where the difference between faith and historical testimony is discussed.

[16] ST IIa IIae, q. 8, a. 6, co.: 'Fides autem est *ex auditu*, ut dicitur *Rom*. 10, [17]. Unde oportet aliqua proponi homini ad credendum non sicut visa, sed sicut audit, quibus per fidem assentiat.'

[17] See also Locke, *Essay*, Book IV, chap. XVI, 14: 'there is one sort of Propositions that challenge the highest Degree of our Assent, upon bare Testimony, whether the thing proposed, agree or disagree with common Experience, and the ordinary course of Things, or no. The Reason whereof is, because the Testimony is of such an one, as cannot deceive, nor be deceived, and that is of God himself. This carries with it Assurance beyond Doubt, Evidence beyond Exception. This is called by a peculiar Name, *Revelation*, and our Assent to it, *Faith*.'

12.2.4 Intrinsic and Extrinsic Evidence

Leibniz captures these insights with a distinction between *evidentia in rebus* and *evidentia in personis*. When I assent to the conclusion of a geometrical demonstration because I have myself gone through the demonstrative process, the reason of my assent is what Leibniz calls *evidentia in rebus* ('evidence in things'). When I assent to the same conclusion because a geometry teacher tells me it necessarily follows from the premises, the reason of my assent is what Leibniz calls *evidentia in personis* ('evidence in persons'), that is, what I know about this person, including their professional standing and their being trustworthy. 'I can admit that *the basis of persuasion is evidence*', he writes:

> provided there is no abuse of this doctrine. For even if that of which we are persuaded is not always evident, yet evidence must be involved in the manner of persuading. For instance, the authority of those by whom we believe that something has happened must be evident to us, even though we do not always perceive how it is attained.... [E]ven in human affairs we do not always need *evidence in things* (as the famous Author [John Toland] requires), provided it exists *in persons*, so that it is made sure by trust in them. (Dutens V, 144–6)

In short: what we know (or, more weakly in most cases, justifiably believe) about the authoritative status of a person grounds faith in the trustworthiness of their testimony.

The distinction between *evidentia in rebus* and *evidentia in personis* could be generalized, I propose, as a distinction between intrinsic and extrinsic evidence.[18] The difference between these two types of evidence is clearer in propositional cognition. In intellectual knowledge expressed in propositions, intrinsic evidence is (immediate or mediated) evidence of the connection between subject and predicate of a proposition (for example, it is seeing that being a triangle implies being three-sided). Extrinsic evidence is seeing that there are good reasons to affirm the connection between subject and predicate although one cannot see that they are connected, or why and how they are connected. For instance, I may have good reasons to affirm the equality between energy and mass times the speed of light squared because I have found this equality stated in many reliable books. But even if I have a rough idea of what energy, mass, and the speed of light are (that is, even if these words have some meaning for me, as opposed to being mere *flatus vocis*), I may be completely unable to see that (or why) energy, mass, and speed of light are in some necessary ways connected.

[18] I take the distinction between intrinsic and extrinsic evidence from Vanni Rovighi 1962: 191 and 1982: 12–13, footnote 3.

Intrinsic evidence, I suggest, grounds knowledge; extrinsic evidence grounds belief; and testimony, in turn, constitutes the paradigmatic case of extrinsic evidence. Moreover, the intrinsic/extrinsic distinction tracks Aquinas's two distinct modes of thinking with assent.[19] As one of the first neo-Thomists crisply summarizes in the early nineteenth century:

> In the first case, the intellect is moved to assent by the object itself [ab ipso obiecto movetur ad assentiendum], and cannot refrain from assenting. In the second case, it is not moved by the object, *because it does not know it* [quia illud non cognoscit], and therefore not necessarily but through a certain choice, as S. Thomas says, voluntarily turn to assenting.[20]

I propose that recognizing the difference between assenting on the basis of intrinsic evidence and assenting on the basis of extrinsic evidence acknowledges an important ontological and phenomenological difference in our mental states—a difference which is overlooked by the orthodoxy which regards testimony as a source, on its own, of individual knowledge as opposed to (reasonable, justified, entitled, . . .) belief.

12.3 Modified Global Reductionism

Even assuming that we are dealing with justified belief rather than knowledge, the question of when and how testimony provides sufficient justification for belief still needs to be answered. In current literature on the epistemology of testimony, there are two competing approaches to this question: reductionism (commonly regarded as inspired by Hume) and non-reductionism (commonly regarded as inspired by Reid).[21]

12.3.1 Reductionism and Non-Reductionism

According to reductionists, in order to accept testimony as reliable, there must be positive reasons which are not themselves of a testimonial kind. That is to say, the justification of testimony reduces to the justification of other cognitive modes,

[19] See Introduction to Part I, sect. I.4 and Chap. 2, sect. 2.1.2.

[20] Buzzetti 1940: 88 (my emphasis). Vincenzo Buzzetti (1777–1824) taught philosophy in Piacenza in the early nineteenth century, writing during this time a substantial exposition of Aristotelian-Thomistic philosophy (*Institutiones Philosophicae*). His work was published in 1940–1941 by a prominent exponent of the Italian neo-Scholastic movement, Amato Masnovo (1880–1955). Cf. Aveling 1907: belief is 'that state of the mind by which it assents to propositions, not by reason of their intrinsic evidence, but because of authority'.

[21] Cf. Lackey 2006: 4–6.

such as sense perception, memory, or inferential reasoning. In turn, reductionism comes in two brands: global reductionists demand positive reasons justifying the belief that testimony is generally reliable; local reductionists demand positive reasons justifying the reliability of a particular testimonial report. For instance, for a global reductionist, experience over time of passers-by generally giving correct information when asked for directions, of waiters truthfully reporting the location of toilets, and so on, justifies belief in the general reliability of testimony, and of belief in a particular new piece of testimony-based information. On the other hand, for a local reductionist, the reliability of what a passer-by is telling me about the road to Larissa needs to be justified by positive reasons, different from testimony, relating specifically to that piece of information. Overall, for a reductionist, testimony is guilty until proved innocent, and its innocence must be proven by reasons not based in testimony.

By contrast, according to non-reductionists, the justification of testimony does not reduce to the justification of non-testimonial modes of cognition. Thus, testimony is itself a basic source of justification of belief: I am justified in believing that this is the road to Larissa merely on the basis of this passer-by saying so, unless I have some specific reason to doubt the reliability of my informant. In brief, testimony is innocent until proved guilty: it is taken to be reliable unless there are positive reasons to doubt its reliability.

Objections have been raised against both positions. Typically, non-reductionists are charged with opening the gates to gullibility and epistemic irrationality: in the present age of innocent-looking fake news, this is surely an increasingly legitimate concern. Reductionists, on the other hand, are charged with setting the bar too high for testimony's justification: given the ubiquity of testimony in our cognitive lives, is it really possible to have any belief's justification which is not already indebted to testimony?[22] As a result of these opposite pressures, qualified or hybrid views have been developed which seek ways of combining reductionism and non-reductionism.[23] The position I propose belongs to this category of qualified or hybrid views: specifically, it is a modified version of global reductionism.

12.3.2 Hume, Reid, and Modified Global Reductionism

As argued in the first part of the chapter, I take the view that testimony does not simply pass on knowledge to a given individual, although it can lead to individual

[22] This objection is at least implicitly raised in a number of contributions, notably, Anscombe 1979; Bonjour 2002; Wolterstorff 2001.

[23] Cf., for instance, Faulkner 2000, and the contributions by Peter Graham, Sanford C. Goldberg, Keith Lehrer, and Jennifer Lackey in Lackey and Sosa 2006.

knowing. A fortiori, on my account, testimony is neither a source of *basic knowledge* (that is, knowledge not grounded in some other knowledge) nor a *basic source* of knowledge (that is, a source which, on its own, produces knowledge).[24] Insofar as Thomas Reid and other non-reductionists think that testimony can be an epistemically basic source not merely of belief but also of knowledge, I disagree with Reid and non-reductionism.[25] That is, I oppose testimonial fundamentalism understood as a view according to which testimony is a foundational epistemic source on a par with perception and memory.[26]

On these matters, I side instead with Hume's view that testimony, on its own, cannot ground knowledge but only belief, although for reasons which are in part different from those of Hume. To have *knowledge* purely based on testimony, Hume suggests, we would need to have an a priori perception of the connection between testimony and reality.[27] However, given that, in general, our belief in the existence of necessary connections, based on 'constant and regular conjunction', does not amount to knowledge that there are any such necessary connections, a fortiori 'our observation of the veracity of human testimony' based on 'the usual conformity of facts to the reports of witnesses' does not amount to knowledge of the existence of any necessary connection between facts and testimonial reports.[28] I agree with Hume that testimony could be, purely by itself, a source of knowledge (as opposed to justified belief) only if we had a priori knowledge of the connection between reality and testimony. Moreover, on my account, individual knowledge is essentially first-person. If this is right, testimony does not, by itself, produce knowledge in an individual, but provides information which is believed in a more or less justified way.

In addition, I side specifically with *global* reductionists in taking the view that the justification of testimony as a source of justified belief should be established in general, and that this justification depends on other cognitive modes. That is, the general reliability of testimony is originally established and constantly reinforced by the fundamental cognitive modes such as sense-perception and memory, which allow a first-hand contact with the object of cognition and the preservation of such contact. A good answer to the objection that, given the pervasiveness of testimony, any belief's justification is already indebted to testimony, is offered, in my view, by

[24] Audi 2006 argues that testimony is a source of basic knowledge but not a basic source of knowledge.

[25] As I will explain below, I am not sure that Reid is a non-reductionist as he is normally taken to be.

[26] Cf. Van Cleve 2006: 59–69 and Coady 1992: 23 and 123. Both interpret Reid as holding that testimony-based beliefs are epistemically basic and are a source not merely of belief but of knowledge. 'Fundamentalism' is the label proposed by Coady 1992: 23.

[27] Hume, *Enquiry*, Part I, sect. 10, pp. 85–6: 'The reason, why we place any credit in witnesses and historians, is not derived from any *connexion*, which we perceive *a priori*, between testimony and reality, but because we are accustomed to find a conformity between them'. Van Cleve 2006: 61–7 rejects testimonial fundamentalism by proposing an argument according to which a foundational source must be an a priori source, and testimony is not an a priori source.

[28] See Hume, *Enquiry*, Part I, sect. 10, pp. 84–5.

Van Cleve (2006: 67–8). If the objection takes the form of claiming that, in principle, there is no case in which corroboration of testimony does not rely on further testimony, it is surely too strong. If it takes the weaker form of claiming that the proportion of cases one can corroborate first-hand is 'vanishingly small',[29] it is far from obvious that this claim undermines reductionism: for reductionism, it is enough that the first-hand verification of the general reliability of testimony is a regular feature of our cognitive life (and, insofar as it is regular, it is not *vanishingly* small), even if, overall, the proportion of first-hand verified testimonial reports is small.

I agree with Reid, however, on non-reductionism *iff* non-reductionism is set in the framework of global reductionism and is limited: (1) to testimony as a source of justified *belief*; and (2) to the 'innocent until proved guilty' rule which justifies (once the general reliability of testimony is established by non-testimonial means) taking testimony to be reliable unless there are positive reasons to doubt its reliability.

In order to flesh-out this position, it is crucial to distinguish, first of all, between a descriptive psychology of testimony and a normative epistemology of testimony.[30] As a descriptive theory of the psychology of testimony, non-reductionism clearly has the upper hand. Reid insightfully notes that the principle of credulity—that is, the 'disposition to confide in the veracity of others, and to believe what they tell us'—'is unlimited in children, until they meet with instances of deceit and falsehood'.[31] The very fact that credulity is 'strongest in childhood', and is then 'limited and restrained by experience', Reid reasons, shows that it is an instinctive feature of our natural constitution ('a gift of nature', as Reid puts it).[32] As far as the *psychology* of testimony is concerned, instinctive credulity treats testimony in a non-reductionist way. Children start out by just believing what they are told; testimony is initially just a basic source of beliefs. Crucially, however, the psychological immediacy and lack of inferentiality of beliefs based on testimony is not sufficient to establish the epistemic status of testimony as a basic source of justified beliefs. The justification of the principle of credulity as a *normative epistemic principle* of the epistemology of testimony comes from other sources of cognition.

Reid mentions 'experience' here, and 'experience' unpacks, in my view, along the lines of global reductionism: that is, unrestricted childish credulity is gradually limited by perceptual verification or falsification of testimonial reports, experiential verification or falsification which is stored by memory, retrieved, and used in rational inference, and so on. In brief, as we grow up, credulity as a mere psychological feature develops into an epistemic principle the justification of which is based on cognitive modes other than testimony. As Reid explains, 'as

[29] Bonjour 2002: 172–3; quoted by Van Cleve 2006: 67.
[30] Cf. Van Cleve 2006: 59.
[31] Reid, *Inquiry*, chap. 6, sect. 24, p. 194.
[32] Reid, *Inquiry*, chap. 6, sect. 24, p. 195.

we find good reason to reject testimony in some cases, so in others we find good reason to rely upon it with perfect security, in our most important concerns'.[33] Immediately after this sentence, in a way remarkably reminiscent of Locke, Reid lists criteria for the evaluation of the reliability of testimony which 'may give an irresistible strength to testimony, compared to which its native and intrinsic authority [that is, the authority merely based on the instinctive psychological feature of credulity] is very inconsiderable'.[34] In sum, it is a *restricted* principle of credulity, limited by experience and shaped by criteria which are not purely testimonial, which 'retains a very considerable degree of strength through life'.[35]

Given these views, I very much doubt that Reid can really be regarded as the founding father of non-reductionism and fundamentalism, as he is normally taken to be. But apart from historical points of Reidian interpretation, the substantive theorical point is the following: the epistemic justification of testimony is set in a global reductionist framework in which the psychological predisposition to credulity is gradually underpinned by an epistemic principle of credulity justified by cognitive modes other than testimony. This epistemic principle 'tallies' (in Reid's phrase) with a complementary principle of veridicity, that is, 'a propensity to speak truth, and to use the signs of language, so as to convey our real sentiments'[36]—another principle the epistemic justification of which ultimately relies, I suggest, on cognitive modes other than testimony. Together, these two principles seem to me to tally also with the long-established legal dictum *Nemo gratis mendax* (no one lies gratuitously).

I propose that it is in this global reductionist framework, and in the context of the justification of *belief*, that the non-reductionist 'innocent until proved guilty' rule applies, and should apply, to testimony. That is, as specific testimonial reports are concerned, not only the psychology of testimony shows that we do go through life following this rule: we are also epistemically justified in doing so. Once the principles of veridicity and of credulity have been justified by fundamental cognitive modes which allow first-person cognitive contact with 'what is', as well as preservation of this contact in various forms, they provide, I contend, a sufficiently robust epistemic underpinning for the 'innocent until proved guilty' rule rightly envisaged by Reid.

[33] Reid, *Inquiry*, chap. 6, sect. 24, p. 195.

[34] Reid, *Inquiry*, chap. 6, sect. 24, p. 195. Reid lists the following criteria: 'The character, the number, and the disinterestedness of witnesses, the impossibility of collusion, and the incredibility of their concurring in their testimony without collusion.'

[35] Reid, *Inquiry*, chap. 6, sect, 24, p. 194.

[36] Reid, *Inquiry*, chap. 6, sect. 24, p. 193.

13
Taxonomy of Belief and Doxastic Faith

In Chapter 11, I have suggested that the 'doxastic family' is a family of mental states constituted by belief and other cognate cognitive modes which entail belief but do not reduce to belief—the latter being, on my account, a cognitive mental state concerned with a certain state of affairs being true or false. Cognate doxastic mental states are states that have belief as one of their elements in combination with other (typically conative/appetitive/affective) factors (for example, trust, hope, love) which play an important role in determining assent. This chapter explores two historical proposals that offer, in my view, illuminating accounts of particularly significant members of this family.

First, I will outline Kant's distinction between three main types of belief (pragmatic belief, theoretical belief, and moral belief), all subsumed by Kant under the broader category of 'assenting' (*Fürwahrhalten*).[1] Although there is a strand in Kant which has led to an anti-realist interpretation of his claims about belief in God,[2] my interest here is in the more traditional strand of Kant's thought—the strand that John Hawthorne and Daniel Howard-Snyder have called the 'conservative Kant'. This is the Kant according to whom beliefs about God include theoretical beliefs, that is, beliefs involving a commitment to the *truth* of what is believed (where believing, *glauben*, must of course not be confused with knowing, *wissen*).[3] Most importantly for my purposes, Kant's fine-grained taxonomy of belief has the merit of bringing to light the distinctive and irreplaceable contribution of belief to human cognition.

Second, I will revisit Aquinas's discussion of faith as a doxastic state.[4] As mentioned at the end of Chapter 11, I do not wish to deny that there may be forms of non-doxastic faith, that is, varieties of faith which do not involve any degree of belief.[5] Even less do I wish to deny that there are crucial aspects

[1] On Kant's category of *Fürwahrhalten*, see Chap. 4, sect. 4.1. [2] See, for instance, Byrne 2007.

[3] For a defence of theoretical belief in 'the conservative Kant' (the Kant favoured, notably, by Allen Wood's account of Kant on religion) see Hawthorne and Howard-Snyder 1996: 239–43. I agree with them that this is the Kantian strand more worthy of engagement (p. 246, n. 18). See also Chignell 2007, to which the section below on Kant is indebted, and the magisterial work on these topics by Allen W. Wood, culminating in Wood 2020.

[4] On the broader framework of Aquinas's discussion, see Chap. 2, sect. 2.1. For a recent defence of the view that genuine propositional religious faith is partly constituted by beliefs see Malcolm and Scott 2017.

[5] Audi 2011: 51–88 offers a detailed discussion of the varieties of faith, some of which are, on his account, non-doxastic. Howard-Snyder (2016 and 2018b) defends a nondoxastic theory of propositional faith, rejecting the view that faith that *p* entails belief that *p*. By contrast, Adams 1995: 85 classifies 'moral faith as a sort of belief'.

Thinking with Assent: Renewing a Traditional Account of Knowledge and Belief. Maria Rosa Antognazza, Oxford University Press. © Maria Rosa Antognazza 2024. DOI: 10.1093/oso/9780198831518.003.0014

of faith which are non-doxastic.[6] Since the foci of the present inquiry are, however, knowledge and belief, I am limiting my discussion to the type of faith which does involve some degree of belief, including, more specifically, doxastic religious faith.[7]

I do take issue, therefore, with alleged descriptions of religion 'from within' according to which religious faith does not really involve belief. These accounts, often claiming Wittgenstenian inspiration, seem to me to reconstruct rather than describe how religious practitioners themselves typically understand what they are engaged in.[8] A recent variation is offered by Arif Ahmed (2020), whose claim that religion does not really involve belief is based on (1) the alleged insensitivity of religious practitioners to the lack of evidence for religious claims, and (2) the alleged lack of 'penetration' into their behaviour of what they claim to believe. For present purposes, however, I suggest continuing to follow what millions of fellow human beings understand themselves to be doing—for example, believing that God exists; thinking it to be true that God exists.[9] Aquinas's account of faith as involving (but certainly not reducing to) belief is more in line with this more traditional understanding of religious faith by people who identify themselves as participants in religion, at least as far as Abrahamic religions are concerned.

It seems to me that one of the merits of Aquinas's proposal is to offer a unified account of faith in both its secular and its religious expressions.[10] Needless to say, also for Aquinas, religious faith has distinctive features, but these features are (and should be) evaluated in a unified framework which applies to faith generally. One of the advantages of this unified approach is to resist double standards when it

[6] The key importance of non-doxastic elements has been stressed in recent literature. See, for instance, Howard-Snyder 2013. It should be noted, however, that the element which according to Howard-Snyder 2013 can stand for belief—namely, 'assuming'—is still construed as a positive *cognitive* stance which, in combination with conative and evaluative elements, is required by faith. Similarly, Buchak's notion of 'acquiescing' is expounded as a species of 'taking the proposition to be true' (2012: n. 1). On whether acceptance (stressed, in particular, by Alston 1996) is or is not a doxastic state, see Chap. 11.

[7] An insightful account of the meaning of religious belief from an atheist's point of view is proposed by Crane 2017. Crane 2017 does not assess the truth or falsity of religion, but offers an account based on two key ideas: the idea of 'religious impulse', that is, the sense religious people have of a dimension transcending ordinary experience, and the idea of 'identification' or 'belonging'.

[8] See so-called Wittgenstenian Fideism (e.g., Phillips 1970; Malcolm 1977; Holmer 1978; for criticism see Nielsen 1973 and Hawthorne and Howard-Snyder 1996: 249–56). From a different perspective, Schellenberg 2005 goes as far as claiming that propositional faith that *p* requires the absence of belief that *p*. According to Schellenberg, 'faith-that . . . entails nonbelief'; 'faith is voluntary' and, as such, 'it cannot either be or entail belief' (2005: 143, 154).

[9] Ahmed 2020 does not dispute that this is the way in which religious practitioners (at least in the main monotheistic religions) typically describe what they engage in. For criticism of the sort of descriptive anthropology of which Ahmed 2020 seems to be a version, see Hawthorne and Howard-Snyder 1996 (esp. 234–5, 250–4), where it is persuasively argued that ordinary theistic beliefs are theoretical beliefs, that is, commitments to *truth*. For a sophisticated account of how maintaining faith and belief in the face of counter-evidence can, in certain cases, not only be rational but serve an important purpose in human life, see Buchak 2017. Cf. also Alston 1991: 262–6.

[10] The merits of a unified account are shown, for instance, by Buchak 2012.

comes to religion.[11] Faith, taken in a broad, general way, is a complex phenomenon of human life, closely related to appetitive states such as hope and love, and involving both cognitive and conative aspects (notably belief and trust). If, in appropriate circumstances, it may be regarded as a valuable (or even indispensable) element in the full range of human flourishing (think of faith in humanity, in justice, in democracy, or of faith that racial discrimination will be defeated, that peace will prevail, and so on), then religious faith cannot be castigated for features that it shares with the more general phenomenon of faith, and which are not regarded, in the general case, as irrational or pernicious. Ditto for belief and religious belief.

13.1 Pragmatic Belief, Theoretical Belief, and Moral Belief as Epistemic Components of Assenting

13.1.1 *Glauben*

'In the transcendental use of reason' (that is, in the use of reason beyond the bounds of experience), Kant writes, 'to have an opinion is of course too little, but to know is also too much' (A823/B851). Accordingly, in the Canon of Pure Reason, he devotes particular attention to the kind of *Fürwahrhalten* which is weaker than knowing but stronger than having an opinion, namely, believing (*glauben*),[12] further distinguishing three species of it: pragmatic belief, theoretical belief, and moral belief. Most importantly, theoretical belief 'explicitly allows for rational assent about things-in-themselves that is based on *theoretical* (rather than just moral or practical) grounds' (Chignell 2007: 335; see also 359). That is, belief is a specific cognitive mode which, also on theoretical grounds, allows a *sui generis* access to a noumenal sphere which is beyond our actual or possible knowledge.[13] In so doing, pure reason opens up 'prospects beyond the bounds of experience' (A830/B858).

[11] On the importance of rejecting double standards see Alston 1991, discussed in Chap. 14, sect. 14.2.1 and Chap. 15, sect. 15.1.

[12] As discussed in Chap. 4, sect. 4.1.1, for Kant, 'having an opinion [*meinen*] is holding something to be true with the consciousness that it is subjectively as well as objectively insufficient'; believing [*glauben*] is holding something to be true with the consciousness that it is subjectively sufficient but objectively insufficient; knowing [*wissen*] is holding something to be true on both subjectively and objectively sufficient grounds (A822/B850).

[13] I agree with Chignell (2007: 335, n. 15) that *Glaube* is a technical term in Kant but I take this to mean that it can be properly understood only in the context of Kant's critical philosophy, not that it is irremediably at odds with the everyday notion of 'belief' (whatever this murky, but often invoked, 'everyday' notion is supposed to be). As I noted in the General Introduction to this book, typically, good philosophical technical notions do not hijack a commonly used word to apply it to something altogether different. Rather, they use a common word in a technical manner to sharpen an amorphous area still broadly recognizable in relevant ways as picked out by that word.

In order to briefly evaluate these three species of belief, it should be noted, first of all, that being conscious that assent is given on objectively insufficient grounds does not equate to irrational assenting, for it does not equate to having objectively sufficient grounds against assenting. Belief is still 'rationally acceptable for anyone in the subject's position' (Chignell 2007: 336). Moreover, believing does not involve a cognitive mistake as in the case of the person who is persuaded: unlike the persuaded person, the person who believes does not mistake her subjectively sufficient grounds for objectively sufficient grounds.[14]

13.1.2 Pragmatic, Theoretical, and Moral Grounds of Believing

This being said, which sort of subjectively sufficient grounds could be involved in believing? A first family of grounds is 'pragmatic'. Pragmatic belief has a 'practical relation' to action: once an end is proposed (say, curing a sick person), it may be hypothetically necessary to assent to certain propositions if one does not know 'of any other conditions at all under which the end could be attained'. So, a doctor holds for true that the cause of sickness is 'consumption' if 'he does not know of anything better' but must take some action to achieve the end. 'I call such contingent beliefs', Kant concludes, 'pragmatic beliefs' (A823/B851—A824/B852).[15] As noted by Chignell, Kantian pragmatic belief appears to correspond to what in present-day literature is often referred to as acceptance: a firm assent that 'differs from belief in being voluntary, justified by nonepistemic merits, and accompanied by a different phenomenology' (Chignell 2007: 343).[16]

A second family of subjectively sufficient grounds is 'theoretical' and supports theoretical belief.[17] I would summarize Kant's position on theoretical belief as follows. There are *theoretical* (as opposed to only pragmatic or moral) *advantages* to some theoretical hypotheses (notably, the theistic hypotheses of a wise author of nature, of an ultimate ground, and of an *ens realissimum*).[18] The truth of these hypotheses cannot, even in principle, be known. Given their logical possibility, however, these hypotheses can be rationally believed (that is, held for true on

[14] Cf. A820/B849 and Ak 24:218. For discussion of persuasion (*Überredung*) in Kant see Chap. 4, sect. 4.1.1.

[15] Cf. Chignell 2007: 337–44. Chignell defines non-epistemic merit as the 'property of an assent that makes it valuable or desirable for a subject—given his or her needs, interests, and goals—but which does not do so by way of directly indicating that the assent is true' (p. 334).

[16] According to Alston 1996, belief is dispositional and involuntary, whereas acceptance is a voluntary mental act of regarding something as true. See also Cohen 1992. I discuss acceptance and its relation to belief and assent in Chap. 4, sect. 4.2.5 and in Chap. 11.

[17] Kant calls this kind of belief 'doctrinal belief [*doctrinale Glaube*]' (A825/B853). *Doctrinale Glaube* means in this context a belief which has theoretical content (a 'doctrine'). I follow therefore Chignell in referring to it as theoretical belief.

[18] See A826/B824; A622/B650; Ak 28: 1034.

subjectively sufficient theoretical grounds). This position is well captured by the following passage from Kant's *Reflexionen* on logic:

> The principle of the self-preservation of reason is the basis of rational Belief, in which the act of assenting has the same degree as in Knowledge [das Fürwahrhalten eben den Grad hat als beym Wissen], but is of another kind which comes not from the cognition of grounds in the object but rather from the true needs of the subject in respect to theoretical as well as practical applications. (Ak 16: 371–2; trans. modified)[19]

What I call 'theoretical advantages' correspond, roughly, to Chignell's non-epistemic merits which are 'still in some important sense theoretical merits' (2007: 349). The notion of 'theoretical advantages' of a hypothesis, I propose, gives more precise content to these non-epistemic but theoretical merits—this is a kind of merit 'which comes not from the cognition of grounds in the object' but from 'true needs' of reason (Ak 16:371–2). To be sure, these theoretical hypotheses are not open to confirmation by knowledge of their truth,[20] but there are other ways in which a theoretical hypothesis can be confirmed in a broader sense: for instance, by confirming its heuristic power or its superiority to new competing hypotheses. Indeed, Kant explicitly writes that 'the outcome of experiments... often confirms [*bestätigt*]' the usefulness of the 'presupposition [*Voraussetzung*] of a wise author of the world' as 'a guide for the investigation of nature' (see A826/B854).

Furthermore, like pragmatic belief,[21] also theoretical belief is accompanied by a voluntary element which justifies the comparison, proposed by Chignell, with the present-day notion of acceptance. It is important to note, however, that the element of voluntariness is not primarily triggered, in this case, by pragmatic or moral considerations but by *theoretical* considerations,[22] that is, by the need for rational explanation expressed by the Principle of Sufficient Reason.[23] In other words, theoretical belief is required by reason to avoid precipitating into the abyss of irrationality. As Kant writes in his *Lecture on Transcendental Theology* (part of his lectures on the philosophical doctrine of religion, given in 1785/86), 'my reason makes it absolutely necessary for me to assume [*annehmen*] a being

[19] Attention to this passage is drawn by Chignell (2007): 349, n. 32.

[20] Chignell (2007: 353) objects to conceiving theoretical beliefs as theoretical hypotheses due to their not being open to confirmation. Cf., however, Chignell's description of the presupposition of a wise author of the world held by the biologist as 'a hypothetically necessary condition of attaining her chosen end' (2007: 347).

[21] Note that Kant regards theoretical beliefs as 'an analogue' of practical judgements (A825/B853).

[22] Note that, for Kant, theoretical belief is concerned with 'merely' theoretical matters (cf. A825/B853). It seems to me that its being triggered by theoretical rather than by pragmatic considerations is what marks the main distinction between pragmatic and theoretical belief.

[23] Chignell rightly stresses that 'the inclusion of Theoretical Belief in Kant's system clearly shows that the Principle of Sufficient Reason (PSR) doesn't go away in the critical philosophy' (2007: 350).

which is the ground of everything possible, because otherwise I would be unable to know [*erkennen*] what in general the possibility of something consists in' (28:1034, trans. Wood and Di Giovanni, 375). In his critical writings, the notion of 'accepting' a theoretical belief as required by rationality is already apparent: 'the entire whole would have to sink into the abyss of nothingness [*Abgrunde des Nichts*] if one did not accept [*annehmen*] something subsisting with its origin in itself and independently outside this infinite contingency, which supports it and at the same time, as the cause of its existence, secures its continuation' (A622/B650, trans. Guyer and Wood, 579).

Another important difference between pragmatic belief and theoretical belief, consonant (if not explicitly stated) with the thrust of Kant's proposal, is the following. In the case of pragmatic belief, there can be, in principle, a nearby possible world in which a subject could have knowledge of the matters of which, in this world, she has merely pragmatic belief. By contrast, in the case of theoretical belief, there is not, even in principle, such a nearby possible world, since the matter at issue cannot be settled within the bounds of possible experience. To put it another way, the relevant world is not a *nearby* one, belonging to the same phenomenal order, but a radically different one, such as the noumenal world.[24]

Finally, a third family of grounds for belief is 'moral'. These grounds support the most well known and frequently discussed type of Kantian belief, namely, 'moral belief'.[25] For Kant the primacy of practical over speculative reason is reflected in the way in which immortality, freedom, and God's existence must be postulated. In the *Critique of Pure Reason*, he defines theoretical cognition as 'that through which I cognize *what exists*', and practical cognition as 'that through which I represent *what ought to exist*' (A632/B660–A634/B662). In the *Critique of Practical Reason* (1788), he explains that the existence of God, immortality, and freedom ought to be postulated (that is, we must voluntarily assent to them)[26] in order to establish reverence for the moral law and the conditions of possibility of its realization (cf. Ak 5: 124–34). Belief in God's existence, immortality, and freedom is required to maintain the rationality of the moral order. Through this kind of moral belief [*Glaube*], we can somehow relate to the noumenal or intelligible world which lies beyond what is knowable.

[24] I take this is what Chignell means to say with his claim that 'a crucial difference between Pragmatic Belief and Theoretical Belief is that the former is assent for which the subject *could* in a nearby possible world have sufficient objective grounds and which *could* thereby count as Knowledge, whereas the latter is assent that *could not* in similar circumstances count as Knowledge' (Chignell 2007: 345). Conversely, I take Chignell does not mean to claim that in a nearby possible world pragmatic belief could count as knowledge if the subject had sufficient objective grounds. As far as I can see, for Kant, knowledge is never a *species* of pragmatic belief since belief is, by definition, a kind of assenting which lacks sufficient objective grounds. If the subject does have sufficient objective (and subjective) grounds, her assenting would simply be knowledge *as opposed to* being pragmatic belief.

[25] Cf. A828/B856–A830/B858.

[26] Cf. Chignell 2007: 355.

In sum, belief plays a crucial, distinctive, and irreplaceable role in extending our rational cognitive grip in ways which are not only practical and moral but also theoretical.

13.2 Faith as a Doxastic State

13.2.1 The Object of Faith Is Not Something Seen or Known

Mutatis mutandis, also for Aquinas, belief plays a key role in extending rational cognition beyond the bounds of what is, strictly speaking, known or knowable.[27] The contrast between seen/not seen, tracking the contrast between known/believed, returns repeatedly throughout the part of the *Summa Theologiae* devoted to faith, emerging as one of the hallmarks of Aquinas's account.[28] Although faith (*fides*), in this context, normally means religious faith, Aquinas acknowledges also a more general sense of faith. The latter differs from the former in its not being directed at the hope of eternal happiness (ST II IIae, q. 4, a. 1). At least some of the epistemic features identified by Aquinas for religious faith apply also to faith taken in this more general sense.

In ST IIa IIae, q. 1 a. 4, Aquinas asks 'whether the object of faith can be something seen [aliquid visum]'; and in the following article he asks 'whether it can be something known [aliquid scitum]'. His answer to both questions is 'no'. When it is said in John's gospel (20:29) that Thomas saw and believed, Aquinas explains, what he saw was different from what he believed: he actually saw a man but believed him to be God.[29] The sense in which seeing applies to believing, he continues, is this: in order to believe one has to *see* the credibility of what is believed, either on account of the evidence of signs or on account of something of this kind.[30] Thus believing is grounded in *seeing* (that is, knowing, understanding) the reasons for believing but is not itself seeing the object of belief. Faith, Aquinas goes on to say, does not ask natural reason 'to demonstrate what is believed' but to inquire 'into those things which lead a man to believe' (ST II IIae, q. 2, a. 1, ad

[27] There are, of course, vast differences between Kant and Aquinas. I am focusing here on a particular, but important, aspect of their thought.

[28] Cf. ST IIa IIae, q. 1–16. See also Aquinas, *Scriptum super Sententiis*, lib. 3 d. 23 q. 2 a. 2. The contrast between seen/not seen, known/believed does not make of Aquinas a fideist (*pace* Pasnau 2013). On the other hand, it is not the case that according to Aquinas 'faith provides one with knowledge' (Hawthorne 2013: here p. 121) (although, of course, I do not deny that for Aquinas certain things about God can be *known*, notably that God exists). It seems to me that Pasnau and Hawthorne's opposed interpretations are both ultimately the result of not taking on board the distinction in kind between knowledge and belief. A much better account of Aquinas on belief is offered, in my view, by the earlier Hawthorne and Howard-Snyder 1996: esp. 235–9.

[29] ST IIa IIae, q. 1, a. 4, ad primum.

[30] ST IIa IIae, q. 1, a. 4, ad secundum: 'non enim crederet, nisi videret ea esse credenda, vel propter evidentiam signorum, vel propter aliquid hujusmodi'.

primum). That is, it is not a matter of demonstrating what is believed but of checking the credibility of what is believed on the basis of signs and testimony.[31]

'All knowledge [scientia]', he claims:

> is acquired through some self-evident, and therefore 'seen', principles [principia per se nota, et per consequens visa]. And for that reason it is necessary that whatsoever is known is, in some way, seen [quaecumque sunt scita aliquo modo esse visa]. Now, as stated above, it is not possible that the same thing should be believed and seen by the same person. Hence it is indeed impossible that the same things be known and believed [scitum et creditum] by the same person. Nevertheless it may happen that what is seen or known [visum vel scitum] by one, is believed [creditum] by another. (ST IIa IIae, q. 1, a. 5)[32]

That is to say, although some things can in principle be known (for example, by demonstration), some people may believe these same things through testimony rather than knowing them.[33] An obvious example is some truth of higher mathematics which, strictly speaking, is known by mathematicians by demonstration but merely believed on the basis of their testimony by most non-mathematicians: 'and thus it can happen that, even in earthly matters, that which is seen or known by one man is believed by another who has not learned its demonstration [id quod est visum, vel scitum ab uno homine... sit ab alio creditum, qui hoc demonstratione non novit]' (ST II IIae q. 1, a. 5).[34] There are, however, things which are not even knowable (at least ordinarily): 'what is ordinarily proposed to all human beings as a matter of belief [proponitur... ut credendum]', Aquinas concludes, 'is generally unknown [est communiter non scitum]: such are the things which are of faith simpliciter; and therefore faith and knowledge are not about the same things [et ideo fides, et scientia non sunt de eodem]' (ST II IIae q. 1, a. 5).

The examples given leave no doubt that Aquinas intends to apply the epistemic distinction in kind between knowing and believing in particular to religious epistemology: in our present condition, we can only believe (as opposed to know) that God is Triune, precisely because we lack a vision of God (that is, we lack the insight into the nature of God which knowledge would require). As long as we live our earthly life, Aquinas reasons, we cannot enjoy the beatific vision already possessed by purely spiritual creatures such as angels. The epistemic status of most of our cognition of God is not, therefore, that of knowledge but of belief.

[31] Cf. ST IIa IIae, q. 2, a. 9, ad secundum; ST IIa IIae, q. 2, a. 9, ad tertium; ST IIa IIae, q. 2, a. 10 ad secundum for the compelling character of demonstration and knowledge, contrasted with faith.

[32] See also IIa IIae, q. 1, a. 5, ad quartum: 'non potest simul idem, et secundum idem esse scitum, et creditum, quia scitum est visum, et creditum est non visum'.

[33] Cf. ST IIa IIae, q. 2, a. 4.

[34] Cf. Aquinas, *Summa contra Gentiles* Book I, chap. 4, on reasons why many people are unable to achieve knowledge of truths which are in principle knowable, and rely instead on belief based on testimony.

13.2.2 Faith, Hope, and the Unseen

Furthermore, faith is of *unseen* things[35] that we hope to be able to see one day:

> those things which we now believe [credimus] about the Trinity, we hope [speramus] to see one day, according to 1 Corinthians 13:[12]: *Now we are seeing a dim reflection in a mirror, but then we shall be seeing face to face*, as the vision angels already have, so that what we believe, they see [quod nos credimus, illi vident]. (ST IIa IIae, q. 1, a. 5)[36]

Like faith, so also hope, Aquinas maintains, regards in fact only unseen (or non-apparent) things: 'according to the Apostle (Romans 8:[25]): *We hope for that which we see not* [*Quod non videmus, speramus*]; because to see the truth is to possess it, and one does not hope for something that he has already: hope is for what one does not have' (ST IIa IIae, q. 4, a. 1); 'hope is always of things which are absent and unseen [non visorum]' (ST IIa IIae, q. 4, a. 1, ad tertium).

'Faith', Aquinas continues:

> is a habit of the mind . . . whereby the intellect assents to what is not manifest [faciens intellectum assentire non apparentibus]. And indeed faith is distinguished by this from all other things which pertain to the intellect: in so far as we say that it is an argument, faith is distinguished from opinion, suspicion, and doubt, by which there is no firm adhesion of the intellect to anything; in so far as we say that it is of non-manifest things, faith is distinguished from knowledge and understanding [distinguitur fides a scientia, et intellectu] the object of which is something manifest. (ST IIa IIae, q. 4, a. 1)[37]

The epistemic status of faith as between opinion and knowledge, he concludes, is also endorsed by other authors according to whom 'faith is that certainty of the mind about absent things [de absentibus] which is above opinion but below knowledge [supra opinionem, et infra scientiam]' (ST IIa IIae, q. 4, a. 1). Once again, the lack of a direct presence to the cognizer of the object of cognition is what marks the difference between faith and knowledge, believing and knowing. On the

[35] ST IIa IIae, q. 4, a. 1: 'the intellect of the believer is convinced to assent by divine authority to those things it does not see'. Aquinas is keen to cite Augustine's authority in support of this position: 'Augustine says: Faith is a virtue by which things that are not seen are believed [creduntur quae non videntur].' Cf. also Heb. 11:1, referred to by Aquinas in ST I, q. 2, a. 2 and commented extensively in ST IIa IIae, q. 4, a. 1. For the Augustine passage, cf. *In Iohannis euangelium tractatus*, tract. 79, PL 35:1379; and *Quaestiones euangeliorum*, lib. 2, q. 39, PL 35:1321.

[36] See also ST IIa IIae, q. 4, a. 1.

[37] Aquinas is commenting on Paul's doctrine in Heb 11:1: 'Est autem fides [*pistis*] sperandorum substantia, rerum argumentum non apparentium.'

other hand, the firmness of assent (based on authoritative, trustworthy testimony) which characterizes faith makes faith epistemically superior to mere opinion.[38]

13.2.3 Faith as a Virtue

Most importantly, the relative epistemic obscurity which characterizes faith (due to the absence of 'clear sight') is essential to its being a *virtue*. Precisely because there is not the same compulsion to assent in faith that there is in knowledge, there is in faith an element of free will (*liberum arbitrium*), and there can therefore be moral value in faith as well.[39] In knowledge as well, Aquinas grants, there is a meritorious element, insofar as there is a voluntary aspect to the attentive consideration of what is knowable. But as regards the assent to what is known, there is no scope for free will 'because the knower is compelled to assent by the force of demonstration [quia sciens cogitur ad assentiendum per efficaciam demonstrationis]' (ST IIa IIae, q. 2, a. 9, ad secundum). In faith, on the other hand, both assent and consideration of the object of cognition are subject to free will and can be, therefore, meritorious.[40] This element of freedom does not imply, however, that it is per se meritorious or acceptable to believe 'lightly' without good reasons. The point is that these reasons are sufficient for belief but not for knowledge, leaving a role for the will to play.[41] More precisely, these reasons 'are not demonstrations which can bring the human intellect to intellectual vision; and therefore they do not cease to be non-manifest things; but they remove obstacles to faith, by showing that what faith proposes is not impossible' (ST IIa IIae, q. 2, a. 10 ad secundum).[42]

Finally, the epistemic obscurity which characterizes faith does not compromise its certainty. This view may appear surprising, given Aquinas's central claims that faith is of the unseen, that reasons for belief do not compel assent, and so on. 'Certainty', however, 'may be considered in two ways. In one way, on the part of its cause: and thus it is said to be more certain that which has a more certain cause;... In another way, on the part of the subject: and thus it is said to be more certain that which the human intellect reaches more fully' (ST IIa IIae, q. 4, a. 8).

[38] Cf. for instance ST II IIae, q. 2, a. 1 and ST IIa IIae, q. 4, a. 1.

[39] ST II IIae, q. 2, a. 9 (*Whether to believe is meritorious*): 'our actions are meritorious in so far as they proceed from free will moved through grace by God... to believe is itself an act of the intellect that assents to divine truth at the command of the will moved by God through grace... hence the act of faith can be meritorious'. On faith as a virtue see Robert Adams 1987: 9–24.

[40] See ST IIa IIae, q. 2, a. 9, ad secundum. Cf. also ST IIa IIae, q. 2, a. 10.

[41] ST IIa IIae, q. 2, a. 9, ad tertium: 'the believer has what is sufficient to lead to belief [sufficiens inductivum ad credendum]... hence he does not believe lightly. However, he does not have what is sufficient to lead to knowledge [sufficiens inductivum ad scientiam]; and therefore, the ground of merit is not eliminated.'

[42] Cf. Aquinas, *Summa Contra Gentiles*, Book I, chaps. 5–7, esp. chap. 7 (*That the truth of reason is not contrary to the truth of the Christian faith*).

Assuming that the cause of faith's certainty is God, faith is the most certain of all intellectual virtues (including—in addition to faith—wisdom, knowledge, and understanding). With respect to the human intellect, however, 'faith is less certain' than knowledge.[43] That is, the certainty of faith of which Aquinas is speaking is not the subjective or psychological certainty of someone whose belief is unshakable even if there are not compelling reasons that determine assent. The relevant kind of certainty is the objective certainty which follows from the premise that 'faith rests on divine truth' (ST IIa IIae, q. 4, a. 8). Crucially, however, the truth of this premise is not known or knowable by the human intellect. Thus, faith is absolutely certain *secundum se* or simpliciter but not *quoad nos*.[44]

This position mirrors Aquinas's answer to the question of whether it is self-evident (*per se notum*) that there is a God.[45] 'Something can be self-evident', Aquinas maintains, 'in two manners. In one manner *secundum se*, and not *quoad nos*. In another manner *secundum se*, and *quoad nos*.' The existence of God is self-evident in the first, but not in the second manner. In short, as far as we are concerned, it is not self-evident that God exists. It takes instead laborious arguments from effects to come to the conclusion that He does, and even so we are not able to know what God is, namely, what is (*quid sit*) God's essence. Similarly, although faith is in itself certain, as far as we are concerned, it is compatible with doubt precisely because faith *is not* knowledge.[46]

The bottom line is that Aquinas is acutely aware of the epistemic gulf between humankind and God, and this awareness is a pillar of his religious epistemology. While he does not embrace the most radical version of apophaticism according to which God is totally ineffable and, therefore, nothing can be said about Him, he leaves no doubt that what we can say about God is at best analogical. There is a strong current of negative theology running through the Christian theological tradition. Aquinas, I contend, contributes to this current in important ways. While he advocates the possibility of religious cognition, he is also firm in drawing its structural limits: of God we can know what He is *not* rather than what He is.[47]

[43] See ST IIa IIae, q. 4, a. 8 (*Whether faith is more certain than knowledge and the other intellectual virtues* [prudence, art, wisdom, and understanding]).

[44] ST IIa IIae, q. 4, a. 8: 'faith is more certain simpliciter, but the other [intellectual virtues] are more certain secundum quid, namely, quoad nos'. Cf. Aquinas, *Scriptum super Sententiis*, lib. 3, d. 23, q. 2, a. 2, qc. 3.

[45] See ST I, q. 2, a. 1.

[46] Contra Plantinga's claim that 'Faith is *Knowledge*' (2000: 256–8). Plantinga's attempt to link this claim to Aquinas (as well as Calvin) rests, in my view, on a significant misunderstanding of Aquinas's position (cf. Plantinga 2000: 167–86 and ST I q. 2, a. 1, ad primum and ad secundum, where Aquinas is in fact saying that any cognition of the existence of God naturally implanted in us is so confused as to be compatible with atheism and materialism, e.g., with the identification of God with the corporeal universe, or of the supreme good with earthly riches). For further discussion of Plantinga's position see Chap. 14.

[47] ST I, q. 3, pr. I agree with interpreters who stress this aspect of Aquinas's thought (including Davies 1992; Marenbon 2007: 237–8; Turner 2013; and, most recently, Hewitt 2020a and 2020b), although Aquinas's complex and nuanced approach resists, in my view, a clear-cut classification as

Overall, his account seems to me to strike a remarkably good balance between cognitive and conative/affective aspects of faith (notably trust). In fact, the very importance of the latter aspects is signalled by the traditional view that, properly speaking, it is not belief but faith which qualifies as a virtue. That is, faith, I propose, is compatible with some degree of voluntariness absent from belief qua spontaneous response to perceived evidence.[48] And it is precisely this degree of *liberum arbitrium* which grounds the meritoriousness needed for a virtue. What is virtuous about it is not doxastic voluntarism but the sort of trust, sustained by hope and love, which makes a father have faith in his son despite his present drastic failings, or a wife have faith that her husband will overcome his drinking habit even if this faith outstrips current reasons for believing that he will.

negative theology/apophaticism (for qualifications see for instance Te Velde 2006: 72–7). On the other hand, it seems to me that some leading interpreters in analytical Anglo-American philosophy underestimate the elements of negative theology in Aquinas's thought.

[48] For a discussion see Chap. 11.

14
Religious Belief I
Reformed Epistemology and Neo-Cartesianism

The next two chapters explore how the framework proposed by this book applies specifically to religious belief. It will be argued that the conception of knowledge and belief as two irreducibly different cognitive modes is especially important in religious epistemology in safeguarding the distinctive epistemological status of religious belief. In fact, I contend that religious belief shows in a particularly striking way that the project of turning belief into knowledge with the addition of necessary and sufficient conditions is misguided, and that a different account of cognition along the lines I have defended is therefore needed. The result is an approach to religious epistemology fundamentally different from that of the highly influential movement known as Reformed Epistemology. This chapter outlines my interpretation of the project of Reformed Epistemology and explains why, in my view, it should be abandoned.

14.1 Reformed Epistemology and Proper Basicality

14.1.1 The Rise of Reformed Epistemology

Traditionally, the epistemic justification of religious belief has been approached in the framework of the justification of any belief, whether religious or secular, in terms of the evidence or reasons which can be provided in support of the belief in question. In religious epistemology, this is the approach followed by natural theology, as exemplified by arguments for the existence of God. Although these arguments have been presented, historically, as 'demonstrations', nowadays they are typically regarded as ways to support the reasonableness of believing in God's existence or as ways to reject charges of irrationality against belief in God. At best, they are thought to make a convincing case for the probability of God's existence,[1] rather than constituting proofs which afford knowledge of the existence of God.

The acknowledgement of this weaker epistemological status is one of the key factors behind the rise, in the early 1980s, of a new brand of religious

[1] Cf. the new version of natural theology developed by Richard Swinburne in his formidable collection of publications (see in particular Swinburne 1993, 2004, 2005).

Thinking with Assent: Renewing a Traditional Account of Knowledge and Belief. Maria Rosa Antognazza, Oxford University Press. © Maria Rosa Antognazza 2024. DOI: 10.1093/oso/9780198831518.003.0015

epistemology that has swept through anglophone analytical religious epistemology and that continues to hold sway especially in North America, namely, Reformed Epistemology.[2] Reformed Epistemology is so called due to the allegiance of its original proponents to the Protestant, 'Reformed' tradition originating from John Calvin. Its founding fathers and most prominent advocates, Alvin Plantinga and Nicholas Wolterstorff,[3] counter the failure of rational arguments to provide religious believers with knowledge of the existence of God with an altogether different approach to the rational justification of religious belief.[4] One of the traits of this alternative approach is a marked anti-intellectualism deployed in defence of the epistemic respectability of the faith of common people. 'Many Reformed thinkers and theologians', Plantinga writes in a ground-breaking paper of 1981, 'have rejected *natural theology* (thought of as the attempt to provide proofs or arguments for the existence of God). They have held not merely that the proffered arguments are unsuccessful, but that the whole enterprise is in some way radically misguided' (Plantinga 1981/1993: 134). In Wolterstorff's more recent words:

> Faith is not the property of the intelligentsia; it inhabits all those to whom God is revealed in Christ. As such, it's OK as it is. It can use the ministrations of Christian theology. But it doesn't need to be rationally grounded to make it acceptable. (Wolterstorff 2005: 269)

In brief, Reformed Epistemology's key claim is that religious belief can be rational, 'warranted', or 'entitled', without any need for believers to appeal to evidence or arguments in support of their beliefs. Indeed, not only do believers not need to be aware of evidence or arguments which might be provided in support of their beliefs: there need not be any such arguments or evidence at all.

14.1.2 Evidentialism and Properly Basic Beliefs

Accordingly, for Wolterstorff, the target of Reformed Epistemology is 'Enlightenment Evidentialism' as chiefly represented by John Locke. In Wolterstorff's interpretation,

[2] In one recent collection on religious epistemology, the editors of the volume note that Reformed Epistemology 'remains the dominant perspective' (Benton, Hawthorne, and Rabinowitz 2018: 'Introduction').

[3] Although William Alston is usually associated with Reformed Epistemology due to some important similarities between his proposal and the views of Plantinga and Wolterstorff, there are also significant differences, notably Alston's stress on doxastic practices and epistemic justification rather than on turning belief into knowledge. In this chapter I will focus on Reformed Epistemology as advanced by Plantinga and Wolterstorff. Reference will be made, however, to aspects of Alston's epistemology which tallies with their approach. Alston's specific proposal about the important contribution made by experiential awareness of God to the grounds of religious belief is discussed in Chap. 15.

[4] See Plantinga's seminal papers 'Is Belief in God Properly Basic?' (1981) and 'Reason and Belief in God' (1983). Although Reformed Epistemology came to prominence in the early 1980s, its roots are deeper and go back at least to the late 1960s. Cf. Plantinga 1967.

Locke holds that rational intuition and sense experience 'evoke in us what we in the twentieth century have called "immediate" or "basic" beliefs—in contrast to *mediate* beliefs, which are those formed in us on the basis of other beliefs'. 'Reason and experience both give us direct cognitive access to certain facts of reality and, when working properly, evoke in us beliefs whose propositional content corresponds to those facts.' However, for Locke, 'neither reason nor experience gives us direct cognitive access to the facts corresponding to our religious beliefs' (Wolterstorff 2005: 252). Thus, for so-called 'Enlightenment Evidentialism', religious beliefs must be rationally grounded in the deliverances of reason and experience in order to be rational ('entitled').

Against this 'evidentialism', Wolterstorff and the Reformed Epistemologists want to advance the view that 'the believer is entitled to his or her beliefs even though they're not rationally grounded' since 'it's not true that religious beliefs in general have to be rationally grounded in the deliverances of reason and experience to be doxastically meritorious'.[5]

The same sharp distinction between basic and non-basic beliefs provides the framework of Plantinga's early work in religious epistemology. A *basic* belief, Plantinga explains, is a belief which is not inferred from, or based on, other beliefs. It is *properly* basic if one is justified, rational, warranted, entitled in holding it in this basic, non-inferential way. Examples of properly basic beliefs include perceptual beliefs, memory beliefs, and beliefs which ascribe mental states to other persons such as '1. I see a tree, 2. I had breakfast this morning, and 3. That person is angry.' Likewise, rational intuition is also a source of properly basic beliefs (for example, '2 + 1 = 3'). On the other hand, non-basic beliefs are beliefs which are based upon (or inferred from) other beliefs (for example, '72 × 71 = 5112').[6] Non-basic beliefs are justified only if they are based on other justified beliefs. The chain of justification, however, must eventually end in basic beliefs which do not depend on other beliefs and provide, therefore, the foundation of our noetic edifice. Plantinga's polemical target is not, therefore, epistemic foundationalism as such but a specific (if historically pervasive) version of foundationalism—'classical foundationalism'.

As characterized by Plantinga, classical foundationalism (which includes Wolterstorff's 'Enlightenment Evidentialism' as, arguably, its most paradigmatic manifestation) grants the status of proper basicality only to beliefs which are 'self-evident, or incorrigible, or evident to the senses' (Plantinga 1981/1993: 141). This shortlist, however, is way too short for Reformed Epistemology. Plenty of other beliefs which do not make the short list (so it is claimed) would be intuitively regarded as basic beliefs, notably, religious beliefs such as 'God exists'. Scores of

[5] Wolterstorff 2005: 248, 265. I leave aside the question of whether this is an accurate interpretation of Locke.

[6] Plantinga 1981/1993: 136, 133.

people (Plantinga argues) hold such belief in a basic way, that is, without propositional evidence or support by reasons or arguments. Why should not 'God exists' count as a *properly* basic belief, Plantinga asks, along with the other properly basic beliefs excluded by classical foundationalism's unjustified and unjustifiable criterion for proper basicality?[7] 'What Reformed thinkers really mean to hold', Plantinga summarizes,

> is that belief in God need not be based on argument or evidence from other propositions at all. They mean to hold that the believer is entirely within his intellectual rights in believing as he does even if he doesn't know of any good theistic arguments (deductive or inductive), even if he doesn't believe that there is any such argument, and even if in fact no such argument exists. They hold that it is perfectly rational to accept belief in God without accepting it on the basis of any other beliefs or propositions at all. In a word, they hold that *belief in God is properly basic.* (Plantinga 1981/1993: 134)

The rationality of such basic belief in God, Plantinga continues, depends on the fact that a properly basic belief is not a *groundless* belief despite its not being based on reasons. This is shown, for instance, by basic perceptual beliefs:

> Upon having experience of a certain sort, I believe I am perceiving a tree.... My having that characteristic sort of experience... plays a crucial role in the formation and justification of that belief. We might say this experience, together, perhaps, with other circumstances, is what *justifies* me in holding it; this is the *ground* of my justification, and, by extension, the ground of the belief itself. (Plantinga 1981/1993: 136)

The upshot is the following. Perceptual beliefs, memory beliefs, and beliefs resulting from rational intuition are *properly* basic just in case they are the direct result of cognitive faculties working properly in the appropriate circumstances. Likewise, basic belief in God is *properly* basic just in case it is the result of a well-functioning cognitive faculty—call it *sensus divinitatis*—working properly in appropriate circumstances.[8] For instance, upon experiencing a beautiful starry sky, I find myself spontaneously believing that God exists, much as upon having a certain characteristic sort of experience, I form the basic (non-inferential) belief that I am perceiving a tree. As in sense-perception the combination of properly functioning eyesight and appropriate visual stimuli result in the basic belief 'I see a

[7] Plantinga 1983: 59 formulates classical foundationalism's criterion for proper basicality as follows: 'A proposition *p* is properly basic for a person *S* if and only if *p* is either self-evident to *S* or incorrigible for *S* or evident to the senses for *S*.'

[8] Plantinga traces the notion of *sensus divinitatis* back to Calvin, although it is debatable whether Plantinga's *sensus divinitatis* corresponds to an accurate reading of Calvin.

tree', so the combination of a properly functioning faculty for being directly aware of God's presence (the *sensus divinitatis*) and appropriate stimuli result in the basic belief 'God exists'.

14.1.3 Analogies and Dis-Analogies

The trouble is that there are also glaring dis-analogies between the two cases. The 'characteristic sort of experience' which leads to the basic belief that I am perceiving a tree is that of seeing a tree, whereas the experience which leads to the basic belief that God exists is that of seeing a beautiful starry sky, not that of seeing God. It seems that some pretty hefty inference is needed to move from the beautiful starry sky to the existence of God. And if inference is needed, the belief loses its all-important status of proper basicality, that is, of belief which does not need reasons or argument to be rationally held. Not to speak of the fact that many people do not find themselves spontaneously believing that God exists upon experiencing a beautiful starry sky—or, at any rate, not with the same kind of regularity with which people experiencing a tree form the belief that they are perceiving a tree.

Moreover, critics are quick to object that Plantinga's plan to substitute the short list of classical foundationalism's basic beliefs with a much longer list opens the gates to epistemic anarchy. Once classical foundationalism's criterion of proper basicality is ditched, it seems disturbingly easy for any belief to claim the epistemic status of proper basicality, and hence the right to be rationally held without supporting reasons, argument, or evidential backing. As for the *sensus divinitatis*, what is there to stop the followers of Linus from claiming that their basic belief that the 'Great Pumpkin' returns every Halloween is the result of an ad hoc properly functioning cognitive faculty (say, the *sensus pumpkinitatis*)?[9]

Plantinga, however, is undeterred. Arguably, a closer analogy can be found in the case of forming basic beliefs about the mental states of other people. 'If I see someone displaying typical pain behaviour, I take it that he or she is in pain', Plantinga notes.[10] His key point, as already argued in his earlier monograph of 1967 on *God and Other Minds*, is that we routinely form and accept beliefs regarding other minds even if there are no 'cogent arguments of the sort required' in support of these beliefs. That is, from the point of view of classical foundationalism's injunction to believe

[9] Rivers of ink have been spilled over the famous Great Pumpkin's objection. I cannot follow here all the twists and turns of the arguments and counter-arguments. For a canonical text on the Great Pumpkin's objection see Plantinga 1983: 74–8.

[10] Plantinga 1981/1993: 136.

> a proposition which is not certain (i.e., self-evident or incorrigible) only on the evidential basis of propositions that *are* certain . . . belief in other minds and belief in God are on an epistemological par. . . . If you flout epistemic duty in accepting the one, then you flout it just as surely in accepting the other; hence if the former is irrational, so is the latter.[11]

But since we grant the rationality of belief in other minds despite the lack of conclusive arguments, so we should grant the rationality of belief in God.

14.2 Epistemic Parity and Neo-Cartesianism

14.2.1 Reliability and Epistemic Circularity

At bottom, what does the work in Plantinga's analogies between belief in God and other beliefs is the demand for epistemic parity between basic beliefs about God and basic beliefs about other matters which are routinely accepted as rational despite the lack of conclusive argumentative support for those beliefs.

A similar rejection of epistemic double-standards is at the core of William Alston's epistemology of religious perceptual beliefs.[12] The Christian Mystical Practice (CMP) of forming beliefs about God, Alston argues, 'is being condemned for features shared by other practices [notably, Sense Perception] that are approved'.[13] Building on suggestions by Thomas Reid, Alston claims that 'the only (external) basis we have for trusting rational intuition and introspection is that they are firmly established doxastic practices,[14] so firmly established that we 'cannot help it'; and we have exactly the same basis for trusting sense perception, memory, non-deductive reasoning, and other sources of belief for which Descartes and Hume were demanding an external validation. They all 'come out of the same shop', and therefore if one of them is suspect so are all the others.'[15]

That is, 'none of our most basic "doxastic" (belief-forming) practices, including introspection, memory, and reasoning of various sorts, can be noncircularly shown to be reliable'. Sense perception is, according to Alston, no exception: none of the attempts to show its reliability escape 'epistemic circularity'. Any

[11] Plantinga 1990: xi–xii ('Preface to the 1990 Paperback Edition').

[12] See Alston 1991: 249–50.

[13] Alston 1991: 199.

[14] A doxastic practice is a belief-forming mechanism. More precisely, it is 'the exercise of a system or constellation of belief-forming habits or mechanisms, each realizing a function that yields beliefs with a certain kind of content from inputs of a certain type' Alston 1991: 155.

[15] Alston 1991: 151. Alston quotes the relevant passages in Reid's *Inquiry*, where the expressions 'cannot help it' and 'came out of the same shop' are found (see, respectively, *Inquiry*, chap. 5, 7, p. 71 and chap. 6, 20, p. 169). I quote and discuss Reid's famous 'mint of Nature' and 'same shop' passage in Chap. 3, sect. 3.2.3 where I note a greater similarity to Hume than Reid himself (and, I dare say, many of his present-day interpreters) seems to realize.

attempt to deliver a knock-down blow against ever resurgent competitors such as Cartesian scepticism or Berkeleyan idealism is doomed to failure. Our inability to show the reliability of our doxastic practices, Alston concludes, 'gives rise to a crisis of rationality'. What is then 'the most rational attitude for us to take toward these practices?'[16] Alston's proposal, for which inspiration from Reid and Wittgenstein is claimed, is markedly practical in character: it is practically rational to engage in any socially established practice as long as we do not have sufficient reasons for regarding it as unreliable.[17] In brief, 'all our established doxastic practices' are 'innocent until proven guilty'.[18] The conclusion is that 'it is prima facie rational to engage in CMP . . . because it is a socially established doxastic practice' and 'we lack sufficient reason for regarding it as unreliable or otherwise disqualified for rational participation'.[19]

Notwithstanding key differences between Plantinga's and Alston's projects,[20] on the issue of the reliability of our belief-forming mechanisms Plantinga adopts a similar stance, drawing from the same passages of Reid: reason is as uncertain as perception since 'they both came out of the same shop'.[21] As some Christian thinkers have recognized, Plantinga claims, 'there aren't any certain foundations of the sort Descartes sought . . . ; there is no sure and certain method of attaining truth by starting from beliefs about which you can't be mistaken'.[22]

14.2.2 Scepticism and Neo-Cartesianism

Now, Plantinga and other Reformed Epistemologists make a great show of being, in their theory of perception, direct realists inspired by Thomas Reid's attack on the Lockean way of ideas.[23] It seems to me, however, that it is not direct realism that bears the weight of Reformed Epistemology's argument. First of all, even if (as implicitly suggested by Wolterstorff)[24] we recast the classical terminology of knowledge and belief in terms of basic beliefs versus mediate beliefs, direct realists of the Reidian kind would agree with the despised 'classical foundationalists' in considering only universal practices (notably, sense perception) as

[16] See Alston 1991: 103 and Chap. 3, devoted in particular to the issue of the reliability of sense perception.

[17] See Alston 1991: 6. [18] Alston 1991: 153. [19] Alston 1991: 223.

[20] For Plantinga's own account of similarities and differences between his project and that of Alston, see Plantinga 2000: 286–9. Among other things, Plantinga stresses that his focus is on warrant rather than justification, and on the specific beliefs of Christianity (the Trinity, the Incarnation, and so on) rather than, generally, on belief in God.

[21] See Plantinga 2000: 220–2. [22] See Plantinga 2000: 436–7.

[23] The case for direct realism in the theory of perception is most compellingly articulated by Alston through his 'Theory of Appearing' (see Alston 1991: 70–7, 186–7). Reformed Epistemology's links with the views of Thomas Reid are discussed by Byrne 2011.

[24] Cf. Wolterstorff 2005: 252.

sources of properly basic beliefs—something which is indeed noted and lamented by Alston.[25]

Second, and most importantly, the weight of Plantinga's argument does not rest on the direct-realist claim that sense-perception puts us in direct cognitive contact with the world, but on the claim that basic beliefs resulting from sense-perception (or rational intuition, memory, and so on) have no better claim to epistemic justification than basic belief about God. The crucial point is that no cognitive faculty has independent justification for the reliability of the beliefs that it produces: that these beliefs are mostly true must be taken, ultimately, on trust.[26] Far from genuinely building on direct realism and its claim of a direct openness of the mind to the world, Plantinga's overarching project is best understood, in my view, as a kind of neo-Cartesianism according to which we can be rescued from a thoroughgoing scepticism about the reliability of our beliefs (including perceptual beliefs and a priori beliefs) only in a theistic framework.[27]

Against this backdrop, it should become clear that the distinction between basic beliefs and non-basic beliefs *is not* the distinction I am drawing between knowledge and belief under a different name. Basic beliefs are *beliefs* in the same sense in which Hume distinguishes belief from knowledge.[28] What really sets them apart from non-basic, inferential beliefs is their being immediate, spontaneous, incorrigible—they are the sort of beliefs we find ourselves having and which Reid describes (in a passage dear to Reformed Epistemologists) as beliefs one 'cannot help'.[29] To cut short a long story told over multiple monumental volumes, for Plantinga, we can be certain that they latch on to 'what is' only if a God of the Christian sort exists.

The neo-Cartesian bent of this project becomes more apparent in the later phase of Plantinga's work in which, under the pressure of objections, he sharpens his epistemic model. It is time, therefore, to shine the spotlight on the epistemic

[25] See Alston 1991: 169 and Byrne 2011: 279, 283.

[26] Cf. Alston (1991)'s claim that all doxastic practices are irremediably circular and can only be self-supporting. Both Alston and Plantinga refer to Reid's claim that belief on 'the existence of external objects' which are perceived is taken 'upon trust' in a way which is not different from all other beliefs, including those originating from reason rather than sense perception (see Reid, *Inquiry*, chap. 6, sect. 20, pp. 168–9; Alston 1991: 151; Plantinga 2000: 221).

[27] Pust 2013: 210–11 stresses that Plantinga's 'pattern of concession with regard to the classical skeptical problems appears in his treatment of our belief that we are persisting things, of our belief (on the basis of memory) that certain things have happened, of our belief that other minds exist, of beliefs formed on the basis of testimony of other persons, of perceptual belief in the external world, *a priori* beliefs, and inductive beliefs'. The latent scepticism and neo-Cartesianism of Plantinga's position is briefly noted by BonJour 1996: 69.

[28] On this distinction in Hume and on its impact on (J)TB+ theories (of which Plantinga's warrant theory is a version), see Chap. 3, sect. 3.2.

[29] Cf. Reid, *Inquiry*, chap. 5, 7, p. 71; Alston 1991: 151. On the surprising similarity between Reid and Hume on this point, see my discussion in Chap. 3, sect. 3.2.

framework in which Plantinga's proposal is located. From its early days onward, Plantinga's proposal takes for granted the twentieth-century epistemological orthodoxy according to which knowledge is a kind of *belief* which meets certain criteria (namely, truth plus some additional, duly de-Gettierized justificatory condition or set of conditions). Plantinga's particular version of the received doctrine, expounded at great length in his massive trilogy on 'warrant', conceives knowledge as warranted true belief.[30]

14.3 Warranted Christian Belief and the Claim That 'Faith is *Knowledge*'

14.3.1 Warrant, Externalism, and Reliabilism

Warrant, Plantinga explains, is 'that property—or better, *quantity*—enough of which is what makes the difference between knowledge and mere true belief' (Plantinga 2000: xi). Warrant is what turns true belief into knowledge. It is 'intimately connected with *proper function*:... a belief has warrant just if it is produced by cognitive processes or faculties that are functioning properly, in a cognitive environment that is propitious for that exercise of cognitive powers, according to a design plan that is successfully aimed at the production of true beliefs' (Plantinga 2000: xi).

Plantinga's approach to belief justification (taken in the loose sense of 'being rationally acceptable') shows here its uncompromising externalism: a belief is (loosely speaking) justified, or (strictly speaking) warranted, if it is the product of a well-functioning belief-forming mechanism. The subject does not need to be aware of this cognitive mechanism, and/or of its proper function, in order for her belief to have warrant. There is no requirement whatsoever for her to be able to give reasons in support of her belief. It is worth noting that in defending externalism Plantinga is sailing with the tide: most present-day epistemologists accept one version or another of externalism,[31] understood as the view that, in order for a belief to be justified or rationally held, the justification status of a belief need not (and most often, is not) directly accessible to the subject. Furthermore, as has been noted, Plantinga's epistemological proposal is at bottom nothing else than a variant of the widely held externalist model which goes under the label of reliabilism.[32] A belief has warrant just in case it is produced by a reliable belief-forming mechanism working in the appropriate circumstances.

[30] Plantinga 1993a, 1993b, 2000.
[31] There are, of course, notable exceptions (cf. Feldman and Conee 2001; Feldman 2014).
[32] See Byrne 2011: 275.

14.3.2 'Faith is Knowledge'

Armed with his version of a well-honed epistemological model still fashionable especially in the USA, Plantinga is now able to claim that:

> what is required for *knowledge* is [i] that belief be produced by cognitive faculties or processes that are working properly, [ii] in an appropriate epistemic environment... [iii] according to a design plan that is aimed at truth, and [iv] is furthermore *successfully* aimed at truth. But according to this model, what one believes by faith (the beliefs that constitute faith) meets these four conditions.[33]

As such, 'Faith is *Knowledge*' (Plantinga 2000: 256–8).

More specifically, 'faith' is identified by Plantinga with a belief-forming process (analogous to sense-perception, memory, or rational intuition) which, when working properly, produces warranted true beliefs.[34] With faith understood in this way, Plantinga's aim in Warranted Christian Belief becomes much bolder than in his earlier work, namely, he now intends to show how 'the full panoply of Christian belief in all its particularity' can enjoy the three main varieties of 'positive epistemic status', that is, justification, rationality, and warrant.[35] Given the epistemological framework in which Plantinga is operating, Christian belief counts, therefore, as knowledge.

Furthermore, on this model, 'it is really the *unbeliever* who displays epistemic malfunction; failing to believe in God is a result of some kind of dysfunction of the *sensus divinitatis*' (2000: 184) due to the noetic effects of sin.[36] More generally, it turns out that only in a theistic framework are all the conditions of warrant fulfilled: only if (a non-deceiving) God exists can we be sure that our cognitive faculties or belief-forming mechanisms work to a design plan that is aimed at truth. The most popular alternative theory, Darwinian natural selection, tells us that evolution aims at survival not at truth.[37] As in Descartes so in Plantinga, it is the existence of (a non-deceiving) God which ultimately rescues us from an engulfing scepticism about the truth of our beliefs, since only a theistic metaphysics can reassure us that our belief-forming mechanisms have been designed to reach truth.[38] In brief,

[33] Plantinga 2000: 256 (ii–v added for clarity purposes).

[34] Cf. Plantinga 2000: 257: 'when these beliefs are accepted by faith and result from the internal instigation of the Holy Spirit, they are produced by cognitive processes working properly... Faith, the whole *process* that produces them, is specifically designed by God himself to produce this very effect... the beliefs in question satisfy the external rationality condition, which is also the first condition of warrant.'

[35] Cf. Plantinga 2000: 241–89 (see, for instance, pp. 241, 252).

[36] On 'the noetic effects of sin' see esp. Plantinga 2000: 213–40.

[37] Cf. Plantinga 2000: 227–40 ('Naturalism and Lack of Knowledge').

[38] According to Wolterstorff and Plantinga (who in turn claim inspiration from Thomas Reid), from a classical Cartesian point of view, a priori beliefs are just as exposed to scepticism as perceptual beliefs and beliefs in other minds. Cf. Pust 2013: 219.

only in a theistic framework can beliefs have warrant sufficient to turn them into knowledge.

There is, however, a key difference. Descartes thought that he had watertight demonstrations of the existence of God. On the contrary, much of the impetus of Reformed Epistemology comes from the acknowledgement that none of the arguments for the existence of God can claim such an exalted demonstrative status. In fact, arguing for the existence of God is precisely what Reformed Epistemology *does not* want to do. God's existence is simply *assumed* (or, in a more distinctly Plantingian terminology, it is simply held as a basic belief). Given the assumption that God exists, or given the basic belief which a religious believer simply finds himself having, Plantinga's project is not to show that this basic belief is true, but that this basic belief is rationally held even in the absence of any argument or evidence for its truth.

As Plantinga puts it, there are two types of objections to belief in the existence of (a Christian) God: de facto objections, that is, objections to the *truth* of this belief (Plantinga 2000: viii), and *de jure* objections, that is, 'arguments or claims to the effect that Christian belief, whether or not true, is at any rate unjustifiable, or rationally unjustified, or irrational' (Plantinga 2000: ix). The main question of *Warranted Christian Belief* is the following: 'is there a viable *de jure* objection to Christian belief? One that is independent of the *de facto* objections and does not presuppose that Christian belief is false?' (2000: x) Plantinga's answer is a resounding 'no': there are no viable *de jure* objections independent of the de facto objections (see especially Plantinga 2000: 190–1).

That is, in his view, all objections to the rationality of holding the belief that God exists (*de jure* question) *presuppose* the falsity of this belief (de facto question). It is only because it has already been assumed that (as a matter of fact) God does not exist, Plantinga argues, that atheistic world-views such as Marxism or Freudianism conclude that it is irrational to believe in God.[39] And, indeed, presupposing or assuming that God does not exist is all that these world-views can really do, given that the de facto question cannot be settled (or, at least, has not been settled) by natural reason one way or the other. If one presupposes, on the contrary, that (as a matter of fact) God exists (that is, if one holds God's existence as a basic belief), then there is a perfectly coherent explanation of why belief in God is rationally held despite the lack of propositional evidence or arguments in support of this belief. In a world-view which includes the existence of God, it makes sense to hold that God has equipped human beings with a properly functioning belief-forming mechanism which, in the presence of appropriate stimuli, lead them to believe that God exists. Assuming (as this world-view does) that it is true that (a Christian) God exists, belief in God's existence is true and warranted. Hence this belief qualifies, in this world-view, as knowledge.

[39] Cf. Plantinga 2000: 135–63.

14.3.3 Fideism and the (J)TB+ Theory of Knowledge

Interestingly, Wolterstorff himself notes the similarity between this approach and the approach of another prominent movement in anglophone analytical religious epistemology, namely, so-called Wittgensteinian Fideism.[40] In a series of notes written between 1948 and 1951 (now published under the title *On Certainty*), Wittgenstein stresses that every belief presupposes a system of beliefs. Together, these beliefs constitute a 'world-view' or a 'form of life'. Any belief can be confirmed or disconfirmed only within the 'world-view' or 'form of life' to which this belief belongs. Wittgensteinian Fideists apply the notions of 'world-view' or 'form of life' to religion, arguing that religion, like all other human activities (including, notably, science), has its own *internal* criteria of meaning and rationality.[41] Despite disagreement with Wittgensteinianism's typical assumption that religious language is non-referential (and hence with its inclination towards anti-realism or fictionalism about religion and God), Wolterstorff draws attention to the fact that for both Wittgensteinianism and Reformed Epistemology religion is a 'world-view' which interprets ordinary reality and ordinary experience in its own, internally coherent, way. This implies that its coherence can be ascertained only from 'within' such a world-view, as opposed to being measured through some 'external' standards.[42]

To conclude, Plantinga's bold claim that the Christian faith, with all its distinctive mysteries (Trinity, Incarnation, and so on), is, in a word, *knowledge*, represents a radical attempt to turn the tables on the failure of the classical arguments for the existence of God to provide knowledge of the existence God.

In my view, however, this attempt results in a general weakening of rationality rather than in a plausible defence of Christian belief from the charge of irrationality. Rather than elevating religious belief to the status to knowledge, all knowledge is reduced to the particular beliefs of incommensurable world-views. Wolterstorff's comparison between Reformed Epistemology and Wittgensteinianism shows that Reformed Epistemology's new project is in fact, at heart, a version of an older and well-attested position, namely fideism. As Wolterstorff himself maintains, 'the Reformed tradition has been fideist, not evidentialist, in its impulse', adding that, in his view, 'that impulse is correct'.[43] Reformed Epistemologists are right in pointing out that their project is profoundly different from the enterprise of natural theology, since at the core of that enterprise is the view that there are shared criteria of meaning and rationality which allow a genuine dialogue among all human beings, whether religious believers or non-believers. Rather than conceiving human beings as playing mutually incommunicable language games, each with its own internally

[40] Cf. Geivett-Sweetman 1992: 8–9, 81–130.

[41] See Geivett-Sweetman 1992: 8–9 ('Introduction').

[42] See Wolterstorff 2005: 245–71.

[43] Wolterstorff 1981/1992: 149.

coherent rules, natural theology builds on the premise that reason is a common language with rules which are shared across world-views.

Most importantly, it seems to me that the very project of turning religious belief into knowledge is misguided. The acknowledgment that natural theology does not provide *knowledge* of the existence of God but, at best, rational arguments for the reasonableness of *believing* in God's existence, is not (I contend) a sign of failure but a reflection of the epistemic status of human cognition with regard to putative supernatural entities. Furthermore, it seems to me that undermining the fundamental difference in kind between belief and knowledge does not ultimately help the cause of religious belief. On the contrary, it compromises the aspect of epistemic uncertainty, and consequently the element of trust, which is traditionally regarded as essential to faith. In short, it compromises the notion of 'faith' itself.

To conclude, Reformed Epistemology's twentieth-century version of fideism is rooted in a mistaken twentieth-century account of knowledge as *a kind of belief* which meets certain criteria. The astute but profoundly problematic consequences drawn by Reformed Epistemology from a flat-out use of this widely endorsed epistemic model constitute, I claim, one of the best illustrations of the untenability of the model itself.

15
Religious Belief II
Perceiving God and Transcendental Realism

This chapter turns to the question of whether a putative 'experiential awareness of God' or '*perception* of God' can provide justification for holding certain beliefs about God, as proposed by the influential and insightful work of William Alston.[1] After outlining Alston's epistemology of religious experience and my objections to a putative *direct* perception of God, I conclude with a positive proposal based on the application to religious epistemology of the account of knowledge and belief defended in this book.

In so doing, I am aware of leaving the resources of another, complementary dimension of religious epistemology virtually untapped: namely, the interpersonal or second-personal perspective of religious cognition, suggestively labelled by Eleonore Stump the 'Franciscan', as opposed to the 'Dominican', approach. This is undoubtedly a key perspective, uniquely suited to tackle a host of issues which are not discussed in this book (notably, the problem of evil). Doing justice to it, however, is a project of its own, as is shown by the perceptive and innovative work that is done in this area, and to which I must limit myself to referring. I will only note that personal, or interpersonal, or second-personal knowledge is yet another crucial and pervasive modality of cognition which is not (at least primarily) propositional. We will do well to keep this in mind before assuming that 'knowing that' is the privileged pathway into an account of cognition.[2]

15.1 Perceiving God

15.1.1 Putative Perceptions of God and Well-Established Doxastic Practices

As pointed out by Plantinga himself, there are significant differences between his project and that of William Alston. Whereas Plantinga tries to show that the

[1] See especially Alston 1991.

[2] Benton 2017 notes that 'propositional knowledge is arguably distinct in kind from objectual and *inter*personal knowledge', the latter being construed as 'knowledge had when two subjects know each other personally, as subjects, from the second-person perspective' (p. 814). See also Benton 2018 (exploring interpersonal knowledge specifically in relation to religious epistemology), and Stump 2009 and 2010.

Thinking with Assent: Renewing a Traditional Account of Knowledge and Belief. Maria Rosa Antognazza, Oxford University Press. © Maria Rosa Antognazza 2024. DOI: 10.1093/oso/9780198831518.003.0016

specific beliefs of the Christian faith (if true) have enough warrant to constitute knowledge, Alston's aim is the justification of belief in God.[3] On the other hand, their views on what could count as knowledge of God remain close. In particular, Alston claims that (de-Gettierized) justified true belief (JTB) is sufficient—although not necessary—for knowledge since a true belief generated by a reliable belief-forming mechanism counts as knowledge.[4] His inquiry (like Plantinga's inquiry) is therefore still conducted in the (J)TB+ framework to which this book objects. I will focus here, however, on Alston's main concern, namely, making a case for theistic belief's justification rather than claiming the status of knowledge for the Christian faith.

As he puts it, the chief aim of his classic monograph, *Perceiving God*, 'is to defend the view that putative direct awareness of God can provide justification for certain kinds of beliefs about God'.[5] It should be noted at the outset that it is neither assumed, nor argued for, that it is true that God exists. Alston's work is a work of epistemology and not an attempt to provide an argument for God's existence based on religious experience. The experiences in question are in fact *putative* direct awareness of God, that is, they are experiences that are taken by the subject to be direct presentations or manifestations of a divine reality. Alston argues 'for the epistemological position that beliefs formed on the basis of such (putative) perceptions are (prima facie) justified',[6] noting the vicinity of his position to the principle of credulity formulated by Richard Swinburne as follows: 'if it seems (epistemically) to a subject that x is present (and has some characteristic), then probably x is present (and has that characteristic); what one seems to perceive is probably so'.[7] The core of Alston's strategy is to show that beliefs based on putative perceptions of God are formed through belief-forming mechanisms which have the same epistemic status of other belief-forming mechanisms commonly taken to produce justified beliefs.

The fundamental notion on which the case is built is that of doxastic practice.[8] Our beliefs, Alston claims, are formed within doxastic practices which are irreducibly plural (each has unique features) and epistemically circular. They have to be taken on trust for the most part, on the basis of exhibiting significant self-support. A socially well-established doxastic practice is rationally engaged in 'provided it and its output cohere sufficiently with other firmly established doxastic practices and their output'.[9] Stock examples of doxastic practices include sense-perception, rational intuition, introspection, and memory. Alston argues,

[3] See Plantinga 2000: 286–9. [4] See Alston 1991: 284–5.

[5] Alston 1991: 9. [6] Alston 1991: 10.

[7] Swinburne 2004: 303. Alston 1991: 195 quotes from the first edition of Swinburne's monograph (1979: 254). For a detailed account of Swinburne's principle of credulity see Swinburne 2001: 141–50. While welcoming the similarity between his position and Swinburne's, Alston claims that by embedding individual beliefs in doxastic practices he is able to make a stronger case for the prima facie justification of beliefs.

[8] Cf. Alston 1991: esp. chap. 4. [9] Alston 1991: 175.

however, that there are other doxastic practices which are socially well established, self-supporting, and therefore prima facie rationally engaged in, although they are shared only by a minority of the population. Such is the refined palate of the wine connoisseur or the refined ear of the musicologist—wine connoisseurs and musicologists form beliefs about the world on the basis of acquired sensitivities to features of their environment that the majority of people are unable to perceive. The mystical practice (MP) of forming beliefs about God on the basis of putative perceptions of God, Alston contends, is another one of such socially well-established doxastic practices, and the Christian Mystical Practice (CMP) qualifies as a more specific version of it. Crucially, the fact that CMP is not universally shared cannot count against its prima facie rationality any more than the fact that only a minority of people engages in the doxastic practice of musicologists.

Two complementary moves support this overall strategy: the rejection of 'epistemic double standards' and the rejection of 'epistemic imperialism'. The former (already discussed in Chap. 14, sect. 14.2.1) consists in 'unwarrantedly making requirements of one practice from which others are exempted'. The latter consists in 'unwarrantedly taking the standards of one doxastic practice as normative for all'. Notably, although some features of sense perception (SP) 'are de rigueur for any respectable practice' (for example, being socially well-established and exhibiting significant self-support), other features of SP are unique to this specific doxastic practice.[10] It would be epistemic imperialist to demand the same features of SP from, say, introspection or rational intuition, let alone from CMP.[11]

15.1.2 Challenges from Dis-Analogies and Religious Diversity

Alston is of course well aware of the dis-analogies between SP and CMP, which are discussed at length and ultimately rejected as sufficient reasons to disqualify CMP as a rationally engaged doxastic practice. The aspect of this defence to which I would like to draw attention regards the difference between the object of SP and the putative object of CMP. The Christian doctrinal scheme which provides the necessary overrider of putative perceptions of God, Alston argues, actually leads us to expect deep differences between SP and CMP.[12] This point is made most effectively by Alston in an earlier paper: the reality CMP claims to put us in touch with, Alston explains, 'is conceived to be vastly different from the physical environment'. It is 'wholly other'. For this reason, 'we can only attain the faintest, sketchiest, and most insecure grasp of what God is like'.[13] If this is right, Alston concludes, it is no wonder that CMP is not like SP in many key respects.

[10] Alston 1991: 199. See also Alston 1991: 249.
[11] See, in particular, Alston 1991: 216–25.
[12] See Alston 1991: 219–22.
[13] Alston 1982 and Alston 1991: 301–2.

I will come back shortly on what should be the import, in my view, of Alston's acknowledgment that, according to major religious traditions (including Judaism, Christianity, and Islam), the nature of God is 'wholly other'. For now, I note that Alston confronts head-on the challenge posed by religious diversity to the claim that CMP (or any other specific MP) has not been shown to be unreliable. Religious pluralism presents us in fact with 'a plurality of incompatible religious perceptual doxastic practices', underpinned by incompatible doctrinal claims.[14]

To meet this challenge, Alston declines to avail himself of John Hick's neo-Kantian way out.[15] According to Hick's widely discussed 'Pluralistic Hypothesis', the world's different religions are all culturally conditioned religious responses to the ambiguity of the universe, none of which can claim to be true of the Real as it is in itself: in its mysterious transcendence, the noumenal Real 'cannot be said to be one or many, person or thing, substance or process, good or evil, purposive or non-purposive'.[16] I agree with Alston that, unless one is prepared to reconceive and reconstruct (rather than describe and evaluate) the systems of religious beliefs as they are understood by the relevant religious communities, this way to diffuse the challenge of contradictory religious claims will not work. The same objection of radical reconstruction applies, as far as I can see, to the approach adopted by D. Z. Phillips and other philosophers of religion influenced by the Wittgensteinian tradition—a radical reconstruction even more jarring in their case since it seems to run contrary to the stated aim of keeping to the task of describing a form of life from *within*.[17] As Alston points out (rightly to my mind), practitioners of the different world religions typically take themselves to be making realist claims about the divine: Christians do mean to say that God is Triune; Muslims and Jews do mean to deny that the latter is the case, not to speak of the even more sharply opposed claims of non-theist religions. In brief, religious realism must face the full force of the challenge posed by incompatible religious claims.

Alston acknowledges that 'religious diversity reduces the rationality of engaging in CMP' but denies that such reduction is of such a magnitude as to render it irrational to continue to engage in it.[18] He is right, however, in granting that the conclusions drawn about the epistemic situation of practitioners of CMP 'hold, *pari passu*, for practitioners of other internally validated forms of MP'—like CMP practitioners, those practitioners are also able 'to rationally engage in their religious doxastic practice despite the inability to show that it is epistemically superior to the competitor'.[19]

[14] Alston 1991: 255–85 (here p. 255). [15] See especially Hick 2004. Cf. Alston 1991: 264–6.
[16] Hick 2004: 246.
[17] See, for instance, Phillips 1970; Malcolm 1977; Holmer 1978. For criticism see Nielsen 1973.
[18] Alston 1991: 275. [19] Alston 1991: 274–5.

15.1.3 A Cumulative Case

Finally, and most importantly, Alston's case for the experiential direct awareness of God as a ground of religious belief is part of a cumulative case: in his own words, the perception of God contributes one strand in a rope which 'has enough strength to do the job' only when other strands are combined together.[20] Other strands of the rope include revelation, tradition, and natural theology.[21] Crucially, these other strands provide the necessary overrider system which allows the evaluation of putative perceptions of God. Alston is in fact very clear that neither his proposal nor the Christian tradition regard claims to perceptions of God as self-validating: if I hear the voice of God telling me to break into my neighbour's house, snatch the barking puppy, and throw it out of the window to stop the noise, the overrider constituted by the Christian doctrinal system of beliefs about God will flush out this alleged perception of God as an hallucination resulting from sleep deprivation.

'Let's take it', Alston concludes, 'that CMP is a functioning, socially established, perceptual doxastic practice with distinctive experiential inputs, distinctive input–output functions, a distinctive conceptual scheme, and a rich, internally justified overrider system. As such, it possesses a prima facie title to being rationally engaged in, and its outputs are thereby prima facie justified.'[22] Since, upon reflection, 'we lack sufficient reason for regarding it as unreliable or otherwise disqualified for rational participation', it is not only prima facie but also unqualifiedly rational to engage in CMP.[23]

15.2 Perceiving God?

15.2.1 God as 'Wholly Other'

There is no doubt, in my mind at least, that Alston has built a brilliantly original, balanced, and sophisticated proposal. There is much in it with which I agree. I disagree, however, with its central claim regarding a direct perception of God. The reasons of this disagreement are principally metaphysical and only derivatively epistemological.

CMP is explicitly construed by Alston along the lines of a *perceptual* model in the framework of a direct realist theory of perception:[24] it postulates

[20] The cumulative nature of the case for the existence of God is also a key feature of Swinburne's proposal.

[21] Alston 1991: 289–92. [22] Alston 1991: 225. [23] Alston 1991: 223.

[24] On this direct realist framework, labelled by Alston 'theory of appearing', see esp. Alston 1991: 70–7, 186–7.

awareness of the divine in the form of a directly perceived object (God).[25] It seems to me, however, that CMP cannot be sufficiently analogous to other *perceptual* doxastic practices (notably, SP) due to the very features of its putative object—features which are identified by the very doctrinal system which serves as the indispensable overrider required by Alston's proposal. As Alston himself points out, according to the Christian overrider system of doctrinal beliefs, God is 'wholly other', transcendent, eternal, immaterial, and so on. If we take seriously (as, I think, we should) the categorical difference between the object of SP and the putative object of CMP, this difference puts a more significant barrier to any perception of God sufficiently analogous to other types of direct perception than Alston's proposal allows. I follow here in the footsteps of the Kantian tradition in thinking that in our present condition of corporeal beings bounded by space and time, there is an ontological, and therefore also an epistemological gap between human beings and any putative noumenal entity not bounded by space and time. In the natural order of things, and for embodied beings for whom any natural perception is mediated by corporeal organs, a direct perception of any such 'wholly other' entity is beyond our ken.

It has been objected by others that Alston wants to have it both ways: to have CMP sufficiently analogous to ordinary sense perception to count as a rationally engaged doxastic practice in a framework of direct realism (such as ordinary sense perception) *and* to defend CMP from the charge of not being analogous to SP on the basis of the difference between their objects. Alston engages with this type of objection by arguing that the positive argument for CMP is based on his theory of doxastic practices, not on the analogy with SP:

> The basic contention is that it is prima facie rational to engage in CMP, not because it is analogous to SP in one or another respect, but because it is a socially established doxastic practice.[26]

What I am challenging, however, is not the existence, in Christianity as in other world religions, of a socially well-established doxastic practice of forming beliefs about God which exhibits significant self-support and to which epistemic double standards and epistemic imperialism should not be applied. I strongly agree with all that. Rather, my contention is that a Christian doxastic practice built on a perceptual model of a *direct perception* of God faces significant (arguably fatal) overriders from both its own internal overrider system and from independent philosophical reasons.

[25] Cf. for instance Alston 1991: 287, 300.

[26] Alston 1991: 223. Cf. Gale 1991, quoted at length in Alston.

15.2.2 Direct and Indirect Experiential Awareness of God

To be clear: I do not wish at all to deny that some experiential awareness of a divine presence is a key and indispensable element in the faith of many (or even most) religious believers. But at least as regards the conception of God in the Christian tradition, it seems to me that the situation is rather that of believing 'there is a mouse under the straw in the barn' than that of 'actually seeing a mouse in the straw', to use Alston's own analogy for marking the difference between the experiential support he is arguing for and other types of experiential support.[27] After all, one of the explicit claims of the Christian overrider system is that 'no one has ever seen God' (John 1:18). The experiential awareness of the type indicated by the 'mouse under the straw' analogy is that of people who interpret certain events in their life, or certain features of their experience (say, a new sense of peace in a time of distress; of hope where there was only desperation) as revealing the presence of a divine being or the existence of a divine dimension that is not *directly* perceived. That is, the direct experience is the sense of peace, of hope, of light, and so on; in the mouse analogy, it is a certain, distinctive movement of the straw. It needs hardly to be said that such theistic interpretations of these experiences face rival, fully naturalistic explanations. But, by the same token, so do naturalistic explanations face the possibility that theists are right, until the de facto question of whether there is or there is not a God has been settled. Until such time, Plantinga and other Reformed Epistemologists do have a point in noting that dismissing theistic interpretations simply begs the question.

Furthermore, I do not wish to deny that, if there is indeed an entity of the kind envisaged by the doctrinal system of monotheistic religions, there may be some supernatural mystical access to this noumenal entity. Given such entity, one may even take a leaf from Plato's *Symposium* (209e–212a) and think of this access as a mystical intuition which goes above and beyond rational cognition and is powered by an appetitive principle (love) rather than by purely cognitive principles. The subject matter of this book, however, is natural cognition during the earthly life of embodied beings who live in space and time. As long as we are in this condition of *homo viator in hac lacrimarum valle*, a central strand of the Christian tradition stresses that we will see in a mirror, dimly, and not face to face.[28] That is why, I contend, there is so much insistence on the need for faith and hope—two theological virtues construed as no longer needed in the beatific vision of the afterlife, where the only theological virtue left is supposed to be love in its highest form of charity. To be sure, Alston notes that on his account there is still need for faith.[29] The way in which the Christian tradition construes human cognition of

[27] Alston 1991: 287. [28] 1 Corinthians 13:12. [29] Alston 1991: 277.

God, however, seems to me to require a stronger element of negative theology than a direct perception of God would allow.

15.3 An Alternative Framework for Religious Epistemology

15.3.1 Religious Epistemology and the Distinction in Kind between Knowledge and Belief

As noted in the course of this book, the shortcomings of the (J)TB+ orthodoxy of the twentieth century have been exposed in recent epistemological work of various stripes, stirring the lively debates which agitate current epistemology. Once the project of turning belief into knowledge through the addition of necessary and sufficient conditions is abandoned, the scene is set also for an approach to religious epistemology which is fundamentally different from that of Reformed Epistemology. My suggestion is that the account of cognition defended in this book offers a good alternative. In particular, I contend that a conception of knowledge and belief as two irreducibly different mental states is especially suited to religious epistemology owing to the distinctive epistemological status of religious belief.

According to the version of the tradition I have revisited and reproposed, although fundamentally different, knowing and believing can both be conceived as ways of 'thinking with assent [cum assensione cogitare]'.[30] As we have seen, according to this model, we 'think with assent': (1) when we *know* something—that is, when the mind's assent is moved 'by the object itself' (we 'see' or 'grasp' it, either literally in sense perception or metaphorically in the case of intellectual perception); and also (2) when we *believe* something—that is, when the mind's assent is not moved 'by its proper object' but by other reasons; here is where justification, marks of truth, warrant, and so on come in.[31] As regards specifically the experiential awareness of God discussed in the section above, on my account, the relevant cognitive mode is thinking with assent of this second kind: that is, assent justified by seeing such-and-such movements in the straw, as it were, and not thinking with assent resulting from directly seeing the object of cognition.

A clear implication of this proposal is that the bar for what, strictly speaking, an individual knows, is set high. Knowing is a cognitive mode sparingly available only in areas which are plausibly within the reach of limited cognitive faculties, and for objects of cognition which are in the same finite order of things. The great majority of what we can pursue in our successful individual cognition is not

[30] ST IIa IIae, q. 2, art. 1.

[31] ST IIa IIae, q. 1, a. 4 (quoted and discussed in the Introduction to Part I and in Chap. 2, sect. 2.1.2). See also ST IIa IIae, q. 1, a. 5.

therefore knowledge but justified true belief with different degrees of justification. While agreeing with the slogan 'knowledge first'[32] (interpreted as the claim that knowledge is ontologically prior to belief), the complementary slogan of this proposal is: 'give belief its due'. It should be fully acknowledged that belief (as opposed to knowledge) is by far the most common and ineliminable mode of one's cognition and that justified belief is mostly reliable in tracking truth. Although in some cases belief may well aim at knowledge,[33] this proposal maintains that the specific contribution of belief to cognition is that of aiming at truth where and when knowledge is out of an individual's cognitive reach (either for objective or for subjective reasons).

As Kant saw very clearly, a prime case of such a situation is putative noumenal entities. If most of what we do in our successful individual cognition is justified true belief, it is hardly surprising that, when the object of cognition is some putative supernatural, noumenal entity, the appropriate cognitive mode is belief rather than knowledge. I do not intend to deny that some things may be known also in the domain of religion, but I contend that a distinctive feature of religious belief is that of being primarily (if not exclusively) about matters which surpass the limits of a finite mind: therefore, the specific epistemic status of what, in that domain, is held by faith is belief, not knowledge.[34] This is in line, I claim, with an illustrious tradition which distinguishes between truths which are 'according to reason' and truths which are 'above reason'—the latter being the proper objects of faith as claims whose logical possibility can be defended, but which surpass the ability of human reason to discover and fully comprehend.[35]

15.3.2 Transcendental Realism

If I had to give a name to my position, I would call it *transcendental realism*, intended as a view according to which the conditions of possibility of the objects of cognition are independent of our thought.[36] Unlike Kantian transcendental idealism, which regards objects in space and time as, to some significant extent, mental constructions, I have taken the view that objects in space and time exist independently of our experience of them (a view that Kant labels, disapprovingly,

[32] See Williamson's remark at the beginning of his *Knowledge and its Limits*: 'If I had to summarize this book in two words, they would be: knowledge first' (2000: 'Preface').

[33] Cf. Williamson 2000: 47–8 (see also p. 1). [34] Cf. ST IIa IIae, q. 1, a. 5.

[35] Cf. Locke, *Essay*, Book IV, chap. XVII, 23 and XVIII, 6 and Leibniz, *Theodicy*, 'Preliminary Discourse', § 23 (GP VI, 64). The view defended by Locke and Leibniz is by no means new: cf. Aquinas, *Summa contra Gentiles*, Book I, chaps. 4–7 (see esp. chap. 5). According to the persuasive interpretation of Kant on religion offered by Wood 2000, an analogous distinction along the lines of rational and reveled religion is also found in Kant (see esp. 2000: 11–14).

[36] Some of these concluding remarks have been inspired by Robert Adams 1987: 5–6. Any misunderstandings or shortcomings are, of course, my sole responsibility.

transcendental realism). We can know these objects in a direct realist way because we are also bodily beings that exist in space and time: as such we belong to the same order of things, that is, corporeal, spatio-temporal, finite beings. Since there is no ontological gap, I do not see that independent existence of objects needs to imply an epistemological gap. That is, I go back to the old insight that like knows like, and that in the same order of things there can be knowledge.[37]

In turn (and in line, this time, with Kant) I am a transcendental realist also about noumena, that is, non-corporeal, non-spatio-temporal things-in-themselves (if there is any such entity). If there is a God as traditionally conceived by theism (eternal, infinite, non-corporeal, and so on), this entity will belong to this noumenal order—an order in which the conditions of possibility of the objects of cognition are, a fortiori, independent of our thought. It is this ontological gap between the (putative) noumenal world and the corporeal world bounded by space and time which explains why the noumenal order is beyond the limits of human knowledge. We can, however, relate to it through a different cognitive mode—a cognitive mode which does not require a 'cognition of grounds in the object' (Ak 16:371–2), that is, does not require a cognitive contact with a putative object of cognition which is beyond our ken. This cognitive mode is belief: one of the feats of belief as a cognitive mode is, I contend, that of opening up *rational* 'prospects' on a dimension which is not only de facto but also *de jure* beyond the grasp of human knowledge.[38]

This is not to say that there is no fact of the matter: a transcendental realist will think that there is—either there is God, or there is not, and, if there is, God will have a certain definite nature. In this respect, Hick's brand of neo-Kantianism goes, in my view, too far in its deconstruction of religion according to which revelation is merely a human, culturally conditioned way to represent the Real. Rather, I point at a much older and pervasive tradition of negative theology and apophaticism which is still consistent with the claim that some religions come significantly closer to truth than others. The question of which one is closer to how things really are, cannot, however, be settled by *knowledge*, or, at least, not by the natural knowledge of which spatio-temporal, corporal beings are capable of, and which is the concern of the present inquiry. The best each religion can do is to present its own motives of *credibility* and leave the rest, as it were, for later (in good time, we will all be confronted with what is what).

This is not to deny, either, that some mystical contact with this different ontological order might be possible. That is, this is not to deny that, if God exists, some religious experiences may be genuine direct awareness of God. But if there were such genuine perception, this perception would constitute some wholly *supernatural* cognitive modality akin to what major religious traditions reserve

[37] This is a key insight already found in Empedocles, as noted at the beginning of Chap. 1.
[38] Cf. A830/B858. As argued by Wood 2020: 3, religion for Kant goes also beyond morality.

for the afterlife—namely the *visio Dei* or beatific vision. On my account, as a vision or perception of its object, a *visio Dei* would certainly count as knowledge—and indeed as the perfect, adequate knowledge of which sense-perception and intellectual perception are limited echoes. (It is certainly not by chance that a conception of the beatific vision as the highest kind of knowledge is shared by all philosophers who embrace some version of it, including those as opposed to traditional theism as Spinoza). The question, however, could not be settled in the framework of the natural cognitive modes to which the present inquiry is devoted. To put it another way, a direct perception of (an eternal, transcendent, infinite ...) God resists naturalization into a cognitive mode sufficiently analogous to other, natural doxastic practices. The ontological gap between natural and supernatural, spatio-temporal and noumenal remain, and with it the epistemological gap which requires 'to deny [*aufheben*] *knowledge*' of a noumenal order, at least as long as we are corporeal beings bounded by space and time.[39]

Given this framework, I agree with Alston that religious belief should be protected from epistemic imperialism: there are features of religious belief which religious believers acknowledge from the outset to be distinctive of it. It would not do, for instance, to fault religious belief because, as far as our earthly condition is concerned, it cannot on many matters progress to knowledge, unlike other—but by no means *all* other—types of belief.

On the other hand, these distinctive features of religious belief should not make us lose sight of the fact that, in general, most of our individual cognition relies on assenting to putative features of reality that are in many cases not only de facto but also *de jure* beyond a direct cognitive contact. Often all we have is testimony, signs, symptoms, motives of credibility. Religious belief is therefore located in a large swath of cognition which shares a great deal of its features. If this is the case, Alston is once again right in demanding that religious belief not be the victim of epistemic double standards.

To summarize: the approach I propose is fully open to the rational justifiability of religious belief, intended as the cognitive element of a broader phenomenon—faith—which involves both cognitive and non-cognitive dimensions (I fully agree that religious faith is an all-embracing form of life, a *Weltanschauung*, and not merely a set of beliefs). Thus, my proposal shares the aim of Plantinga, Alston, and, more generally, Reformed Epistemology of defending religious belief from the charge of irrationality but regards the attempt of turning religious belief into knowledge as ill-judged. *Pace* Reformed Epistemology, the best way to provide epistemic justification for religious belief remains the tried and tested one of giving reasons for believing something that cannot, typically, be known. This does not mean that every religious believer must be able to produce formal arguments in

[39] Kant, *Critique of Pure Reason* (Bxxx).

order to fulfil her epistemic duties as a rational human being. But there must be reasons for believing something which can be produced, if not by every individual, at least by someone in the community.[40] As a distinguished critic of Plantinga has stressed, 'conscientious believers as well as objectors live by the evidentialist canon. There *is* deficiency in a faith that can give no reason, even if not everyone who holds such a faith is epistemically deficient.'[41] According to my proposal, religious belief, like any other belief, does need justification which is, ultimately, grounded in what we know about the world—namely, in our perception of some object or understanding of some truth.

[40] Cf. Leibniz, *Examen Religionis Christianae* (A VI, 4, 2362).

[41] Kretzmann 1992/2000: 105.

General Conclusion

In this book I have developed an account of knowledge and belief that revisits and renews some historical insights. My proposal, I claim, is both traditional and novel: traditional insofar as it recovers a prominent strand of thought which traverses Western philosophy; novel insofar as, in so doing, it offers a model of cognition which is significantly different from most present-day views. If I had to summarize this proposal in a few words, I would use two complementary slogans: 'knowledge first' but 'give belief its due!'[1]

I.1 The Distinction in Kind between Knowledge and Belief

Part I of the book focused on the distinction in kind between knowledge and belief traceable in a long tradition going back to Parmenides and Plato, and spanning philosophical movements and thinkers as diverse as Aristotle, Epicureanism, Stoicism, Aquinas, Descartes, Spinoza, Leibniz, Locke, Hume, Kant, Oxford Realism, and neo-Scholasticism. In this tradition, I have tracked a strand of thought according to which there are two fundamentally distinct modes of cognition which can be roughly identified by a contrast between 'seeing' and 'not-seeing'. The state of 'seeing' (or 'grasping') is regarded as the most fundamental, primitive cognitive mode. I have used the term 'knowledge' as a shorthand to refer to a family of cognate mental states characterized by this *sui generis* cognitive 'seeing' or 'grasping'. Successful cognition, I argue, must be ultimately founded upon an underived apprehension of 'what is' in which the object of cognition is directly present to a cognitive subject. Construed, at its most fundamental, as this apprehension, knowledge has ontological priority as well as cognitive primacy over other cognitive modes. It is in this sense that the proposed account of cognition is a knowledge-first epistemology.

There could be no successful cognition, I contend, without this primitive contact between mind and reality, but what an *individual* knows (and can know) is limited because, primarily or paradigmatically, knowledge is akin to acquaintance and, in intellectual cognition, involves understanding. Its primitive mode is a non-discursive, non-propositional perception which can take the form

[1] For the slogan 'knowledge first', see Williamson 2000: v.

Thinking with Assent: Renewing a Traditional Account of Knowledge and Belief. Maria Rosa Antognazza, Oxford University Press. © Maria Rosa Antognazza 2024. DOI: 10.1093/oso/9780198831518.003.0017

of sense-perception or of intellectual perception. On this primitive perception of 'what is' are based discursive modes of knowledge in which the evidence of 'what is' is followed step-by-step by inference. Likewise, on this primitive perception are based other cognitive modes such as memory and recognition, in which the original cognitive contact with 'what is' can be preserved (albeit with varying degrees of success). Knowing, on my account, therefore includes types of inferential reasoning, memory and recognitional abilities, and thereby can extend much further than one might initially think. Even so, however, the epistemic status of being 'knowledge' (strictly speaking and for a given individual) is less liberally given in my proposal than in other accounts.

According to the traditional strand of thought which I have followed, this mental state of seeing or grasping is contrasted with another mode of cognition in which the object of cognition is *not* directly seen or grasped. As a shorthand for this cognitive mode, I have used the term 'belief'.[2] Believing lacks the direct perception or presence of the object of cognition which characterizes knowing. Since believing essentially lacks what knowing essentially has, knowledge cannot be a species of belief for the same reason that seeing cannot be a species of not-seeing.

The claim that knowledge is, instead, a species of belief which meets certain criteria—a claim expressed by the many variations of (J)TB+ analyses of knowledge—is nowadays in retreat. Although by no means silenced, it is no longer repeated by a choir of voices as an undisputed orthodoxy which merely needs to work out more precisely the correct conditions that, added to belief, turn it into knowledge. The increasingly orthodox doctrine, propelled by the surge of knowledge-first epistemology, is the claim that knowledge, although not a species of belief, entails belief.[3] In the order of explanation, it is argued, knowledge has conceptual priority. Notwithstanding this conceptual priority, 'if S knows that A then S believes that A'.[4]

The position advanced in this book is more radical and significantly different. I have maintained that, according to a long and fruitful tradition which should be recovered, knowing and believing are mutually exclusive mental states: they cannot both be held by the same person at the same time and in the same respect. A genuinely non-sceptical philosophy of cognition, I claim, acknowledges a distinction in kind between knowledge and belief of this sort. That is, according to the interpretation I offer, the main battle line in the history of epistemology is drawn between the affirmation of a natural mental state in which there is a cognitive contact between cognizer and cognized, 'mind' and 'reality' (whatever

[2] More precisely, this cognitive mode may be indicated by terms such as *doxa, pistis, zann, opinio, opinari, fides, credere* (with their derivatives in Romance languages); *Glaube, glauben, Meinung, meinen, belief, believing, opinion, opining, credence.*

[3] Williamson 2000.

[4] Williamson 2000: 4–5, 41–8.

the ontological nature of this 'reality') and the rejection of such a natural mental state. For the former position, there is a mental state which is different in kind from belief, and which is constituted by the presence of the object of cognition to the cognitive subject, with no gap between them. For the latter position, all our cognition is belief, and the question becomes how and when belief is permissible, and whether the gap may or may not be bridged. The battle of non-sceptical philosophy of cognition is won, in my view, at the very beginning: the tradition I commend resists scepticism not by arguing that the gap between cognizer and *cognitum* can be bridged, but by arguing that there is no gap to start with. To put it another way, this tradition starts from the natural assumption that, in cognition, we do make contact with reality, shifting the burden of proof that we do not on the sceptic, and denying that the sceptic has come up with compelling reasons to think that we do not. If, on the other hand, an original gap is conceded, the battle is lost forever.

I.2 Thinking with Assent

In developed human cognition, the difference in kind between knowledge and belief is tracked (I contend) by two fundamentally distinct ways of 'thinking with assent'. Drawing inspiration from some passages of Aquinas's *Summa Theologiae* which incorporate insights of ancient and early medieval thought, I suggest that we think with assent: (1) when we *know* something, that is, when the mind's assent is moved 'by the object itself' (we 'see' or 'grasp' it, either in sense-perception and in intellectual perception, or in discursive reasoning in which the cognitive contact with 'the object itself' is maintained); (2) when we *believe* something, that is, when the mind's assent is not moved 'by its proper object' but by other reasons; here is where justification, signs, marks, symptoms, testimony, warrant, and so on are relevant.[5]

Furthermore, on the account I propose, assent and belief are kept distinct, as they are kept distinct in a long tradition including Stoicism, Aristotelian–Thomist Scholasticism, Kantian philosophy, and Newman's brand of British empiricism. Indeed, I argue that some of the key problems which have beset twentieth-century epistemology, and continue to beset current debates, are rooted not only in the conflation between knowledge and belief but in the further conflation between assent and belief. These conflations derive, at least in part, from failing to recognize that the adoption of the category of 'belief' as the umbrella under which to group qualitatively different elements of cognition is not a mere terminological accident. On the contrary, it is the result of a post-Humean sceptical

[5] ST IIa IIae, q. 1, a. 4 (quoted and discussed in the Introduction to Part I and in Chap. 2, sect. 2.1.2). See also ST IIa IIae, q. 1, a. 5.

outlook according to which, due to the fallibility of our cognitive faculties, there is no certainty in our cognition and all we can really achieve is belief. This sceptical outlook manifests itself in the so-called 'standard' analysis of knowledge as a kind of belief—a conception increasingly regarded as a philosophical cul-de-sac.

In particular, the difference between assent and belief is, on my account, the following. Assent is the implicit mental 'yes' which may be either the immediate, compelled response to the 'evidentness', 'seeableness' of the object of cognition, or the mental 'yes' of a 'decision' (to use Cook Wilson's expression) which follows a process of deliberation in which reasons, signs, symptoms, testimony, pros and contra are weighted. Assent is, in its nature, simple and indivisible: it is an indivisible mental affirmation that the matter is as we have judged it to be—that is, manifestly such-and-such, or uncertain, or doubtful, or fairly likely, or very probable, and so on. By contrast, believing is a specific mental state or mental act in which assent is not compelled by the presence of the object itself, but is moved by reasons which are extrinsic to the object of cognition. Depending on the strength of these reasons, there will be lower or higher degrees of belief that the relevant state of affairs is such-and-such. In some cases, these reasons may be so strong as to force assent: such is the case in which one cannot but believe that so-and-so is the case even if so-and-so is not directly presenting itself. In many other cases, these reasons will ground degrees of belief not high enough to determine, on their own, assent to a certain state of affairs being so-and-so. In such cases, other, typically conative, factors (drives, desires, trust, hope, love...) will concur in determining assent. Most importantly, I claim, whether assent is compelled by epistemic reasons (as in higher degrees of belief), or whether it is determined by both epistemic and non-epistemic reasons/cognitive and conative factors (as in lower degrees of belief), belief is still ontologically different from knowledge—that is, it is still ontologically different from a mental state in which assent is moved by the presence of the object of cognition itself, as opposed to a mental state in which assent is determined by external (epistemic and non-epistemic) reasons of varying degree of strength.

Assent and belief are therefore distinct, on my account, as on/off versus scalar states. The tension resulting from the attribution of incompatible features—being on/off and being scalar—to the same state (belief) is only thinly veiled, I claim, by the technical use of two broadly synonymous terms to indicate 'full' belief versus 'scalar' belief (aka credence). What is needed is a full acknowledgement that two different elements of cognition have been conflated, and that the simple and indivisible mental act of affirming can be the result either of 'clear sight' (*manifesta visio*) or of a process of deliberation in which signs, traces, signals, symptoms, and testimony are evaluated in the absence of clear sight of what is what.

Finally, I argued that 'assent' should also be kept distinct from another on/off category which has received sustained attention in recent epistemology, namely 'acceptance'. As understood in most contemporary literature, acceptance is voluntary in nature. This voluntariness does not sit well with knowledge or with very high degrees of belief, but it is interestingly complementary, I maintain, to lower degrees of belief. Assent, on the other hand, as the implicit mental 'yes' which is relevant not only to knowledge and belief but also to involuntary and voluntary aspects of cognition, is a broader category than acceptance.

II.1 The Distinction between Subject and Object, and the Nature of Their Cognitive Contact

Within this historical and theoretical framework, Part II of the book has investigated the phenomenology and ontology of cognition. I begin by proposing an account of how we arrive, in the first place, at the distinction between 'subject' and 'object', I and not-I. Focusing on why and how subject and object, I and not-I, are distinct—I claim—is of key importance for understanding the nature of knowledge itself. This distinction, I suggest, is grounded in the phenomenology of two distinct ways in which something is present in experience. Some aspects of what is present are experienced (lived, *erlebt*) as modes of whatever it is that unifies these modes of being: these are affective and conative/appetitive states such as feeling cold and wishing to warm up. Other aspects of what is present (say, the white of snow) are experienced as 'other' than this complex of affective and conative/appetitive states.

Building on these phenomenological observations, I have offered a positive proposal which construes individual knowledge as essentially or paradigmatically first-person and which is grounded in a conception in which cognitive and conative/appetitive aspects of sensitive and rational beings are fundamentally integrated and play complementary roles. Individual knowledge is essentially first-personal in the sense that its object-directedness requires a built-in awareness of the self as the unifying perspective from which an *aliud* (a not-self, an object) is apprehended. This is a first-order awareness which is crucially distinct from the second-order awareness which requires a reflexive cognitive act—a distinction which I propose to flesh out in terms of 'first-person knowledge' versus 'self-knowledge'.

Furthermore, I propose: (1) that the 'self' or 'subject' is first given through the affective and the conative/appetitive states of a sentient being (that is, through a sense of what 'it is like' for a sentient organism to *be* that organism); (2) that these affective and/or conative/appetitive states are qualitatively different from mental states in which something is phenomenologically given as *other* than the subject, whatever the ontological status of this 'other'; (3) that cognition is, most fundamentally, a primitive presence of something *other* than the subject to a perceiving subject (by which I mean nothing more than a being which can have some form of *awareness* of this presence), and (4) that this fundamental cognitive mode, of which pre-verbal children and many non-human animals are capable, is what knowledge primitively is.

What is gained by establishing that any sentient being capable of awareness of an *aliud qua aliud* is capable of the first, most primitive version of knowledge—I contend—is an antidote against scepticism. The reason for maintaining that there *is* a primitive contact between mind and world is what I call 'naturalism': that is, human beings are, first of all, simply a species of perceiving beings which share with other perceiving beings the natural ability to connect with, and respond to, their physical environment *as* their physical environment. If it is granted that primitive sentient beings successfully perceive and respond to their surroundings, thereby showing a primitive contact between perceiver and perceived, there is no reason for denying such contact to human perceivers. And if so, scepticism loses its initial and all-important foothold. Going forward, it will be a matter of making a case for higher, vastly more sophisticated types of apprehension of 'what is'; but the starting point of these cases will be a cognitive contact between mind and world as opposed to a gap which needs to be (and ultimately cannot be) bridged.

On this basis, I have explored the nature of the cognitive contact between subject and object, outlining and defending a historical tradition that explains this contact in terms of intentionality. According to this tradition, cognitive intentionality is intrinsically relational: the very idea at its core—the presence to a subject of some information about some object—implies a relation between a subject and an object. At its root is the ancient doctrine, going back to Empedocles and Democritus, that cognition requires some sort of similarity between cognizer and cognized. This insight is developed by Aristotle and the Aristotelian tradition into the view that to be capable of cognition means to have the potentiality of becoming similar to the cognized, and that the actualization of this potentiality consists in a *sui generis* identification of perceiver with perceived, knower with known, in which they maintain their ontological distinction. For this strand of thought, in its formal reality (that is, in itself, according to its own nature), knowing is a modification of the subject (that is, a cognitive act is an 'accident' of the mind); according to its objective reality, however, the nature of knowing is not that of being a modification of the mind but of referring to something other than the mind. This distinction between formal and objective reality, developed in medieval and early modern philosophy, allows an account in which there are only two really distinct *res* involved in cognition: the mind (of which cognitive acts are modifications or qualities) and some thing other than the mind (whatever the formal reality of this thing might be). In turn, the object of cognition can be considered in two ways: in itself (that is, formally, according to its own nature) and qua cognized. What is crucial is that there is only one object considered in two ways: the distinction between object in its formal reality and object qua cognized is a mere distinction of reason; being cognized is a mode of being of the cognized thing itself, and not a modification of the mind or a tertium quid representing the object in the mind.

Furthermore, I have noted that being intentionally aware—*s'apercevoir*, as Antoine Arnauld puts it—is something more than its material conditions. Neither the material conditions of the subject nor the material conditions of the object are sufficient to explain the intentional presence of objects to a subject. One should be wary, therefore, of confusing two different (albeit interrelated) orders of problems. The first problem is what are the physical and psychological conditions and mechanisms which make knowledge possible? This is the issue of the efficient causes of cognition—an issue which constitutes the proper subject-matter of the natural sciences (physics, biology, neuroscience, empirical psychology, and so on). The second problem is how best to understand and describe the primitive experience we all have of perceiving/being aware of things/having objects intentionally present. This is the issue of the nature, or formal cause, of cognition. It is this second issue, I claim, which is the proper subject-matter of epistemology and philosophy of mind. My conclusion is that individual knowledge is a *sui generis* and undefinable but primitively experienced intentional presence of an *aliud*. In Max Scheler's phrase, primarily or paradigmatically, knowing is 'consciousness of something' founded upon the immediate 'presence and self-givenness of things'.[6]

II.2 Objects, Acts, and Faculties

Having discussed the origin of the distinction between subject and object, and the nature of their contact in a cognitive act, I have turned to the question of which kinds of entities are involved in cognition, and which kind of entity is knowledge itself. The ancient–medieval tradition which explains the ontology of cognition in terms of objects, acts, and faculties is revisited and reproposed. There is no need, I claim, to add a fourth element to this ontology, namely, representational content. Although it may be useful, in certain contexts, to treat object and content as conceptually distinct, this is a distinction of reason and not a real distinction. Content, I contend, is ontologically reducible to objects and acts.

My exploration of objects has started from sensible objects and how they are grasped, respectively, in sense-perceptual and intellectual cognition. All that has real, mind-independent existence, I claim, is individual; all really existing, extra-mental things are fully determinate particulars. The main upshot of the investigation of how we grasp these individuals is that cognition is a process of progressive determination of what is apprehended in an indeterminate way first by the senses and then by the intellect—a process which can never fully exhaust

[6] Scheler 1957: 397.

the richness of fully determinate individuals. Denying adequate knowledge of individuals is different, however, from denying knowledge. Although not *all* aspects of an individual can be known, *some* can and are known. That is, senses and intellect do latch on to 'what is', although they cannot exhaust what it is in its full determinacy.

Concrete individuals are not, however, the only objects of thought. I have suggested that there are also some objects which do not have extra-mental existence (that is, they need a mind thinking them) but which are not reducible to psychological features of the human mind—for example, ideal mathematical objects. These objects, I claim, have their own logically necessary natures, wholly independent of what individual cognitive subjects think (rightly or wrongly) of them. It is this nature which constitutes the object towards which intentionality is directed when ideal mathematical objects are thought, whatever the more precise ontological status of such objects might be. Furthermore, I have noted that there are some objects of human cognition which are purely imaginary (the god Jupiter, centaurs, golden mountains). Their nature, I claim, is that of being logical possibilities with contingent natures. On the other hand, on my account, there are no impossible (that is, logically contradictory) objects. Without going more precisely into the exceedingly difficult issue of what the nature of logical possibility might be, I commend a tradition drawing attention to the following: the phenomenology of thinking about an ideal triangle or about the god Jupiter is not that of thinking about a feature of the mind, but that of thinking of something 'other' than mind, whatever the more precise ontological status of this 'other' might be.

Most importantly, the result of this thinking is not a new ontological category of objects (intentional objects, mental contents, mental representations, and the like) but merely a *mode of being* of objects which, in themselves, have their own formal reality, their own nature (sensible or not-sensible, mind-independent or mind-dependent, real or ideal or imaginary . . .), whatever that is more precisely. These objects in themselves (that is, according to their formal reality, whatever that is) are the objects of cognition. This account, I claim, offers the following answer to the problem posed to intentionality by so-called non-existing objects: (1) intentionality is relational and, as a relation, it requires a referent; (2) the ontological status of this referent, however, can vary; (3) although there are different ontological categories of objects, there is no need for a specific, additional ontological category of *intentional* objects: objects in themselves, with their own formal reality, are the objects towards which a cognitive intentional relation is directed.

After discussing the first element in the ontology of cognition—objects—I have turned to the discussion of the other two: acts and faculties (tracking, respectively, occurrent and dispositional cognition). Three main types of cognitive mental acts are explored: apprehension, judgement, and reasoning. Although in fully developed rational beings the mental acts of apprehension, judgement, and reasoning are logically expressed (respectively) by concepts, propositions, and propositional argumentation, the relevant mental acts should not be identified with the logical entities which express them. This distinction between mental acts and their logical expression provides space, in my view, for the full acknowledgment of pre-conceptual and pre-propositional versions of apprehension and judgement which are manifested, for instance, in the behaviour of pre-verbal children and non-rational animals.

Furthermore, in relation to these three main types of cognitive mental acts, I have argued that: (1) in the case of assent to present objects or states of affairs (a case central to the conception of knowledge defended in this book), the distinction between the apprehension of what is present and the mental act of acknowledgement of this presentation (that is, judgement) is merely a distinction of reason; (2) judging and reasoning—or, generally speaking, the mental activity of thinking with assent in developed human beings—span knowing, believing, and their cognates; (3) whether an act of judgement (an act of thinking with assent) is an act of knowing as opposed to an act of believing depends on whether assent is compelled by an original cognitive contact with 'what is'; (4) there are key mental activities such as memory, recognition, and inference which can retain and extend a cognitive contact with 'what is'; insofar as they do so, they extend knowing; (5) on the other hand, these activities are also relevant to cognitive modes lacking a direct contact with 'what is'; they span, therefore, both knowing and believing.

In turn, I started my discussion of faculties and the dispositional aspect of cognition by reproposing the Aristotelian distinction between *actus primus* and *actus secundus* of a faculty. According to its *actus primus*, a faculty is an actual property of a subject; according to its *actus secundus*, a faculty is a potentiality which is not always actualized. Ontologically, I suggest, faculties are natural properties or qualities of the mind which manifest its essence or nature. Although they have an aspect of potentiality (faculties are not always exercised), I have followed the Aristotelian tradition in thinking that their exercise (that is, the passage from potentiality to actuality) does not mark a change in ontological category: both potential and actual states therefore fall under the category of qualities or properties of the mind. Thus, a cognitive ability and its exercise (an act of cognition) are related as a potential state of the mind and an actual state of the mind in which potentiality is actualized.

In addition to cognitive faculties or powers, I noted, there are powers of a different sort which (I claim) are complementary and equally important in understanding the activity of cognitive beings. These are the conative/appetitive powers of sensible and rational beings, which include the distinctive appetitive faculty of rational beings, namely, the will. As I try to show, both in relation to the original distinction between subject and object and as regards the interplay between belief and will, only a philosophical anthropology in which cognitive and conative powers—perception and appetite—are fundamentally integrated can properly account for human cognition.

Finally, the ontology of cognition in terms of objects, acts, and faculties, summarized above, leads to the following proposal as regards the object of knowledge and the object of belief: negatively, neither the object of knowledge nor the object of belief are normally or primarily propositions, although fully developed human knowledge and/or belief are typically articulated and expressed in propositions; positively, what one knows are objects in themselves, that is, objects as they are according to their formal reality, whatever that is. If these objects are mind-independent, fully determinate individuals, our knowledge of them will always be *inadequate* and *indeterminate*. If they are abstract entities (such as mathematical or logical entities, or imaginary entities) our knowledge of them can be in principle adequate precisely in virtue of their abstract nature, although most people will still know them inadequately and indeterminately.

As for the object of belief, I argue, in some cases it may be the same as the object of knowledge, but assent to it being so-and-so will not be determined by a cognitive presence of the objects of cognition themselves but by reasons which are, as it were, external to the object (for example, the testimony of a trustworthy authority or the symptoms normally associated with an illness). In these cases, the difference between knowing and believing will be found in *how* one assents to this state of affairs rather than in *what* one assents to. In other cases—and, paradigmatically, when the putative entities/states of affairs are not even in principle open to the sort of cognitive contact with the object of cognition required by knowledge—the object of belief will be imagined or conceived entities and states of affairs which may or may not correspond to 'what is'.

Most importantly, the indeterminacy which characterizes human cognition has momentous consequences, including its accounting for the fact that people who know the *same* object will grasp it in different ways, that is, there will be different modes of presentation of the same object to different knowers (for example, inadequate or not fully determinate knowledge of Venus results in Venus being known by someone as Hesperus and by someone else as Phosphorus). This point, I contend, has great anti-sceptical relevance. A key mistake of scepticism, I claim, is that of being, at bottom, an all-or-nothing position: either we infallibly know such-and-such or nothing is certain. Now, such infallibility would require not only infallible faculties (which as limited, fallible beings we do not have) but also an adequate (that is, fully determinate) knowledge of the relevant object. Acknowledging the structural indeterminacy of human cognition when it comes to anything which has extra-mental existence provides an important path of resistance to scepticism. We only ever grasp some very limited aspects of a concrete object or state of affairs. The aspects with which we *do* connect, however, are known with certainty even if most aspects of that very object/state of affairs are not known at all. The latter limitation plays a key role in accounting for the fallibility of our overall judgements about the object/state of affairs with which we have made contact. Moreover, in the progressive determination of what is indeterminately apprehended, not everything is present to the senses and/or the intellect. Indeed, most of what contributes to fully determining the identity of this individual (or state of affairs) is not (and, in many cases, cannot be) present. This is why we have to rely so often on a different and complementary cognitive mode, namely, belief.

III.1 The Distinctive Contribution of Belief

It is clear that (as in the best Early Modern tradition) my proposal sets the bar for individual knowledge very high. Individual knowing, on my account, does extend to discursive reasoning, and does involve capacities such as memory and recognition; yet, it is a cognitive mode more sparingly available than according to other accounts. A key aim of my project has been therefore to stress the distinctive and irreplaceable contribution to human cognition of a complementary cognitive mode: belief. Belief too, I argue, is a cognitive mental state in which a cognizer assents to a certain state of affairs as being true or false. Although irreducibly distinct from knowledge, it is not (I claim) a 'botched' kind of cognition. Rather, belief accomplishes something different from knowledge: namely, it extends our cognitive grip on reality and/or the world when (for objective or subjective reasons) we are unable to know. It has its own standards (justification, degrees of probability, level of support by reasons, and so on) and, when they are applied in a robust way, it enjoys remarkable success in tracking truth.

Given this distinctive contribution to cognition, Part III of this book is devoted to a further exploration of belief and the doxastic family (defined as a family of cognate mental states which entail belief but do not reduce to belief). This part of the inquiry has tackled, first of all, the vexed question of whether belief is voluntary or involuntary, claiming that a satisfactory answer to this question requires the distinction between assent and belief proposed by this book. On this basis, I have proposed the following threefold account: (1) belief is a spontaneous (that is, in this context, involuntary) response to epistemic reasons (reasons which concern the truth or falsity of the putative state of affairs which is the object of belief); (2) notwithstanding the spontaneity of belief, the will has a key role to play in determining assent; (3) acknowledging this role of the will does not amount to doxastic voluntarism.

Both an indirect and a direct role of the will are identified. To start with, the will plays an indirect role in belief-formation by directing attention to reasons in support of believing such-and-such to be the case. Furthermore, in cases of genuine epistemic uncertainty, the will plays a direct role in determining assent via conative factors such as hope, trust, wishes, and drives. A number of these cases, I suggest, map onto the mental act that the literature calls 'acceptance'. Many such cases entail, in my view, some degree of belief, but this degree of belief is insufficient on its own to determine a certain course of action, and needs therefore to be complemented by voluntary (conative/appetitive) factors. What the resulting actions have in common is that they manifest assent to the obtaining of a state of affairs which outstrips purely doxastic considerations. Finally, I claim, the will plays a direct role in determining assent also in theoretical contexts. That is to say, theoretical judgements in which assent is not compelled by clear sight of the object of cognition are in themselves 'decisions'. As such, they have a genuine volitional element which does not consist in directly influencing belief but in *ending enquiry*. It is this conative/appetitive element, I argue, that allows us to move on, as opposed to stagnating in a mental life of endlessly entertaining and not assenting due to the lack of clear sight.

My main conclusion is the following. The fact that, in highly probable cases as well as in cases of natural, incorrigible, or instinctive belief, assent and belief align, makes their distinction often invisible. Yet, acknowledging their distinction serves to dispel a number of pseudo-problems on the divide between voluntarism and anti-voluntarism. As a spontaneous response to epistemic reasons, it is not belief which is voluntary; the volitional element is constituted by the conative factors which contribute to determining assent in situations of epistemic uncertainty. It is these factors, rather than our spontaneous response to epistemic reasons, that normally bear the weight of moral responsibility. A shift from an ethics of belief to an ethics of assent may therefore be in order. More generally, it seems to me that, by distinguishing between belief and assent, my proposal acknowledges the fundamental integration of the cognitive and conative aspects of mental life without resorting to doxastic voluntarism.

Next, I have tackled the issue of testimony. On my account, testimony plays a crucial role in our epistemic lives as the source of most of our beliefs, but does not, *on its own*, produce individual knowledge (although it may, and often does, *lead* to individual knowing). To put it another way, as the source of many of one's beliefs, testimony is as important to my story as it is to other stories. The difference is that, on my account, it is a central plank of a story about our remarkable cognitive success in reliably tracking 'what is' if and when 'what is' is beyond the reach of one individual's knowledge. It is not part of a story about how knowledge is transmitted to an individual because, I claim, knowledge is not transferable to individuals as a parcel which is simply passed on.[7] In this framework, the distinction between intrinsic and extrinsic evidence tracks the two distinct ways of 'thinking with assent' constituted by knowing and believing. Intrinsic evidence, I suggest, grounds knowledge; extrinsic evidence grounds belief; in turn, testimony constitutes the paradigmatic case of extrinsic evidence.

[7] This claim has key implications for education. On this model, the primary aim of education is to guide students to see for themselves. Only secondarily, or instrumentally as a means to its primary aim, education is a process by which information is passed on.

Assuming then that what we are dealing with is justified belief rather than knowledge, my account of when and how testimony provides sufficient justification for belief takes the form of a modified version of global reductionism. That is, in my view, the general reliability of testimony is originally established and constantly reinforced by the fundamental cognitive modes which allow a first-hand contact with the object of cognition and the preservation of such contact, such as sense-perception and memory. It is in this global reductionist framework, I argue, that the non-reductionist 'innocent until proved guilty' rule applies, and should apply, to testimony.

Overall, while acknowledging that the bar for individual knowledge is set high, I resist the charge that it is set *too* high. First of all, those who think that knowledge is a species of belief are hardly in a position to complain that, on my account, too much of what people normally take to be knowledge ends up being, in fact, belief. Unlike them, I argue for a mental state which is ontologically different from *any* sort of belief, whereas for them all our cognition is, at bottom, *some* sort of belief. Second, one should distinguish between what is distributively known by an individual and what is collectively known by a community. My focus in this inquiry is on what is known by an *individual*. Much of what is not known (as opposed to justifiably believed) by that individual can still count as collectively known by a community.[8] In fact, the Socratic humility proposed by this book for claims to individual knowledge magnifies the importance of collective knowing: there are many matters on which we cannot even in principle claim individual knowledge and must instead trust the collective knowledge of appropriate communities of experts. Third and most importantly, restricting what is, rigorously speaking, known by a given individual does not equate to restricting the scope of that individual's successful cognition. Justified true belief (JTB) greatly broadens such cognition beyond the limits of what an individual strictly knows.

III.2 Religious Belief and Transcendental Realism

Finally, I have proposed to apply the account of knowing and believing outlined by this book to a particular type of belief: namely, religious belief. Specifically, my account offers an alternative to the project of Reformed Epistemology, especially as it is represented by Plantinga's claim that 'faith is knowledge'. Adopting the twentieth-century orthodoxy according to which knowledge is a kind of belief which meets certain criteria, Plantinga offers a strongly externalist and reliabilist version of this doctrine which construes knowledge as warranted true belief. If true and warranted, Plantinga argues, Christian belief counts therefore as knowledge.

[8] I agree with Bird 2010 that social knowing is an *analogue* of individual knowing. As such it has its own distinctive features, not all of which are applicable to individual knowing.

By contrast, I defend a view according to which a distinction in kind between knowing and believing is especially important in religious epistemology in order to safeguard the distinctive epistemological status of religious belief and religious faith. Rather than elevating religious belief and religious faith to the status of knowledge, it seems to me that Reformed Epistemology ends up reducing all knowledge to the particular beliefs of incommensurable world-views. In so doing, far from offering a plausible defence of Christian belief from the charge of irrationality, its project results in a general weakening of rationality. Furthermore, I argue that undermining the fundamental difference in kind between belief and knowledge does not ultimately help the cause of religious belief. On the contrary, this move compromises the aspect of epistemic uncertainty, and consequently the element of trust, which is traditionally regarded as essential to faith. In short, it compromises the notion of 'faith' itself.

As regards William Alston's defence of a putative direct perception of God, my main objection is the following. The very doctrinal system which serves as the indispensable overrider required by Alston's notion of rationally engaged doxastic practices construes God as 'wholly other'. If one takes seriously (as, I think, one should) the categorical difference between the objects of natural perception and the object of mystical practices, a putative direct perception of (an eternal, transcendent, infinite...) God resists naturalization into a cognitive mode sufficiently analogous to other, natural doxastic practices.

The alternative framework for religious epistemology which I propose instead takes as crucial the categorical difference between a putative eternal, noumenal dimension not bounded by space and time, and the corporeal, spatio-temporal order of which we are part and of which we have experience. This framework could be called 'transcendental realism', intended as the view that the conditions of possibility of the objects of cognition are independent of our thought. According to the realist metaphysics endorsed by this book, objects in space and time exist independently of our experience of them. Renewing the ancient Heraclitean insight that 'like knows like', I take the view that we can know these mind-independent objects in a direct realist way because we are also embodied beings which exist in space and time: as such we belong to the same order of things (that is, corporeal, spatio-temporal, finite beings), and in this same order of things a cognitive contact of the sort relevant to human knowledge is possible.

On the other hand, if there is a God as traditionally conceived by theism (eternal, infinite, non-corporeal, and so on), this entity will belong to a different (call it 'noumenal') order of things—an order in which the conditions of possibility of the objects of cognition are also, and a fortiori, independent of our thought. The ontological gap between the spatio-temporal corporeal world and this (putative) noumenal world explains why the latter is beyond the limits of human *knowledge*. We can, however, relate to it through a different cognitive mode—a cognitive mode which does not require a cognitive contact with an object of cognition which is beyond our ken. This cognitive mode is *belief.* If much of our cognition relies on assenting to putative features of reality that in many cases are not only de facto but also *de jure* beyond the direct cognitive contact required by knowledge, it is hardly surprising that the appropriate mode of cognition is not knowledge but belief when the putative object of cognition is a noumenal, supernatural entity.

Religious belief therefore shares key features of a cognitive mode which contributes in a systematic and irreplaceable way to successful human cognition. As such, it should not be unfairly subjected to epistemic double-standards that castigate features in religious belief which are accepted in belief more generally. On the other hand, religious belief (like any other belief) *does,* on my account, need justification which is ultimately grounded in what we know about the world—namely, in our perception of some object or understanding of some truth. In conclusion, I propose to include religious belief, in its own unique manner, under the two complementary slogans that summarize the project of this book: 'knowledge first' but 'give belief its due!'

Bibliography

1. Abbreviations

A: Leibniz, G. W. *Sämtliche Schriften und Briefe*, ed. Academy of Sciences of Berlin. Series I–VIII (Darmstadt; Leipzig; Berlin, 1923 ff). Cited by series, volume, and page.

A/B: Kant, Immanuel. *Kritik der reinen Vernunft*, 1st edn 1781 ('A' followed by page number)/2nd edn 1787 ('B' followed by page number). In Ak, Vols 3 and 4. Trans. as *Critique of Pure Reason*, ed. and trans. Paul Guyer and Allen W. Wood (Cambridge: Cambridge University Press, 1998). Cited as A/B.

Ak: *Kant's gesammelte Schriften*, ed. Königlichen Preußischen (later Deutschen) Akademie der Wissenschaften. (Berlin: Georg Reimer/Walter De Gruyter, 1900–). Cited by volume and page.

Allen: Plato, *Republic*, trans. R. E. Allen (New Haven and London: Yale University Press, 2006).

AT: René Descartes, *Oeuvres de Descartes*, ed. Charles Adam and Paul Tannery, 11 vols (Paris: Léopold Cerf, 1897–1909). Cited as AT followed by volume and page. Translations are from CSM.

Auriol, I *Sent.*: Auriol, Peter, *Commentariorum in Primum Librum Sententiarum*, ed. by C. Sarnano (Rome: Ex Typographia Vaticana, 1596).

BJHP: *British Journal for the History of Philosophy*.

Crisp: Aristotle, *Nicomachean Ethics*, ed. and trans. Roger Crisp (Cambridge: Cambridge University Press, 2000).

CSM: René Descartes, *The Philosophical Writings of Descartes*, trans. John Cottingham, Robert Stoothoff, and Dugald Murdoch, 3 vols (Cambridge: Cambridge University Press, 1988).

DK: Diels, H. (ed.), *Die Fragmente der Vorsokratiker*. 6th edn. Rev. W. Kranz, 9th edn (Berlin: Weidmann, 1960).

Dutens: G. W. Leibniz, *Opera omnia, nunc primum collecta, in classes distributa, praefationibus et indicibus exornata*, ed. L. Dutens, 6 vols (Geneva: De Tournes, 1768). Cited by volume, part (if relevant), and page.

Gill: Plato, *Symposium*, trans. Christopher Gill (London: Penguin Books, 1999).

GP: G. W. Leibniz, *Die Philosophischen Schriften*, ed. C. I. Gerhardt, 7 vols (Berlin: Weidmannsche Buchhandlung, 1875–1890; reprint, Hildesheim: Olms, 1960–1961). Cited by volume and page.

Griffith: Plato, *The Republic*, ed. G. R. F. Ferrari, trans. Tom Griffith (Cambridge: Cambridge University Press, 2000).

GRUA: G. W. Leibniz, *Textes inédits d'après les manuscrits de la Bibliothèque Provinciale de Hanovre*, ed. G. Grua, 2 vols (Paris: PUF, 1948).

Grube/Reeve: Plato, *Republic*, trans. G. M. A. Grube, rev. C. D. C. Reeve (Indianapolis: Hackett, 1992).

Husserliana: *Husserliana: Edmund Husserl—Gesammelte Werke*, ed. Lothar Eley (The Hague/Dordrecht: Nijhoff/Kluwer, 1950–).

LCL: *Loeb Classical Library*, followed by volume number.

LCL 123: Plato, *Theaetetus. Sophist*, trans. Harold North Fowler (Cambridge, MA: Harvard University Press, 1921).

Lee/Johansen: Plato, *Timaeus and Critias*, trans. Desmond Lee, trans. rev. by T. K. Johansen (London: Penguin Books, 2008).

LM: Laks, André and Glenn W. Most (trans. and eds), *Early Greek Philosophy* Vol. V: *Western Greek Thinkers*, Part 2 (LCL, 528) (Cambridge, MA: Harvard University Press, 2016).

Locke, *Essay*: John Locke, *An Essay concerning Human Understanding*, 1690 (2nd edn, 1694), in *The Clarendon Edition of the Works of John Locke*, ed. P. H. Nidditch (Oxford: Clarendon Press, 1975).

NE: G. W. Leibniz, *New Essays on Human Understanding*, ed. and trans. Peter Remnant and Jonathan Bennett (Cambridge: Cambridge University Press, 1981).

OCT: *Oxford Classical Texts* (or *Scriptorum Classicorum Bibliotheca Oxoniensis*), including Plato and Aristotle's original texts (Oxford: Clarendon Press).

OED: *Oxford English Dictionary*: https://www.oed.com/.

QDP: Thomas Aquinas, *Quaestiones disputatae de potentia Dei*.

Ross: Aristotle, *Nichomachean Ethics*, trans. W. D. Ross, in *The Basic Works of Aristotle*, ed. Richard McKeon (New York: Random House, 1941), 927–1112.

Sedley/Long: Plato, *Meno and Phaedo*, ed. David Sedley, trans. Alex Long (Cambridge: Cambridge University Press, 2011).

Shields: Aristotle, *De Anima*, trans. Christopher Shields (Oxford: Clarendon Press, 2016).

Smith: Aristotle, *De Anima*, trans. J. A. Smith, in *The Complete Works of Aristotle*, ed. Jonathan Barnes, Vol. I (Princeton: Princeton University Press, 1984).

SEP: Edward N. Zalta (ed.), *The Stanford Encyclopedia of Philosophy*: https://plato.stanford.edu/archives (precise edition used indicated in each reference).

ST: Aquinas, Thomas. *Summa Theologiae*. Textum Leoninum (Rome: Ex Typographia Senatus, 1886–1887).

SVF: *Stoicorum Veterum Fragmenta*, ed. H. von Armin (repr. Stuttgart: Teubner, 1979).

Wadding: John Duns Scotus, *Opera Omnia*, ed. Luke Wadding, 12 vols (Lyons: Sumptibus Laurentii Durand, 1639; repr. Hildesheim: Georg Olms Verlagsbuchhandlung, 1968): http://www.logicmuseum.com/wiki/Wadding_1639.

2. Works Written before 1800 (see also Abbreviations)

Aquinas, Thomas, *Compendium theologiae seu Brevis compilatio theologiae*, in *Sancti Thomae de Aquino Opera Omnia*, t. 42. (Rome: Editori di San Tommaso, 1979).

Aquinas, Thomas, *Quaestio disputata de spiritualibus creaturis*, ed. J. Cos, in *Sancti Thomae de Aquino Opera Omnia*, t. 24.2. (Rome; Paris: Commissio Leonina-Les Éditions du Cerf, 2000).

Aquinas, Thomas, *Quaestiones disputatae de anima*, ed. B.-C. Bazán, in *Sancti Thomae de Aquino Opera Omnia*, 24.1 (Rome; Paris: Commissio Leonina-Les Éditions du Cerf, 1996).

Aquinas, Thomas, *Quaestiones disputatae de potentia*, in *Corpus Thomisticum* https://www.corpusthomisticum.org/iopera.html.

Aquinas, Thomas, *Quaestiones disputatae de veritate*, ed. A. Dondaine, in *Sancti Thomae de Aquino Opera Omnia*, t. 22, 3 Vols, 5 fasc. (Rome: Editori di S. Tommaso, 1970–1976).

Aquinas, Thomas, *Scriptum super Sententiis magistri Petri Lombardi*, I–II, ed. P. Mandonnet, Vols 1–2 (Paris: Lethielleux, 1929); III–IV d. 22, ed. M. F. Moos, Vols 3–4 (Paris: Lethielleux, 1933 and 1947); IV dd. 23–50, t. 7.2. (Parma: Fiaccadori, 1858).

Aquinas, Thomas, *Sentencia Libri de Anima*, ed. R.-A. Gauthier, in *Sancti Thomae de Aquino Opera Omnia*, t. 45.1 (Rome; Paris: Commissio Leonina-Vrin, 1984).

Aquinas, Thomas, *Sententia Libri Metaphysicae*, in *Corpus Thomisticum* https://www.corpusthomisticum.org/iopera.html.

Aquinas, Thomas, *Summa contra Gentiles*, in *Corpus Thomisticum* https://www.corpusthomisticum.org/iopera.html.

Arnauld, Antoine, *Des vraies et des fausses idées* (1683), in *Oeuvres philosophiques*, ed. C. Jourdain (Paris: Ladrange, 1843). English trans: *On True and False Ideas*, trans. E. J. Kremer (Lewiston: Edwin Mellen Press, 1990), trans. Stephen Gaukroger (Manchester: Manchester University Press, 1990).

Augustine, *Confessiones*. Available online at https://www.thelatinlibrary.com/.

Augustine, *De Quantitate Animae*, Latin text, with English translation (London: Herder, 1933).

Augustine, *De Praedestinatione Sanctorum Liber Unus*, in *S. Aurelii Augustini Opera Omnia* (*Patrologia Latina* 44), ed. J.-P. Migne (Paris, 1879).

Augustine, *Quaestiones euangeliorum*; *In Iohannis euangelium tractatus*, in *S. Aurelii Augustini Opera Omnia* (*Patrologia Latina* 35), ed. J.-P. Migne (Paris, 1864).

Augustine, *De Trinitate*, trans. Arthur West Haddan in *Nicene and Post-Nicene Fathers*, first series, Vol. 3, ed. Philip Schaff (Buffalo, NY: Christian Literature Publishing Co., 1887.) Rev. and edited for New Advent by Kevin Knight: http://www.newadvent.org/fathers/130111.htm.

Averroes (Ibn Rushd) of Cordoba, *Averrois Cordubensis Commentarium Magnum in Aristotelis De Anima Libros*, ed. F. Stuart (Crawford, Cambridge, MA: Medieval Academy of America, 1953). Trans. R. C. Taylor, *Long Commentary on the De Anima of Aristotle* (New Haven: Yale University Press, 2009).

Berkeley, George, *A Treatise Concerning the Principles of Human Knowledge* [1710], ed. Kenneth Winkler (Indianapolis; Cambridge: Hackett, 1982).

Buridan, John, *Summulae de Dialectica*, trans. Gyula Klima (New Haven; London: Yale University Press, 2001).

Burgersdijk, Franco (1660), *Institutionum logicarum libri duo* (Cambridge: Apud Joann. Field). 1st edn, Leiden: 1626.

Chillingworth, William, *Works* (Philadelphia, PA: Hooker, 1840).

Cicero, *Academica*, in LCL 268.

Cicero, *De Oratore*, in LCL 348.

Clarke, Samuel, *The Works* (London: Printed for John and Paul Knapton, 1738; repr., New York: Graland Publishing, 1978).

Diogenes Laertius, *Vitae Philosophorum* (*Lives of Eminent Philosophers*), in OCT and LCL 184–5.

Eisenhardt, Johann, *De fide historica commentarius* (Helmstedt: Müller, 1679).

Eusebius, *Praeparatio Evangelica*, in *Patrologiae Graecae*, Vol. 21 (Paris: J-P. Migne, 1857).

Hervaeus Natalis, *De secundis intentionibus. Distinctiones I & II*. Critical edn with introduction and indices by J. Dijs (Zupthen: Koninklijke Wöhrmann, 2012).

Hume, David, *A Treatise of Human Nature* [1739–1740], ed. L. A. Selby-Bigge, 2nd edn rev. P. H. Nidditch (Oxford: Clarendon Press, 1978).

Hume, David, *An Enquiry concerning Human Understanding* [publ. 1748 under the title *Philosophical Essays concerning Human Understanding*], ed. Tom L. Beauchamp (Oxford: Oxford University Press, 2000).

Kant, Immanuel, *Prolegomena to Any Future Metaphysics* [1783], trans. and ed. Gary Hatfield, rev. edn (Cambridge: Cambridge University Press, 2004).

Kant, Immanuel, *Critique of Pure Reason*, ed. and trans. Paul Guyer and Allen W. Wood (Cambridge: Cambridge University Press, 1998).

Kant, Immanuel, *Religion and Rational Theology*, ed. and trans. Allen W. Wood and George di Giovanni (Cambridge: Cambridge University Press, 1996).

Leibniz, G. W., 'Lettres et fragments inédits', ed. Paul Schrecker, *Revue philosophique de la France et de l'Étranger* 118 (1934): 5–134.

Leibniz, G. W., *Elementa juris naturalis. Philosophical Writings on Jurisprudence and Natural Law, 1667–1672*, ed. and trans. Lucy Sheaf (Oxford: Oxford University Press, forthcoming).

Locke, John, *A Letter Concerning Toleration* (London: Awnsham Churchill, 1689). Modern edn: *A Letter Concerning Toleration and Other Writings*, ed. James H. Tully (Indianapolis: Hackett, 1983).

Locke, John, *Essays on the Law of Nature*, ed. W. von Leyden (Oxford: Oxford University Press, 1954).

Locke, John, *Drafts for the Essay Concerning Human Understanding, and Other Philosophical Writings*, Vol. 1: Drafts A and B, ed. Peter H. Nidditch and G. A. J. Rogers (Oxford: Oxford University Press, 1990).

Malebranche, Nicolas, *De la recherche de la verité* [1674–1675; 3rd edn 1677–1678], in *Oeuvres complètes de Malebranche*, ed. A. Robinet, 20 Vols (Paris: J. Vrin, 1958–1984).

Ockham, William of, *Scriptum in Librum Primum Sententiarum Ordinatio: Distinctiones II-III* (abbreviated as *I Sent.)*, in *Opera Theologica*, Vol. II (St. Bonaventure, NY: The Franciscan Institute, 1970).

Ockham, William of, *Quodlibeta Septem*, in *Opera Theologica*, Vol. IX (St. Bonaventure, NY: The Franciscan Institute, 1980).

Ockham, William of, *Summa Logicae*, in *Opera Philosophica*, Vol. I (St. Bonaventure, NY: The Franciscan Institute, 1974).

Olivi, Peter John, 'Quaestiones in II librum Sententiarum, q. 76', in Dominik Perler and Sonja Schierbaum (eds), *Selbstbezug und Selbstwissen: Texten zu einer mittelalterlichen Debatte* (Frankfurt am Main: Klostermann, 2014), 138–48.

Pascal, Blaise, *Pensées* (2nd edn, Paris: Guillaume Desprez, 1670).

Peter of Spain, *Tractatus called afterwards Summule logicales* [*c.*1230], first critical edition from the manuscripts, with an introduction by L. M. de Rijk (Assen: van Gorcum, 1972).

Plotinus, *Enneads*, in *Plotini Opera*, ed. Paul Henry and H.-R. Schwyzer, Vols I–III (Oxford: Clarendon Press, 1964–1982).

Reid, Thomas, *An Inquiry into the Human Mind on the Principles of Common Sense* [1764], ed. Derek R. Brookes (Edinburgh: Edinburgh University Press, 1997).

Reid, Thomas, *Essays on the Intellectual Powers of Man* [1788], ed. Derek R. Brookes and Knud Haakonssen (Edinburgh: Edinburgh University Press, 2002).

Scotus, John Duns, *Opus Oxoniense*, in Wadding, Vols V.1–X.

Scotus, John Duns, *Ordinatio*, in Duns Scotus, *Opera Omnia*, ed. K. Balić and others, 20 vols (Vatican City: Typis Polyglottis Vaticanis, 1950–2013).

Scotus, John Duns, *Quodlibetum*, in Wadding.

Scotus, John Duns, *Reportatio I-A*, 2 vols, ed. and trans. Allan B. Wolter and Oleg V. Bychov (St Bonaventure, NY: Franciscan Institute, 2004–2008).

Sextus Empiricus, *Pyrrhoniae Hypotyposes*, in LCL 273.

Sextus Empiricus, *Adversus Mathematicos*, in LCL 291, 311, and 382.

Spinoza, Baruch, *Tractatus de Intellectus Emendatione* [1st ed. 1677], in Benedictus de Spinoza. *Opera*, Vol. 2, ed. Carl Gebhardt (Heidelberg: C. Winter, 1925), trans. Samuel Shirley, in Spinoza, *Complete Works* (Indianapolis: Hackett, 2002).

Spinoza, Baruch, *Ethica Ordine Geometrico Demonstrata* 1st edn 1677], in Benedictus de Spinoza. *Opera*, Vol. 2, ed. Carl Gebhardt (Heidelberg: C. Winter, 1925).
Suarez, Francisco, *De Anima*, in *Opera omnia*, Vol. 3, ed. A. D. M. André (Paris: Vivès, 1856).
Suarez, Francisco, *Disputationes Metaphysicae*, in *Opera omnia* 25–6, ed. Carolus Berton (Paris: Vivès, 1861).
Thomasius, Christian, *Dissertatio de fide juridica* (Halle: Salfeldius, 1699).
Wilkins, John, *Of the Principles and Duties of Natural Religion* (London: Maxwell, 1675).

3. Works Written after 1800

Adams, Marilyn McCord (1987), *William Ockham*, 2 vols (Notre Dame, IN: University of Notre Dame Press).
Adams, Marilyn McCord (1995), 'Praying the Proslogion: Anselm's Theological Method', in Thomas D. Senor (ed.), *The Rationality of Faith and the Plurality of Belief* (Ithaca, NY: Cornell University Press), 13–39.
Adams, Robert M. (1987), *The Virtue of Faith and Other Essays in Philosophical Theology* (Oxford: Oxford University Press).
Adams, Robert M. (1994), *Leibniz: Determinist, Theist, Idealist* (Oxford: Oxford University Press).
Adams, Robert M. (1995), 'Moral Faith', *Journal of Philosophy* 92: 75–95.
Adamson, Peter (2022), *Don't Think for Yourself: Authority and Belief in Medieval Philosophy* (Notre Dame, IN: University of Notre Dame Press).
Adler, J. (2002), *Belief's Own Ethics* (Cambridge, MA: MIT Press).
Aertsen, Jan (1992), 'Truth as Transcendental in Thomas Aquinas', *Topoi* 11: 159–71.
Ahmed, Arif (2020), 'Belief and Religious 'Belief'', *Religious Studies* 56: 80–94.
Algra, K., Barnes, J., Mansfeld, J., and Schofield M. (eds) (1999), *The Cambridge History of Hellenistic Philosophy* (Cambridge: Cambridge University Press).
Alston, William (1982), 'Religious Experience and Religious Belief', in Geivett and Sweetman (1992): 295–303; repr. from *Noûs* 16 (1982).
Alston, William (1991), *Perceiving God: The Epistemology of Religious Experience* (Ithaca: Cornell University Press).
Alston, William (1996), 'Belief, Acceptance and Religious Faith', in J. Jordan and D. Howard-Snyder (eds), *Faith, Freedom, and Rationality* (Lanham, MD: Rowman & Littlefield).
Alston, William (2007), 'Audi on Nondoxastic Faith', in Mark Timmons, John Greco, and Alfred R. Mele (eds), *Rationality and the Good: Critical Essays on the Ethics and Epistemology of Robert Audi* (Oxford: Oxford University Press), 123–38.
Alvarez, Maria (2010), *Kinds of Reasons: An Essay in the Philosophy of Action* (Oxford: Oxford University Press).
Amerini, Fabrizio (2009), 'Realism and Intentionality: Hervaeus Natalis, Peter Aureoli, and William Ockham in Discussion', in Stephen F. Brown, Thomas Dewender, and Theo Kobusch (eds), *Philosophical Debates at Paris in the Early Fourteenth Century* (Leiden: Brill).
Amerini, Fabrizio (2013), *Tommaso d'Aquino e l'intenzionalità* (Pisa: ETS).
Antognazza, Maria Rosa (2014), 'Primary Matter, Primitive Passive Power, and Creaturely Limitation in Leibniz', *Studia Leibnitiana* 46/2: 167–86.

Antognazza, Maria Rosa (2015), 'The Benefit to Philosophy of the Study of its History', *BJHP* 23/1: 161–84.

Antognazza, Maria Rosa (ed.) (2018), *The Oxford Handbook of Leibniz* (Oxford: Oxford University Press).

Antognazza, Maria Rosa, and Segala, Marco (eds) (2022), *Intuition in the History of Philosophy*: special issue of *BJHP*.

Anscombe, G. E. M. (1975), 'The First Person', in Samuel Cuttenplan (ed.), *Mind and Language*: Wolfson College Lectures 1974 (Oxford: Clarendon Press), 21–36.

Anscombe, G. E. M. (1976), 'The Subjectivity of Sensation', in G. E. M. Anscombe, *Metaphysics and the Philosophy of Mind: Collected Philosophical Papers Volume II* (Oxford: Basil Blackwell, 1981), 44–56.

Anscombe, G. E. M. (1979), 'What is it to Believe Someone?', in C. F. Delaney (ed.) *Rationality and Religious Belief* (Notre Dame: University of Notre Dame Press).

Asmis, Elizabeth (1999), 'Epicurean Epistemology', in Algra, Barnes, Mansfeld, and Schofield (1999), 260–94.

Audi, Robert (2006), 'Testimony, Credulity, and Veracity', in Lackey and Sosa (2006): 25–49.

Audi, R. (2008). 'Belief, Faith and Acceptance,' *International Journal for Philosophy of Religion* 63: 87–102.

Audi, Robert (2011), *Rationality and Religious Commitment* (Oxford: Clarendon Press).

Austin, J. L. (1962), *Sense and Sensibilia* (New York: Oxford University Press).

Austin, J. L. (1979), 'Truth', in J. L. Austin, *Philosophical Papers*, ed. J. O. Urmson and G. J. Warnock (Oxford: Oxford University Press), pp. 117–33. First published in *Proceedings of the Aristotelian Society Supplementary* 24 (1950), 111–28.

Aveling, Francis (1907), 'Belief', *The Catholic Encyclopedia*, Vol. 2 (New York: Robert Appleton). Online at http://www.newadvent.org/cathen/02408b.htm.

Ayers, Michael (1991), *Locke: The Arguments of the Philosophers*, 2 vols (London: Routledge).

Ayer, A. J. (1956), The Problem of Knowledge (London: Macmillan).

Ayers, Michael (1998a), 'Theories of Knowledge and Belief', in Garber and Ayers (1998), Vol. 2: 1003–61.

Ayers, Michael (1998b), 'Ideas and Objective Being', in Garber and Ayers (1998), Vol. 2: 1062–107.

Ayers, Michael (2019), *Knowing and Seeing: Groundwork for a New Empiricism* (Oxford: Oxford University Press).

Ayers, Michael (2021), 'Response to Comments and Criticisms', *Grazer Philosophische Studien* 98: 600–27.

Ayers, Michael, and Antognazza, Maria Rosa (2019), 'Knowledge and Belief from Plato to Locke', in Ayers (2019), 3–33.

Austin, J. L. (1962), *Sense and Sensibilia* (New York: Oxford University Press).

Austin, J. L. (1979), 'Truth', in J. L. Austin, *Philosophical Papers*, ed. J. O. Urmson and G. J. Warnock (Oxford: Oxford University Press), pp. 117–33. First published in *Proceedings of the Aristotelian Society Supplementary* 24 (1950), 111–28.

Aveling, Francis (1907), 'Belief', *The Catholic Encyclopedia*, Vol. 2 (New York: Robert Appleton). Online at http://www.newadvent.org/cathen/02408b.htm.

Barnes, J. (1982), 'The Beliefs of a Pyrrhonist', *Proceeding of the Cambridge Philological Society* 28: 1–28.

Bayne, Tim, and Hattiangadi, Anandi (2013), 'Belief and its Bedfellows', in N. Nottelmann (ed.), *New Essays on Belief: Constitution, Content, and Structure* (Basingstoke: Palgrave Macmillan), 124–44.

Bénveniste, Émile (1969), *Le Vocabulaire des Institution Indo-Européennes* (Paris: Les Éditions de Minuit).

Bengson, John (2015), 'The Intellectual Given', *Mind* 124: 707–60.

Benton, Matthew A. (2017), 'Epistemology Personalized', *Philosophical Quarterly* 67/269: 813–34.

Benton, Matthew A. (2018), 'God and Interpersonal Knowledge', *Res Philosophica* 95/3: 421–47.

Benton, Matthew A., Hawthorne, John, and Rabinowitz, Dani (eds) (2018), *Knowledge, Belief, and God: New Insights in Religious Epistemology* (Oxford: Oxford University Press).

Bird, Alexander (2010), 'Social Knowing', *Philosophical Perspectives* 24/1: 23–56.

Bird, Alexander (2016), 'Overpowering: How the Power Ontology Has Overreached Itself', *Mind* 125: 341–83.

Bird, Alexander (2022), *Knowing Science* (Oxford: Oxford University Press).

Bishop, John (2007), *Believing by Faith: An Essay in the Epistemology and Ethics of Religious Belief* (Oxford: Oxford University Press).

Black, Carolyn (1971), 'Knowledge without Belief', *Analysis* 31/5: 152–8.

Black, Deborath (1998), 'Logic in Islamic Philosophy', in Edward Craig (ed.), *Routledge Encyclopedia of Philosophy* (London: Routledge): doi:10.4324/9780415249126-H017-1

Bluck, R. S. (1963), 'Knowledge by Acquaintance in Plato's Theaetetus', *Mind* 72: 259–63.

BonJour, Laurence (1996), 'Plantinga on Knowledge and Proper Function,' in Jonathan L. Kvanvig (ed.), *Warrant in Contemporary Epistemology: Essays in Honor of Plantinga's Theory of Knowledge* (Lanham: Rowman & Littlefield), 47–71.

BonJour, Laurence (2002), *Epistemology: Classic Problems and Contemporary Responses* (Lanham, MD: Rowman & Littlefield).

Booth, Anthony Robert (2022), 'Ought to Believe, Simpliciter,' *Episteme*. p. 1: https://doi.org/10.1017/epi.2021.53.

Bratman, M. (1992), 'Practical Reasoning and Acceptance in a Context', *Mind* 102: 1–15.

Brentano, Franz (1874), *Psychologie vom empirischen Standpunkt* (Leipzig: Duncker & Humblot). New editions: (1924, repr. 1973), ed. Oskar Kraus (Leipzig: Felix Meiner Verlag). Trans. Antos C. Rancurello, Dailey B. Terrell, and Linda L. McAlister (1995), *Psychology from an Empirical Standpoint* (London: Routledge).

Brentano, Franz (1903/1987), 'Von der Natur der Vorstellung (Ein Diktat aus dem Nachlass 1903)', *Conceptus* 21: 25–31.

Brentano, Franz (1911), *Von der Klassifikation der psychischen Phänomene, Psychologie vom empirischen Standpunkt*, Vol. 2 (Leipzig: Duncker & Humblot).

Brentano, Franz (1930), *Wahrheit und Evidenz*, ed. Oskar Kraus (Leipzig: Felix Meiner Verlag). Trans. as Brentano 1966.

Brentano, Franz (1966), *The True and the Evident*, trans. Roderick M. Chisholm, Ilse Politzer, and Kurt Fischer (London: Routledge). A trans. of Brentano 1930.

Brentano, Franz (1968), *Kategorienlehre*, ed. Alfred Kastil, 2nd edn (Hamburg: Felix Meiner Verlag).

Brentano, Franz (1982), *Deskriptive Psychologie*, ed. Roderick M. Chisholm and Wilhelm Baumgartner (Hamburg: Felix Meiner Verlag).

Brewer, Bill (2011), *Perception and its Objects* (Oxford: Oxford University Press).

Brewer, Bill (2021), 'The Presidential Address: The Objectivity of Perception', *Proceedings of the Aristotelian Society*: https://doi.org/10.1093/arisoc/aoaa018.

Brunschwig, Jacques (1999), 'Introduction: The Beginnings of Hellenistic Epistemology', in Algra, Barnes, Mansfeld, and Schofield (1999), 229–59.

Buchak, Lara (2012), 'Can it be Rational to Have Faith?', in *Probability in the Philosophy of Religion* (Oxford: Oxford University Press), 225–47.
Buchak, Lara (2014), 'Rational Faith and Justified Belief', in T. O'Connor and L. Goins (eds), *Religious Faith and Intellectual Virtue* (Oxford: Oxford University Press), 49–73.
Buchak, Lara (2017), 'Faith and Steadfastness in the Face of Counter-Evidence', *International Journal for Philosophy of Religion* 81: 113–33.
Burnyeat, Myles (1982), 'Idealism and Greek Philosophy: What Descartes Saw and Berkeley Missed', *Philosophical Review* 91/1: 3–40.
Burnyeat, Myles (1984), 'Aristotle on Understanding Knowledge', in E. Berti (ed.), *Aristotle on Science: The Posterior Analytics*. Proceedings of the Eighth Symposium Aristotelicum (Padua: Editrice Antenore), 97–139.
Burnyeat, Myles, and Michael Frede (eds) (1998), *The Original Sceptics: A Controversy* (Indianapolis: Hackett).
Burnyeat, Myles (unpublished), 'Carneades was no Probabilist': https://www.scribd.com/document/341395731/Carneades-Was-No-Probabilist.
Buzzetti, Vincenzo (1940), *Institutiones philosophicae*, Vol. I: *Logicam et metaphysicam complectens*, ed. Amato Masnovo (Piacenza: Merlini).
Byrne, Peter (2007), *Kant on God* (Aldershot: Ashgate).
Byrne, Peter (2011), 'Reidianism in Contemporary English-Speaking Religious Epistemology', *European Journal for Philosophy of Religion* 3/2: 267–84.
Carriero, John (2013), 'Epistemology Past and Present', *Proceedings of the Aristotelian Society* 113: 175–200.
Carter, J. Adam, Jarvis, Benjamin W., and Rubin, Katherine (2016), 'Belief without Credence', *Synthese* 193: 2323–51.
Cassam, Quassim (2009), 'Can the Concept of Knowledge be Analysed?', in Greenough and Pritchard (2009), 12–30.
Chignell, Andrew (2007), 'Belief in Kant', *Philosophical Review* 116: 323–60.
Chignell, Andrew (2018), 'The Ethics of Belief', in SEP (spring 2018): https://plato.stanford.edu/archives/spr2018/entries/ethics-belief/.
Chisholm, Roderick M. (1957), 'Intentional Inexistence', in Roderick M. Chisholm, *Perceiving: A Philosophical Study* (Ithaca: Cornell University Press), 168–85.
Chisholm, Roderick M. (1966), *Theory of Knowledge* (Englewood Cliffs, N.J.: Prentice Hall).
Clifford, W. K. (1879), 'The Ethics of Belief', in W. K. Clifford, *Lectures and Essays*, Vol. 2 (London: Macmillan), 177–211. Originally published in *Contemporary Review*, 1877.
Coady, C. A. J. (1992), *Testimony: A Philosophical Study* (Oxford: Clarendon Press).
Cohen, Jonathan (1992), *An Essay on Belief and Acceptance* (Oxford: Clarendon Press).
Coffey, Peter (1917), *Epistemology or the Theory of Knowledge* (London: Longmans, Green).
Cook Wilson, John (1926), *Statement and Inference with other Philosophical Papers*, 2 vols (Oxford: Clarendon Press). Repr. Bristol 2002.
Coppens, Charles (1891), *A Brief Text-Book of Logic and Mental Philosophy* (New York: Schwartz, Kirwin, and Fauss).
Craig, Edward (1990), *Knowledge and the State of Nature* (Oxford: Clarendon Press).
Crane, Tim (2001), *Elements of Mind: An Introduction to the Philosophy of Mind* (Oxford: Oxford University Press).
Crane, Tim (2006), 'Brentano's Concept of Intentional Inexistence', in M. Textor (ed.), *The Austrian Contribution to Analytic Philosophy* (London: Routledge), 20–35.
Crane, Tim (2013), *The Objects of Thought* (Oxford: Oxford University Press).
Crane, Tim (2017), *The Meaning of Belief: Religion from an Atheist's Point of View* (Cambridge, MA: Harvard University Press).

Crane, Tim, and French, Craig (2017), 'The Problem of Perception', in SEP (spring 2017): https://plato.stanford.edu/archives/spr2017/entries/perception-problem/.

Crivelli, Paolo (2004), *Aristotle on Truth* (Cambridge: Cambridge University Press).

Crivelli, Paolo (2022), 'Intuition, Discursive Thought, and Truth in Aristotle', in Antognazza and Segala (2022): 1–12.

Cross, Richard (2014), *Duns Scotus's Theory of Cognition* (Oxford: Oxford University Press).

Davidson, Donald (1975/2001), 'Thought and Talk', in S. Guttenplan (ed.), *Mind and Language* (Oxford: Oxford University Press), 7–23; also in Donald Davidson, *Inquiries into Truth and Interpretation* (Oxford: Oxford University Press, 2001), 155–70 (quotations are from this edition).

Davidson, Donald (1982), 'Rational Animals', *Dialectica* 36/4: 317–27.

Davies, Brian (1992), *The Thought of Thomas Aquinas* (Oxford: Oxford University Press).

De Sousa, Ronald B. (1971), 'How to Give a Piece of Your Mind: Or, the Logic of Belief and Assent', *Review of Metaphysics*, 25/1: 52–79.

Dubray, Charles (1910), 'Knowledge', *The Catholic Encyclopedia*. Vol. 8 (New York: Robert Appleton): http://www.newadvent.org/cathen/08673a.htm.

Ducasse, Curt J. (1968), 'Moore's Refutation of Idealism', in Paul A. Schilpp (ed.), *The Philosophy of G. E. Moore* (La Salle: Open Court), 225–51.

Dutand, Julien (2015), 'The Legend of the Justified True Belief Analysis', *Philosophical Perspectives* 29: 95–145.

Engel, Pascal (1998), 'Believing, Holding True, and Accepting', *Philosophical Explorations*, 1/2: 140–51.

Engel, Pascal (1999), 'Dispositional Belief, Assent, and Acceptance', *Dialectica* 53/3–4: 211–26.

Engel, Pascal (ed.) (2000), *Believing and Accepting* (Dordrecht: Kluwer Academic).

Engel, Pascal (2012), 'Trust and the Doxastic Family', *Philosophical Studies* 161: 17–26.

Faulkner, Paul (2000), 'The Social Character of Testimonial Knowledge', *Journal of Philosophy* 97: 581–601.

Feldman, Richard (2014), 'Justification is Internal', in Matthias Steup, John Turri, and Ernest Sosa (eds), *Contemporary Debates in Epistemology*, 2nd edn (Oxford: Blackwell), 337–50.

Feldman, Richard, and Conee, Earl (2001), 'Internalism Defended', *American Philosophical Quarterly*, 38/1: 1–18.

Fine, Gail (1979), 'Knowledge and *Logos* in the *Theaetetus*', *Philosophical Review* 88: 366–97.

Fine, Gail (1990), 'Knowledge and Belief in Republic V–VII', in Stephen Everson (ed.), *Cambridge Companions to Ancient Thought: I Epistemology* (Cambridge: Cambridge University Press), 85–115.

Fine, Kit (1982), 'First-Order Modal Theories iii: Facts', *Synthese*, 53: 43–122.

Fodor, Jerry (1975), *The Language of Thought* (New York: Crowell).

Fodor, Jerry (1981), *Representations* (Cambridge, MA: MIT Press).

Fonnesu, Luca (2015), 'Kant on Private Faith and Public Knowledge', *Rivista di Filosofia* 106: 361–90.

Flew, Anthony (1970), 'Belief by H. H. Price', *Mind* 79/315: 454–60.

Floridi, Luciano (2002), *Sextus Empiricus: The Transmission and Recovery of Pyrrhonism* (Oxford; New York: Oxford University Press).

Frankish, Keith (2007), 'Deciding to Believe Again', *Mind* 116: 523–47.

Frede, Michael (1984), 'The Sceptic's Two Kinds of Assent and the Question of the Possibility of Knowledge', in Richard Rorty, J.B. Schneewind, and Quentin Skinner (eds), *Philosophy in History* (Cambridge: Cambridge University Press 1984); also in Burnyeat and Frede (1998), 127–52.

Frede, Michael (1999), 'Stoic Epistemology', in Algra, Barnes, Mansfeld, and Schofield (1999), 295–322.

Frege, Gottlob (1914), *Logik in der Mathematik*, in his *Nachgelassene Schriften*, ed. Hans Hermes, Friedrich Kambartel, and Friedrich Kaulbach (Hamburg: Meiner Verlag), 219–70.

Frege, Gottlob (1918–1919), 'Der Gedanke', *Beiträge zur Philosophie des deutschen Idealismus I*: 58–77.

Frege, Gottlob (1977), 'Thoughts: A Logical Inquiry', in Gottlob Frege, *Logical Investigations*, ed. P. T. Geach, trans. P. T. Geach and R. H. Stoothoff (Oxford: Basil Blackwell), 1–30.

Frey, Christopher (2013), 'Phenomenal Presence', in Uriah Kriegel (ed.), *Phenomenal Intentionality* (Oxford: Oxford University Press), 71–92.

Fricker, Elizabeth (2006), 'Testimony and Epistemic Autonomy', in Jennifer Lackey and Ernest Sosa (eds), *The Epistemology of Testimony* (Oxford: Clarendon Press), 225–50.

Fricker, Elizabeth (2009), 'Is Knowing a State on Mind? The Case Against', in Greenough and Pritchard (2009), 31–59.

Friedman, Russell L (1999), 'Peter Auriol on Intentions and Essential Predication', in R. L. Friedman and S. Ebbesen (eds), *Medieval Analyses in Language and Cognition: Acts of the Symposium, the Copenhagen School of Medieval Philosophy, January 10–13, 1996* (Copenhagen Royal Danish Academy of Sciences and Letters), 415–30.

Friedman, Russell L (2000), 'Peter Auriol on Intellectual Cognition of Singulars', *Vivarium* 38: 177–93.

Friedman, Russell L. (2016), 'Peter Auriol', in SEP (winter 2016): https://plato.stanford.edu/archives/win2016/entries/auriol/.

Gale, Richard (1991), *On the Nature and Existence of God* (Cambridge: Cambridge University Press).

Garber, Daniel, and Ayers, Michael (eds) (1998), *The Cambridge History of Seventeenth-Century Philosophy*, 2 vols (Cambridge: Cambridge University Press).

Geivett, R. Douglas, and Sweetman, Brendan (eds) (1992), *Contemporary Perspectives on Religious Epistemology* (New York; Oxford: Oxford University Press).

Gendler, Tamar S. (2008a), 'Alief and Belief', *Journal of Philosophy* 105: 634–63.

Gendler, Tamar S. (2008b), 'Alief in Action', *Mind and Language* 23: 552–85.

Gerson, Lloyd P. (1994), *Plotinus* (London; New York: Routledge).

Gerson, Lloyd P. (ed.) (1996), *The Cambridge Companion to Plotinus* (Cambridge: Cambridge University Press).

Gerson, Lloyd P. (2009), *Ancient Epistemology* (Cambridge: Cambridge University Press).

Gerson, Lloyd P. (2022), 'Intuition in Plato and the Platonic Tradition', in Antognazza and Segala (2022): 579-96.

Gettier, Edmund (1963), 'Is Justified True Belief Knowledge?' *Analysis* 23: 121–3.

Ghisalberti, Alessandro (1975), *Giovanni Buridano. Dalla metafisica alla fisica* (Milan: Vita e Pensiero).

Goldberg, Sanford (2015), *Assertion: On the Philosophical Significance of Assertoric Speech* (Oxford: Oxford University Press).

Goldman, Alvin (1976), 'Discrimination and Perceptual Knowledge', *Journal of Philosophy* 73: 771–91.

Goldman, Alvin (2009), 'Williamson on Knowledge and Evidence', in Greenough and Pritchard (2009), 73–91.

Gómez-Torrente, Mario (2019), 'Logical Truth', in SEP (spring 2019): https://plato.stanford.edu/archives/spr2019/entries/logical-truth/.

Gonzalez, Francisco J. (1996), 'Propositions or Objects? A Critique of Gail Fine on Knowledge and Belief in "Republic" V', *Phronesis* 41/3: 245–75.

Gonzalez, Francisco J. (1998), 'Nonpropositional Knowledge in Plato', *Apeiron* 31: 235–84.

Gould, Stephen Jay (1992), *Bully for Brontosaurus* (London: Penguin).

Greco, John (2003), 'Knowledge as Credit for True Belief', in Michael DePaul and Linda Zagzebski (eds), *Intellectual Virtue: Perspectives from Ethics and Epistemology* (Oxford: Oxford University Press), 111–34.

Greenough, Patrick, and Duncan Pritchard (eds) (2009), *Williamson on Knowledge* (Oxford: Oxford University Press).

Guttenplan, Samuel (1994), 'Belief, Knowledge and the Origins of Content', *Dialectica* 48: 287–305.

Haddock, Adrian, 'On "The Subjectivity of Sensation", and Some Related Matters': unpublished draft paper.

Harcourt, Edward (2000), 'The First Person: Problems of Sense and Reference', in Roger Teichmann (ed.), *Logic, Cause, and Action: Essays in Honour of Elizabeth Anscombe* (Cambridge: Cambridge University Press), 25–46.

Hawthorne (as O'Leary-Hawthorne), John, and Howard-Snyder, Daniel (1996), 'Are Beliefs about God Theoretical Beliefs? Reflections on Aquinas and Kant', *Religious Studies* 32: 233–58.

Hawthorne, John (2013), 'Aquinas on Faith and Knowledge: Response to Robert Pasnau', in John Marenbon (ed.), *Continuity and Innovation in Medieval and Modern Philosophy* (Oxford: Oxford University Press), 119–33.

Hewitt, Simon (2020a), 'Disowning the Mystery: Stump's Non-Apophatic Aquinas', *Medieval Mystical Theology* 1: 3–14.

Hewitt, Simon (2020b), *Negative Theology and Philosophical Analysis* (Cham: Palgrave Macmillan).

Hick, John (1989/2004), *An Interpretation of Religion: Human Responses to the Transcendent* (New Haven: Yale University Press); quoted from 2nd edn (Basingstoke: Palgrave Macmillan, 2004).

Hinton, J. M. (1967), 'Visual Experiences', *Mind* 76/302: 217–27.

Hinton, J. M. (1973), *Experiences* (Oxford: Oxford University Press).

Höfler, Alois (1890), *Philosophische Propädeutik*, Erster Theil: *Logik*, in Zusammenarbeit mit A. Meinong (Vienna: Tempsky/ Freitag).

Holmer, Paul L. (1978), *The Grammar of Faith* (New York: Harper Collins).

Holton, Richard (2017), 'Facts, Factives, and Contrafactives', *Proceedings of the Aristotelian Society Supplementary* 91: 245–66.

Howard-Snyder, Daniel (2013), 'Propositional Faith: What It Is and What It Is Not', *American Philosophical Quarterly* 50: 357–72.

Howard-Snyder, Daniel (2016), 'Does Faith Entail Belief?, *Faith and Philosophy* 33: 142–62.

Howard-Snyder, Daniel (2018a), 'Pistis, fides, and Propositional Belief', *Religious Studies* 54: 585–92.

Howard-Snyder, Daniel (2018b), 'Three Arguments for Thinking that Faith Does Not Entail Belief', *Pacific Philosophical Quarterly* 100/1: 114–28.

Hunter, Bruce (2021), 'Clarence Irving Lewis', SEP (spring 2021): https://plato.stanford.edu/archives/spr2021/entries/lewis-ci/

Husserl, Edmund (1900/2nd edn, 1913): *Logische Untersuchungen*. Erster Band: Prolegomena zur reinen Logik. Text der 1. und der 2. Auflage (Halle: Niemeyer).

Trans. (1975), *Logical Investigations: First Part. Prolegomena to Pure Logic.* Text of the first and second edition (The Hague: Nijhoff).

Husserl, Edmund (1901/2nd edn 1913), *Logische Untersuchungen. Zweiter Band. Untersuchungen zur Phänomenologie und Theorie der Erkenntnis. I. Teil* (Halle a.d.S.: Max Niemeyer). Trans. (1984), *Logical Investigations: Second Part. Investigations Concerning Phenomenology and the Theory of Knowledge.* In two volumes (The Hague, Netherlands: Martinus Nijhoff).

Husserl, Edmund (1913), *Ideen zu einer reinen Phänomenologie und phänomenologische Philosophie* (Halle: Niemeyer). Trans. Fred Kersten (1982), *Ideas Pertaining to a Pure Phenomenology and to a Phenomenological Philosophy, First Book: General Introduction to a Pure Phenomenology* (The Hague: Martinus Nijhoff).

Husserl, Edmund (1933), *Ideas: General Introduction to Phenomenology*, trans. B. Gibson (repr. London: Routledge, 2012).

Hyman, John (1999), 'How Knowledge Works', *Philosophical Quarterly* 49: 433–51.

Hyman, John (2014), 'The Most General Factive Stative Attitude', *Analysis* 74/4: 561–5.

Hyman, John (2015), *Action, Knowledge, and Will* (Oxford: Oxford University Press).

Hyman, John (2017), 'Knowledge and Belief', *Aristotelian Society Supplementary* 91: 267–88.

Inoue, Haruko (2018), 'Personal Identity Regarding the Passions in Hume's *Treatise*', *History of Philosophy Quarterly*, 35/3: 241–58.

Jacob, Pierre (2019), 'Intentionality', in SEP (spring 2017): https://plato.stanford.edu/archives/win2019/entries/intentionality/.

Jackson, Elizabeth (2019a), 'Belief and Credence: Why the Attitude-Type Matters', *Philosophical Studies* 176/9: 2477–96.

Jackson, Elizabeth (2019b), 'Belief, Credence, and Faith', *Religious Studies* 55: 153–68.

Jackson, Elizabeth (2020), 'The Relationship between Belief and Credence', *Philosophy Compass* 15/6: https://doi.org/10.1111/phc3.12668.

Jackson, Frank (1986), 'What Mary Didn't Know', *Journal of Philosophy* 83/5: 291–5.

James, William (1896), 'The Will to Believe', *The New World: A Quarterly Review of Religion, Ethics and Theology* 5: 327–47.

Jay, C. (2015), 'Testimony, Belief and Non-Doxastic Faith: The Humean Argument for Religious Fictionalism', *Religious Studies* 52/2: 247–61.

Jordan, J. (2006), *Pascal's Wager: Pragmatic Arguments and Belief in God* (Oxford: Oxford University Press).

Kemp Smith, Norman (1941), *The Philosophy of David Hume* (Macmillan: London).

Kenny, Anthony (1989), *The Metaphysics of Mind* (Oxford: Oxford University Press).

Klima, Gyula (2013), 'Three Myths of Intentionality Versus Some Medieval Philosophers', *International Journal of Philosophical Studies* 21/3: 359–76.

Klima, Gyula (ed.) (2015), *Intentionality, Cognition, and Mental Representation in Medieval Philosophy* (New York: Fordham University Press).

Kornblith, Hilary (2002): *Knowledge and its Place in Nature* (Oxford: Oxford University Press).

Kosman, A. (1973), 'Understanding, Explanation, and Insight in the *Posterior Analytics* 374–392', in E. N. Lee, A. P. D. Mourelatos, and R. M. Rorty (eds), *Exegesis and Argument: Studies in Greek Philosophy Presented to Gregory Vlastos* (New York: Humanities Press).

Kremer, Michael (2016), 'A Capacity to Get Things Right: Gilbert Ryle on Knowledge', *European Journal of Philosophy* 25/1: 25–46.

Kretzmann, Norman (1992/2000), 'Evidence and Religious Belief', in B. Davies (ed.), *Philosophy of Religion: A Guide and Anthology* (New York; Oxford: Oxford University Press, 2000), 95–107; edited extract from 'Evidence against Anti-Evidentialism', in K. J. Clark (ed.), *Our Knowledge of God* (Dordrecht: Kluwer Academic Press, 1992).

Kretzmann, Norman (1993), 'Philosophy of Mind', in Norman Kretzmann and Eleonore Stump (eds), *The Cambridge Companion to Aquinas* (Cambridge: Cambridge University Press), 128–59.

Kriegel, Uriah (2007), 'Intentional Inexistence and Phenomenal Intentionality', *Philosophical Perspectives* 21: 307–40.

Kriegel, Uriah (2011), *The Sources of Intentionality* (Oxford: Oxford University Press).

Kriegel, Uriah (2016), 'Brentano's Mature Theory of Intentionality', *Journal for the History of Analytical Philosophy* 4/2: 1–15.

Kurath, Hans, Kuhn, Sherman M., Lewis, Robert E., and McSparran, Frances (eds) (2000–), *Middle English Dictionary* (Ann Arbor, MI: Regents of the University of Michigan): https://quod.lib.umich.edu/m/middle-english-dictionary/dictionary.

Lackey, Jennifer (2006), 'Introduction', in Lackey and Sosa (2006), 1–21.

Lackey, Jennifer, and Sosa, Ernest (eds) (2006), *The Epistemology of Testimony* (Oxford: Clarendon Press).

Laporte, Jean (1945), *Le rationalisme de Descartes* (Paris: Presses Universitaires de France).

Lehrer, Keith (1990), *Knowledge* (Boulder, CO: Westview).

Le Morvan, Pierre (2004), 'Arguments against Direct Realism and How to Counter Them', *American Philosophical Quarterly* 41/3: 221–34.

Le Morvan, Pierre (2017), 'Knowledge before Gettier', *BJHP* 25/6: 1216–38.

Leo XIII (1879), *Aeterni Patris*: https://www.vatican.va/content/leo-xiii/en/encyclicals/documents/hf_l-xiii_enc_04081879_aeterni-patris.html.

Lesher, J. H. (1992), *Xenophanes of Colophon: Fragments, a Text and Translation with a Commentary* (Toronto: University of Toronto Press).

Lesher, J. H. (2001), 'On Aristotelian Ἐπιστήμη as "Understanding"', *Ancient Philosophy* 21: 45–55.

Levy, Neil, and Mandelbaum, Eric (2014), 'The Powers that Bind: Doxastic Voluntarism and Epistemic Obligation', in J. Matheson and R. Vitz (eds), *The Ethics of Belief: Individual and Social* (Oxford: Oxford University Press), 12–33.

Lewis, C. I. (1946), *An Analysis of Knowledge and Valuation* (La Salle, IL: Open Court).

Littlejohn, Clayton (2013), 'The Russellian Retreat', *Proceedings of the Aristotelian Society* 113/3: 293–320.

Long, A. A. and D. N. Sedley (1987), *The Hellenistic Philosophers*, 2 vols (Cambridge: Cambridge University Press).

Longworth, Guy (2018), 'Enough is Enough: Austin on Knowing', in Savas L. Tsohatzidis (ed.), *Interpreting J. L. Austin* (Cambridge: Cambridge University Press), 186–205.

Longworth, Guy, and Wimmer, Simon (2022), 'Cook Wilson on Knowledge and Forms of Thinking'. *Synthese* 200, 276: https://doi.org/10.1007/s11229-022-03748-1.

Lycan, W. G. (2006), 'On the Gettier Problem Problem', in S. Hetherington (ed.), *Epistemology Futures* (Oxford: Oxford University Press).

Maher, P. (1986), 'The Irrelevance of Belief to Rational Action', *Erkenntnis* 24/3: 363–84.

Malcolm, Finlay, and Scott, Michael (2017), 'Faith, Belief, and Fictionalism', *Pacific Philosophical Quarterly* 98/S1: 257–74.

Malcolm, Norman (1977), 'The Groundlessness of Belief', in Stuart C. Brown (ed.), *Reason and Religion* (Ithaca: Cornell University Press), 143–57; repr. in Norman Malcolm,

Thought and Knowledge: Essays (Ithaca, NY: Cornell University Press, 1977), 199–216: https://doi.org/10.7591/9781501738760-010.

Marcus, Ruth Barcan (1983), 'Rationality and Believing the Impossible', *Journal of Philosophy* 80/6: 321–38. Also in Marcus (1995a), 143–62.

Marcus, Ruth Barcan (1990), 'Some Revisionary Proposals about Belief and Believing', *Philosophy and Phenomenological Research*, 50 (suppl.): 133–53. Also in Marcus (1995a), 233–56.

Marcus, Ruth Barcan (1995a), *Modalities* (Oxford: Oxford University Press).

Marcus, Ruth Barcan (1995b), 'The Anti-Naturalism of Some Language-Centered Accounts of Belief', *Dialectica* 49/2–4: 113–29.

Marenbon, John (2007), *Medieval Philosophy: An Historical and Philosophical Introduction* (London; New York: Routledge).

Marenbon, John (ed.) (2013), *Continuity and Innovation in Medieval and Modern Philosophy: Knowledge, Mind and Language* [Proceedings of The British Academy 189] (Oxford: Oxford University Press).

Marion, Mathieu (2000a), 'Oxford Realism: Knowledge and Perception I', *BJHP* 8/2: 299–338.

Marion, Mathieu (2000b), 'Oxford Realism: Knowledge and Perception II', *BJHP* 8/3: 485–519.

Marion, Mathieu (2016), 'John Cook Wilson', in SEP (spring 2016): https://plato.stanford.edu/archives/spr2016/entries/wilson/.

Maritain, Jacques (1948), *Distinguer pour unir ou Les degrés du savoir*, rev. and enlarged new edn (Paris: Desclée De Brouwer).

McDowell, John H. (1982), 'Criteria, Defeasibility and Knowledge', *Proceedings of the British Academy* 68: 455–79.

McDowell, John H. (1994), *Mind and World* (Cambridge, MA: Harvard University Press, 1994; reissued with a new introduction, 1996).

McDowell, John H. (1995), 'Knowledge and the Internal', *Philosophy and Phenomenological Research* 55: 877–93.

McDowell, John H. (2011), *Perception as a Capacity for Knowledge* (Milwaukee: Marquette University Press).

McGrath, Matthew, and Frank, Devin (2018), 'Propositions', in SEP (spring 2018): https://plato.stanford.edu/archives/spr2018/entries/propositions/.

Millar, Alan (2007), 'What the Disjunctivist is Right About', *Philosophy and Phenomenological Research* 74/1: 176–98.

Millar, Alan (2014), 'Perceptual Knowledge and Background Beliefs', in Dylan Dodd and Elia Zardini (eds), *Scepticism and Perceptual Justification* (Oxford: Oxford University Press), 128–48.

Millar, Alan (2019), *Knowing by Perceiving* (Oxford: Oxford University Press).

Moore, G. E. (1903), 'The Refutation of Idealism', *Mind* 12: 433–53.

Moravcsik, Julius M. E. (1979), 'Understanding and Knowledge in Plato's Philosophy', *Neue Hefte für Philosophie* 15/16: 53–69.

Morris, Thomas V. (1986), 'Pascalian Wagering', in Geivett and Sweetman (1992), 257–69; repr. from *Canadian Journal of Philosophy*, 16/3: 437–53.

Moser, Paul K. (ed.) (2002), *The Oxford Handbook of Epistemology* (Oxford: Oxford University Press).

Moss, Jessica (2021), *Plato's Epistemology: Being and Seeming* (Oxford: Oxford University Press).

Moss, Jessica, and Whitney Schwab (2019), 'The Birth of Belief', *Journal of the History of Philosophy* 57/1: 1–32.

Mugnai, Massimo (2018), 'Essences, Ideas, and Truths in God's Mind and in the Human Mind', in Antognazza (2018), 11–26.

Mulligan, Kevin, and Barry Smith (1985), 'Franz Brentano on the Ontology of Mind', *Philosophy and Phenomenological Research* 45: 627–44.

Myers-Schulz, Blake, and Schwitzgebel, Eric (2013), 'Knowing That P without Believing That P', *Noûs* 47/2: 371–84.

Nadler, Steven (1989), *Arnauld and the Cartesian Philosophy of Ideas* (Princeton, NJ: Princeton University Press).

Nagel, Thomas (1974), 'What is it Like to be a Bat?', *Philosophical Review* 83/4: 435–50.

Nes, Anders (2016), 'Assertion, Belief, and "I believe": Guarded Affirmation', *Linguistics and Philosophy* 39: 57–86.

Newman, John Henry (1870/1895), *An Essay in Aid of a Grammar of Assent* (London: Burns & Oates). Quoted from 1895 edn (London: Longmans, Green).

Nielsen, Kai (1973), *Scepticism* (London: Macmillan).

O'Brien, Lucy (2007), *Self-Knowing Agents* (Oxford: Oxford University Press).

Orlando, Eleonora (2012), Review of Uriah Kriegel, *The Sources of Intentionality*, in *Notre Dame Philosophical Reviews*: https://ndpr.nd.edu/reviews/the-sources-of-intentionality/.

Osorio-Kupferblum, Naomi, and Sickinger, Mira Magdalena (2021), 'Preface: Book Symposium on Ayers' *Knowing and Seeing* (OUP 2019)', *Grazer Philosophische Studien* 98: 489–94.

Panaccio, Claude (2004), *Ockham on Concepts* (Aldershot: Ashgate).

Pappas, George (2023), 'Internalist vs. Externalist Conceptions of Epistemic Justification', in SEP (spring 2023): https://plato.stanford.edu/archives/spr2023/entries/justep-intext/.

Pasnau, Robert (1997), *Theories of Cognition in the Later Middle Ages* (Cambridge: Cambridge University Press).

Pasnau, Robert (2002), *Thomas Aquinas on Human Nature: A Philosophical Study of Summa theologiae Ia 75–89* (Cambridge: Cambridge University Press).

Pasnau, Robert (2008), 'Id Quo Cognoscimus', in Simo Knuuttila and Pekka Kärkkäinen (eds), *Theories of Perception in Medieval and Early Modern Philosophy* (Dordrecht: Springer), 131–51.

Pasnau, Robert (2013), 'Divisions of Epistemic Labour: Some Remarks on the History of Fideism and Esotericism', in John Marenbon (ed.), *Continuity and Innovation in Medieval and Modern Philosophy* (Oxford: Oxford University Press), 83–117.

Pasnau, Robert (2014), 'Epistemology Idealized', *Mind* 122: 987–1021.

Pasnau, Robert (2017), *After Certainty: A History of Our Epistemic Ideals and Illusions* (Oxford: Oxford University Press).

Perler, Dominik (2000), 'Essentialism and Direct Realism. Some Late Medieval Perspectives', *Topoi* 19: 111–22.

Perler, Dominik (2004), *Theorien der Intentionalität im Mittelalter*, 2nd edn (Frankfurt: Klostermann).

Perler, Dominik (2013), 'What Are Faculties of the Soul? Descartes and His Scholastic Background', *Proceedings of the British Academy* 189: 9–38.

Perler, Dominik (2015), 'Introduction' and 'Faculties in Medieval Philosophy', in Dominik Perler (ed.), *The Faculties: A History* (Oxford: Oxford University Press), 3–18 and 97–139.

Perler, Dominik (2017), 'Self-Knowledge in Scholasticism', in Ursula Renz (ed.), *Self-Knowledge: A History* (New York; Oxford: Oxford University Press), 114–30.

Perler, Dominik (2019), 'What is a Person? Olivi and the Franciscan Tradition', Handout for Conference on 'The *Summa Halensis*: Philosophy and Reception' (Oxford, 24 September 2019).

Phillips, D. Z. (1970), *Faith and Philosophical Enquiry* (London: Routledge & Kegan Paul).

Phillips, J., Buckwalter, W., and Cushman, F. et al. (2021), 'Knowledge before Belief', *Behavioral and Brain Sciences* 44, e140: 1–75. doi:10.1017/S0140525X20000618.

Plantinga, Alvin (1967), *God and Other Minds: A Study of the Rational Justification of Belief in God* (Ithaca: Cornell University Press).

Plantinga, Alvin (1981), 'Is Belief in God Properly Basic?', *Noûs* 15/1: 41–51. Repr. in R. Douglas Geivett and Brendan Sweetman (eds), *Contemporary Perspectives on Religious Epistemology* (Oxford: Oxford University Press, 1993), 133–41 (references are to this edition).

Plantinga, Alvin (1983), 'Reason and Belief in God,' in Alvin Plantinga and Nicholas Wolterstorff (eds), *Faith and Rationality: Reason and Belief in God* (Notre Dame, IN: University of Notre Dame Press), 16–93.

Plantinga, Alvin (1990), *God and Other Minds: A Study of the Rational Justification of Belief in God* (Ithaca: Cornell University Press): reprinted with new preface.

Plantinga, Alvin (1993a), *Warrant: The Current Debate* (New York; Oxford: Oxford University Press).

Plantinga, Alvin (1993b), *Warrant and Proper Function* (New York; Oxford: Oxford University Press).

Plantinga, Alvin (2000), *Warranted Christian Belief* (New York; Oxford: Oxford University Press).

Platts, M. (1979), *Ways of Meaning* (London: Routledge & Kegan Paul).

Poston, (2023), 'Internalism and Externalism in Epistemology', *Internet Encyclopedia of Philosophy*: https://iep.utm.edu/int-ext/.

Pojman, L. P. (1986), 'Faith without Belief', *Faith and Philosophy* 3: 157–76.

Price, H. H. (1969), *Belief* (London: George Allen & Unwin).

Prichard, H. A. (1950), *Knowledge and Perception: Essays and Lectures*, ed. W. D. Ross (Oxford: Clarendon Press).

Priest, Graham (2016), *Towards Non-Being: The Logic and Metaphysics of Intentionality*, 2nd edn (Oxford: Oxford University Press).

Pust, Joel (2013), 'Skepticism, Reason, and Reidianism,' in Albert Casullo and Joshua C. Thurow (eds), *The A Priori in Philosophy* (Oxford: Oxford University Press), 205–25.

Putnam, H. (1994), 'Sense, Nonsense, and the Senses: An Inquiry into the Powers of the Human Mind', *Journal of Philosophy* 91: 445–517.

Quine, W. V. O. (1969), 'Epistemology Naturalized', in W. V. O. Quine, *Ontological Relativity and Other Essays* (New York: Columbia University Press), 69–90.

Renz, Ursula (2017a), 'Introduction', in Ursula Renz (ed.), *Self-Knowledge: A History* (New York; Oxford: Oxford University Press), 1–18.

Renz, Ursula (2017b), 'Self-Knowledge as a Personal Achievement', *Proceedings of the Aristotelian Society* 117/3: 253–72.

Renz, Ursula (2018), *The Explainability of Experience: Realism and Subjectivity in Spinoza's Theory of the Human Mind* (Oxford: Oxford University Press).

Renz, Ursula (2019), 'Spinozist Cognitive Psychology: Spinoza's Concept of the Imagination', in Rudolf Meer, Giuseppe Motta, and Gideon Stiening (eds), *Konzepte der Einbildungskraft in der Philosophie, den Wissenschaften und den Künsten des 18. Jahrhunderts* (Berlin: De Gruyter), 11–25.

Reynolds, Steven L. (2011), 'Doxastic Voluntarism and the Function of Epistemic Evaluations', *Erkenntnis* 75: 19–35.

Rickaby, John (1889), *The First Principles of Knowledge*. Online at https://maritain.nd.edu/jmc/aristotl.htm.

Rizzier, Aaron (2017), 'The Practice of Assertion under Conditions of Religious Ignorance', *European Journal for Philosophy of Religion* 9: 27–39.

Rollinger, Robin D. (2009), 'Brentano's Psychology and Logic and the Basis of Twardowski's Theory of Presentations', *Baltic International Yearbook of Cognition, Logic and Communication* 4: 1–23.

Rott, Hans (2001), *Change, Choice and Inference: A Study of Belief Revision and Nonmonotonic Reasoning* (Oxford: Clarendon Press).

Rowett, Catherine (2018), *Knowledge and Truth in Plato* (Oxford: Oxford University Press).

Russell, Bertrand (1910–1911), 'Knowledge by Acquaintance and Knowledge by Description', *Proceedings of the Aristotelian Society* 11: 108–28.

Russell, Bertrand (1940), *An Inquiry into Meaning and Truth* (London: Allen & Unwin).

Russell, Bertrand (2010), *The Philosophy of Logical Atomism* (London: Routledge).

Ryle, Gilbert (1949), *The Concept of Mind* (London: Hutchinson).

Sayre, Kenneth M., *Belief and Knowledge: Mapping the Cognitive Landscape* (Lanham, MD: Rowman & Littlefield, 1997).

Scheler, Max (1957), *Phänomenologie und Erkenntnistheorie* (1913–1914), in *Gesammelte Werken*, Bd 10: *Schriften aus dem Nachlaß*, Bd 1: *Zur Ethik und Erkenntnislehre* (Bern/Munich: Francke-Verlag).

Schellenberg, J. L. (2005), *Prolegomena to a Philosophy of Religion* (Ithaca, NY: Cornell University Press).

Schofield, Malcolm (1999), 'Academic Epistemology', in Algra, Barnes, Mansfeld, and Schofield (1999), 323–51.

Schwitzgebel, Eric (2019), 'Belief', in SEP (fall 2019): https://plato.stanford.edu/archives/fall2019/entries/belief/.

Scott, Michael (2017), 'Religious Assertion', in J. L. Kvanvig (ed.), *Oxford Studies in Philosophy of Religion* 8: 269–93.

Scribano, Emanuela (2006), *Angeli e beati. Modelli di conoscenza da Tommaso a Spinoza* (Bari: Laterza).

Searle, John R. (1983), *Intentionality: An Essay in the Philosophy of Mind* (Cambridge: Cambridge University Press).

Sedley, David (2004), *The Midwife of Platonism: Text and Subtext in Plato's Theaetetus* (Oxford: Oxford University Press).

Sedley, David (2019), 'The *Timaeus* as Vehicle for Platonic Doctrine', *Oxford Studies in Ancient Philosophy* 56: 45–71.

Sellars, Wilfrid (1956/1963), 'Empiricism and the Philosophy of Mind', in *Minnesota Studies in the Philosophy of Science*, Vol. I, ed. H. Feigl and M. Scriven (Minneapolis, MN: University of Minnesota Press): 253–329. Originally presented at the University of London Special Lectures in Philosophy for 1956 as 'The Myth of the Given: Three Lectures on Empiricism and the Philosophy of Mind'; repr. in *Science, Perception and Reality* (London: Routledge & Kegan Paul, 1963), 129–94, with additional footnotes.

Stevenson, Leslie (2003), 'Opinion, Belief or Faith, and Knowledge', *Kantian Review* 7: 72–101.

Shaffer, Michael J. (2013), 'Doxastic Voluntarism, Epistemic Deontology, and Belief-Contravening Commitments', *American Philosophical Quarterly* 50: 73–82.

Shields, Christopher, and Robert Pasnau (2016), *The Philosophy of Aquinas* (Oxford: Oxford University Press).

Shope, Robert K. (1983), *The Analysis of Knowing* (Princeton, NJ: Princeton University Press).

Shope, Robert K. (2002), 'Conditions and Analyses of Knowing', in Paul K. Moser (ed.), *The Oxford Handbook of Epistemology* (Oxford: Oxford University Press), 25–70.

Slote, Michael A. (1974), *Metaphysics and Essence* (Oxford: Basil Blackwell).

Snowdon, Paul (1980), 'Perception, Vision and Causation', *Proceedings of the Aristotelian Society* 80: 175–92.

Sosa, Ernest (2001), 'Human Knowledge, Animal and Reflective', *Philosophical Studies* 106/3: 193–6.

Sosa, Ernest (2007), *A Virtue Epistemology*, Vol. I of *Apt Belief and Reflective Knowledge* (Oxford: Clarendon Press).

Sosa, Ernest (2009), *Reflective Knowledge*, Vol. II of *Apt Belief and Reflective Knowledge* (Oxford: Clarendon Press).

Soteriou, Matthew (2016), *Disjunctivism* (London: Routledge).

Stalnaker, R. (1984), *Inquiry* (Cambridge, MA: MIT Press).

Steup, Matthias, and Neta, Ram (2020), 'Epistemology', in SEP (fall 2020): https://plato.stanford.edu/archives/fall2020/entries/epistemology/.

Strawson, P. F. (1992), *Analysis and Metaphysics: An Introduction to Philosophy* (Oxford: Oxford University Press).

Strawson, P. F. (1998), 'Reply to John Searle', in Lewis Edwin Hahn (ed.), *The Philosophy of P. F. Strawson* (La Salle, IL: Open Court), 402–4.

Stump, Eleonore (2003), *Aquinas* (London: Routledge).

Stump, Eleonore (2009), 'The Problem of Evil: Analytic Philosophy and Narrative', in Oliver D. Crisp and Michael C. Rea (eds), *Analytic Theology* (Oxford: Oxford University Press), 251–65.

Stump, Eleonore (2010), *Wandering in Darkness: Narrative and the Problem of Suffering* (Oxford: Oxford University Press).

Stumpf, C. (1939), *Erkenntnislehre* I (repr. Lengerich: Pabst Science, 2011).

Sutton, J. (2005), 'Stick to What You Know', *Nous* 39/3: 359–96.

Sutton, J. (2007), *Without Justification* (Cambridge, MA: MIT Press).

Swinburne, Richard (1993), *The Coherence of Theism*, 2nd edn (Oxford: Oxford University Press).

Swinburne, Richard (1996), *Is There a God?* (Oxford: Oxford University Press).

Swinburne, Richard (2001), *Epistemic Justification* (Oxford: Clarendon Press).

Swinburne, Richard (2004), *The Existence of God*, 2nd edn (Oxford: Oxford University Press).

Swinburne, Richard (2005), *Faith and Reason*, 2nd edn (Oxford: Oxford University Press).

Tachau, Katherine H. (1988), *Vision and Certitude in the Age of Ockham: Optics, Epistemology and the Foundations of Semantics, 1250–1345* (Leiden: Brill).

Taieb, Hamid (2018a), *Relational Intentionality: Brentano and the Aristotelian Tradition* (Cham: Springer).

Taieb, Hamid (2018b), 'What is Cognition? Peter Auriol's Account', *Recherches de Théologie et Philosophie médiévales* 85/1: 109–34.

Tebben, Nicholas (2018), 'Belief Isn't Voluntary, but Commitment Is', *Synthese* 195: 1163–79.

Te Velde, Rudi (2006), *Aquinas on God* (Aldershot: Ashgate).

Textor, Mark (2017a), *Brentano's Mind* (Oxford: Oxford University Press).

Textor, Mark (2017b), 'Towards a Neo-Brentanian Theory of Existence', *Philosophers' Imprint* 17/6: 1–20.

Tor, Shaul (2015), 'Parmenides Epistemology and Two Parts of his Poem', *Phronesis* 60/1: 3–39.

Tor, Shaul (2017), *Mortal and Divine in Early Greek Epistemology: A Study of Hesiod, Xenophanes and Parmenides* (Cambridge: Cambridge University Press).

Tor, Shaul (2020), 'Xenophanes on the Ethics and Epistemology of Arrogance', in D. Wolfsdorf (ed.), *Early Greek Ethics* (Oxford: Oxford University Press), 19–36.

Trabattoni, Franco (2016), *Essays on Plato's Epistemology* (Leuven: Leuven University Press).

Travis, Charles, and Kalderon, Mark (2013), 'Oxford Realism', in Michael Beaney (ed.), *The Oxford Handbook of The History of Analytic Philosophy* (Oxford: Oxford University Press), 488–517.

Trego, Kristell (2016), 'Intention et réalité: Avicenne et les origins du concept de *ma'nâ*', *Revue Philosophique de Louvain* 114/3: 445–60.

Turner, Denys (2013), *Aquinas: A Portrait* (New Haven: Yale University Press).

Turri, John (2011), 'Manifest Failure: The Gettier Problem Solved', *Philosophers' Imprint* 11/8: 1–11.

Twardowski, Kasimir (1894). *Zur Lehre vom Inhalt und Gegenstand der Vorstellungen. Eine psychologische Untersuchung* (Vienna: Hölder).

Urmson, J. O. (1988), 'Prichard and Knowledge', in J. Dancy, J. M. E. Moravcsik, and C. C. W. Taylor (eds), *Human Agency: Language, Duty and Value* (Stanford, CA: Stanford University Press), 11–24.

Vahid, Hamid (2009), 'Alston on Belief and Acceptance in Religious Faith', *Heythrop Journal* 50/1: 23–30.

Van Cleve, James (2006), 'Read on the Credit of Human Testimony', in Lackey and Sosa (2006), pp. 50–74.

Vanni Rovighi, Sofia (1962), *Elementi di Filosofia*. Vol. I (Brescia: La Scuola).

Vanni Rovighi, Sofia (1963–1979), *Gnoseologia* (Brescia: Morcelliana).

Vanni Rovighi, Sofia (1965), *L'antropologia filosofica di San Tommaso d'Aquino* (Milan: Vita e Pensiero).

Vanni Rovighi, Sofia (1978a), 'L'intenzionalità della conoscenza secondo P. Aureolo', in *Studi di filosofia medioevale*, II: *Secoli XIII e XIV* (Milan: Vita e Pensiero), 275–82. Originally published in *L'homme et son destin, d'après les penseurs du Moyen Age: actes du Premier Congrès international de philosophie médiévale. Louvain-Bruxelles, 28 août–4 septembre 1958* (Louvain: Nauwelaerts, 1960), 673–80).

Vanni Rovighi, Sofia (1978b), 'Una fonte remota della teoria husserliana dell'intenzionalità', in *Studi di filosofia medioevale*, II: *Secoli XIII e XIV* (Milan 1978), 283–98. Originally published in *Omaggio a Husserl* (Milan: Saggiatore, 1960), 49–65.

Vanni Rovighi, Sofia (1982), *Istituzioni di Filosofia* (Brescia: La Scuola).

Vendler, Zeno (1972), *Res Cogitans: An Essay in Rational Psychology* (Ithaca, NY: Cornell University Press).

Vetter, Barbara (2015), *Potentiality: From Dispositions to Modality* (Oxford: Oxford University Press).

Wedin, Michael V. (2014), *Parmenides' Grand Deduction: A Logical Reconstruction of the Way of Truth* (Oxford: Oxford University Press).

Williamson, Timothy (1995), 'Is Knowing a State of Mind?', *Mind* 104: 533–65.

Williamson, Timothy (2000), *Knowledge and its Limits* (Oxford: Oxford University Press).

Williamson, Timothy (2009), 'Replies to Critics', in Greenough and Pritchard (2009), 279–384.

Williamson, Timothy (2014), 'Knowledge First', in M. Steup. J. Turri, and E. Sosa (eds), *Contemporary Debates in Epistemology*, 2nd edn (Oxford; Chichester: Wiley Blackwell), 1–9.

Williamson, Timothy (2018), 'Hyman on Knowledge and Ability', *Philosophy and Phenomenological Research* XCVII/1: 243–8.

Wittgenstein, Ludwig (1953), *Philosophical Investigations* (Oxford: Basil Blackwell).
Wodehouse, Helen (1908), 'Judgment and Apprehension', *Mind* 17/3: 359–67.
Wodehouse, Helen (1909), 'Knowledge as Presentation', *Mind* 18/1: 391–9.
Wodehouse, Helen (1910), *The Presentation of Reality* (Cambridge: Cambridge University Press).
Wolterstorff, Nicholas (1981/1992), 'Is Reason Enough?', in Geivett and Sweetman (1992), 142–9; repr. from *The Reformed Journal* 31 (1981), 21–4.
Wolterstorff, Nicholas (1996), *John Locke and the Ethics of Belief* (Cambridge: Cambridge University Press).
Wolterstorff, Nicholas (2001), *Thomas Reid and the Story of Epistemology* (Cambridge: Cambridge University Press).
Wolterstorff, Nicholas (2005), 'Religious Epistemology,' in William J. Wainwright (ed.), *The Oxford Handbook of Philosophy of Religion* (Oxford: Oxford University Press), 245–71.
Wood, Allen W. (2020), *Kant and Religion* (Cambridge: Cambridge University Press).
Woolf, Raphael (2015), *Cicero: The Philosophy of a Roman Sceptic* (Abingdon; New York: Routledge).
Zagzebski, Linda (1994), 'The Inescapability of Gettier Problems', *Philosophical Quarterly* 44/174: 65–73.
Zagzebski, Linda (1996), *Virtues of the Mind: An Inquiry into the Nature of Virtue and the Ethical Foundations of Knowledge* (Cambridge: Cambridge University Press).
Zagzebski, Linda (1999), 'What is Knowledge?', in John Greco and Ernest Sosa (eds), *The Blackwell Guide to Epistemology* (Oxford: Blackwell), 92–116.
Zamulinski, Brian (2008), 'Christianity and the Ethics of Belief', *Religious Studies* 44: 333–46.
Zupko, Jack (2018), 'John Buridan', in SEP (fall 2018): https://plato.stanford.edu/archives/fall2018/entries/buridan/.

Index

For the benefit of digital users, indexed terms that span two pages (e.g., 52–53) may, on occasion, appear on only one of those pages.